The Jesus I Never Knew: "This is the best book about Jesus I have ever read, probably the best book about Jesus in the whole century."

LEWIS B. SMEDES

❖

Reaching for the Invisible God: "A brilliant book. It is both profound and simple, the best blend, in my view. Simple is neither shallow, nor simplistic. The sections on doubt and God's 'absence' are classics."

RICK WARREN, pastor and author, *The Purpose Driven Life*

❖

Prayer: Does It Make Any Difference?: "I have never read a book on prayer that touched me so deeply. I believe that a hundred years from now people will be reading this book."

BRENNAN MANNING

❖

"Reading *A Skeptics Guide to Faith* is like sitting in a darkened room and watching it slowly fill with light. It's Philip Yancey at his most stirring and insightful."

STEVE CHALKE, pastor and author

❖

What's So Amazing about Grace?: "This is beyond a doubt the very best book I have read from a Christian author in my life."

DR. ROBERT A. SEIPLE, president and CEO of Council
for America's First Freedom, and former president of World Vision

PHILIP YANCEY

Grace Notes

366 Daily Inspirations with a Fellow Pilgrim

ZONDERVAN®
.com

ZONDERVAN

Grace Notes
Copyright © 2009 by Someone Cares Charitable Trust.

Requests for information should be addressed to:

Zondervan, 3900 *Sparks Dr. SE, Grand Rapids, Michigan 49546*

This edition: ISBN 978-0-310-34515-2 (softcover)

Library of Congress Cataloging-in-Publication Data

Yancey, Philip. Grace notes : daily readings from a fellow pilgrim / Philip Yancey.
    p. cm.
    Includes bibliographical references and index.
    ISBN 978-0-310-28772-8 (hardcover, jacketed) 1. Devotional calendars. I. Title.
    BV4811.Y36 2009
    242'.2--dc22   2009026484

Cover design by Jeff Gifford
Cover photo by Hermitage Museum, St. Petersburg / SuperStock
Interior design by Beth Shagene

First printing December 2015 / *Printed in the United States of America*

A writer should strive to be a person on whom nothing is lost.
HENRY JAMES

CONTENTS

PREFACE

I have been writing full time for three decades, long enough for a publisher to propose this book of readings drawn from twenty-some books and numerous articles. As I read through them I feel a bit like Rip Van Winkle, going over experiences and thoughts from as long as twenty or thirty years ago. I've doubted, believed, doubted again, changed, grown.

I have also been privileged to travel widely, to observe the church at work in a variety of cultures, and to interview some fascinating people, both exemplary and blameworthy. Always I return to my office and sort out these encounters in articles and books. I find that other people have a romantic view of a writer's life, which I feel a need to correct. I once got a letter from a student inquiring whether I might need an intern. "I could do research for you, or office work. Or perhaps just sit and watch you write."

I sent her a polite turndown, though this is what I should have responded: *Young woman, are you crazy? No, you can't watch me write! I can't bear to have anyone in the same room. Writing is an act of utmost privacy and paranoia, and no one dare cross that barrier. Plus, you would soon get bored out of your mind. Why don't you stare at a rock all day or watch a TV screen with the power off—far more exciting than watching someone write.*

Alone in a room, the writer sits with a notepad or computer keyboard and manipulates abstract symbols, arranging and rearranging them. As Philip Roth explains the process, "I turn sentences around. That's my life. I write a sentence and I turn it around. Then I look at it and I turn it around again. Then I have lunch. Then I come back in and write another sentence. Then I have tea and turn the new sentence around. Then I read the two sentences over and turn them both around. Then I lie down on my sofa and think. Then I get up and throw them out and start from the beginning." Roth has described my day precisely.

Of all the arts, writing is the meekest. Painters use color and sculptors work with three dimensions, both media so much more arresting than the writer's thin marks of abstraction. Other art forms—movies, painting, dance, music—we encounter directly, sensually; only writing requires an intermediate step, literacy, for a person to perceive it. Show a copy of *King Lear* to an Amazon Indian tribe and they'll see something resembling pepper sprinkled on a page.

Surveys reveal that writers rank very high on the list of addiction-prone professionals. They chain-smoke, mainline caffeine, and turn to alcohol at an alarming rate. Why? Every day a writer must cope with a deep-seated paranoia: I have nothing to say, I've said it all before, I'm a fake and a hypocrite, I write in clichés. In addition, writing is such a disembodied act that we unconsciously seek ways to involve other body parts, even if it means moving a cup, glass, or wrapped tobacco tube from table to mouth and back. Fortunately, I live in Colorado, an outdoorsy state that daily beckons me to reconnect with the planet in more healthy ways (and in the process, avoid writing).

When I speak before audiences, I feel as if I have just emerged from a cave to face bright lights and microphones. "What are the five greatest trends confronting the church today?" someone asks, and I blink into the light. "How do you see your influence in the world?" someone else asks. To all such questions I want to reply, "How should I know—I've been sitting in my basement office." Instead, I smile politely and try to say something sensible.

❖

The question, "Have you always wanted to be a writer?" inevitably comes up as well. I have to confess that like most young boys I wanted to be a fireman or a baseball player. Later, while attending graduate school at Wheaton College, I needed a job to pay tuition bills. When I knocked on the doors of various Christian organizations headquartered nearby, the only offer came from Harold Myra, then publisher of *Campus Life*, a magazine for teenagers. That first year I filed reports on campus issues, wrote brochure copy, organized photo files, and generally acted as editorial errand boy.

Harold had created an ethos that valued writing above all else, and he mentored his young staff writers with endless patience. Leaning back in his creaky wooden chair he would say, "Philip, this article is 80 percent of the way there," which I soon understood to be a euphemism for "This article stinks and you might as well start over." I literally learned on the job, working on active verbs, then sentence syntax, then paragraphs and article structure, and ultimately books. Writing can be learned—I knew almost nothing when I started.

I found that the process of mulling over life experiences and ordering them on paper fit my cautious, introverted personality. I could interview people and observe the world through the safety screen of a journalist. My time at *Campus Life* provided superb training, as I know no more daunting challenge than writing about matters of faith for spoiled American teenagers. I learned that the reader controls the transaction, not the writer; fail to hold the reader's attention and you're out of a job.

Many Christian books are written by experts of some sort: a pastor, theologian, professor, or other specialist. I began my career as a journalist, by definition a generalist or nonexpert, and ever since have clung to that identity. Only later did I find my own voice, the voice of an earnest pilgrim, wounded by the church, sifting through faith issues and finding my way back. I feel blessed, truly, to have a profession that allows me to work out on paper what I struggle with internally, a calling that mirrors my own biography.

After a decade at *Campus Life* I felt enmeshed in the management details of publishing. I was spending my time studying circulation figures and reviewing marketing budgets instead of writing. I took the plunge, scary at the time, to go freelance, simultaneously moving from the suburbs to downtown Chicago as if to underscore that break.

Many of the selections in this book stem from that period. City living opened up a new world, especially since my wife worked as a social worker among the urban needy. We lived right downtown, near Wrigley Field, and Chicago proved a stimulating setting for a journalist. If I hit writer's block I would take a walk and within a few minutes would see someone have an epileptic fit, get tossed out of a bar, or scream at a passing motorist.

In the meantime *Campus Life* joined a stable of magazines published by *Christianity Today*, and I began contributing regularly to that magazine. Alternating issues with Chuck Colson, I took on a monthly column, of which this collection contains several samples. I also began traveling internationally, sometimes to research articles, other times on tours arranged by my book publishers. I learned to value a different perspective on the U.S. and the version of Christianity that has flourished here. For someone cynical about the religious-industrial complex in the U.S., I suggest a simple cure: visit places like Brazil, the Philippines, or China, and spend time among people who receive the gospel as unadorned good news.

In 1992 we made the dramatic move from downtown Chicago to the foothills of the Rocky Mountains in Colorado. I worked in a basement office in both places, but what a difference. Out my casement window in Chicago I could see people's knees walking past, and wildlife consisted of pigeons and squirrels. Now out my window I see Ponderosa pines and snow-capped mountains, and a parade of foxes, deer, elk, skunks, marmots, bears, and bobcats—and even an occasional mountain lion—wander through the yard.

We moved in part because life had become too cluttered in Chicago and in part because I sensed a change in focus in my writing. As a journalist I had written other people's stories; now it was time to turn attention inward, toward more reflective and personal writing. I needed to examine my own faith and record steps along the journey. I still marvel that I can actually make a living doing so. Others who work in various professions have to deal with faith struggles as a sideline, outside their work arena. I get paid to do what I would do anyway.

In the process, I've kept that identity of journalist. I feel called to represent the ordinary pilgrim in the pew. Perhaps because I grew up in an unhealthy church background, I shy away from representing the Christian establishment in any formal sense. I am not ordained and have no organization whose reputation I need to protect. Rather, I'm a freelancer, free to explore my own questions wherever they lead me, without worrying about the fallout. I go to the experts and learn all that I can, then translate the answers I find helpful into a readable form.

❖

Every writer who touches on spirituality can identify with Thomas Merton's concern that his books expressed the spiritual life so confidently and surely when actually he was plagued by insecurities, doubts, and even terrors. I often have the impression that the words I write have more lasting value than my life, and I sense that the higher I reach in my writing about the spiritual life, the more I misrepresent my own disorderly life. It is far easier, I find, to edit words than to edit life. When I get letters from readers telling me how my words have affected them, I want to protest, "Yes, but you don't know me—talk to my wife!" Words grant to writers of faith a vicarious power that we do not deserve.

Several times I have written about my years attending a Christian college, without identifying it by name. I had not realized how much I upset people there until I revisited the campus and spoke with some of the teachers and administration. "Why do you hurt us?" asked one professor. "Why concentrate only on the negative? We've given you the Alumnus of the Year award, and you turn around and lambaste us every chance you get!" I tried simply to listen, rather than defend myself. I knew he was reacting against the unfair power of words, my words, which through my books have gone out across the country, presenting one limited and inadequate point of view and causing him embarrassment.

Why do we do it, we writers? "Of making many books there is no end," sighed the Teacher of Ecclesiastes some three millennia ago, and a quarter million new ones will appear in the U.S. this year alone. Still we keep at it, cranking out more and more words, with the potential to bring harm as well as comfort. All writing involves a kind of arrogance. As I write this sentence, I have the chutz-pah to believe it will be worth your time to read it. *I, a person you probably have never met, hereby request your attention. Subject yourself to my words and thoughts. Listen to me, please, without the opportunity for reciprocation.*

I think we do it because we have nothing else to offer than a point of view. Everything I write is colored by my family, my upbringing in the South and in fundamentalism, my back-roads pilgrimage. I can only write with passion about my own experience, not yours. Yet somehow my rendering of church, family, and halting steps toward faith may provoke a response in the reader, like the harmonic overtones from a plucked guitar string. As Walker Percy said, a writer may help reveal what the reader knows but does not know that he or she knows.

I have written about the "toxic church" I grew up in: a legalistic, angry, racist church in the South. I joke about being "in recovery" from that church, learn-ing along the way that much presented as absolute truth was in fact wrong. As a result, when I began writing I saw myself as someone on the edge, more com-fortable asking questions than proposing answers. My early book titles (*Where Is God When It Hurts, Disappointment with God*) betray what I struggled with and how I positioned myself.

I once described the people I tend to hear from as "borderlanders," those caught in a no-person's-land between faith and disbelief. Some approach the church cautiously, attracted to Jesus but turned off by his followers. Some have fled the church due to bad experiences, yet still yearn for the consolation they felt there. I've spent time in the borderlands myself and want to honor those wandering on the edges, the misfits.

I do not try to defend the church, but instead identify with those it has wounded and point them toward the good news of the gospel. Jesus said that the truth will set us free and that he came to give life in all its fullness. If it's not setting you free and enlarging life, then it's not Jesus' message. If it doesn't sound like good news, it's not the gospel.

Words are my business, so I pick a word and turn it around and take it apart and mull it over. I did that with the word *grace*. I noticed forms of the word appearing in unlikely places: the sports pages (graceful athlete), parking lots (one-hour grace period), music scores (grace note). That prompted a closer look, because all these uses of the word are positive and appealing whereas Chris-tians often have a negative reputation. People think of Christians as uptight and judgmental. Odd, I thought, that grace has come to convey the opposite of God's intent, as it is lived out through us. From there, the book *What's So Amazing About Grace?* took shape.

I wish I could say, "Let me tell you about my ten-year-plan, my strategy of expressing my faith within a postmodern cultural context." Hardly. I bounce from one topic to another depending on what's bothering me at the time. Looking back, I see themes recurring through the years, themes such as suffering and grace. I also see my writing as spiraling in from the margins of faith toward its center. Consider the topics of my recent books — Jesus, grace, prayer — all central to faith.

If someone had suggested twenty years ago that I would write a book on prayer, I would have laughed out loud. It took years for me to sense the desire to explore such a topic. The desire, I say, not the competence: I approached that book too with the stance of a journalist, bringing a list of questions to those who might suggest some answers. We have the inestimable privilege of communicating with the God of the Universe, and yet for many people prayer remains a boring, lifeless ritual. Can that change? Do I truly believe in prayer? I start asking questions like that, and they lead to a book.

In truth, I write my books for myself. I take an issue that puzzles and intrigues me and dive in, not knowing where I'll emerge. Someone may eventually dive in behind me, but while I'm writing the book I'm alone, grappling with issues and herding words (like small animals, they keep trying to escape). Writing has afforded me a way to work out my faith, word by word. And to my astonishment my words have helped encourage others in their faith.

❖

In the old days of hand-rolled cigars, Cuba had a tradition of hiring lectors to read to the workers on the factory floor. Working in silence, they listened hour after hour to literature read aloud. It helped the time pass and, the foremen noticed, also helped the workers' morale. The cigar-rollers enjoyed *The Count of Monte Cristo* so much that they wrote Alexandre Dumas for permission to name a cigar after the novel — the origin of the still-popular "Montecristo" cigar. I doubt that Dumas had a Cuban cigar factory in mind when he wrote the novel, but the portability of words allowed him to cross an ocean, enter another language, and visit that distant place.

Words allow a writer to leap across the gap and enter the consciousness of other human beings. The transaction between writer and reader usually takes place in secret, at a place and time unknown to the one who initiated it. I never see anyone reading one of my books, though I hear from readers who assure me they've done so. I hope that something I write may give companionship to those who doubt, comfort to those who suffer, and grace to those who have felt little of it from the church.

I once got a letter from Indonesia written in fractured English: "I been reading your book *The Jesus I Never Knew*. These truly a blessing. I read them three times. many times i couldn't sleep at night thinking what you wrote. Your book help me see Jesus not only a person who lived and died on earth 2000 ago, but also a real person that risen 2000 ago that still reacheable until today."

On a trip to Lebanon in 1998 I met a woman who said she had read my book *Disappointment with God* during the Lebanese civil war. She kept it in a basement bomb shelter. When the artillery fire intensified around her high-rise apartment building, she would make her way with a flashlight down the darkened stairway, light a candle, and read my book. I cannot describe how humbling it was for me to hear that at a moment when Christians were dying for their faith, when the most beautiful city of the Middle East was being reduced to rubble, at that moment words I wrote from my apartment in Chicago somehow brought her solace.

Another woman in Beirut wrote that my book *What's So Amazing about Grace?* helped improve her attitude toward the P.L.O. guerrillas who had stolen her apartment. I read such letters and think to myself, *I really had in mind a chronic illness not a civil war, and neighbors who play loud music not guerrillas who move in uninvited.* Again and again God has surprised me by using words written with mixed motives by my impure self to bear fruit in ways I never could have imagined.

A friend once said to me, "The words you write, the books you publish, they're like your children. You do the best you can with them, but eventually they go out there and take on a life of their own. You can't control where they go or what impact they have." How true. This book pulls together selections from my "children" written over several decades, appearing in twenty-two books and forty-five different articles as well as a few unpublished selections. Reviewing them, I give thanks for the privilege of working with words and for the unlikely linkages they make possible.

"We read to know that we're not alone," said one of the students tutored by C. S. Lewis in the movie *Shadowlands*. True, and those of us who write do so in desperate hope that we're not alone.

Philip Yancey, Colorado, Spring 2009

NOTE TO THE READER

Grace Notes pulls together 366 daily readings taken from the writings of Philip Yancey. All have been edited for length, and in addition some have undergone minor editorial changes for the sake of transition and clarity.

Readings corresponding to particular days (for example, 9/11) fall on that day, and some thematic material falls in the appropriate season (for example, political themes tend to cluster around election time, and Christmas themes appear in December). In addition, some of the readings follow the church calendar, which introduces a problem: dates for major events in the church calendar vary from year to year. We have arbitrarily placed such readings on an early date, so that readings related to Jesus' death and resurrection begin on March 13 and continue through April 1. Ideally, a reader who follows the church calendar should begin these readings two weeks before Easter, skipping ahead to later readings until that date arrives. Similarly a reading for the ascension and a cluster of readings related to Pentecost are placed on May 5 and May 15–18, even though the actual days will vary from year to year.

A Descriptive Bibliography at the end of the book gives further information on the original sources for these extracts.

January

Rosetta Stone

Step back for a moment and contemplate God's point of view. A spirit un-bound by time and space, God had borrowed material objects now and then—a burning bush, a pillar of fire—to make an obvious point on planet Earth. Each time, God adopted the object in order to convey a message and then moved on. In Jesus, something new happened: God *became* one of the planet's creatures, an event unparalleled, unheard-of, unique in the fullest sense of the word.

The God who fills the universe imploded to become a peasant baby who, like every infant who has ever lived, had to learn to walk and talk and dress himself. In the incarnation, God's Son deliberately "handicapped" himself, ex-changing omniscience for a brain that learned Aramaic phoneme by phoneme, omnipresence for two legs and an occasional donkey, omnipotence for arms strong enough to saw wood but too weak for self-defense. Instead of overseeing a hundred billion galaxies at once, he looked out on a narrow alley in Nazareth, a pile of rocks in the Judean desert, or a crowded street of Jerusalem.

Because of Jesus we need never question God's desire for intimacy. Does God really want close contact with us? Jesus gave up Heaven for it. In person he reestablished the original link between God and human beings, between seen and unseen worlds.

In a fine analogy, H. Richard Niebuhr likened the revelation of God in Christ to the Rosetta stone. Before its discovery scholars could only guess at the meaning of Egyptian hieroglyphics. One unforgettable day they uncovered a dark stone that rendered the same text in three different languages. By com-paring the translations side by side, they mastered hieroglyphics and could now see clearly into a world they had known only in a fog.

Niebuhr goes on to say that Jesus allows us to "reconstruct our faith." We can trust God because we trust Jesus. If we doubt God, or find him incompre-hensible, unknowable, the very best cure is to gaze steadily at Jesus, the Rosetta stone of faith.

Reaching for the Invisible God (135 – 39)

Magnifying Glass of Faith

I also envision Jesus as the "magnifying glass" of my faith, a phrase that needs some explanation. I am the proud owner of *The Oxford English Dictionary*, which contains every word in the English language. By joining a book club, I obtained a special one-volume edition for only $39.95. It contains the full text of the dictionary, with the one drawback of typesetting shrunken so small that no one on earth can read it unaided. Next, I purchased a splendid magnifying glass — the kind jewelers use, the size of a dinner plate, mounted on a swivel arm. With that, and the occasional assistance of another, hand-held magnifying glass, I can pore over the shades of meaning of any word in English.

I have learned about magnifying glasses, using my dictionary. When I train the glass on a word, the tiny print shows up crisp and clear in the center, or focal point, while around the edges it grows progressively distorted. In an exact parallel, Jesus has become the focal point of my faith, and increasingly I am learning to keep the magnifying glass of my faith focused on Jesus. In my spiritual journey as well as in my writing career I have long lingered in the margins, pondering unanswerable questions about the problem of pain, the conundrums of prayer, providence versus free will, and other such matters. When I do so, everything becomes fuzzy. Looking at Jesus, however, restores clarity.

I admit that many standard Christian doctrines bother me. What about hell? What of those who die without ever hearing about Jesus? I fall back on the response of Bishop Ambrose, mentor of Augustine, who was asked on his deathbed whether he feared facing God at judgment. "We have a good Master," Ambrose replied with a smile. I learn to trust God with my doubts and struggles by getting to know Jesus. If that sounds evasive, I suggest it accurately reflects the centrality of Jesus in the New Testament. We start with him as the focal point and let our eyes wander with care into the margins.

By looking at Jesus, I gain insight into how God feels about what goes on down here. Jesus expresses the essence of God in a way that we cannot misconstrue.

Reaching for the Invisible God (139 – 40)

God Came Close

What difference did Jesus make? Both for God and for us, he made possible an *intimacy* that had never before existed. In the Old Testament, Israelites who touched the sacred Ark of the Covenant fell down dead; but people who touched Jesus, the Son of God in flesh, came away healed. To Jews who would not pronounce or even spell out the letters in God's name, Jesus taught a new way of addressing God: *Abba*, or "Daddy." In Jesus, God came close.

Augustine's *Confessions* describes how this closeness affected him. From Greek philosophy he had learned about a perfect, timeless, incorruptible God, but he could not fathom how an oversexed, undisciplined person like himself could relate to such a God. He tried various heresies of the day and found them all unsatisfying, until he met at last the Jesus of the Gospels, a bridge between ordinary human beings and a perfect God.

The book of Hebrews explores this startling new advance in intimacy. First the author elaborates on what was required just to approach God in Old Testament times. Only once a year, on the Day of Atonement — Yom Kippur — could one person, the high priest, enter the Most Holy Place. The ceremony involved ritual baths, special clothing, and five separate animal sacrifices; and still the priest entered the Most Holy Place in fear. He wore bells on his robe and a rope around his ankle so that if he died and the bells stopped ringing, other priests could pull out his body.

Hebrews draws the vivid contrast: we can now "approach the throne of grace with confidence," without fear. Charging boldly into the Most Holy Place — no image could hold more shock value for Jewish readers. Yet at the moment of Jesus' death, a thick curtain inside the temple literally ripped in two from top to bottom, breaking open the Most Holy Place. Therefore, concludes Hebrews, "Let us draw near to God."

Jesus contributes at least this to the problem of disappointment with God: because of him, we can come to God directly. We need no human mediator, for God's own self became one.

Disappointment with God (124 – 25)

Prozac Jesus

H ow would Jesus have scored on a personality profile test?
The personality that emerges from the Gospels differs radically from the image of Jesus I grew up with, an image I now recognize in some of the older Hollywood films about Jesus. In those films, Jesus recites his lines evenly and without emotion. He strides through life as the one calm character among a cast of flustered extras. Nothing rattles him. He dispenses wisdom in flat, measured tones. He is, in short, the Prozac Jesus.

In contrast, the Gospels present a man who has such charisma that people will sit three days straight, with empty stomachs, just to hear his riveting words. He seems excitable, impulsively "moved with compassion" or "filled with pity." The Gospels reveal a range of Jesus' emotional responses: sudden sympathy for a person with leprosy, exuberance over his disciples' successes, a blast of anger at cold-hearted legalists, grief over an unreceptive city, and then those awful cries of anguish in Gethsemane and on the cross.

I once attended a men's movement retreat designed to help men "get in touch with their emotions" and break out of restrictive stereotypes of masculinity. As I listened to other men tell of their struggles to express themselves and to experience true intimacy, I realized that Jesus lived out an ideal for masculine fulfillment that nineteen centuries later still eludes most men. Three times, at least, he cried in front of his disciples. He did not hide his fears or hesitate to ask for help: "My soul is overwhelmed with sorrow to the point of death," he told them in Gethsemane; "Stay here and keep watch with me." How many strong leaders today would make themselves so vulnerable?

Jesus quickly established intimacy with the people he met. Whether talking with a woman at a well, a religious leader in a garden, or a fisherman by a lake, he cut instantly to the heart of the matter, and soon these people revealed to Jesus their innermost secrets. Jesus drew out a hunger so deep that people crowded around him just to touch his clothes.

The Jesus I Never Knew (88 – 89)

Seeing Upside Down

Taking God's assignment seriously means that I must learn to look at the world upside down, as Jesus did. Instead of seeking out people who stroke my ego, I find those whose egos need stroking; instead of important people with resources who can do me favors, I find people with few resources; instead of the strong, I look for the weak; instead of the healthy, the sick. Is not this how God reconciles the world to himself? Did Jesus not insist that he came for the sinners and not the righteous, for the sick and not the healthy?

The founder of the L'Arche homes for the mentally disabled, Jean Vanier, says that people often look upon him as mad. The brilliantly educated son of a governor general of Canada, he recruits skilled workers (Henri Nouwen was one) to serve and live among damaged people. Vanier shrugs off those who second-guess his choices by saying he would rather be crazy by following the foolishness of the gospel than the nonsense of the values of our world. Furthermore, Vanier insists that those who serve the deformed and damaged benefit as much as the ones whom they are helping. Even the most disabled individuals respond instinctively to love, and in so doing they awaken what is most important in a human being: compassion, generosity, humility, love. Paradoxically, they replenish life in the very helpers who serve them.

In India I have worshiped among leprosy patients. Most of the medical advances in the treatment of leprosy came about as a result of missionary doctors, who alone were willing to live among patients and risk exposure to study the dreaded disease. As a result, Christian churches thrive in most major leprosy centers.

In Myanmar, I have visited homes for AIDS orphans, where Christian volunteers try to replace parental affection the disease has stolen away. In Jean Vanier's center in Toronto, I have watched a scholarly priest lavish daily care on a middle-aged man so mentally handicapped that he could not speak a word. The most rousing church services I have attended took place in Chile and Peru, in the bowels of a federal prison. Among the lowly, the wretched, the downtrodden, the rejects, God's kingdom takes root.

Rumors of Another World (202 – 3)

Penniless Gourmets

Overwhelmed by how many people the church never touched, Marcel Roussel began work in 1949 amid the poverty and despair of post-war France. He concluded that the church could not merely wait, but rather must actively pursue people of need, especially in the workplace. Had not Jesus served as a carpenter and Paul as a tentmaker? "Everywhere," concluded Roussel, "in prisons, hotels and work sites, we can help reestablish a dialogue with God." He recruited a group of young women known as Missionary Workers for just that purpose.

At first the Missionary Workers took jobs in factories and came together only for prayer and study. But within a few years Father Roussel envisioned a restaurant where the Missionary Workers would live and "shine as a light to the world."

The first such restaurant, L'Eau Vive, opened in Belgium in 1960. Its success soon led to others, including the Agua Viva in Lima, Peru, where I dined on a visit in 1987.

Agua Viva soon began to attract the wealthy and powerful of Lima. Only a few clues announce to the visitor the restaurant's spiritual intent. The inside cover of the menu proclaims "Jesus lives! For this we are happy." And each evening at 10:30 the waitresses appear together to sing a vespers hymn for their patrons.

Besides these clues, says Sister Marie, the work itself should stand as a witness. "Don't ask us how our prayer life is going; look at our food. Is your plate clean and artfully arranged? Does your server treat you with kindness and love? Do you experience serenity here? If so, then we are serving God."

In the spirit of Brother Lawrence, the workers cook, wait on tables, scrub floors, worship, all to the glory of God. But the Missionary Workers have introduced a modern twist: they proffer gourmet meals in order to serve the poor of Lima.

Later that day, mothers from the slums of Lima will fill the same elegant room for classes on basic hygiene, child-raising, and physical and spiritual health. Once off duty in the restaurant, all staff members devote themselves to the poor, carrying out social programs that are funded by profits from the restaurant.

"The Penniless Gourmets," *Christianity Today,*
January 15, 1988 (12 – 13, 15)

Getting a Life

"The glory of God is a person fully alive," said the second-century theologian Irenaeus. Sadly, that description does not reflect the image many people have of modern Christians. Rightly or wrongly, they see us rather as restrained, uptight, repressed—people less likely to celebrate vitality than to wag our fingers in disapproval.

Where did Christians get the reputation as life-squelchers instead of life-enhancers? Jesus himself promised, "I am come that they might have life, and that they might have it more abundantly." What keeps us from realizing that abundant life?

Author Frederick Buechner decided once to turn his literary skills to exploring the lives of saints. The first three he chose—Brendan, Godric, and the biblical Jacob—surprised him, for the more he researched them, the more skeletons in the closet he uncovered. What made this unsavory trio saintly? he asked himself. He finally settled on the word "life-giver." Passionate, risk-taking, courageous, each of the three made those around him feel more alive, not less.

When I heard Buechner give that definition of saintliness, I thought immediately of my friend Bob. His parents worried about his spiritual state, concerned that he was spending too little time "in the Word" and in church. But I have never met anyone more fully alive. He took in stray animals, did carpentry chores for friends, climbed mountains, sky-dived, learned to cook, built his own house. Although Bob rarely used religious words, I noticed that everyone around him, including me, felt more alive after spending time with him. He radiated the kind of pleasure in the world of matter that God must feel. By Buechner's definition, at least, Bob was a saint.

I have known other life-giving Christians. A devout Presbyterian named Jack McConnell invented the Tine test for tuberculosis, helped develop Tylenol and MRI imaging, and then devoted his retirement to recruiting retired physicians to staff free medical clinics for the poor. Overseas I have met missionaries who repair their own vehicles, master several languages, study the local flora and fauna, and give shots if no doctor is available. Often these life-givers have difficulty finding a comfortable fit in staid American churches. Paradoxically, the life-givers I have known seem most abundant with life themselves.

"Back Page" column, *Christianity Today,*
October 23, 2000 (128)

World's Hardest Profession

I once had dinner in an Amish home where I heard about their unusual procedure for choosing a pastor. In that part of the country few Amish acquire education beyond the eighth grade, and almost none have theological training. The entire congregation votes for any male members who show pastoral potential, and those who receive at least three votes move forward to sit at a table. Each has a hymn book in front of him, and inside his randomly chosen hymn book one of the men finds a card designating him as the new pastor. For the next year he gets to preach two sermons a week, averaging ninety minutes in length.

"What if the person selected doesn't feel qualified?" I asked my Amish friend. He looked puzzled, then replied, "If he did feel qualified, we wouldn't want him. We want a humble man, one who looks to God."

I don't recommend the Amish method of pastoral call (though it does have intriguing parallels with the Old Testament system of drawing lots), but his last comment got me thinking. Thomas Merton once said that most of what we expect pastors and priests to do — teach and advise others, console them, pray for them — should in fact be the responsibility of the rest of the congregation.

In our modern fixation with job descriptions and career competency, do we neglect the most important qualification of a pastor, the need to know God? I recall that the Hindu Gandhi, leader of half a billion people, even in the heat of negotiations over independence refused to compromise his principle of observing every Monday as a day of silence. He believed failure to honor that day of spiritual nourishment would make him less effective throughout the other six days.

I wonder how much more effective our spiritual leaders would be if we granted them one day a week as a time of silence for reflection, meditation, and personal study. I wonder how much more effective our churches would be if we made the pastor's spiritual health — not his or her efficiency — our number one priority.

"Back Page" column, *Christianity Today*,
May 21, 2001 (104)

Shadow Mentor

I first encountered C. S. Lewis through his space trilogy. It had an undermining effect on me. He made the supernatural so believable that I could not help wondering, *What if it's really true?*

I was attending college in the late 1960s, just a few years after Lewis's death in 1963. I wrestled with his books as with a debate opponent and reluctantly felt myself drawn, as Lewis himself had been, kicking and screaming all the way into the kingdom of God. Since then he has been a constant companion, a kind of shadow mentor who sits beside me urging me to improve my writing style, my thinking, my vision.

As my shadow mentor, Lewis has taught me a style of approach that I try to follow in my own writings. To quote William James, "In the metaphysical and religious sphere, articulate reasons are cogent for us only when our inarticulate feelings of reality have already been impressed in favor of the same conclusion." In other words, we rarely accept a logical argument unless it fits an intuitive sense of reality. The writer's challenge is to nurture that intuitive sense — as Lewis had done for me with his space trilogy before I encountered his apologetics.

Lewis's background of atheism and doubt gave him a lifelong understanding of and compassion for readers who would not accept his words. He had engaged in a gallant tug-of-war with God, only to find that the God on the other end of the rope was entirely different from what he had imagined. Likewise, I had to overcome an image of God badly marred by an angry and legalistic church. I fought hard against a cosmic bully only to discover a God of grace and mercy.

I doubt C. S. Lewis ever anticipated the wild success of his books and then the movies and even spin-off products based on his books that would become available. If informed of that fact during his life, he would likely have shrunk back in alarm. We writers are not nouns, he used to say. We are mere adjectives, pointing to the great Noun of truth. Lewis did that, faithfully and masterfully, and because he did so many thousands have come to know and love that Noun. Including me.

"Back Page" column, *Christianity Today,*
July 2008 (62)

Theology from Dirty Jokes

C. S. Lewis had the literary gift of one-liners. His tongue lodged securely in cheek, he once said something like this: In the absence of any other evidence, the essentials of natural theology could be argued from the human phenomena of dirty jokes and attitudes toward death.

Let's start with dirty jokes. They dwell almost exclusively on the subjects of excretion and reproduction, two of the most "natural" processes on earth; yet in our smirks and double entendres we treat them as unnatural, even comical. Functions we share with all other animals somehow, to humans alone, seem strange.

As for death, humans act even less animal-like in its presence. Nature treats death as a normal, everyday occurrence. Only we humans treat it with shock and revulsion, as though we can't get used to the reality, universal though it may be.

Lewis suggests that these anomalies (like the more commonly cited human conscience) betray a permanent state of disunity within human beings. An individual person is a spirit made in the image of God but merged with a body of flesh. Dirty jokes and an obsession with death express a rumbling sense of discord about this in-between state. We *should* feel dissonance; we are, after all, immortal beings in mortal surroundings. We lack unity because long ago a gap fissured open between our mortal and immortal parts; theologians trace the fault line back to the fall.

According to the biblical view of humanity, it is natural that we blush at excretion and rear back from death. Such actions seem odd because they *are* odd. In all of earth there are no exact parallels of spirit and immortality poured into matter. The discomfiture we feel may be our most accurate human sensation, reminding us we are not quite "at home" here.

C. S. Lewis used hyperbole: one would be hard-pressed to derive most essential theology from dirty jokes and our attitudes toward death. But one might be harder pressed to deny all natural theology in the face of these and other rumors of transcendence.

I Was Just Wondering (19 – 21)

The Problem of Pleasure

Why is sex fun? Why is eating fun? Why are there colors?

It struck me the other day, after I had read my umpteenth book on the problem of pain, that I have never even seen a book on "the problem of pleasure." Nor have I met a philosopher who goes around shaking his or her head in perplexity over the basic question of why we experience pleasure.

Where did pleasure come from? That seems to me a huge question—the philosophical equivalent, for atheists, to the problem of pain for Christians. Don't atheists and secular humanists have an equal obligation to explain the origin of pleasure in a world of randomness and meaninglessness?

One person, at least, faced the issue squarely. In his indispensable book *Orthodoxy*, G. K. Chesterton traced his own Christian conversion to the problem of pleasure. He found materialism too thin to account for the sense of wonder and delight that sometimes marks the world, a sense that gives an almost magical dimension to such simple human acts as sex, and childbirth, and artistic creation.

Pleasure is at once a great good and a grave danger. If we start chasing pleasure as an end in itself, along the way we may lose sight of the One who gave us such good gifts as sexual drive, taste buds, and the capacity to appreciate beauty. As Ecclesiastes tells it, a wholesale devotion to pleasure will, paradoxically, lead to a state of utter despair.

Somehow Christians have gotten a reputation as anti-pleasure, and this despite the fact that they believe pleasure was an invention of the Creator himself. We Christians have a choice. We can present ourselves as uptight bores who sacrificially forfeit half the fun of life by limiting our indulgence in sex, food, and other sensual pleasures. Or we can set about enjoying pleasure to the fullest, which means enjoying it in the way the Creator intended.

Not everyone will accept the Christian philosophy of pleasure as a gift best enjoyed within the bounds of the Creator's intent. Some skeptics will scoff at any insistence on moderation. For these skeptics, I have a few simple questions. Why is eating fun? Why are there colors? I'm still waiting for a good explanation that does not include the word God.

I Was Just Wondering (32 – 36)

◆

Moments of Suspension

I will never forget one encounter with art's wondrous power. I was visiting Rome, and the first day I arose well before dawn and took a bus to the Tiber River, just outside Vatican City. I stood on the bridge colonnaded with Bernini's angels and watched the sun rise. Slowly, quietly, I walked the few blocks to St. Peter's. I strolled its vast spaces at a time so silent that each of my steps echoed off its graceful walls. Except for a few faithful nuns kneeling in prayer, I was alone.

After a while I climbed stairs to the roof, where I could examine the statues and look out over the plaza. I saw a long line snaking outside in the plaza. They were not tourists, rather a choir of two hundred strong bused in from Germany. As they filed in, I stood on the balcony of the dome designed by Michelangelo. Beneath me, the choir formed a large circle under the dome and began to sing a cappella. Some of the words were in Latin, some in German, it did not matter. Inside that magnificent sheltering dome with its perfect acoustics, I was virtually suspended in their music. I had the feeling that if I lifted my arms, the medium itself would support me.

Michelangelo, arguably the greatest artist who has ever lived, later confessed that his work had crowded out his own faith. As his life drew to a close, he penned these lines:

> So now, from this mad passion
> Which made me take art for an idol and a king
> I have learnt the burden of error that it bore
> And what misfortune springs from man's desire . . .
> The world's frivolities have robbed me of the time
> That I was given for reflecting upon God.

Perhaps. But Michelangelo and others like him have through their labors helped turn us from the world's frivolities and given us time for such reflection. For this one moment inside St. Peter's I had inhabited a glorious space not on earth, a moment of time not in time. Art had done its work.

From "A Goad, a Nail, and Scribbles in the Sand,"
First Things, February 2009 (38)

◆

Messiah Sighting

In 1993 I read a news report about a "Messiah sighting" in the Crown Heights section of Brooklyn, New York. Twenty thousand Lubavitcher Hasidic Jews live in Crown Heights, and in 1993 many of them believed the Messiah was dwelling among them in the person of Rabbi Menachem Méndel Schneerson.

Word of the rabbi's public appearance spread like a flash fire through the streets of Crown Heights, and Lubavitchers in their black coats and curly sideburns were soon dashing down the sidewalks toward the synagogue where the Rabbi customarily prayed.

The rabbi was ninety-one years old. He had suffered a stroke the year before and had not been able to speak since. When the curtain finally pulled back, those who had crowded into the synagogue saw a frail old man in a long beard who could do little but wave, tilt his head, and move his eyebrows. No one in the audience seemed to mind, though. "Long live our master, our teacher, and our rabbi, King, Messiah, forever and ever!" they sang in unison, over and over, building in volume until the rabbi made a small, Delphic gesture with his hand, and the curtain closed. They departed slowly, savoring the moment, in a state of ecstasy.

When I first read the news account I nearly laughed out loud. Who are these people trying to kid—a nonagenarian mute Messiah in Brooklyn? (He died in 1994.) And then it struck me: I was reacting to Rabbi Schneerson exactly as people in the first century had reacted to Jesus. A Messiah from Galilee? A carpenter's kid, no less?

The scorn I felt as I read about the rabbi and his fanatical followers gave me a clue to the responses Jesus faced throughout his life. His neighbors asked, "Isn't his mother's name Mary, and aren't his brothers James, Joseph, Simon and Judas? Where did this man get this wisdom and these miraculous powers?" Other countrymen scoffed, "Nazareth! Can anything good come from there?" His own family tried to put him away, believing he was out of his mind. The religious experts sought to kill him. As for the whipsaw commoners, one moment they judged him "demon-possessed and raving mad," the next they forcibly tried to crown him king.

The Jesus I Never Knew (41 – 42)

Undesirables

Jesus was a Jew ... yet in some ways Jesus did not act like a Jew. The very architecture of the temple expressed Jewish belief in a ladder of hierarchy reaching
higher and higher toward God. Gentiles and "half-breeds" like the Samaritans
could enter the outer Court of the Gentiles; a wall separated them from the
next partition, which admitted Jewish women. Jewish men could proceed one
stage further, and then only priests could enter the sacred areas.

The society was, in effect, a religious caste system based on steps toward holiness, and the Pharisees scrupulosity reinforced the system daily. All their rules
on washing hands and avoiding defilement were an attempt to make themselves
acceptable to God. Had not God set forth lists of desirable (spotless) and undesirable (flawed, unclean) animals for use in sacrifice? Had not God banned
sinners, menstruating women, the physically deformed, and other "undesirables"
from the temple?

In the midst of this tight religious caste system, Jesus appeared, with no
qualms about socializing with children or sinners or even Samaritans. He
touched, or was touched by, the "unclean": those with leprosy, the deformed, a
hemorrhaging woman, the lunatic and possessed. Although Levitical laws prescribed a day of purification after touching a sick person, Jesus conducted mass
healings in which he touched scores; he never concerned himself with the rules
of defilement after contact with the sick or even the dead.

Indeed, Jesus turned upside down the accepted wisdom of the day. Pharisees
believed that touching an unclean person polluted the one who touched. Yet
when Jesus touched a person with leprosy, Jesus did not become soiled—the
leprous became clean. When an immoral woman washed Jesus' feet, *she* went
away forgiven and transformed. When Jesus defied custom to enter a pagan's
house, the pagan's servant was healed. As Walter Wink puts it, "The contagion
of holiness overcomes the contagion of uncleanness."

In short, Jesus moved the emphasis from God's holiness (exclusive) to God's
mercy (inclusive). Instead of the message "No undesirables allowed," he proclaimed, "In God's kingdom there are no undesirables."

"Unwrapping Jesus," *Christianity Today*,
June 17, 1996 (30)

Losing the Culture Wars

I once addressed the topic "Culture Wars" before a large gathering that was tilted toward the liberal Democratic persuasion and included a strong minority of Jews. I had been selected as the token evangelical Christian on a panel that included the presidents of the Disney Channel and Warner Brothers, as well as the president of Wellesley College.

To prepare for my talk, I went through the Gospels for guidance, only to be reminded how unpolitical Jesus was. Today, each time an election rolls around Christians debate whether this or that candidate is "God's man" (or woman) for the White House. I had difficulty imagining Jesus pondering whether Tiberius, Octavius, or Julius Caesar was "God's man" for the empire.

I was also struck by what happens when Christians lose the culture wars. In waves of persecution during the 1960s and 1970s, for instance, Chinese believers were fined, imprisoned, and tortured. Yet despite this government oppression, a spiritual revival broke out that could well be the largest in the history of the church. As many as fifty million believers gave their allegiance to an invisible kingdom even as the visible kingdom made them suffer for it.

When my turn came to speak, I said that the man I follow, a Palestinian Jew from the first century, had also been involved in a culture war. He went up against a rigid religious establishment and a pagan empire. The two powers, often at odds, conspired together to eliminate him. His response? Not to fight, but to give his life for these his enemies, and to point to that gift as proof of his love. Among the last words he said before death were, "Father, forgive them, for they know not what they do."

After the panel, a television celebrity came up to me whose name every reader would recognize. "I've got to tell you, what you said stabbed me right in the heart," he said. "I was prepared to dislike you because I dislike all right-wing Christians and I assumed you were one. I don't follow Jesus—I'm a Jew. But when you told about Jesus forgiving his enemies, I realized how far from that spirit I am. I have much to learn from the spirit of Jesus."

"Unwrapping Jesus," *Christianity Today*,
June 17, 1996 (30–31)

◇

No Shortcuts

I believe most of the questions about guidance, the "how-tos," are misdirected. They are the typically impatient demands of us Americans who want a short-cut to the "magic," the benefit of relating to Almighty God. There is no short-cut, no magic, at least not that anyone can reduce to a three-point outline. There is only the possibility of a lifetime search for intimacy with a God who, as the psalmists discovered, sometimes seems close and sometimes far, sometimes seems loving and sometimes forgetful.

Does God guide? Yes, I believe. Most times God guides in subtle ways, by feeding ideas into our minds, speaking through a nagging sensation of dissatisfaction, inspiring us to choose better than we otherwise would have done, bringing to the surface hidden dangers of temptation, and perhaps by rearranging certain circumstances. (God may also still guide through visions, dreams, and prophetic utterances, but I cannot speak to these forms as they lie outside my field of experience.) God's guidance will supply real help, but in ways that will not overwhelm my freedom.

Yet, I cannot help thinking this whole issue of divine guidance, which draws throngs of seekers to seminars and sells thousands of books, is powerfully overrated. It deserves about as much attention as the Bible devotes to the topic.

The sociologist Bronislaw Malinowski suggested a distinction between magic and religion. Magic, he said, is when we manipulate the deities so that they perform our wishes; religion is when we subject ourselves to the will of the deities. True guidance cannot resemble magic, a way for God to give us shortcuts and genie bottles. It must, rather, fall under Malinowski's definition of religion. If so, it will occur in the context of a committed relationship between you and your God. Once that relationship exists, divine guidance becomes not an end in itself but merely one more means God uses in nourishing faith.

Guidance booklet (15–16)

◇

Night Guidance

I have a confession to make. For me, at least, guidance only becomes evident when I look backward, months and years later. Then the circuitous process falls into place and the hand of God seems clear. But at the moment of decision I feel mainly confusion and uncertainty. Indeed, almost all the guidance in my life has been subtle and indirect.

I think, for example, of a major crossroad in my career. While working for *Campus Life* magazine, I felt the constant tug between two irreconcilable directions. One pulled me toward management, business, marketing, budgeting; the other pulled me toward editorial directing and writing. For many months I tried both, unable to decide. Each field offered opportunities for ministry and similar rewards. I enjoyed both roles. Most advisers around me counseled me toward the management role because of the organization's existing needs. I often prayed about this issue but never received any concrete guidance.

Over time I began to notice a trend, however: a battle with insomnia. Externally, I handled the pressures of management well and stayed healthy to all appearance. But often I would have bouts of insomnia, so severe that I would get only one or two hours' sleep at night. It took me almost a year to notice a further detail: I slept when I worked on writing projects, I did not sleep when I worked in management. I tried to ignore the signs for another few months, but they became almost comically evident (if insomnia can ever be considered comical).

For a time I would work one full week on writing projects, then one full week on management. It was true. I slept like a baby (truthfully, more like a colicky baby) during writing weeks and slept hardly at all during management weeks. Could this be divine guidance? I wondered. I had heard of God speaking through dreams, but through insomnia?

The situation never changed, and finally I concluded the message of insomnia was as direct a form of guidance as I would get. Now that I look back on it, it seems startlingly direct.

Guidance booklet (17 – 18)

◆

A Backward Look

I think of the circumstances that led to some of the books I have written. *Where Is God When It Hurts?* came out of a rejection. Back in 1975 I had what I thought to be a wonderful idea for a book. I had just discovered *Devotions upon Emergent Occasions* by John Donne, a meditation written as Donne suffered from a life-threatening illness. The concepts were superb, but the King James–era English made them impenetrable to many modern readers. I wrote several publishers, proposing to do for *Devotions* what Ken Taylor had done for the King James Version: a *Living Donne*, perhaps, or *John Donne Redone*. I spent long hours working up samples. Everyone judged the idea fine as a literary exercise but totally unmarketable as a contemporary book.

My boss at the time, Harold Myra, had a constructive suggestion. "The problem," he said, "is not just the dated language, but the dated context and even dated way of thinking. Why don't you do your own book on the problem of pain and suffering, using modern examples." *Where Is God When It Hurts?* was born.

While researching that book, I met Paul Brand, a world authority on the subject of pain. I came to know him "by chance," when my wife cleaned out a supply closet at the warehouse of a Christian relief organization. "There's an article on pain in this international conference report that I think you'll like," she told me. Dr. Brand's unique perspective so fascinated me that I arranged for a meeting as soon as possible. I ultimately learned of a scuffed-up transcript of some devotional talks he had kept in a file drawer for twenty years. That transcript became the genesis of *Fearfully and Wonderfully Made* and *In His Image*.

Looking back, the hand of God seems evident in those and many other choices. I had always thought of guidance as forward-looking. Yet in my own experience I have found the direction to be reversed. For me, guidance only becomes clear as I look backward. As for the present, my focus must be my relationship to God. Am I responding with obedience and trust?

"Life must be understood backwards; but ... it must be lived forward," said Kierkegaard.

Guidance booklet (18 – 20)

Showing Up

I learned early on never to ask myself, "Do you feel like running today?" I just do it. Why? I can think of many reasons. Regular exercise allows me to eat what I want without worrying about weight gain. It does long-term good for my heart and lungs. It allows me to do other activities, such as skiing and mountain climbing. All these benefits represent a kind of "deferred gratification."

As with physical exercise, much of the benefit of prayer comes as a result of consistency, the simple act of showing up. The writer Nancy Mairs says she attends church in the same spirit in which a writer goes to her desk every morning, so that if an idea comes along she'll be there to receive it. I approach prayer the same way. Many days I would be hard-pressed to describe a direct benefit. I keep on, though, whether it feels like I am profiting or not. I show up in hopes of getting to know God better, and perhaps hearing from God in ways accessible only through quiet and solitude.

For years I resisted a regular routine of prayer, believing that communication with God should be spontaneous and free. As a result I prayed infrequently and with little satisfaction. Eventually I learned that spontaneity often flows from discipline. Leonardo da Vinci spent ten years drawing ears, elbows, hands, and other parts of the body in many different aspects. Then one day he set aside the exercises and painted what he saw. Likewise, athletes and musicians never become great without regular practice. I found that I needed the discipline of regularity to make possible those exceptional times of free communication with God.

The English word *meditate* derives from a Latin word which means "to rehearse." Virgil speaks of a shepherd boy "meditating" on his flute. Often my prayers seem like a kind of rehearsal. I go over basic notes (the Lord's Prayer), practice familiar pieces (the Psalms), and try out a few new tunes. Mainly, I show up.

Prayer: Does It Make Any Difference? (165 – 66)

Doing It Right

I'll never pray like Martin Luther.... I'll never have the spirit of Mother Teresa." Agreed. We are not called to duplicate someone else on earth but to realize our authentic selves. "For me to be a saint means for me to be myself," said Thomas Merton.

I learned long ago that I could never match my wife's instinctive skills as a social worker or hospice chaplain. When I meet someone in dire straits, I start to interview them. When my wife meets them, she immediately tunes in to their concerns. Our prayer practices reflect another difference: I tend to pray in scheduled, ordered times while she prays in spurts throughout the day.

Apart from the requirement that we be authentic before God, there is no prescribed way to pray. Each of us presents a unique mix of personality, outlook, training, gifts, and weaknesses, as well as a unique history with church and with God. As Roberta Bondi says, "If you are praying, you are already 'doing it right.'"

Over the years the church has repeatedly shifted its emphasis in prayer. Early Christians prayed for strength and courage. Then the state church composed majestic prayers. The Middle Ages stressed penitence and a plea for mercy. Later, Anselm and Bernard of Clairvaux led a rediscovery of the love and mercy of God, and St. Francis called forth a carefree joy. Meister Eckhart, Teresa of Avila, and the Quaker George Fox explored the interior, mystical silence of the heart while Brother Lawrence practiced God's presence in mundane work. Luther steered toward practical devotion, even as Calvin emphasized the majesty of God.

The diversity continues today. I have stood in a Russian Orthodox cathedral and watched grandmothers weep though they understood barely a word of the Old Slavonic prayers. I have listened as Korean Presbyterians in Chicago sang hymns and prayed loudly through the night. In some African-American churches, you can barely hear the prayer for all the cries of "Amen!" and "Now listen, Lord!" In Japan, during congregational prayer, everyone prays at once, aloud. Members of a Chinese house church in Germany continue the stringent practices of the mother country, sometimes praying three days straight while fasting. In Ukraine worshipers stand to pray; in Africa they dance.

Prayer: Does It Make Any Difference? (190–91)

◆

Jesus and Stormin' Norman

When time came to teach the Beatitudes to my class at LaSalle Street Church in Chicago, I followed my regular routine of previewing the movies about Jesus. Since I drew from fifteen different movies, the task of locating and viewing all the right portions consumed several hours of my time each week, much of it spent waiting for the VCR to fast-forward or reverse to the appropriate scenes. To relieve boredom while the VCR whirred and clicked its way to the right places, I had CNN playing on the TV monitor in the foreground. As the machine sped, say, to the eight-minute-twenty-second mark of Cecil B. DeMille's *King of Kings*, I caught up on news from around the world. Then I hit the "play" button and was transported back into first-century Palestine.

A lot was happening in the world in 1991 the week I taught the Beatitudes. In a ground campaign that lasted a scant one hundred hours, allied forces had achieved a stunning victory over Iraq in the Gulf War that liberated Kuwait. Like most Americans, I could hardly believe the long-feared war had ended so quickly, with so few American casualties. As my VCR searched through the celluloid frames of Jesus in the background, various commentators on-screen were illustrating with charts and maps exactly what had transpired in Kuwait. Then came General Norman Schwarzkopf.

CNN announced an interruption in scheduled programming: they would shift to live coverage of the morning-after press conference by the commander of allied forces. For a time I tried to continue preparing for my class. I watched five minutes of Pasolini's version of Jesus delivering the Beatitudes, then several minutes of General Schwarzkopf's version of allied troops bearing down on Kuwait City.

Soon I abandoned the VCR altogether—Stormin' Norman proved entirely too engaging. He told of the "end run" around Iraq's elite Republican Guard, of a decoy invasion by sea, of the allied capability of marching all the way to Baghdad unopposed. He credited the Kuwaitis, the British, the Saudis, and every other participant in the multinational force. A general confident in his mission and immensely proud of the soldiers who had carried it out, Schwarzkopf gave a bravura performance. I remember thinking, *That's exactly the person you want to lead a war.*

[Continued on January 22]

The Jesus I Never Knew (106–7)

Beatitudes in Reverse

[Continued from January 21]

The briefing ended, CNN switched to commercials, and I returned to the VCR tapes. Max von Sydow, a blond, pasty Jesus, was giving an improbable rendition of the Sermon on the Mount in *The Greatest Story Ever Told*. "Blessed ... are ... the ... poor ... in spirit," he intoned in a slow, thick Scandinavian accent, "for ... theirs ... is ... the ... kingdom ... of ... heaven." I had to adjust to the languid pace of the movie compared to General Schwarzkopf's briefing, and it took a few seconds for the irony to sink in: I had just been watching the Beatitudes in reverse!

Blessed are the strong, was the general's message. Blessed are the triumphant. Blessed are the armies wealthy enough to possess smart bombs and Patriot missiles. Blessed are the liberators, the conquering soldiers.

The bizarre juxtaposition of two speeches gave me a feeling for the shock waves the Sermon on the Mount must have caused among its original audience, Jews in first-century Palestine. Instead of General Schwarzkopf, they had Jesus, and to a downtrodden people yearning for emancipation from Roman rule, Jesus gave startling and unwelcome advice. If an enemy soldier slaps you, turn the other cheek. Rejoice in persecution. Be grateful for your poverty.

The Iraqis, chastened on the battlefield, got a nasty measure of revenge by setting fire to Kuwait's oil fields; Jesus enjoined not revenge but love for one's enemies. How long would a kingdom founded on such principles survive against Rome?

"Happy are the bombed-out and the homeless," Jesus might as well have said. "Blessed are the losers and those grieving for fallen comrades. Blessed are the Kurds still suffering under Iraqi rule." Any Greek scholar will tell you the word "blessed" is far too sedate and beatific to carry the percussive force Jesus intended. The Greek word conveys something like a short cry of joy, "Oh, you lucky person!"

"How lucky are the unlucky!" Jesus said in effect.

The Jesus I Never Knew (107)

Future Rewards

One summer I met with a group of Wycliffe Bible Translators at their austere headquarters in the Arizona desert. Many lived in mobile homes, and we convened in a concrete block building with a metal roof. I was impressed with the dedication of these professional linguists who were preparing for a life of poverty and hardship in remote outposts. They loved to sing one song especially: "So send I you, to labor unrewarded, to serve unpaid, unloved, unsought, unknown ..." The thought occurred to me that the song has it slightly wrong: these missionaries were not planning to labor unrewarded. They served God, trusting in turn that God would make it worth their while—if not here, then in eternity.

In the mornings I went jogging along dirt roads that coiled among the stands of saguaro cacti. Wary of rattlesnakes and scorpions, I mostly kept my head down looking at the road, but one morning on a new route I glanced up to see a shimmering resort looming before me, almost like a mirage. I discovered two Olympic swimming pools, aerobic workout rooms, a cinder jogging trail, lush gardens, a baseball diamond, soccer fields, and horse stables. The facilities, I learned, belonged to a famous eating disorder clinic that caters to movie stars and athletes.

I jogged slowly back to the jumble of buildings at the Wycliffe base, keenly aware of their contrast to the gleaming architecture of the eating disorder clinic. One institution endeavored to save souls, to prepare people to serve God here and in eternity; the other endeavored to save bodies, to prepare people to enjoy this life. It seemed obvious which institution the world honors.

In the Beatitudes, Jesus honored people who may not enjoy many privileges in this life. To the poor, the mourners, the meek, the hungry, the persecuted, the poor in heart, he offered assurance that their service would not go unrecognized. They would receive ample reward. Wrote C. S. Lewis, "We are half-hearted creatures, fooling about with drink and sex and ambition when infinite joy is offered us, like an ignorant child who wants to go on making mud pies in a slum because he cannot imagine what is meant by the offer of a holiday at the sea."

The Jesus I Never Knew (110 – 11)

◆

A Just God After All

Among many Christians an emphasis on future rewards has fallen out of fashion. My former pastor Bill Leslie once observed, "As churches grow wealthier and more successful, their preference in hymns changes from 'This world is not my home, I'm just a passin' through' to 'This is my father's world.'" In the United States, Christians have grown so comfortable that we no longer identify with the humble conditions Jesus addressed in the Beatitudes.

Yet we dare not discount the value of future rewards. One need only listen to the songs composed by American slaves to realize this consolation of belief. "Swing low, sweet chariot, comin' for to carry me home." "When I get to heaven, goin' to put on my robe, goin' to shout all over God's heaven." "We'll soon be free, we'll soon be free, when the Lord will call us home." They had little hope in this world but abiding hope in a world to come.

I no longer scorn the eternal rewards mentioned in the Beatitudes as "pie in the sky." What good does it do to hope for future rewards? What good did it do the Anglican hostage Terry Waite to believe that he would not spend the rest of his life chained to a door in a filthy Beirut apartment, but that a world of family and friends and mercy and love and music and food and good books awaited him if he could just find the strength to hang on a little longer? What good did it do the slaves to believe that God was not satisfied with a world that included back-breaking labor and masters armed with bullwhips and lynching ropes? To believe in future rewards is to believe that the long arm of the Lord bends toward justice, to believe that one day the proud will be overthrown and the humble raised up and the hungry filled with good things.

The prospect of future rewards in no way cancels out our need to fight for justice now, in this life. Rather, it allows us to believe in a just God after all. Like a bell tolling from another world, Jesus' promise of rewards proclaims that no matter how things appear, there is no future in evil, only in good.

The Jesus I Never Knew (111–12)

◆

God's Gamble

"There are two things we cannot do alone," said Paul Tournier: "one is to be married and the other is be a Christian." In my pilgrimage with the church, I have learned that the church plays a vital, even necessary role. We are God's "new community" on earth.

I am aware, painfully aware, that the ideal church is a mirage. Many churches offer more entertainment than worship, more uniformity than diversity, more exclusivity than outreach, more law than grace. Nothing troubles my faith more than my disappointment with the visible church.

Still, I must remind myself of Jesus' words to his disciples: "You did not choose me, but I chose you." The church was God's risk, God's "gamble," so to speak. I have even come to see in the church's flawed humanity a paradoxical sign of hope. God has paid the human race the ultimate compliment by choosing to live within us vessels of clay.

Several times I have read the Bible straight through, from Genesis to Revelation, and each time it strikes me that the church is a culmination, the realization of what God had in mind from the beginning. The body of Christ becomes an overarching new identity that breaks down barriers of race and nationality and gender and makes possible a community that exists nowhere else in the world. Simply read the first paragraph from each of Paul's letters to diverse congregations scattered throughout the Roman Empire. They are all "in Christ," and that matters even more than their race or economic status or any of the other categories humanity may devise.

My identity in Christ is more important than my identity as an American or as a Coloradan or as a white male or as a Protestant. Church is the place where I celebrate that new identity and work it out in the midst of people who have many differences but share this one thing in common. We are charged to live out a kind of alternative society before the eyes of the watching world, a world that is increasingly moving toward tribalism and division.

Church: Why Bother? (37 – 38)

◆

Midnight Church

I once visited a "church" that manages, with no denominational headquarters or paid staff, to attract millions of devoted members each week. It goes by the name Alcoholics Anonymous. I went at the invitation of a friend who had just confessed to me his problem with drinking. "Come along," he said, "and I think you'll catch a glimpse of what the early church must have been like."

At twelve o'clock on a Monday night I entered a ramshackle house that had been used for six other sessions already that day. Acrid clouds of cigarette smoke hung like tear gas in the air, stinging my eyes. It did not take long, however, to understand what my friend had meant with his comparison to the early church.

The "sharing time" worked like the textbook description of a small group, marked by compassionate listening, warm responses, and many hugs. Each person attending gave a personal progress report on his or her battle with addiction. We laughed a lot, and we cried a lot. Mostly, the members seemed to enjoy being around people who could see right through their façades. There was no reason not to be honest; everyone was in the same boat.

AA owns no property, has no headquarters, no media center, no staff of well-paid consultants and investment counselors who jet across the country. The original founders of AA built in safeguards that would kill off anything that might lead to a bureaucracy, believing their program could work only if it stayed at the most basic, intimate level: one alcoholic devoting his or her life to help another. Yet AA has proven so effective that 250 other kinds of twelve-step groups, from Chocoholics Anonymous to cancer patient groups, have sprung up in conscious mimicry of its technique.

For my friend, immersion into Alcoholics Anonymous has meant salvation in the most literal sense. He knows that one slip could—no, will—send him to an early grave. More than once his AA partner has responded to his calls at 4:00 a.m., only to find him slouched in the eerie brightness of an all-night restaurant where he is filling a notebook, like a punished schoolchild, with the single sentence, "God, help me make it through the next five minutes."

Church: Why Bother? (48 – 50)

Alcoholic Teachers

Alcoholics Anonymous meets needs in a way that the local church does not—or at least did not for my friend. I asked him to name the one quality missing in the local church that AA had somehow provided. He stared at his coffee for a long time and then he said softly this one word: dependency.

"None of us can make it on our own—isn't that why Jesus came?" he explained. "Yet most church people give off a self-satisfied air of piety or superiority. I don't sense them consciously leaning on God or on each other. Their lives appear to be in order. An alcoholic who goes to church feels inferior and incomplete."

"It's a funny thing," he said at last. "What I hate most about myself, my alcoholism, was the one thing God used to bring me back to him. Because of it, I know I can't survive without God. I have to depend on him to make it through each and every day. Maybe that's the redeeming value of alcoholism. Maybe God is calling us alcoholics to teach the saints what it means to be dependent on him and on his community on earth."

From my friend's midnight church I learned the need for humility, total honesty, and radical dependence—on God and on a community of compassionate friends. As I thought about it, these qualities seemed exactly what Jesus had in mind when he founded his church.

Alcoholics Anonymous came out of a discovery by Bill Wilson. On his own, Bill had stayed sober for six months until he made a trip out of town, where a business deal fell through. Depressed, wandering a hotel lobby, he heard familiar sounds of laughter and of ice tinkling in glasses. He headed toward the bar, thinking "I need a drink."

Suddenly a brand new thought came to him: "No, I don't need a drink—I need another alcoholic!" Walking instead toward the lobby telephones, he began the sequence of calls that put him in touch with Dr. Bob Smith, who would become AA's cofounder.

Church is a place where I can say, unashamedly, "I don't need to sin. I need another sinner."

Church: Why Bother? (51 – 52)

Caring for Nobodies

A slight man with graying hair entered the room where we had agreed to meet. He apologized for the blood on his lab coat, explaining that he had just been dissecting armadillos, the only nonhuman species known to harbor leprosy bacilli. He wore outdated clothes, lived in a rented bungalow on the Louisiana hospital grounds, and drove an economical, rundown automobile. At heart, Paul Brand was still a missionary, unimpressed by and unaccustomed to relative prosperity and fame.

That first visit lasted a week. I sat beside Brand as he studied the ulcerated limbs of patients and visited the labs. At night in their wooden house, I would share a rice-and-curry meal with him and his wife, Margaret, a respected ophthalmologist. Then Paul would prop up his bare feet, and I would turn on the tape recorder for discussions that ranged from leprology and theology to world hunger and soil conservation.

Every topic I brought up, he had already thought about in some depth. He quoted Shakespeare and discussed the derivation of Greek, Hebrew, and Latin words. During breaks he taught me such things as how to select a ripe fig (watch the ones butterflies light on several times, testing, before flitting on to their preferred overripe fruit) and how African weaver birds build their elaborate nests using only one foot and a beak.

The conversations that stand out are those in which he recalled individual patients in India, "nobodies" on whom he had lavished medical attention. When he began his pioneering work, he was the only orthopedic surgeon in the world working among fifteen million victims of leprosy. He and Margaret performed several dozen surgical procedures on some of these patients, restoring rigid claws into usable hands through innovative tendon transfers, remaking feet, forestalling blindness, transplanting eyebrows, fashioning new noses.

He told me of his patients' family histories, the rejection they had experienced as the disease presented itself, the trial-and-error treatments of doctor and patient experimenting together. Almost always his eyes would moisten and he would wipe away tears as he remembered their suffering. To him these, among the most neglected people on earth, were not nobodies, but people made in the image of God, and he devoted his life to try to honor that image.

In the Likeness of God (12 – 14)

True Humility

We made an odd couple, Dr. Brand and I. He was a silver-haired surgeon characterized by proper British reserve, and I an eager young journalist in my mid-twenties with bushy Art Garfunkel – style hair. I had interviewed many subjects: actors and musicians, politicians, successful business executives, Olympic athletes, Nobel laureates, and Pulitzer Prize winners.

Something attracted me to Dr. Brand at a deeper level than I had felt with any other interview subject. My father died just after my first birthday, and in many ways Dr. Brand became a father-figure to me. Already an adult when I met him, I didn't have to go through teenage rebellion and the agony of individuation. I sat at his feet from the first day we met.

For perhaps the first time, I encountered genuine humility. The apostle Paul pointed to Jesus as an example of humility: "Your attitude should be the same as that of Christ Jesus: Who, being in very nature God, did not consider equality with God something to be grasped, but made himself nothing, taking the very nature of a servant, being made in human likeness." Meeting Dr. Brand, I realized that I had misconstrued humility as a negative self-image. Paul Brand obviously knew his gifts: he had finished first throughout his academic career and had attended many awards banquets honoring his accomplishments. Yet he recognized his gifts as just that, *gifts* from a loving Creator, and used them in a Christlike way of service.

When I first met him, Dr. Brand was still adjusting to life in the United States. Everyday luxuries made him nervous, and he longed for a simple life close to the soil. He knew presidents, kings, and celebrities, yet he rarely mentioned them. He talked openly about his failures and always tried to deflect credit for his successes to his associates. Most impressive to me, the wisest and most brilliant man I have ever met devoted much of his life to some of the lowest people on the planet: members of the Untouchable caste in India afflicted with leprosy.

In the Likeness of God (14 – 15)

◆

Hands That Would Not Be Silenced

I got a call in June 2003 informing me that Dr. Brand had fallen while carrying a box of books to the second-floor office in his cottage. He had hit his head on the banister and was now lying in a coma in a Seattle hospital. My wife and I were due to leave in a few days for a trip to New Zealand, and after some persistent calls United Airlines allowed us to reroute the trip through Seattle.

In an email I read on the plane, Dr. Brand's daughter Pauline recalled a scene from *The Lion, the Witch and the Wardrobe*: "It's when the two girls find Aslan's body shaved and bound up, and see that although such things had been done in order to strip the lion of his dignity they have only succeeded in emphasizing it. That's how it is with Dad's poor half-shaved head, and the ugly semicircle of staples from the surgery, and the multitude of tubes taped to his face, neck and chest. Within it all, there is his grand old face...."

By his bedside, suddenly I was overcome with emotion and could not speak. For nearly thirty years Paul Brand had been the towering giant in my life, the one to whom I turned for guidance, wisdom, inspiration, and faith. Now only a shell was left, the physical body we had written about. I bent over and kissed the smooth, babylike skin on his shaven head.

His left hand grasped out for something to hold, and I put my hand in his. Incredibly, almost eerily, he began examining it with his fingers, running his own fingers up and down mine, squeezing, testing, analyzing. As I stood there, he did the same thing with his own right hand, which lay useless at his side. The instincts of fifty years of hand surgery had so imprinted on the synapses of his brain that even with much of it destroyed, this remained. Often he had told me that he could remember his patients' hands better than their faces. Now he could not speak, probably could not think, could barely breathe, but still he reached out with the hands that had brought healing to so many.

[Continued on January 31]

In the Likeness of God (21–23)

◆

Intoxicating Goodness

[Continued from January 30]

A few days later, from an email received halfway around the world, I learned Paul Brand had taken his last breath on July 8, a week before his eighty-ninth birthday. All that week, at unexpected times—waking up, in the shower, while praying—I would find myself sobbing. "What's wrong?" my wife asked the first few times. "I miss Dr. Brand," was my only answer. A phrase kept going through my mind: *I am not ready to walk alone.*

When it came my turn to speak at the memorial service, first I removed my shoes and socks and stood barefoot. It seemed somehow appropriate to honor in this small way a man who slipped off his own shoes at any opportunity, who lobbied against "No shoes, no shirt, no service" policies, and who had spent thousands of hours investigating how best to protect the insensitive feet of his leprosy patients, for whom tight shoes or rough sandals represented danger.

I still am not ready to walk alone. But that I walk at all on this perilous journey of faith depends in large part on the strength I received from a giant of faith against whom I leaned for thirty years as one leans against a towering tree of the forest. As we heard in that memorial service, the colonnade left by Paul Brand stretches long and far, spanning continents, affecting not just fellow surgeons, but nurses, leprosy patients, neighbors, and ordinary people whose lives he touched.

I know no one who better illustrates Jesus' most-quoted statement, that "whoever loses his life for my sake will find it." From the perspective of a success-obsessed culture, an orthopedic surgeon spending his professional life among some of the poorest and most oppressed people on the planet is an example of "losing his life." Yet Dr. Brand lived as full and rich a life as anyone I know, combining humility, gratitude, and a grand sense of adventure.

I feel privileged to have had some role, as his coauthor, in shining a light on his life. You need only meet one saint to believe, and I had the inestimable privilege of spending leisurely hours getting to know a distinguished and faithful follower of Jesus. For that, Paul Brand, I thank you.

In the Likeness of God (23–26)

February

◆

Two Worlds

A story is told about Rabbi Joseph Schneerson, a Hasidic leader during the early days of Russian communism. The rabbi spent much time in jail, persecuted for his faith. One morning in 1927, as he prayed in a Leningrad synagogue, secret police rushed in and arrested him. They took him to a police station and worked him over, demanding that he give up his religious activities. He refused. The interrogator brandished a gun in his face and said, "This little toy has made many a man change his mind." Rabbi Schneerson answered, "This little toy can intimidate only that kind of man who has many gods and but one world. Because I have only one God and two worlds, I am not impressed by this little toy."

The theme of "two worlds," or two kingdoms, emerges often in Jesus' teaching, and two stories in Luke 16 draw a sharp distinction between the two worlds. "What is highly valued among men is detestable in God's sight," Jesus says, commenting on the story of the shrewd manager. The second story, of the rich man and Lazarus, elaborates on that difference in values between the two worlds. The rich man prospers in this world yet neglects to make any provision for eternal life and thus suffers the consequences. Meanwhile a half-starved beggar, who by any standard would be judged a failure in this life, receives an eternal reward.

Jesus tells such stories to a Jewish audience with a tradition of wealthy patriarchs, strong kings, and victorious heroes. But Jesus keeps emphasizing his stunning reversal of values. People who have little value in this world (the poor, the persecuted—people like Lazarus) may in fact have great stature in God's kingdom. Consistently he presents the visible world as a place to invest for the future, to store up treasure for the life to come.

In a question that brings the two worlds starkly together, Jesus asks, "What good will it be for a man if he gains the whole world, yet forfeits his soul?" (Matthew 16:26).

Meet the Bible (453)

◆

Money Worries

Jesus has more to say on money than almost any other topic. Yet two thousand years later Christians have trouble agreeing on exactly what he *does* say. One reason is that he rarely gives "practical" advice. He avoids comment on specific economic systems and, as in Luke 12, refuses to get involved in personal disputes about finances. Jesus sees money primarily as a *spiritual* force.

One pastor boils down money issues into three questions:

1. How did you get it? (Did it involve injustice, cheating, oppression of the poor?)
2. What are you doing with it? (Are you hoarding it? Exploiting others? Wasting it on needless luxuries?)
3. What is it doing to you?

Although Jesus speaks to all three of these issues, he concentrates on the last one. As he explains it, money operates much like idolatry. It can catch hold and dominate a person's life, diverting attention away from God. Jesus challenges people to break free of money's power — even if it means giving it all away.

Luke 12 offers a good summary of Jesus' attitude toward money. He does not condemn all possessions ("your Father knows that you need [food, drink, and clothes]"). But he strongly warns against putting faith in money to secure the future. As his story of the rich man shows, money will ultimately fail to solve life's biggest problems.

Jesus urges his listeners to seek treasure in the kingdom of God, for such treasure can benefit them in this life and the next one too. "Do not worry," he says. Rather, trust God to provide your basic needs. To emphasize his point, he brings up the example of King Solomon, the richest man in the Old Testament. To most nationalistic Jews, Solomon is a hero, but Jesus sees him in a different light: Solomon's wealth has long since vanished — and even in his prime he was no more impressive than a common wildflower. Better to trust in the God who lavishes care on the whole earth than to spend your life worrying about money and possessions.

Meet the Bible (455 – 56)

From Tents to Malls

In early 2009 I toured with a team from the U.K. in Arabian Gulf countries. We saw strange sights: women in full black robes speaking through their veils on iPhones or Blackberries while strolling along a beach among bikini-clad Europeans. Or a man walking through a shopping mall trailed by his four wives.

Just two generations ago the locals were Bedouins traipsing across the desert in camel caravans. Now as few as 10 percent of the population comprises local Arab citizens; the rest are workers imported from places like India and the Philippines, as well as well-heeled business people.

I spoke in four of the United Arab Emirates as well as in Kuwait. These countries have only a handful of local, Muslim-background believers: seven here, twelve there, all of whom live at risk since conversion can be punished by death. Yet the governments allow Christian churches to serve the international community as long as they don't try to proselytize locals. One allotted church building may serve dozens (in Kuwait as many as seventy-five) of congregations, all of whom take turns using the facility. God must smile at the rare phenomenon of church unity—enforced by Islamic governments!

The first missionaries, over a century ago, served well and left a good impression. The clinic founded by Samuel Zwemer, for example, still has the address "Post Office Box 1" in Bahrain. We led a worship service at the well-equipped Oasis Hospital in Abu Dhabi, founded by missionaries in 1960, where doctors and midwives have safely delivered seventeen members of the royal family. Nationwide, infant mortality has dropped from 50 percent to 1 percent.

I have great respect for the Christian workers who choose this part of the world. While staying in a guest house, I met a lovely young couple serving in Afghanistan, in an area under constant threat of violence from the Taliban. In that culture men and women simply do not appear in public together, so they can't go out on a "date," and would have nowhere to go regardless. They hear cries from a wife being beaten next door and can do nothing but tend to her wounds. And they are trying to teach basic education to a country that has only 37 percent literacy.

[Continued on February 4]

Unpublished trip notes, Middle East, 2009

The Garbage Church

[Continued from February 3]

From the Gulf countries we traveled to Cairo, Egypt. The city's monochrome brown buildings sprawl along potholed roads for miles in every direction. Some four thousand people move here from the country each day, adding to the population of 22 million. Unlike the Gulf countries, Egypt has a historic community of Christians, some 10 percent of the population, who trace back to the apostle Mark.

On Sunday we visited the "garbage church" in a suburb called Mokkatam. A sprawling slum of 30,000 people has grown up around the process of garbage-picking. With no formal garbage industry, Cairo relies on individuals who roam the streets and collect garbage in plastic bags. After transporting the haul to this slum, they spread out the garbage and sort out recyclable plastic and metal, which they sell for a modest income.

About thirty years ago someone discovered the entrance to a large cave near the slum, and over time Coptic Christians moved 140,000 tons of rock out of the cave to form a 3000-seat auditorium. (They did this mostly at night during Muslim fast periods, after the guards went home to eat.) The church outgrew that facility and now meets in a 13,000-seat amphitheater likewise hewn out of rock. A Polish sculptor has carved biblical scenes in the rock and the grounds are beautifully planted, forming an oasis of beauty in a desert of poverty.

Middle Eastern converts to Christianity are very rare, though we managed to meet some at a secret gathering of "Muslim-background believers." Virtually every one told of a dream or vision that prompted them to take the courageous step of leaving Islam.

Each country has its own distinctiveness. Kuwaiti drivers are crazy; Bahrain serves up alcohol and prostitutes to the repressed folks from Saudi Arabia who drive there across a causeway; Qatar hosts the TV network Al Jazeera, which shows in almost every Arab home. It's a different part of the world indeed, and one that remains at the center of world attention. I observed an alien culture, heard pleas for Americans not to judge all Middle Easterners by a few terrorists, and returned grateful that I live in a democracy with guarantees of human rights and decent treatment of women and minorities.

Unpublished trip notes, Middle East, 2009

The Dachau Call

I used to meet with a gentle and wise pastor who, while serving in World War II, had participated in the liberation of the Dachau concentration camp. I asked him about the experience.

"A buddy and I were assigned to one boxcar. Inside were human corpses, stacked in neat rows, exactly like firewood. Our job was like moving furniture to a designated area. I spent two hours in the boxcar, and the negative emotions came in waves, all but the rage. It stayed, fueling our work.

"Then we turned our attention to the SS officers in charge of Dachau, who were being held under guard in a bunkhouse. The captain asked for a volunteer to escort a group of twelve SS prisoners to an interrogation center nearby. A few minutes after they disappeared into the trees, we heard the rattly burp of a machine gun. Soon Chuck, the volunteer, came strolling out, smoke still curling from the tip of his weapon. 'They all tried to run away,' he said with a kind of leer.

"It was on that day that I felt called by God to become a pastor. First, there was the horror of the corpses in the boxcar. I knew beyond doubt that I must spend my life serving whatever opposed such evil—serving God.

"Then came the incident with Chuck. I had a nauseating fear that the captain might call on me to escort the next group of SS guards, and an even more dread fear that if he did, I might do the same as Chuck. The beast that was within those guards was also within me."

After a pause he continued, "I do see a connection in my work now. Without being melodramatic, I sometimes wonder what might have happened if a skilled, sensitive person had befriended the young, impressionable Adolf Hitler as he wandered the streets of Vienna in his confused state. The world might have been spared all that bloodshed—spared Dachau. I never know who might be sitting in that chair you're occupying right now.

"And even if I end up spending my life with 'nobodies' … I learned in the boxcar that there's no such thing. I learned that day in Dachau what 'the image of God' in a human being is all about."

I Was Just Wondering (76 – 80)

Forward to the Past

One rainy Saturday morning I decided to scrap my list of chores and go to a movie. I soon found myself in a theater watching *Following the Fuhrer,* a film about the Third Reich. In this, his second film on Hitler's Germany, director Erwin Leiser tried to recreate everyday life. In between familiar news clips he spliced small, dramatized vignettes of life in Germany.

The film explores the thick gray border between *what will come clear* to later history and what actually happens in everyday life. Now, looking back, the evils of Nazism loom large, and film footage of bombing runs, mass rallies, and concentration camps document that evil. But at the time ordinary German citizens responded to those evils with small, quotidian choices made in a fog of confusion.

As I walked home I reflected. We do not like to think of evil as banal; we prefer our evil characters larger than life, like Adolf Hitler. Because of Hitler, we can take a kind of perverse comfort in the knowledge that someone is worse than we are; and thus, ironically, his horrible extremism may tempt us to discount our own lesser forms of intolerance or idolatry.

My thoughts turned closer toward home, to the United States. What will *come clear* to filmmakers who, forty years from now, will rummage through news clips of our time? Will we be a shining beacon of freedom? Will we go down in history primarily as the civilization whose weapons made possible the abolition of all humanity? How will our million abortions a year look a few decades from now? Our own materialism and decadence?

Then, as my thoughts turned inward and I wondered how an Erwin Leiser of the twenty-first century would splice together scenes from my life with news clips of these confusing times, I felt a sense of helplessness and doom such as I have not felt since the 1960s.

Arriving home, I took out a piece of leftover pizza from a cardboard box in the refrigerator and heated it in the microwave. Then I decided to do my list of Saturday chores after all. I spent the rest of the afternoon pressing flexible caulking around the windows in my house.

I Was Just Wondering (144 – 48)

Not an Arm-Twister

Sometimes I wonder how Jesus would have fared in this day of mass media and high-tech ministry. I can't picture him worrying about the details of running a large organization. I can't see him letting some makeup artist improve his looks before a TV appearance. And I have a hard time imagining the fund-raising letters Jesus might write.

Investigative reporters on television like to do exposés of evangelists who claim powers of supernatural healing with little evidence to back them up. In direct contrast, Jesus, who had manifest supernatural powers, tended to downplay them. Seven times in Mark's gospel he told a healed person, "Tell no one!" When crowds pressed around him, he fled to solitude, or rowed across a lake.

We sometimes use the term "savior complex" to describe an unhealthy syndrome of obsession over solving others' problems. Ironically, the true Savior seemed remarkably free of such a complex. He had no compulsion to convert the entire world in his lifetime or to cure people who were not ready to be cured.

I never sense Jesus twisting a person's arm. Rather, he stated the consequences of a choice, then threw the decision back to the other party. For example, he once answered a wealthy man's question with uncompromising words, then let him walk away. Mark pointedly adds this comment about the man who rejected Jesus' advice, "Jesus looked at him and loved him."

In short, Jesus showed an incredible respect for human freedom. Those of us in ministry need the kind of "Savior complex" that Jesus demonstrated. As Elton Trueblood has observed, the major symbols of invitation that Jesus used had a severe, even offensive quality: the yoke of burden, the cup of suffering, the towel of servanthood. "Take up your *cross* and follow me," he said, in the least manipulative invitation that has ever been given.

"Unwrapping Jesus," *Christianity Today,*
June 17, 1996 (31)

◆

What Did He Look Like?

Despite a preponderance of scholarship, we still lack certain basic information about Jesus. The four gospels skip over nine-tenths of his life. We have only one scene from his adolescence and know nothing about his schooling. Details of his family life are so scant that scholars still debate how many brothers and sisters he had. The facts of biography considered essential to modern readers simply did not concern the gospel writers.

We also know nothing about Jesus' shape or stature or eye color. The first semirealistic portraits of Jesus did not appear until the fifth century, and these were pure speculation; until then the Greeks had portrayed him as a young, beardless figure resembling the god Apollo.

I once showed to a class several dozen art slides portraying Jesus in a variety of forms — African, Korean, Chinese — and then asked the class to describe what they thought Jesus looked like. Virtually everyone suggested he was tall (unlikely for a first-century Jew), most said handsome, and no one said overweight. I showed a BBC film on the life of Christ that featured a fat actor in the title role, and some in the class found it offensive. We prefer a tall, handsome, and above all slender Jesus.

One tradition dating back to the second century suggested Jesus was a hunchback, and in the Middle Ages Christians widely believed that Jesus had suffered from leprosy. In all the Bible I can find only one physical description of sorts, a prophecy written hundreds of years before Christ's birth. Here is Isaiah's portrayal, in the midst of a passage that the New Testament applies to the life of Jesus:

> Just as there were many who were appalled at him — his appearance was so disfigured beyond that of any man and his form marred beyond human likeness.... He had no beauty or majesty to attract us to him, nothing in his appearance that we should desire him. He was despised and rejected by men, a man of sorrows, and familiar with suffering. Like one from whom men hide their faces he was despised, and we esteemed him not.

Evidently, our glamorized representations of Jesus say more about us than about him.

"Unwrapping Jesus," *Christianity Today,*
June 17, 1996 (31)

Untaming Jesus

In writing a book about Jesus, one impression struck me more forcefully than any other: we have tamed him. The Jesus I learned about as a child was sweet and inoffensive, the kind of person whose lap you want to climb onto: someone like television's cuddly Mister Rogers, only with a beard. Indeed Jesus did have qualities of gentleness and compassion that attracted little children. Mister Rogers, however, he assuredly was not.

I realized this fact when I studied the Sermon on the Mount. "Blessed are the poor. Blessed are the persecuted. Blessed are those who mourn." These sayings have a soft, proverbial ring to them — unless you happen to know someone poor, persecuted, or mourning. The homeless huddling over heating grates in our major cities, the tortured prisoners whose pictures are distributed by Amnesty International, the families of terrorists' victims — who would think of calling them blessed, or "lucky"?

In all the movies made about Jesus' life, surely the most provocative — and perhaps the most accurate — portrayal of the Sermon on the Mount appears in a low-budget BBC production entitled *Son of Man*. Roman soldiers have just invaded a Galilean village to exact vengeance for some trespass against the empire. They have strung up Jewish men of fighting age, shoved their hysterical wives to the ground, even speared babies. Into that tumultuous scene of blood and tears and keening for the dead strides Jesus with eyes ablaze. "I tell you: Love your enemies and pray for those that persecute you," he shouts above the groans.

You can imagine the villagers' response to such unwelcome advice. The Sermon on the Mount did not soothe them; it infuriated them.

I came away from my study of Jesus both comforted and terrified. Jesus came to earth "full of grace and truth," said John: his truth comforts my intellectual doubts even as his grace comforts my emotional doubts. And yet I also encountered a terrifying aspect of Jesus, one that I had never learned about in Sunday school. Did anyone go away from Jesus' presence feeling satisfied about his or her life?

Few people felt comfortable around Jesus; those who did were the type no one else felt comfortable around. The Jesus I met in the Gospels was anything but tame.

"Unwrapping Jesus," *Christianity Today,*
June 17, 1996 (31 – 32)

A Slower, Gentler Way

The temptation in the desert reveals a profound difference between God's power and Satan's power. Satan has the power to coerce, to dazzle, to force obedience, to destroy. Humans have learned much from that power, and governments draw deeply from its reservoir. Human beings can force other human beings to do just about anything they want. Satan's power is external and coercive.

God's power, in contrast, is internal and noncoercive. Such power may seem at times like weakness. In its commitment to transform gently from the inside out and in its relentless dependence on human choice, God's power may resemble a kind of abdication. As every parent and every lover knows, love can be rendered powerless if the beloved chooses to spurn it.

"God is not a Nazi," said Thomas Merton. Indeed God is not. The Master of the Universe would become its victim, powerless before a squad of soldiers in a garden. God became weak for one purpose: to let human beings choose freely for themselves what to do with him.

Søren Kierkegaard wrote about God's light touch: "Omnipotence which can lay its hand so heavily upon the world can also make its touch so light that the creature receives independence." Sometimes, I concede, I wish that God used a heavier touch. My faith suffers from too much freedom, too many temptations to disbelieve. I want God to overwhelm me, to overcome my doubts with certainty, to give Final Proofs of God's existence and concern.

I want God to take a more active role in human affairs and in my personal history as well. Why must God "sit on his hands"? I want quick and spectacular answers to my prayers, healing for my diseases, protection and safety for my loved ones. I want a God without ambiguity, One to whom I can point for the sake of my doubting friends.

When I think these thoughts, I recognize in myself a thin, hollow echo of the challenge that Satan hurled at Jesus two thousand years ago. God resists those temptations now as Jesus resisted them on earth, settling instead for a slower, gentler way.

The Jesus I Never Knew (76 – 77)

◆

Miracle of Restraint

The more I get to know Jesus, the more impressed I am by what Ivan Karamazov called "the miracle of restraint." The miracles Satan suggested, the signs and wonders the Pharisees demanded, the Final Proofs I yearn for—these would offer no serious obstacle to an omnipotent God. More amazing is Jesus' *refusal* to perform and to overwhelm. God's terrible insistence on human freedom is so absolute that he granted us the power to live as though he did not exist, to spit in his face, to crucify him. All this Jesus must have known as he faced down the Tempter in the desert, focusing his mighty power on the energy of restraint.

I believe God insists on such restraint because no pyrotechnic displays of omnipotence will achieve the response God desires. Although power can force obedience, only love can summon a response of love, which is the one thing God wants from us. "I, when I am lifted up from the earth, will draw all men to myself," Jesus said. John adds, "He said this to show the kind of death he was going to die." God's nature is self-giving; he bases his appeal on sacrificial love.

I remember listening to a broken man relate the story of his prodigal son. Jake, the son, could not keep a job, wasted all his money on drugs and alcohol, and rarely called home. Jake's father described to me his feeling of helplessness in words not unlike those Jesus used about Jerusalem. "If only I could bring him back, and shelter him and try to show how much I love him," he said. Then he added, "The strange thing is, even though he rejects me, Jake's love means more to me than that of my other three, responsible children. Odd, isn't it? That's how love is."

I sense in that final four-word sentence more insight into the mystery of God's restraint than I have found in any book of theodicy. Why does God stay with the slow, unencouraging way of making righteousness grow rather than avenging it? *That's how love is.* Love has its own power, the only power ultimately capable of conquering the human heart.

The Jesus I Never Knew (78)

◆

Divine Shyness

This quality of restraint in Jesus—one could almost call it a divine shyness—took me by surprise. I realized, as I absorbed the story of Jesus in the Gospels, that I had expected from him the same qualities I had met in the Southern fundamentalist church of my childhood. There, I often felt the victim of emotional pressures. Doctrine was dished out in a "Believe and don't ask questions!" style. Wielding the power of miracle, mystery, and authority, the church left no place for doubt. I also learned manipulative techniques for "soul-winning," some of which involved misrepresenting myself to the person I was talking to. Yet now I am unable to find any of these qualities in the life of Jesus.

If I read church history correctly, many other followers of Jesus have yielded to the very temptations he resisted. Dostoevsky shrewdly replayed the temptation scene in the torture cell of the Grand Inquisitor. How could a church founded by the one who withstood the temptation carry out an Inquisition of forced belief that lasted half a millennium? Meanwhile, in a milder Protestant version in the city of Geneva, officials were making attendance at church compulsory and refusal to take the Eucharist a crime. Heretics there too were burned at the stake.

To its shame, Christian history reveals unrelieved attempts to improve on the way of Christ. Sometimes the church joins hands with a government that offers a shortcut path to power. "The worship of success is generally *the* form of idol worship which the devil cultivates most assiduously," wrote Helmut Thielicke about the German church's early infatuation with Adolf Hitler. "We could observe in the first years after 1933 the almost suggestive compulsion that emanates from great successes and how, under the influence of these successes, men, even Christians, stopped asking in whose name and at what price."

Sometimes the church grows its own mini-Hitlers, men with names like Jim Jones and David Koresh, who understand all too well the power represented in miracle, mystery, and authority. And sometimes the church simply borrows the tools of manipulation perfected by politicians, salesmen, and advertising copywriters.

The Jesus I Never Knew (80 – 81)

Children and Lovers

A friend stopped me the other day with some exciting news. She spent ten minutes re-creating for me the first steps of her year-old nephew. *He could walk!* Later I realized how bizarre we would have sounded to an eavesdropper. Almost everybody can walk. What was the big deal?

It struck me that infancy provides a rare luxury, a quality of *specialness* that nearly vanishes for the rest of life. The limelight of special attention may reignite when time comes for romance. To a lover every mole is cute, every weird hobby a sign of lively curiosity. Once again we are blessed with specialness—for a while, anyway, until the tedium of life chases it away.

Thinking about our treatment of children and lovers gave me further appreciation for some biblical metaphors. More than any other word pictures, God chooses "children" and "lovers" to describe our mutual relationship.

The Old Testament abounds with husband-bride imagery. God woos people, and dotes on them like a lover doting on his beloved. When they fail to respond, God feels hurt, spurned, like a jilted lover. The New Testament often uses the same imagery, picturing the church as "the bride of Christ." Shifting metaphors, it also announces that we are God's children, with all the rights and privileges of worthy heirs. Jesus (the "only begotten" Son of God) came, we're told, to make possible our adoption as sons and daughters in God's family. God looks upon us as we might look upon our own child, or our lover.

Infinity gives God a capacity we do not have: God can treat all of creation with unrelieved specialness. As I read the Bible, it seems clear that God satisfies an eternal appetite by loving individual human beings. I imagine God views each halting step forward in my spiritual "walk" with the eagerness of a parent watching a child take the very first step.

And perhaps, when the secrets of the universe are revealed, we will learn an underlying purpose of parenthood and romantic love. It may be that God has granted us these times of *specialness* to awaken us to the mere possibility of infinite love. Of that love, our most intimate experiences here on earth are mere glimpses.

I Was Just Wondering (163–66)

◆

Romance Business

Have you ever thought about how heavily our Gross National Product depends on romantic love? It dominates the arts: turn on any pop music station and try to find a song that does *not* feature that theme. In publishing, Gothic romances outsell every other line of books. And is there a television soap opera or comedy without a steamy romance woven into the plot?

Entire industries exist to capitalize on romantic love: the fashion, jewelry, and cosmetic trades all tempt us to perfect techniques of attraction between man and woman. Phrases like "catching a man" and "hunting a woman" have come to summarize a fact of life in our culture and, we assume, in every culture. This is the way life is, we think.

Ah, but herein lies a remarkable phenomenon: still today, in our international global village, over half of all marriages occur between a man and woman who have never felt a twinge of romantic love and might not even recognize the sensation if it hit them. Teenagers in most parts of Africa and Asia take for granted the notion of marriages arranged by parents in the same way we take for granted romantic love.

In the U.S. and other Western-style cultures, people tend to marry because they are attracted to another's appealing qualities. Over time, these qualities can change; the physical attributes, especially, will deteriorate with age. Meanwhile, unexpected surprises may surface.

In contrast, the partners in an arranged marriage do not center their relationship on mutual attractions. Having heard your parents' decision, you accept that you will live for many years with someone you now barely know. Thus the overriding question changes from "Whom should I marry?" to "Given this partner, what kind of marriage can we construct together?"

I doubt seriously that the West will ever abandon the notion of romantic love, no matter how poorly it serves as a basis for family stability. But in my conversations with Christians from different cultures I have begun to see how "the spirit of arranged marriages" might transform other attitudes. We may have something to learn in our practical expectations of the Christian life, for example.

[Continued on February 15]

I Was Just Wondering (172 – 74)

68

Spirit of Arranged Marriages

[Continued from February 14]

To take one example, I have always found strange the modern theological fixation with the problem of suffering. People in our society live longer, in far better health, with less physical pain than any in history. Yet our artists, playwrights, philosophers, and theologians stumble over themselves in search of new ways to rephrase the ancient questions of Job. Why does God allow so much suffering? Why doesn't God intervene?

Significantly, the outcries do not come from the Third World — where misery abounds — or from persons like Alexander Solzhenitsyn who endured great suffering. The cry of anguish comes primarily from those of us in the comfortable, narcissistic West. In thinking through this odd trend, I keep coming back to the parallel of arranged marriages.

In this view, we need "the spirit of arranged marriages" in our relationship with God. God made me the way I am: with my peculiar facial features, my handicaps and limitations, my body build, my mental capacity. I can spend my life resenting this quality or that one, and demanding that God change my "raw material." Or I can humbly accept myself, flaws and all, as the raw material God can work with. I do not go in with a list of demands that must be met before I take the vow. Like a husband in an arranged marriage, I pre-commit to God regardless of how it may work out. This involves risk, of course. I am unsure of what the future will hold.

You might say that faith means taking a vow "for better or worse, in sickness and health," to love God and cling to God *no matter what*. Happily, "the spirit of arranged marriage" works two ways: God also pre-commits to me. Faith means believing God has taken that same vow, and Jesus Christ offers the proof. God does not accept me conditionally, on the basis of my performance. God keeps the vow regardless, and therein is grace.

I Was Just Wondering (174 – 76)

The Hardship Ladder

The German pastor/theologian Helmut Thielicke once observed that "American Christians have an inadequate theology of suffering." Who could disagree? More, how could we expect a theology of suffering to emerge from a society that has survived nearly two centuries without a foreign invasion, solves all meteorological discomfort with "climate control," and prescribes a pill for every twinge of pain?

I have found at least five biblical approaches to suffering, and if we focus on one of these approaches exclusively, we risk not only an inadequate, but a heretical theology of suffering.

Stage 1: A person living right should never suffer.

Stage 2: Good people do endure hardships, but they will always get relief.

Stage 3: All things work together for good.

Stage 4: Faithful people may be called to suffer.

Stage 5: Holy indifference.

Stage 1: A person living right should never suffer. We have such "prosperity gospel" thoughts almost as a reflex. You would have to go back to Exodus and Deuteronomy to understand the source of this theology: God's covenant with the Israelites. God had guaranteed prosperity if the people would follow him faithfully, but the Israelites broke the terms of that covenant.

Stage 2: Good people do endure hardships, but they will always get relief. The author of many of the psalms of lament seems to believe, "If I can just convince God of my righteousness, then God will surely deliver me. There must be some mistake involved." I have come to see such self-justifying psalms as psalms of preparation. They help an entire nation understand that sometimes righteous people do suffer, and sometimes they don't get delivered.

Stage 3: All things work together for good. That famous phrase from Romans 8 is often distorted to imply "Only good things will happen to those who love God." Ironically, Paul meant just the opposite. In the remainder of the chapter, he defines what kind of "things" he is talking about: trouble, hardship, persecution, famine, nakedness, danger, sword. Yet, he insists, "*in all these things* we are more than conquerors"; no amount of hardship can separate us from the love of God.

[Continued on February 17]

I Was Just Wondering (182–84)

◆

Suffering's Graduate School

[Continued from February 16]

Stage 4: Faithful people may be called to suffer. The book of 1 Peter explains this new twist on hardship. Far from stage 1, where the righteous expect an immunity from suffering, this theology assumes persecution. Those believers following "in his steps" will, like Christ, suffer unjustly.

Stage 5: Holy indifference. The apostle Paul reached the exalted state described in a passage like Philippians 1, in which Paul can hardly decide whether it's better to die and be with Christ or to stay awhile and continue his ministry. His values seem topsy-turvy. Clearly, his stint in prison he sees as desirable, for that "hardship" has brought about many good results. Wealth, poverty, comfort, suffering, acceptance, rejection, even death or life—none of these circumstances matter much to Paul. Only one thing matters *ultimately*: the surpassing goal of exalting Christ, a goal that can be accomplished in any set of circumstances.

It bothers some people, I know, to list a series of biblical stages without a tidy formula resolving them into a grand scheme. For such people, I simply recommend contemplating stage 1 in the light of stage 5. Curiously, Paul's advanced state of holy indifference to pain puts him right back in stage 1. For Paul, a person living right did not suffer—not in any permanent sense, at least. And God could use all the events of Paul's life, whether painful or pleasurable, as a tool to advance the kingdom.

I have met few people who have attained the lofty state of stage 5, which may confirm Helmut Thielicke's comment about the United States. How can a nation so singularly blessed be expected to master such advanced faith? We must turn instead to the Christians in places like Pakistan or North Korea or Iran for a lesson in the graduate school of suffering. Alas, it seems we devote more time and energy debating the possibilities of stage 1—or at least yearning for those "good old days" when the U.S. won all its wars and the economy soared.

I Was Just Wondering (185–86)

◆

Limits of Miracles

Jesus, who presumably could work a wonder any day of his life if he wanted, seemed curiously ambivalent about miracles. With his disciples, he used them as proof of who he was ("Believe me when I say that I am in the Father and the Father is in me; or at least believe on the evidence of the miracles themselves"). But even as he performed them, he often seemed to downplay them. Mark records seven separate occasions when Jesus told a person he had healed, "Tell no one!"

Jesus knew well the shallow effect of miracles in Moses' day, and in Elijah's: they attracted crowds, yes, but rarely encouraged long-term faithfulness. He was bringing a hard message of obedience and sacrifice, not a sideshow for gawkers and sensation-seekers. (Sure enough, the true skeptics of his day—much like people today—explained away his powers.)

With remarkable consistency, the Bible's accounts show that miracles—the dramatic, show-stopping miracles that many of us still long for—simply do not foster deep faith. For proof, we need look no further than the transfiguration, when Jesus' face shone like the sun and his clothes became dazzling. To the disciples' astonishment, Moses and Elijah appeared in a cloud with them. God spoke audibly. It was too much to take and the disciples fell down, terrified.

Yet what effect did this stupendous event have on Peter, James, and John? Did it permanently silence their questions and fill them with faith? A few weeks later, when Jesus needed them the most, they all forsook him.

Although Jesus' miracles were far too selective to solve every human disappointment, they served as *signs* of his mission, previews of what God would someday do for all creation. For people who experienced them—the paralytic lowered like a chandelier for cleaning—the healings offered convincing proof that God was visiting earth. For everyone else, they awakened longings that will not be fulfilled until a final restoration ends all pain and death.

The miracles did just what Jesus had predicted. To those who chose to believe him, they gave even more reason to believe. But for those determined to deny him, the miracles made little difference. Some things just have to be believed to be seen.

Disappointment with God (116 – 18)

◇

Denying Myself

What are the implications of Jesus' statement that I need to lose my life for his sake? What does he mean, specifically, when he says I should deny that self I have come to know fairly well over the years, take up a cross, and follow him?

Jesus meant something important by his statements on denying the self or the gospel writers would not have repeated them so often. After much reflection, I have come to these conclusions about what he meant.

Self-denial first strikes at my basic identity. I am by nature a selfish creature, and I spend my time with a body and personality unique in all the world. It inevitably follows that I begin viewing the world through a viewpoint, making value judgments based on how things align with my perspective, and imposing my likes and dislikes on others around me.

In his essay, "The Trouble with X," C. S. Lewis points out that we spot a fatal flaw in almost everyone we meet, even our closest friends. We say about them, "He's a very fine fellow, and I enjoy his company. If only it weren't for his ..." Yet we almost never see that fatal flaw in ourselves. We rationalize our weaknesses, explaining them away with references to our backgrounds or our good intentions.

Denying myself starts with a full and repentant acceptance of the fatal flaw within me. Regardless of my accomplishments, my sophistication, my admirable traits, I must come to the humbling ground where I acknowledge I am not different from, but like every person who has ever lived. I am a sinner.

I cannot imagine a more difficult stumbling block in Christianity. It is relatively easy to inspire people with the Christian ethic of love; much liberal humanism is built on similar feelings. But every mechanism of self-protection within me cries out against this painful, renouncing step of identifying myself as a sinner. In that act I lose all the collected aspects of my identity and am known simply as a rebel against God.

[Continued on February 20]

Open Windows (209 – 10)

—◆—

Mirrors and Glass

[Continued from February 19]

Fortunately, however, I do not remain in that humbled state. "Christianity is strange," says Pascal. "It bids man recognize that he is vile, even abominable, and bids him desire to be like God. Without such a counterpoise, this dignity would make him horribly vain, or this humiliation would make him terribly abject." Where sin abounded grace did much more abound.

After going through the humiliating act of losing myself by letting go of that protective pride, I suddenly find myself with a new identity: the exalted state that Paul describes as "in-Christness." No longer must I defend my thoughts, my values, my actions. I trade those in for the identity I am given as a son of God. I relinquish the responsibility for setting my ethical standards and my worldview.

My sense of competition quickly fades. No longer do I have to bristle through life, racking up points to prove myself. My role has ideally become to prove God, to live my life in such a way that people around me recognize Jesus and his love, not the other set of qualities that separate me from the world.

I have found this process to be healthy, relaxing, and wholly good. All of us will realize it incompletely, but I believe the extent to which we realize it will determine our psychological health. Tensions and anxieties flame within me the moment I forget I am living my life for the one-man audience of Christ and slip into living my life to assert myself in a competitive world.

Previously, my main motivation in life was to do a painting of myself, filled with bright colors and profound insights, so that all who looked upon it would be impressed. Now, however, I find that my role is to be a mirror, to brightly reflect the image of God through me. Or perhaps the metaphor of stained glass would serve better, for, after all, God will illumine through my personality and body.

Open Windows (210 – 11)

◆

Two Cheers for Guilt

L ove means never having to say you're sorry," proclaimed a sappy romance novel from the 1970s. I have come to believe the opposite, that love means precisely having to say you're sorry. A sense of guilt, vastly underappreciated, deserves our gratitude, for only such a powerful force can nudge us toward repentance and reconciliation with those we have harmed.

Yet guilt represents danger as well. I have known Christians who go through life with a hyper-attention to defects, terrified that they are somehow offending one of God's laws. A mature Christian learns to discriminate between false guilt inherited from parents, church, or society and true guilt as a response to breaking God's laws clearly revealed in the Bible.

A second danger flows directly from the first. Some people tend to wallow in guilt, as if unaware that guilt, like physical pain, is directional. Just as the physical body speaks to us in the language of pain so that we will attend to the injury site, the soul speaks to us in the language of guilt so that we will take the steps necessary for healing. The goal in both is to restore health.

In his book *Legends of our Time*, Elie Wiesel tells of a visit to his home town of Sighet, in Hungary. Twenty years before, Wiesel and all other Jews in that town had been rounded up and deported to concentration camps. To his dismay, he found that the current residents of the town had simply erased the memory of those Jews. It struck Wiesel that forgetting one's sins may be as great an evil as committing them in the first place, for what is forgotten can never be healed.

In my reading of spiritual masters, I have noticed that persons we now view as saintly have a finely calibrated sense of sin. Aware of God's ideal, aspiring to holiness, free of the vanity and defensiveness that blind most people, they live in full awareness of falling short.

True saints do not get discouraged over their faults, for they recognize that a person who feels no guilt can never find healing. Paradoxically, neither can a person who wallows in guilt. The sense of guilt only serves its designed purpose if it presses us toward a God who promises forgiveness and restoration.

"Back Page" column, *Christianity Today*,
November 18, 2002 (112)

Criticizing Jesus

When a new leader starts making waves, opposition surely follows. While on earth, Jesus makes an extravagant claim: he claims to be the Messiah, sent from God. And opposition to him springs up soon after the wild surge of popularity in Galilee. Mark 2 tells of three different criticisms that people will make against Jesus throughout his life.

He blasphemes. The teachers of the law are scandalized by Jesus forgiving sins. "Who can forgive sins but God alone?" they mutter. Jesus readily agrees that only God can forgive sins — that is his point, exactly.

Throughout his life, Jesus faces strongest opposition from the most pious followers of Old Testament law; they can never accept that the awesome, distant God of Israel could take up residence inside a human body. Eventually, they have Jesus executed for making that claim. (People who accept Jesus as a "good man and enlightened teacher" today often overlook the scenes where Jesus blatantly identifies himself with God. When the Pharisees react violently to Jesus in his day, it is because they have heard him correctly — they simply refuse to believe him.)

He keeps disreputable company. Jesus shows a distinct preference for the most unseemly sort of people. He offends politicians and religious leaders by calling them names. Even after becoming famous, he dines with an outcast tax collector and his low-life friends. On hearing the gossip about this strange behavior, Jesus says simply, "It is not the healthy who need a doctor, but the sick. I have not come to call the righteous, but sinners."

He goes against tradition. To the Pharisees, it seems Jesus' disciples are playing fast and loose with the holy Sabbath. Jesus' response: It's time for a new cloth; the old one has been patched together long enough. Before long, he will introduce the "new covenant." God has some major changes in store for the human race, and the narrow, confining covenant with the Israelites simply can't hold all those changes.

Meet the Bible (427 – 28)

The Mystery That Never Goes Away

The story about the sower of seed summarizes well the mixed results Jesus himself gets while on earth. We who live two thousand years later, with such events as Christmas and Easter marked plainly on our calendars, may easily miss the sheer incredulity that greets Jesus in the flesh.

Neighbors have watched him play in the streets; Jesus is simply too familiar for them to believe he was sent from God. "Isn't this the carpenter?" they ask. "Isn't this Mary's son and the brother of James, Joseph, Judas and Simon?... What's this wisdom that has been given him, that he even does miracles!" (Mark 6:3, 2).

Not even Jesus' family can easily reconcile the wondrous and the ordinary. Mark mentions that one time Jesus' mother and brothers arrive to take charge of him because they have concluded, "He is out of his mind" (3:21). Neither can common people make up their minds about Jesus. They judge him "raving mad" (John 10:20) one moment, then forcibly try to crown him king the next.

The scribes and Pharisees, who pore over the Prophets, should have the clearest notion of what the Messiah will look like. But no group causes Jesus more trouble. They criticize his theology, his lifestyle, and his choice of friends. When he performs miracles, they attribute his power to Satan and demons.

When a storm nearly capsizes the boat transporting Jesus, he yells into the wind, "Quiet! Be still!" The disciples shrink back in terror. What kind of person can shout down the weather, as if correcting an unruly child? That scene helps convince them Jesus is unlike anyone else on earth. Yet it suggests a reason for their confusion about him. Jesus has, after all, fallen asleep in the boat from sheer fatigue, a symptom of his human frailty.

The early church will argue for three centuries about exactly what happened when God became man, but their creeds will do little to dispel the sense of mystery. In a way, Jesus is just like everyone else — he has a race, an occupation, a family background, a body shape. In a way, he is something entirely new in the history of the universe. In between those two statements lies the mystery that never completely goes away.

Meet the Bible (431 – 32)

◆

Out of Control

The last weekend of February 2007, I spoke at a historic church in Los Alamos, New Mexico. When I spoke to the community on the subject of prayer that evening, I related some of my mountain-climbing adventures. For instance, on the day my wife and I summitted Mt. Wilson we were still well above the safety of timberline when dark clouds moved in. Lightning struck closer and closer. "What do we do?" I asked our experienced companion.

"There's really not much you can do," he replied. "The granite rock conducts electricity. I'd recommend separating by at least a hundred yards or so — that way if one of us gets hit, another can go for help. And squat down with your feet together to make yourself as small a target as possible."

My wife and I looked at each other. Finally I shrugged and said, "Honey, we've had a good life. Let's go together." We ditched our buzzing hiking poles and squatted down, as our friend suggested, but side by side, holding hands. For the next hour we got pummeled by rain, hail, sleet, snow, and a mixture of all at once, all the while counting the seconds between each lightning bolt that sizzled around us and the blast of thunder that followed.

"I learned an important life lesson," I told the folks who had gathered in the United Church. "I am not in control. I must tell you, as a freelance writer I'm something of a control freak. I have to be. Since I have no boss telling me what to do, I have to organize my own life, and most of the time I go around feeling like I'm in control. As I learned atop Mt. Wilson, that's an illusion."

I went on to say that this mountain-climbing lesson actually applies all the time. "Even when I think I'm in control, I'm not. I could die of a heart attack right in front of you before finishing this sentence." Some in the audience laughed nervously. "Or I could have an auto accident driving back to Denver tomorrow — probably far more likely than getting hit by lightning on Mt. Wilson." More laughter.

How eerily prophetic those words would prove to be.

[Continued on February 25]

Trip notes, later included in some editions
of *Prayer: Does It Make Any Difference?*

The Longest Day

[Continued from February 24]

Sunday morning, driving back from Los Alamos to Denver, I turned down a small, remote road just over the Colorado border, more for variety in scenery than anything else. Snow had fallen a few days before, and several times I was surprised by patches of ice on the road. Suddenly, as I headed downhill into one curve, my Ford Explorer began to fishtail. I fought it until the right rear tire slipped off the pavement and grabbed soft dirt. Then the Explorer rolled sideways, over and over, five times in all.

The noise was deafening, a crescendo of glass, plastic, and metal breaking all at once. Every window shattered, spilling skis, boots, ice skates, my laptop computer, and luggage across the Colorado countryside.

Finally the rolling stopped, with the vehicle in an upright position. I turned off the ignition, unbuckled my seatbelt, and ducked under the collapsed roof to stumble to the ground. My nose was bleeding, I had cuts on my face, legs, and arms, and I felt a searing pain in my upper back, just below the neck. My belongings were strewn over a hundred feet, and I wandered the desert landscape searching for my laptop and cell phone.

A few minutes later a car pulled over. A well-dressed couple got out, ran to the scene, and started giving orders. They were both certified Emergency Medical Technicians, and the husband headed up the ambulance corps for the county. They led me to their car, called for an ambulance, and sat beside me holding my head in a fixed position. "How did you happen to come down this remote road early on a Sunday morning?" I asked after they had stabilized my neck.

"We're Mormons," the woman replied. "We've just started a mission church in the tiny town of San Luis, and we're driving over to help them get on their feet."

Thus began one of the longest, most memorable days of my life. When the ambulance came, attendants strapped me into a rigid body board, taping my head still and immobilizing it with a neck brace. We drove almost an hour to reach the town of Alamosa, where I was transferred with much jostling and bumping onto a gurney and into a hospital emergency room.

[Continued on February 26]

Trip notes, later included in some editions
of Prayer: Does It Make Any Difference?

◆

Threat to Life

[Continued from February 25]

For two hours I lay in a most uncomfortable position on the body board, awaiting results from CAT scans. Then the doctor came in. "There's no easy way to say this, Mr. Yancey . . ." I had a broken neck, specifically the C–3 vertebra in a "comminuted" or pulverized fashion. The good news was that the break did not occur in the spinal cord channel itself. If it had, I would likely have ended up paralyzed like Christopher Reeve. The bad news was that a bone fragment may well have nicked a major artery.

"We have a jet standing by if needed to airlift you to Denver for surgery," the doctor explained. "We'll do another CAT scan, this time with an iodine dye solution to reveal any possible leakage from the artery. I must emphasize, this is a life-threatening situation. You may want to contact your loved ones."

In all, I lay strapped onto that body board for seven hours that day, plenty of time to think through my life. I've written articles on people whose lives have been instantly changed by an accident that left them paraplegic or quadriplegic. I had narrowly missed that fate. But if my artery was leaking, an artery that feeds the brain, or if it formed a blood clot, well, I soon faced a fate worse than paralysis.

As I lay there, contemplating what I had just been teaching in Los Alamos about prayer, and facing for the first time the imminent possibility of death, I felt surprisingly peaceful. I reflected on what a wonderful life I have had, with a life-giving marriage partner, adventures in more than fifty countries, work that allows me both meaning and near-total freedom, and connections through my writing with people I've never met.

I looked back on my life and felt little regret. And as I thought of what may await me, I felt deep trust. Although no one raised in the kind of church environment I grew up in totally leaves behind the acrid smell of fire and brimstone, I had an overwhelming sense of trust in God. I have come to know a God of compassion and mercy and love.

[Continued on February 27]

Trip notes, later included in some editions
of *Prayer: Does It Make Any Difference?*

Daze of Grace

[Continued from February 26]

As it happened, thank God—oh, yes, thank God—the results turned out far better than I could have hoped. The scans revealed no arterial leakage. The hospital released me within an hour of my wife's arrival, fitted with a stiff neck brace that kept my head from moving for the next twelve weeks. After several months of physical therapy, the fractures healed, and I am left only with some residual soreness and vertebrae that are slightly misaligned. I may need surgery for spinal fusion sometime later, but in almost every way I have resumed normal life.

Looking back now, I see many coincidences—God-incidences?—that contributed to a good outcome. The EMT-trained Mormons traveling that route early on a Sunday morning. The most experienced X-ray technician, normally off-duty on weekends, filling in for a sick colleague. The emergency room doctor, a star graduate of an elite medical school, returning to his small Colorado town to be of service. And, most of all, the injury itself, serious but not nearly as catastrophic as the alternatives.

I now look back on that long day, spent strapped to a body board in an ambulance and then emergency room, as a unique gift. All of us will face death, some through a long degenerative illness like cancer and others through an abrupt accident. I had something in between, a window of time in which I lay suspended between life and nonlife, with the very real possibility of death within a few minutes or hours and yet an opportunity to emerge with overwhelming good news and another chance at life.

I hope that I never forget that window of time or what I saw through it. For a few weeks after the accident I walked around in a "daze of grace," looking at the sky, trees, grass, my wife, my friends, with newly washed eyes. Even as my battered body brought new aches and pains to my attention, life held surprises around every corner, fresh promptings to gratitude and joy. Each day I awoke with a profound sense of gratitude for the simplest things: birds flitting from tree to tree, the sound of a creek flowing around rocks and ice near our home, the ability to move a finger, to dress myself.

[Continued on February 28]

Trip notes, later included in some editions
of Prayer: Does It Make Any Difference?

◆

All That Matters

[Continued from February 27]

Word of the accident got out, and over the next few months I was overwhelmed by support from friends, family, and people I have never met. In the act of writing I spill something of my soul onto the printed page, and through the cards and letters that came in I realized a remarkable link can forge even with strangers. One person wrote me that Quakers have a phrase they were exercising on my behalf: "holding you in the light." I felt held, truly.

My wife, while working as a hospice chaplain, observed a striking difference in the way that believers and unbelievers face death. Both feel fear and pain and grief. But Christians have an almost palpable contribution in the mysterious linkage that comes through prayer. It's the difference between a hospice visitor saying "I will pray for you—honest, every day," and someone saying, "Good luck. Best wishes."

Recently, a spate of authors have been trumpeting a kind of triumphalist atheism. I can understand why someone would choose atheism, but I cannot understand why such a stance might seem like good news, something worth trumpeting. Lying helpless, strapped to a body board, I would have felt utterly and inconsolably alone, except for my faith that I lay in the hands of a God who loves me and promises a future beyond death.

I am trying to keep before me the crystalline vision I had while lying strapped down for seven hours. I have learned how thin is the thread that separates life from nonlife, and how comforting is the knowledge that I am not alone on this journey. I have learned these things in a way that I doubt I will ever forget. What we spend so much time and energy on (finances, image, achievement) matters so little in the face of imminent death.

What matters reduces down to a few basic questions. *Who do I love? Who will I miss? How have I spent my life? Am I ready for what's next?* The challenge is, How do I keep those questions in the forefront as I come to my desk each day and face piles of paper and blinking electronic messages?

Trip notes, later included in some editions
of *Prayer: Does It Make Any Difference?*

Chess Master

In high school, I took pride in my ability to play chess. I joined the chess club and, during lunch hour, could be found sitting at a table with other nerds, poring over books with titles like *Classic King Pawn Openings*. I studied techniques, won most of my matches, and put the game aside for twenty years. Then, in Chicago, I met a truly fine chess player who had been perfecting his skills long since high school.

When we played a few matches, I learned what it is like to play against a master. Any classic offense I tried, he countered with a classic defense. If I turned to more risky, unorthodox techniques, he incorporated my bold forays into his winning strategies. Although I had complete freedom to make any move I wished, I soon reached the conclusion that none of my strategies mattered very much. His superior skill guaranteed that my purposes inevitably ended up serving his own.

Perhaps God engages our universe, the creation, in much the same way. God grants us freedom to rebel against its original design, but even as we do so we end up ironically serving the eventual goal of restoration. If I accept that blueprint — a huge step of faith, I confess — it transforms how I view both good and bad things that happen. Good things, such as health, talent, and money, I can present to God as offerings to serve divine purposes. And bad things too — disability, poverty, family dysfunction, failures — can be "redeemed" as the very instruments that drive me to God. Many people find that a persistent temptation, even an addiction, is the very wound that causes them to turn in desperation to God, so that the wound forms a beginning point for new creation.

A skeptic might accuse me of flagrant rationalization, arguing backward to make evidence fit a prior conclusion. Yes, exactly. A Christian begins with the conclusion that a good God will restore creation to its original design, and sees all history as proceeding toward that end. When a Grand Master plays a chess amateur, victory is assured no matter how the board may look at any given moment.

"Back Page" column, *Christianity Today*,
May 22, 2000 (112)

March

◆

Church Checkup

As an experiment, my wife and I decided to go through the Yellow Pages under "Churches" and visit each of the twenty-four listed in our local phone book. With an intuition difficult to explain, I could usually sense the "aliveness" of a congregation within five minutes. Were people conversing in the foyer? Did I hear the sound of laughter? What activities and issues did the bulletin board highlight?

To my surprise, the aliveness factor had little to do with theology. In two of the most conservative churches, members slumped to their seats and glumly went through the motions. A very liberal church showed the most energy in community and global outreach programs.

I now have a clear picture of the qualities to look for in a healthy church.

1. *Diversity.* As I read accounts of the New Testament church, no characteristic stands out more sharply than this one. Beginning with Pentecost, the Christian church dismantled the barriers of gender, race, and social class that had marked Jewish congregations. Paul, who as a rabbi had given thanks daily that he was not born a woman, slave, or Gentile, marveled over the radical change: "There is neither Jew nor Greek, slave nor free, male nor female, for you are all one in Christ Jesus."

When I walk into a new church, the more its members resemble each other, and resemble me, the more uncomfortable I feel.

2. *Unity.* Of course, diversity only succeeds in a group of people who share a common vision. In his great prayer in John 17, Jesus stressed one request above all others: "that they may be one." The existence of 38,000 denominations worldwide demonstrates how poorly we have fulfilled Jesus' request. Perhaps a whiff of this fragrance is what I detect when I visit a new church and sense its "aliveness."

3. *Mission.* The church, said Archbishop William Temple, is "the only cooperative society in the world that exists for the benefit of its non-members." Some churches, especially those located in urban areas, focus on the needs of immediate neighborhoods. Others adopt sister churches in other countries, support relief and development agencies, and send mission teams abroad. Saddest of all are those churches whose vision does not extend beyond their own facility and parking lot.

"Back Page" column, *Christianity Today,*
November, 2008 (119)

◆

It Takes All Kinds

Every church I have attended includes a measure of diversity. I think back fondly on two people in the church of my childhood in Atlanta, Georgia —people I took turns sitting with when my mother was off teaching Sunday school. I loved sitting with Mrs. Payton because she had a stole, a garish bit of frippery that consisted of two minks biting each other's tails. All during the service I would play with the hard, shiny eyes, the sharp, pointed teeth, and the soft skin and floppy tails of those animals. Mrs. Payton's minks helped me endure many a wearisome sermon.

Mr. Ponce wore no animals around his neck, but I knew no kinder person anywhere. He had six children of his own, and he seemed happy only when a child was occupying his lap. He was a huge man, and I could sit there contentedly for an entire service without his leg falling asleep. He praised the pictures I drew on the church bulletin, and drew funny faces in my hands that would smile and wink when I moved my fingers a certain way.

I remember Mr. Ponce for his kindness, and also for an enormous sprout of nasal hair, easily visible when I looked up from his lap. If you had asked me then who I liked best, probably Mr. Ponce would get the edge. My own father died when I was only a year old, and Mr. Ponce provided for me a comforting male presence.

Later, when I grew older and more sophisticated, I learned the facts: Mrs. Payton was rich, which accounted for the animals around her neck. Her family owned a successful Cadillac dealership. Mr. Ponce, on the other hand, drove a garbage truck and barely brought in enough money to support his large family. When I learned these facts, I realized to my shame that as an adult I probably would not have befriended Mr. Ponce. We probably would have shared few interests.

I am glad, very glad, that the church of Jesus Christ in my childhood included both of these friends. I now see that the church should be an environment where both Mrs. Payton of the hairy stole and Mr. Ponce of the hairy nose feel equally welcome.

Church: Why Bother? (53 – 54)

◆

Basil's Visit

I joined a delegation of Christians as it visited Russia in 1991, at the time of the Soviet Union's collapse. As we encountered unvarying politeness and respect for Christianity, it was easy to lose sight of how radically the nation was changing in its attitude toward religion. Basil's visit brought a jarring reminder.

Basil had been listening, incredulous, to reports on state radio that Christians from the U.S. were meeting with the Supreme Soviet and the KGB. The new openness toward religion seemed so inconceivable to Basil that he got on a night train and made the fourteen-hour journey from Moldavia in order to see us.

Basil had broad, hulking shoulders and the rugged, weather-beaten features of a farmer. He had a most peculiar smile: two front teeth on the top row were missing, and when he smiled gold fillings in the back molars gleamed faintly through the gap.

When Basil opened his mouth and the first sound came out, I jumped. Basil spoke at the decibel level of a freight train. I have never heard a louder voice from any human being. We soon learned why.

In 1962 Basil was arrested and sent to a labor camp for distributing Christian literature. At first Basil was perplexed. Why should he be punished for serving God? But then one morning he saw in a flash that God had provided a new opportunity.

Every morning before sunup prisoners from the labor camp had to assemble in an open space for roll call. Camp commanders insisted on strict punctuality from prisoners, but not from guards. As a result, thousands of prisoners stood outdoors for several minutes each morning with nothing to do. Basil, who loved to preach, decided to start a church.

As he was recounting this story in the hotel room, Basil spoke louder and faster, gesturing passionately with his arms like an opera singer. Every few sentences the translator, Alex, grabbed Basil's flailing arm and asked him to please slow down and lower his voice. Each time Basil apologized, looked down at the floor, and began again in a pianissimo that within three seconds crescendoed to a fortissimo. His voice had no volume control, and the reason traced back to that early morning scene in the labor camp.

[Continued on March 4]

Praying with the KGB (40 – 42)

The Two-Minute Church

[Continued from March 3]

Basil preached daily to a truly captive audience. Typically, he had about two minutes before the guards arrived, rarely as long as five minutes, and as a result it often took him two weeks to deliver a single sermon. He had to shout to be heard by several thousand prisoners, a strain that made him hoarse until his voice adapted. Over the years — ten years in all — of speaking outdoors to thousands, he developed the habit of speaking at top volume and breakneck speed, a habit he could never break.

Released from prison in 1972, Basil devoted his energies to building an unregistered church in his village. Now, after nineteen years, opposition had faded away and he had just laid the last cement block and covered the church with a roof. He had come to Moscow, he said, to thank us for all we were doing, to bring us fresh fruit from Moldavia, and to ask Alex Leonovich, a Russian-American evangelist known for his radio broadcasts, to speak at the dedication of his church.

"There were many years when I had no encouragement," Basil said. By now he was weeping openly and his voice cracked but did not drop one decibel. "The words of this man, Brother Leonovich, I carried in my heart. He was the one who encouraged me when my hands were tied behind my back." He then reached over, grabbed Alex by the shoulders, and kissed him in the Russian style once, twice, fifteen times — one for each year, he said, that he had waited for Alex to return to Russia.

"And now, such changes, I can hardly believe them," Basil said in closing. "When Billy Graham came in 1959 they let him appear on a balcony but not speak. To think that you are here, able to talk with the leaders of our country. Brothers and sisters, be bold! Where I come from the believers are praying for you at this minute. We believe your visit will help reach our country for God. God bless you all!"

Suddenly, I burned with shame. Here we were: nineteen professionals who made a good living from our faith, sitting in a luxurious hotel. What did we know about the kind of bedrock faith needed in this nation of people who had endured such suffering?

Praying with the KGB (42 – 43)

◆

Three Tears

Three times that we know of, suffering drove Jesus to tears. He wept when his friend Lazarus died. I remember one dreadful year when three of my friends died in quick succession. Grief, I found, is not something you get used to. My experience of the first two deaths did nothing to prepare me for the third. Grief hit like a freight train, flattening me. It left me gasping for breath, and I could do nothing but cry. Somehow, I find it comforting that Jesus felt something similar when his friend Lazarus died.

Another time, tears came to Jesus when he looked out over Jerusalem and realized the fate awaiting that fabled city. I sense in that spasm of emotional pain something akin to what a parent feels when a son or daughter goes astray, flaunting freedom, rejecting everything he or she was brought up to believe. Or the pain of a man or woman who has just learned a spouse has left. Not even God, with all power, can force a human being to love.

Finally, Hebrews tells us, Jesus "offered up loud cries and tears to the one who could save him from death." But of course he was not saved from death. Is it too much to say that Jesus himself asked the question that haunts me, that haunts most of us at one time or another: Does God care? What else can be the meaning of his quotation from that dark psalm, "My God, my God, why have you forsaken me?"

Again, I find it strangely comforting that when Jesus faced pain he responded much as I do. He experienced sorrow, fear, abandonment, and something approaching even desperation. Yet he endured because he knew that at the center of the universe lived his Father, a God of love he could trust regardless of how things appeared at the time.

Jesus' response to suffering people provides a glimpse into the heart of God. God is not the unmoved Absolute, but rather the Loving One who draws near.

The Jesus I Never Knew (160 – 61)

◇

Writers as Earthworms

I once heard a writer describe other writers as the earthworms of society. "We aerate the soil," she said. By tunneling through *humus*, the essentially human, writers let in air and light, at the same time creating spaces that readers can fill on their own. Books have a certain decorum about them because the earthworms who have created the tunnel are not staring you in the face, intimidating you into agreeing with them. They have digested the dirt and moved on.

For years, whenever I attended a church or Christian meeting, I would put on defensive armor. I trusted Christian speakers about as much as most people trust the Jehovah's Witnesses who appear at the door. I knew their tricks all too well: their ability to play on emotions like stringed instruments, their backstage hypocrisy. Books, though, were another matter. I could read them at my own pace, letting my emotions respond in a more authentic, less manipulated way.

Books keep religious writers honest. You can't lock an auditorium door or browbeat your audience or go into a trance. You stick the naked word on a page and it speaks for itself. As a result, Liz Curtis Higgs gives *Mere Christianity* a one-page test, then reads another, and another, and before long she has read the entire book and begun a steady return to faith. Chuck Colson, in very different circumstances, picks up the same book and has the uncanny sense that Lewis has perfectly diagnosed his spiritual disease, pride.

I doubt seriously that C. S. Lewis, an Oxford don, had anyone resembling Liz Curtis Higgs or Chuck Colson in mind when he wrote the book. He was delivering radio addresses in order to bring hope and spiritual renewal to a Britain devastated by World War II. Writers, and I speak from humble experience here, have little inkling of who will respond to our books, and what impact they will have.

Foreword to *Indelible Ink: 22 Prominent Christian Leaders Discuss the Books that Shape Their Faith* (x)

◇

Getting It Wrong

I love my work and cannot imagine doing anything else. I begin, however, with a deep sense of humility, an awareness that we writers are little more than Peeping Toms at the keyhole of reality.

I once wrote about a friend of mine named Larry, one of the most fascinating people I've ever known. A bisexual, he has a history of liaisons with people of both genders. A recovering alcoholic, he attends AA sessions almost daily, has twenty years of sobriety behind him, and has gone on to become a substance-abuse counselor for others. Raised Mennonite, he rebelled by serving in Vietnam, but has since become a doctrinaire pacifist.

Along the way Larry became a Christian. He says he was converted by two hymns, "Just As I Am," and "Amazing Grace." As he heard the words of those hymns, it sunk in for the first time that God really did want him just as he was; God's grace was that amazing. In his own way, Larry has been following God ever since. Larry states his dilemma this way: "I guess I'm caught somewhere between 'Just as I am' and 'Just as God wants me to be.'"

I wrote about Larry briefly in an introduction to an article for *Christianity Today*, changing a few details to protect his privacy. A few weeks later I got a phone call from my friend. "I saw the article," he said. I waited. And then came these devastating words: "Philip, I've lived all my life trying to be a real person, a three-dimensional person. You've reduced me to a two-paragraph illustration."

Larry was right, of course. At that moment I realized he had identified what we writers do: we reduce. We reduce the magnificence of human beings to statistics, and illustrations, and article leads. Journalism—and indeed all art—is not reality but a mere portrayal or depiction that will never do it justice. I try to remind myself of that every time I turn to the keyboard. I will do my best to render truth, but I will fail. I will never get it right. That too is part of the pilgrim journey of this calling.

"The Literature of Fact: On the Writer as Journalist,"
from *A Syllable of Water: Twenty Writers
of Faith Reflect Upon Their Art* (165–67)

When the Economy Collapses

During a tumultuous week in 2008 in which global stock markets declined by seven *trillion* dollars, I got a call from *Time* magazine. "How should a person pray during a crisis like this?" the editor asked. As we spoke, we came up with a three-stage approach to prayer.

The first stage is simple, an instinctive cry for "Help!" Look at Jesus' prayer in Gethsemane. With sweat falling like blood, he felt "overwhelmed with sorrow to the point of death." His prayer, however, changed from "Take this cup from me" to "May your will be done." Prayer relieved him of anxiety, reaffirmed his trust in a loving Father, and emboldened him to face the cross.

If I pray with intent to listen as well as talk, I can enter into a second stage, that of meditation and reflection. Okay, my life savings has virtually disappeared. What can I learn from this seeming catastrophe? A Sunday school song came to mind: *The wise man built his house upon the rock . . . And the wise man's house stood firm.* And then, *The foolish man built his house upon the sand . . . Oh, the rain came down and the floods came up . . .*

A time of crisis presents a good opportunity to identify the foundation on which I construct my life. If I place my ultimate trust in financial security, or in the government's ability to solve my problems, I will surely watch the house crumble. (*And the foolish man's house went "splat!"*)

The same week of financial collapse, Zimbabwe's inflation rate hit a record 231 million percent. Which leads me to the third stage of prayer in crisis times: I need God's help in taking my eyes off my own problems in order to look with compassion on the truly desperate.

In the days of a collapsing Roman empire, Christians stayed behind to nurse plague victims, and wet nurses gathered up babies abandoned along the roadside. What a testimony it would be if during hard times Christians resolved to increase their giving to build houses for the poor, combat AIDS in Africa, and announce kingdom values to a decadent, celebrity-driven culture.

Such a response defies all logic. Unless, of course, we take seriously the moral of Jesus' simple tale about building houses on a sure foundation.

"Back Page" column, *Christianity Today,*
January 2009 (80)

Mormons, Pharisees, and Evangelicals

A pamphlet I read on Mormonism praised certain characteristics: industriousness, self-reliance, resistance to government interference. Mormons point to upright living, high achievement, and sterling citizenship as primary proofs of their faith.

Despite the obvious appeal of all these qualities, something nagged at me as I read the pamphlet. The virtues it extolled brought to my mind not Mormons but evangelicals. Virtually every word could have been written in a brochure promoting evangelicals. Do we not want to be known for good citizenship, industriousness, righteousness, and temperance?

One of Walker Percy's characters in *The Second Coming* comments:

> I am surrounded by Christians. They are generally speaking a pleasant and agreeable lot, not noticeably different from other people.... But if they have the truth, why is it the case that they are repellent precisely to the degree that they embrace and advertise the truth?... A mystery: If the good news is true, why is not one pleased to hear it?

His last question rings loud. Could it be that Christians, eager to point out how good they are, neglect one basic fact—that the gospel comes as a eucatastrophe, a spectacularly good thing happening to spectacularly bad people?

Since evangelicals have been busily reading into the *Congressional Record* biblical rationales on abortion, the Department of Education, tobacco subsidies, and sundry Supreme Court decisions, I would propose an important and corrective balance. In our churches, why not spend more time discussing the implications of Jesus' parable of the righteous man and the tax collector? One man thanked God for his blessings, that he was not a robber, evildoer, adulterer, or tax collector. He fasted twice a week and tithed his income. The other had a questionable morality, not much in the way of a résumé, and a thoroughly inadequate theology. One prayed eloquently; the other said seven simple words, "God, have mercy on me, a sinner." Yet which one went home justified?

Curiously, the righteous Pharisees had little historical impact, save for a brief time in a remote corner of the Roman Empire. But Jesus' disciples—an ornery, undependable, and hopelessly flawed group—became drunk with the power of a gospel that offered free forgiveness to the worst sinners and traitors. Those disciples managed to change the world.

I Was Just Wondering (98 – 101)

◆

The Company He Kept

Jesus was the friend of sinners. They liked being around him and yearned for his company. Meanwhile, legalists found him shocking, even revolting. What was Jesus' secret that we have lost?

"You can know a person by the company he keeps," the proverb goes. Imagine the consternation of people in first-century Palestine who tried to apply that principle to Jesus of Nazareth. The Gospels mention eight occasions when Jesus accepted an invitation to dinner. Three of these were normal social occasions among friends. The other five, however, defy all rules of social propriety.

Once, Jesus dined with Simon the Leper. Because of my work with Dr. Paul Brand, a leprosy specialist, I too have dined with leprosy patients, and I can tell you that two thousand years of medical progress have done little to lessen the social stigma of the disease. One refined, educated man in India told me of the day he sat weeping in a car outside a church as his daughter got married within. He dared not show himself, lest all the guests leave. Nor could he host the traditional wedding banquet, for who would enter the home of a leper?

In Palestine, stern laws enforced the stigma against leprosy: the afflicted had to live outside city walls and yell, "Unclean!" when they approached anyone. Yet Jesus ignored those rules and reclined at the table of a man who wore that stigma as part of his name. To make matters worse, during the course of the meal an uninhibited woman poured expensive perfume on Jesus' head. According to Mark, Judas Iscariot left the meal in disgust and went straight to the chief priests to betray Jesus.

At least one other time Jesus accepted hospitality from a prominent Pharisee. Like double agents, the religious leaders were following him around and inviting him to meals while scrutinizing his every move. Provocatively, despite it being the Sabbath, Jesus healed a man from dropsy, and then he drew a stinging contrast between the social-climbing banquets of the Pharisees and God's banquet spread for "the poor, the crippled, the blind and the lame." The Gospels record no other meals with prominent citizens, and I can easily understand why: Jesus hardly made for a soothing dinner guest.

The Jesus I Never Knew (149 – 50)

◇

Subversive Faith

In 2004 I visited Hungary to speak at a Youth for Christ staff conference and then took a train to Austria to spend a weekend at a castle affiliated with IFES, the international version of InterVarsity. Both venues had people from Eastern Europe attending, and I heard some amazing stories.

Most of those I met from Ukraine, Latvia, and such countries were raised by atheists and converted as teenagers. Sergey, for instance, converted when he was twelve. He would tell his parents he was going to the outhouse (no indoor bathrooms, of course) and climb over the fence to pray with his Christian neighbors. Faith was truly a subversive act. Sergey now heads up a national prayer ministry that links thousands of Eastern Europeans by email.

Peter, from Hungary, would help Westerners smuggle in Bibles in black plastic bags, which his parents would surreptitiously distribute. Oleg, from Moldova, reported that Protestants vote for Communist candidates in elections because the church has become so complacent; they want to restore the purity that the church had when it was undergoing persecution.

One day in Budapest I visited the House of Terror, a controversial state-of-the-art museum that documents the sad twentieth-century history of Hungary, a nation sandwiched between Nazi and Soviet powers. The people there have a tradition of being conquered: by Attila the Hun, the Mongols, the Muslims, and then the Nazis and the Russians. The museum occupies a building that served as headquarters first for the Nazi SS and then later the Russian KGB. Dungeons and torture rooms are preserved intact, and the listening machines and propaganda devices characteristic of totalitarianism are carefully displayed.

Shortly after returning to the U.S. I watched presidential candidate John Kerry's concession speech in which he said the great thing about our country is that the next morning after the election, we're all still Americans. After spending several hours in the House of Terror, that lesson sank in deep.

Unpublished trip notes, Hungary 2004

Never Again?

On the road again, the summer of 2008, I spent a full day at Auschwitz, where the scale of mass murder beggars the mind. The three hundred barracks at Auschwitz stretched over fields covering many acres, but prisoners were brought there to die and not to live. Crematoriums worked around the clock to dispose of the gassed bodies, burning as many as 10,000 corpses per day—one and a half million people in all, most of them Jews.

Auschwitz is a haunting place because it seems so methodical and organized, as if some massive corporation had hired consultants to devise a program of pure evil. Think of the impact of 9/11 on the U.S., and then imagine that being repeated day after day for four years—not by terrorists but by an established government against its own citizens.

Various nations (Holland, France, etc.) have "adopted" barracks to tell the stories of their citizens killed at Auschwitz, and of course Israel has set up several displays too. Tour guides lead their groups to displays marked with names like "Extermination Techniques" or "Plunder." One barrack depicts the living conditions in which eight hundred prisoners were crammed into a room designed for two hundred. One displays torture devices used against prisoners; another details medical experiments in which prisoners were deliberately infected or burned to test various treatments, or doused in tanks of freezing water to study resuscitation procedures.

The "Plunder" building shows thousands of shoes taken from prisoners, a huge heap of spectacles, and a mound of human hair filling a glass display case sixty feet long (the Allies found two tons of human hair stored in warehouses at Auschwitz). You can visit an execution wall where thousands were shot, and then the infamous "shower rooms" in which naked Jews were herded to be gassed. For years nothing grew at Auschwitz, for the chimneys had spit out a fine bone loam that covered the ground. Now the grounds are lush and green, incongruously resembling a college campus with walkways and brick dormitories.

The slogan "Never Again" takes on the force of a scream at Auschwitz, and yet in our own lifetime, in Rwanda and Yugoslavia and Darfur, history has repeated itself, though perhaps not on the same scale of evil efficiency.

Unpublished trip notes, Poland 2008

◆

It Happened One Afternoon

The cross is the central image of Christianity, vivid proof that, in Flannery O'Connor's words, the world "has, for all its horror, been found by God to be worth dying for." During Holy Week I found myself reflecting not so much on the theoretical rationale for the atonement as on its practical outworking. When a questioner tried to pin down the theologian Karl Barth on when he had been "saved," Barth replied, "It happened one afternoon in A.D. 34 when Jesus died on the cross." Love finds a way to overcome all obstacles to uniting with the beloved, no matter the cost.

At the same time, the cross reveals the limits of human achievement. Pontius Pilate had Jesus' "crime"—KING OF THE JEWS—posted in three languages, an ironic tribute to the travesty of justice. A public spectacle it was when the most refined religious authorities of the day ganged up on an innocent man and the most renowned justice system carried out the sentence.

Thomas Merton comments, "No one saw the Resurrection. Everyone saw the Crucifixion. Everyone does see the crucifixion. The cross is everywhere." It should give us pause, this sign of contradiction, when we're now tempted to look to politics or science to solve the deepest human problems. Christ exposed as false gods the very powers and authorities in which men and women take most pride and invest most hope.

At the same time, the cross brings to light an unexpected quality of the godhead: humility. In Paul's words, Jesus, "being in very nature God, did not consider equality with God something to be grasped, but ... humbled himself and became obedient to death—even death on a cross!" The poor and disadvantaged respond by instinct to this personal identification, as shown in the sermons in Appalachia or the base communities in Latin America that center on the cross. Novelists know it too: Graham Greene, George Bernanos, and Ignazio Silone all made the sacrament commemorating Jesus' death the centerpiece of their finest works.

Whatever else we may say about it, the atonement fulfills the Jewish principle that only one who has been hurt can forgive. At Calvary, God chose to be hurt.

"Back Page" column, *Christianity Today,*
May 2009 (96)

◆

Hidden God

Human longing for the actual presence of God may crop up almost any-where. But we dare not make sweeping claims about the promise of God's intimate presence unless we take into account those times when God seems absent. The great saints encountered it, Job encountered it, and at some point nearly everyone must face the fact of God's hiddenness.

Some would argue that God does not hide. One religious bumper sticker reads, "If you feel far from God, guess who moved?" But the guilt implicit in the slogan may be false guilt: the book of Job details a time when, apparently, it was God who moved. Even though Job had done nothing wrong and pled desperately for help, God still chose to stay hidden. (If you ever doubt that an encounter with God's hiddenness is a normal part of the pilgrimage of faith, simply browse the works of the Christian mystics, men and women who have spent their lives in personal communion with God. Search for one, just one, who does not describe a time of severe testing, "the dark night of the soul.")

For those who suffer, and those who stand beside them, Job offers up an important lesson. Doubts and complaints are valid responses, not symptoms of weak faith — so valid, in fact, that God made sure the Bible included them all. One does not expect to find the arguments of God's adversaries — say, Mark Twain's *Letters from the Earth* or Bertrand Russell's *Why I Am Not a Christian* — bound into the Bible, but nearly all of them make an appearance, if not in Job, then in the Psalms or Prophets. The Bible seems to anticipate our disappointments, as if God grants us in advance the weapons in opposition, as if God too understands the cost of sustaining faith.

And, because of Jesus, perhaps God does understand. At Gethsemane and Calvary in some inexpressible way God himself was forced to confront the hiddenness of God. "God striving with God" is how Martin Luther summarized the cosmic struggle played out on two crossbeams of wood. On that dark night, God learned the full extent of what it means to feel God-forsaken.

Disappointment with God (232–33)

◆

Tale of Two Traitors

The name "Judas," once common, has all but disappeared. No parent wants to name a child after the most notorious traitor in history. And yet now, to my own surprise, as I read the Gospel accounts it is Judas's *ordinariness*, not his villainy, that stands out. The Gospels contain no hint that Judas had been a "mole" infiltrating the inner circle to plan this perfidy.

How, then, could Judas betray the Son of God? Even as I ask the question I think of the remaining disciples fleeing from Jesus in Gethsemane and of Peter swearing, "I don't know the man!" when pressured in a courtyard and of the Eleven stubbornly refusing to believe reports of Jesus' resurrection. Judas's act of betrayal differed in degree, but not in kind, from many other disloyalties.

Judas was not the first or the last person to betray Jesus, merely the most famous. Shusaku Endo, the Christian novelist in Japan, centered many of his novels on the theme of betrayal. To Endo, the most powerful message of Jesus was his unquenchable love even for — *especially* for — people who betrayed him. When Judas led a lynch mob into the garden, Jesus addressed him as "Friend." The other disciples deserted him but still he loved them. His nation had him executed; yet while stretched out naked in the posture of ultimate disgrace, Jesus roused himself for the cry, "Father, forgive them."

I know of no more poignant contrast between two human destinies than that of Peter and Judas. Both assumed leadership within the group of Jesus' disciples. Both saw and heard wondrous things. Both went through the same dithery cycle of hope, fear, and disillusionment. As the stakes increased, both denied their Master. There, the similarity breaks off. Judas, remorseful but apparently unrepentant, accepted the logical consequences of his deed, took his own life, and went down as the greatest traitor in history. He died unwilling to receive what Jesus had come to offer him. Peter, humiliated but still open to Jesus' message of grace and forgiveness, went on to lead a revival in Jerusalem and did not stop until he had reached Rome.

The Jesus I Never Knew (193 – 94)

◆

Ordeal of Shame

In a memoir of the years before World War II, Pierre Van Paassen tells of an act of humiliation by Nazi storm troopers who had seized an elderly Jewish rabbi and dragged him to headquarters. In the far end of the same room, two colleagues were beating another Jew to death. They stripped the rabbi naked and commanded that he preach the sermon he had prepared for the coming Sabbath in the synagogue. The rabbi asked if he could wear his yarmulke, and the Nazis, grinning, agreed. It added to the joke. The trembling rabbi proceeded to deliver in a raspy voice his sermon on what it means to walk humbly before God, all the while being poked and prodded by the hooting Nazis, and all the while hearing the last cries of his neighbor at the end of the room.

When I read the Gospel accounts of the imprisonment, torture, and execution of Jesus, I think of that naked rabbi standing humiliated in a police station. I still cannot fathom the indignity, the *shame* endured by God's Son on earth, stripped naked, flogged, spat on, struck in the face, garlanded with thorns.

Jewish leaders as well as Romans intended the mockery to parody the crime for which the victim had been condemned. *Messiah, huh? Great, let's hear a prophecy.* Wham. *Who hit you, huh?* Thunk. *C'mon, tell us, spit it out, Mr. Prophet. For a Messiah, you don't know much, do you?*

It went like that all day long, from the bullying game of Blind Man's Bluff in the high priest's courtyard, to the professional thuggery of Pilate's and Herod's guards, to the catcalls of spectators up the long road to Calvary, and finally to the cross itself where Jesus heard a stream of taunts.

I have marveled at, and sometimes openly questioned, the self-restraint God has shown throughout history, allowing the Genghis Khans and the Hitlers and the Stalins to have their way. But nothing—nothing—compares to the self-restraint shown that dark Friday in Jerusalem. With every lash of the whip, every fibrous crunch of fist against flesh, Jesus must have mentally replayed the temptation in the wilderness and in Gethsemane. Legions of angels awaited his command. One word, and the ordeal would end.

The Jesus I Never Knew (199 – 200)

◆

Disarming Power

I t took time for the church to come to terms with the ignominy of the cross. Not until the fourth century did the cross become a symbol of the faith. (Scholars note that the crucifixion did not become common in art until all who had seen a real one died off.)

Now, though, the symbol is everywhere: artists beat gold into the shape of the Roman execution device, baseball players cross themselves before batting, and candy confectioners even make chocolate crosses for the faithful to eat during Holy Week. Strange as it may seem, Christianity has become a religion of the cross — the gallows, the electric chair, the gas chamber, in modern terms.

Normally we think of someone who dies a criminal's death as a failure. Yet the apostle Paul would later reflect about Jesus, "Having disarmed the powers and authorities, he made a public spectacle of them, triumphing over them by the cross." What could he mean?

On one level I think of individuals in our own time who disarm the powers. The racist sheriffs who locked Martin Luther King Jr. in jail cells, the Soviets who deported Solzhenitsyn, the Czechs who imprisoned Václav Havel, the Filipinos who murdered Benigno Aquino, the South African authorities who imprisoned Nelson Mandela — all these thought they were solving a problem, yet instead all ended up unmasking their own violence and injustice. Moral power can have a disarming effect.

When Jesus died, even a gruff Roman soldier was moved to exclaim, "Surely this man was the Son of God!" He saw the contrast all too clearly between his brutish colleagues and their victim, who forgave them in his dying gasp. The pale figure nailed to a crossbeam revealed the ruling powers of the world as false gods who broke their own lofty promises of piety and justice. Religion, not irreligion, accused Jesus; the law, not lawlessness, had him executed. By their rigged trials, their scourgings, their violent opposition to Jesus, the political and religious authorities of that day exposed themselves for what they were: upholders of the status quo, defenders of their own power only. Each assault on Jesus laid bare their illegitimacy.

The Jesus I Never Knew (202 – 3)

◆

Sneak Preview

(A Reading for Good Friday)

I wish someone with the talents of Milton or Dante would render the scene that must have transpired in hell on the day that Jesus died. No doubt an infernal celebration broke out. The snake of Genesis had struck at the heel of God; the dragon of Revelation had devoured the child at last. God's Son, sent to Earth on a rescue mission, had ended up dangling from a cross like some ragged scarecrow. Oh, what a diabolical victory!

Oh, what a short-lived victory. In the most ironic twist of all history, what Satan meant for evil, God meant for good. Jesus' death on the cross bridged the gap between a perfect God and a fatally flawed humanity. On the day we call Good Friday, God defeated sin, routed death, triumphed over Satan, and got his family back. In that act of transformation, God took the worst deed of history and turned it into the greatest victory. No wonder the symbol never went away; no wonder Jesus commanded that we never forget.

Because of the cross, I have hope. It is through the Servant's wounds that we are healed, said Isaiah — not his miracles. If God can wrest such triumph out of the jaws of apparent defeat, can draw strength from a moment of ultimate weakness, what might God do with the apparent failures and hardships of my own life?

Nothing — not even the murder of God's own Son — can end the relationship between God and human beings. In the alchemy of redemption, that most villainous crime becomes our healing strength.

The fatally wounded healer came back on Easter, the day that gives a sneak preview of how all history will look from the vantage point of eternity, when every scar, every hurt, every disappointment will be seen in a different light. Our faith begins where it might have seemed to end. Between the cross and the empty tomb hovers the promise of history: hope for the world, and hope for each one of us who lives in it.

The Jesus I Never Knew (273 – 74)

◆

Distress Signals

W hy did Jesus have to suffer and die? The question deserves an entire book, and has prompted many books, but among the answers the Bible gives is this most mysterious answer: suffering served as a kind of "learning experience" for God. Such words seem faintly heretical, but I am merely following Hebrews: "Although he was a son, he learned obedience from what he suffered" (5:8). Elsewhere, that book tells us that the author of our salvation was made perfect through suffering (2:10).

These words, full of fathomless mystery, surely mean at least this: the incarnation had meaning for God as well as for us. On one level, of course, God understood physical pain, having designed the marvelous nervous system that carries it to our brains as a warning against harm. But had a Spirit ever felt physical pain? Not until the incarnation. In thirty-three years on earth he learned about poverty, and about family squabbles, and social rejection, and verbal abuse, and betrayal. And he learned too about pain. What it feels like to have an accuser leave the red imprint of his fingers on your face. What it feels like to have a whip studded with metal lash across your back. And what it feels like to have a crude iron spike pounded through muscle, tendon, and skin. On earth, God learned all that.

In some incomprehensible way, because of Jesus, God hears our groans differently. The author of Hebrews marveled that whatever we are going through, God too has gone through. "For we do not have a high priest who is unable to sympathize with our weaknesses, but we have one who has been tempted in every way, just as we are—yet was without sin" (4:14). We have a high priest who, having graduated from the school of suffering, "is able to deal gently with those who are ignorant and are going astray, since he himself is subject to weakness" (5:2). Because of Jesus, God understands, truly understands, our groans.

We need no longer cry into the abyss, "Hey, are you listening?" By joining us on earth, Jesus gave visible, historical proof that God hears our groans, and even groans them with us.

"Distress Signals," *Christianity Today*,
October 8, 1990 (34–35)

The Day with No Name

The church I grew up in skipped past the events of Holy Week in a rush to hear the cymbal sounds of Easter. We never held a service on Good Friday. We celebrated the Lord's Supper only once a quarter. We saved our best clothes, our rousing hymns, and our few sanctuary decorations for Easter.

When I studied the Gospels I learned that, unlike my church, the biblical record slows down rather than speeds up when it gets to Holy Week. The Gospels, said one early Christian commentator, are chronicles of Jesus' final week with increasingly longer introductions.

The author and preacher Tony Campolo delivers a stirring sermon: "It's Friday, but Sunday's Comin'." The disciples who lived through both days, Friday and Sunday, learned, preaches Campolo, that when God seems most absent he may be closest of all, when God looks most powerless he may be most powerful, when God looks most dead he may be coming back to life. They learned never to count God out.

Campolo's sermon skips one day, though. The other two days have earned names on the church calendar, Good Friday and Easter Sunday, but in a real sense we live our lives on Saturday, the day with no name.

Perhaps that is why the authors of the Gospels devoted so much more space to Jesus' last week than to the several weeks when he was making resurrection appearances. They knew that the history to follow would often resemble Saturday, the in-between day, more than Sunday, the day of rejoicing.

Can we trust that God can make something holy and beautiful and good out of a world that includes Sudan and Rwanda and inner-city ghettos in the richest nation on earth? Human history grinds on, between the time of promise and fulfillment. It's Saturday on planet Earth; will Sunday ever come?

"Unwrapping Jesus," *Christianity Today*,
June 17, 1996 (33 – 34)

◆

Jesus and Burnout

My pastor in Chicago, Bill Leslie, used the illustration of an old hand-operated pump. He sometimes felt like such a pump, he said. Everyone who came along would reach up and pump vigorously a few times, and each time he felt something drain out of him. Finally, he was approaching a point of "burnout," when he had nothing more to give. He felt dry, desiccated.

In the midst of this period, Bill went on a weeklong retreat and expressed these thoughts to his designated spiritual director, a very wise nun. He expected her to offer soothing words about what a wonderful, sacrificial person he was. Instead, she said, "Bill, there's only one thing to do if your reservoir is dry. You've got to go deeper." He realized on that retreat that for his outward journey to continue, he needed to give a higher priority to his inner journey.

In the record of Jesus' ministry on earth, I see only one time when he approached a state resembling anything like "burnout." In the garden of Gethsemane, Jesus fell prostrate on the ground and prayed. Sweat fell from him like drops of blood. His prayers took on an uncharacteristic tone of pleading. He "offered up prayers and petitions with loud cries and tears to the one who could save him from death," Hebrews says (5:7), but of course Jesus knew he would not be saved from death. As that awareness grew inside him, Jesus felt distress.

Somehow, in Gethsemane Jesus worked through that crisis by transferring the burden to the Father. It was God's will he had come to do, after all, and his prayer resolved into the words, "Yet not as I will, but as you will" (26:39).

I pray for that sense of detachment, of *trust*. I pray that I could see my work, my life, as an offering to God each day. God and God alone is qualified to help me negotiate the slippery path between love for others and love for myself.

Church: Why Bother? (96 – 98)

◇

View from the Future

A wise man named Joe Bayly once said, "Don't forget in the darkness what you have learned in the light." Yet sometimes the darkness descends so thickly that we can barely remember the light. Surely it seemed that way to Jesus' disciples.

During the Last Supper Jesus made the ringing declaration, "In this world you will have trouble. But take heart! I have overcome the world" (John 16:33). At that moment, eleven of the twelve would gladly have given their lives for him; later that evening Simon Peter actually pulled a sword in Jesus' defense.

Yet by the next day all eleven had lost faith. Those triumphant words from the previous night must have cruelly haunted them as they watched him — safely, at a distance — anguish on the cross. It appeared as though the world had overcome God. All of them slipped away in the darkness. Peter swore with an oath he'd never known the man.

The disciples' problem, of course, was a matter of perspective. Yes, the memory of light from the past had been extinguished, but a few days later those same men would encounter the dazzling light of Easter. On that day, they learned that no darkness is too great for God. They learned what it means to judge the present by the future. Ignited by Easter hope, those former cowards went out and changed the world.

Today half the world celebrates the back-to-back holidays Good Friday and Easter. That darkest Friday is now called Good because of what happened on Easter Sunday; and because it happened Christians have hope that God will someday restore this planet to its proper place under God's reign.

It is a good thing to remember, when we encounter dark, disturbing times, that we live out our days on Easter Saturday. As the apostle Paul expressed it, "I consider that our present sufferings are not worth comparing with the glory that will be revealed in us" (Romans 8:18). It was no accident, I believe, that Jesus spoke his triumphant words, I HAVE OVERCOME THE WORLD, even as Roman soldiers were buckling on weapons for his arrest. He knew how to judge the present by the future.

Where Is God When It Hurts? (229 – 30)

◆

Pain's Alchemy

Christianity contains within it paradoxes that would make little sense apart from Jesus' life and death. Consider one paradox: although poverty and suffering are "bad things" that I rightly spend my life fighting against, yet at the same time they can be called "blessed." This pattern of bad transmuted into good finds its fullest expression in Jesus. By taking it on himself, Jesus dignified pain, showing us how it can be transformed. He gave us a pattern he wants to reproduce in us.

Jesus Christ offers the perfect example of all the biblical lessons about suffering. Because of Jesus, I can never say about a person, "She must be suffering because of some sin she committed"; Jesus, who did not sin, also felt pain. God has never promised that tornadoes will skip our houses on the way to our pagan neighbors' and that microbes will flee from Christian bodies. We are not exempt from the tragedies of this world, just as God was not exempt. Remember, Peter earned Jesus' strongest rebuke when he protested against the need for Christ to suffer (Matthew 16:23–25).

We feel pain as an outrage; Jesus did too, which is why he performed miracles of healing. In Gethsemane he did not pray, "Thank you for this opportunity to suffer," but rather pled desperately for an escape. And yet he was willing to undergo suffering in service of a higher goal. In the end he left the hard questions ("if there be any other way . . .") to the will of the Father, and trusted that God could use even the outrage of his death for good.

In the ultimate alchemy of all history, God took the worst thing that could possibly happen—the appalling execution of the innocent Son—and turned it into the final victory over evil and death. It was an act of unprecedented cunning, turning the design of evil into the service of good, an act that holds within it a promise for all of us. The unimaginable suffering of the cross was fully redeemed: it is by his *wounds* that we are healed (Isaiah 53:5), by his weakness that we are made strong.

Where Is God When It Hurts? (230–31)

The Suffering God

From the Old Testament we can gain much insight into what it "feels like" to be God. But the New Testament records what happened when God learned what it feels like to be a human being. Whatever we feel, God felt. Instinctively, we want a God who not only knows about pain but shares in it; we want a God who is affected by our own pain. As the young theologian Dietrich Bonhoeffer scribbled on a note in a Nazi prison camp, "Only the Suffering God can help." Because of Jesus, we have such a God. Hebrews reports that God can now sympathize with our weaknesses. The very word expresses how it was done: "sympathy" comes from two Greek words, *sym pathos*, meaning "suffer with."

Would it be too much to say that, because of Jesus, God understands our feelings of disappointment with God? How else can we interpret Jesus' tears, or his cry from the cross? One could almost pour our questions of God's seeming unfairness, silence, and hiddenness into that dreadful cry, "My God, my God, why have you forsaken me?" God's Son "learned obedience" from his suffering, says Hebrews. A person can only learn obedience when tempted to disobey, can only learn courage when tempted to flee.

Why didn't Jesus brandish a sword in Gethsemane, or call on his legions of angels? Why did he decline Satan's challenge to dazzle the world? For this reason: if he had done so, he would have failed in his most important mission — to become one of us, to live and die as one of us. It was the only way God could work "within the rules" he had set up at creation.

All through the Bible, especially in the Prophets, we see a conflict raging within God. On the one hand God passionately loved the people he had made; on the other hand, God had a terrible urge to destroy the evil that enslaved them. On the cross, God resolved that inner conflict, for there God's Son absorbed the destructive force and transformed it into love.

Disappointment with God (128)

Stumbling Block

Jesus' death is the cornerstone of the Christian faith, the most important fact of his coming. What possible contribution to the problem of pain could come from a religion based on an event like the cross, where God's own self succumbed to pain?

The apostle Paul called the cross a "stumbling block" to belief, and history has proved him out. Jewish rabbis question how a God who could not bear to see Abraham's son slain would allow his own Son to die. The Koran teaches that God, much too gentle to allow Jesus to go to the cross, substituted an evildoer in his place. Even today, U.S. television personality Phil Donahue explains his chief objection to Christianity: "How could an all-knowing, all-loving God allow His Son to be murdered on a cross in order to redeem my sins? If God the Father is so 'all-loving,' why didn't He come down and go to Calvary?"

All of these objectors have missed the main point of the gospel, that in some mysterious way it *was* God who came to earth and died. God was not "up there" watching the tragic events conspire "down here." God was *in Christ*, said Paul, reconciling the world to himself. In Luther's phrase, the cross showed "God struggling with God." If Jesus was a mere man, his death would prove God's cruelty; the fact that he was God's Son proves instead that God fully identifies with suffering humanity. On the cross, God absorbed the awful pain of this world.

To some, the image of a pale body glimmering on a dark night whispers of defeat. What good is a God who does not control the Son's suffering? But another sound can be heard: the shout of a God crying out to human beings, "I LOVE YOU." Love was compressed for all history in that lonely figure on the cross, who said that he could call down angels at any moment on a rescue mission, but chose not to—because of us. At Calvary, God accepted the unbreakable terms of justice.

And thus the cross, a stumbling block to some, became the cornerstone of Christian faith. Any discussion of how pain and suffering fit into God's scheme ultimately leads back to the cross.

Where Is God When It Hurts? (227–28)

Invisible Impact

In the Old Testament, faithful believers seemed shocked when suffering came their way. They expected God to reward their faithfulness with prosperity and comfort. But the New Testament shows a remarkable change. As Peter advised suffering Christians, "This suffering is all part of the work God has given you. Christ, who suffered for you, is your example. Follow in his steps" (1 Peter 2:21 LB).

Other passages go further, using phrases I will not attempt to explain. Paul speaks of "sharing in his [Christ's] sufferings" and says he hopes to "fill up in my flesh what is still lacking in regards to Christ's afflictions."

Harry Boer, a chaplain during World War II, spent the final days of that war among marines in the Pacific Theater. "The Second Division saw much action, with great losses," he writes. "Yet I never met an enlisted man or an officer who doubted for a moment the outcome of the war. Nor did I ever meet a marine who asked why, if victory was so sure, we couldn't have it immediately. It was just a question of slogging through till the enemy gave up."

According to Paul, at the cross Christ triumphed over the cosmic powers—defeating them not with power but with self-giving love. The cross of Christ may have assured the final outcome, but battles remain for us to fight. Significantly, Paul prayed "to know Christ and the power of his resurrection and the fellowship of sharing in his sufferings"—embracing both the agony and the ecstasy of Christ's life on earth (Philippians 3:10).

We will never know, in this life, the full significance of our actions here, for much takes place invisible to us. When a pastor in an oppressive country goes to prison for his peaceful protest, when a social worker moves into an urban ghetto, when a couple refuses to give up on a difficult marriage, when a parent waits with undying hope and forgiveness for the return of an estranged child, when a young professional resists mounting temptations toward wealth and success—in all these sufferings, large and small, there is the assurance of a deeper level of meaning, of a sharing in Christ's own redemptive victory.

Where Is God When It Hurts? (231–32)

◆

Easter Start

I believe in the resurrection primarily because I have gotten to know God. I know that God is love, and I also know that we human beings want to keep alive those whom we love. I do not let my friends die; they live on in my memory and my heart long after I have stopped seeing them. For whatever reason —human freedom lies at the core, I imagine—God allows a planet where a man dies scuba-diving in the prime of life and a woman dies in a fiery crash on the way to a church missions conference. But I believe—if I did not believe this, I would not believe in a loving God—that God is not satisfied with such a blighted planet. Divine love will find a way to overcome. "Death, be not proud," wrote John Donne: God will not let death win.

One detail in the Easter stories has always intrigued me: Why did Jesus keep the scars from his crucifixion? Presumably he could have had any resurrected body he wanted, and yet he chose one identifiable mainly by scars that could be seen and touched. Why?

I believe the story of Easter would be incomplete without those scars on the hands, the feet, and the side of Jesus. When human beings fantasize, we dream of pearly straight teeth and wrinkle-free skin and sexy ideal shapes. We dream of an unnatural state: the perfect body. But for Jesus, being confined in a skeleton and human skin *was* the unnatural state. The scars are, to him, an emblem of life on our planet, a permanent reminder of those days of confinement and suffering.

I take hope in Jesus' scars. From the perspective of heaven, they represent the most horrible event that has ever happened in the history of the universe. Even that event, though, Easter turned into a memory. Because of Easter, I can hope that the tears we shed, the blows we endure, the emotional pain, the heartache over lost friends and loved ones, all these will become memories, like Jesus' scars. Scars never completely go away, but neither do they hurt any longer. We will have re-created bodies, a re-created heaven and earth. We will have a new start, an Easter start.

The Jesus I Never Knew (218 – 19)

◇

A Bright Light

Author Henri Nouwen tells the story of a family he knew in Paraguay. The father, a doctor, spoke out against the military regime there and its human rights abuses. Local police took their revenge on him by arresting his teenage son and torturing him to death. Enraged townsfolk wanted to turn the boy's funeral into a huge protest march, but the doctor chose another means of protest. At the funeral, the father displayed his son's body as he had found it in the jail—naked, scarred from the electric shocks and cigarette burns and beatings. All the villagers filed past the corpse, which lay not in a coffin but on the blood-soaked mattress from the prison. It was the strongest protest imaginable, for it put injustice on grotesque display.

Isn't that what God did at Calvary? "It's God who ought to suffer, not you and me," say those who bear a grudge against God for the unfairness of life. The curse word expresses it well: God be damned. And on that day, God was damned. The cross that held Jesus' body, naked and marked with scars, exposed all the violence and injustice of this world. At once, the cross revealed what kind of world we have and what kind of God we have: a world of gross unfairness, a God of sacrificial love.

No one is exempt from tragedy or disappointment—even God was not exempt. Jesus offered no immunity, no way *out* of the unfairness, but rather a way *through* it to the other side. Just as Good Friday demolished the instinctive belief that this life is supposed to be fair, Easter Sunday followed with its startling clue to the riddle of the universe. Out of the darkness, a bright light shone.

A friend of mine, struggling to believe in a loving God amid much pain and sorrow, blurted out this statement: "God's only excuse is Easter!" The language is nontheological and harsh, but within that phrase lies a haunting truth. The cross of Christ may have overcome evil, but it did not overcome unfairness. For that, Easter is required, a bright clue that someday God will restore all physical reality to its proper place.

Disappointment with God (185 – 86)

◆

Radical Shift

In my study of the Bible, I was struck by a radical shift in its authors' attitudes about suffering, a shift that traces directly back to the cross. When New Testament writers speak of hard times, they express none of the indignation that characterized Job, the prophets, and many of the psalmists. They offer no real explanation for suffering, but keep pointing to two events — the death and resurrection of Jesus — as if they form some kind of pictographic answer.

The apostles' faith, as they freely confessed, rested entirely on what happened on Easter Sunday. Those disciples soon learned what they had failed to learn in three years with their leader: when God seems absent, he may be closest of all. When God seems dead, he may be coming back to life.

The three-day pattern — tragedy, darkness, triumph — became for New Testament writers a template that can be applied to all our times of testing. We can look back on Jesus, the proof of God's love, even though we may never get an answer to our "Why?" questions.

Good Friday demonstrates that God has not abandoned us to our pain. The evils and sufferings that afflict our lives are so real and so significant that God willed to share and endure them. God too is "acquainted with grief." On that day, Jesus himself experienced the silence of God — it was Psalm 22, not Psalm 23, that he quoted from the cross.

And Easter Sunday shows that, in the end, suffering will not triumph. Therefore, "Consider it pure joy ... whenever you face trials of many kinds," writes James; and "In this you greatly rejoice, though now for a little while you may have had to suffer grief in all kinds of trials," writes Peter; and "We also rejoice in our sufferings," writes Paul. The apostles go on to explain what good can result from such "redeemed suffering": maturity, wisdom, genuine faith, perseverance, character, and many rewards to come.

It's a matter of time, Paul says. Just wait: God's miracle of transforming a dark, silent Friday into Easter Sunday will someday be enlarged to cosmic scale.

Disappointment with God (211 – 12)

Hope behind Barbed Wire

On a visit to Virginia I met one of my heroes: Jürgen Moltmann. To my surprise the German theologian in person exuded a charm and sense of humor that belie his scholarly works.

Moltmann was planning on a career in quantum physics until he was drafted at age eighteen at the height of World War II. Assigned to anti-aircraft batteries in Hamburg, he saw compatriots incinerated in the fire-bombings there. The question "Why did I survive?" haunted him. After surrendering to the British, the young soldier spent the next three years in prison camps in Belgium, Scotland, and England. As he learned the truth about the Nazis, Moltmann felt an inconsolable grief about life.

Moltmann had no Christian background, but an American chaplain gave him an army-issue New Testament and Psalms, signed by President Roosevelt. "If I make my bed in hell, behold thou art there," the prisoner read. Could God be present in that dark place? As he read on, Moltmann found words that perfectly captured his feelings of desolation. He became convinced that God "was present even behind the barbed wire — no, most of all behind the barbed wire."

Later Moltmann was transferred to Norton Camp, an educational camp in England run by the YMCA. The local population welcomed the German prisoners, bringing them homemade food, teaching them Christian doctrine, and never adding to the burden of guilt the prisoners felt over Nazi atrocities.

Upon release, Moltmann began to articulate his theology of hope. We exist in a state of contradiction between the cross and the resurrection. Surrounded by decay, we nonetheless hope for restoration, a hope illuminated by the "foreglow" of Christ's resurrection.

Jesus gives a foretaste of a future time when the planet will be restored to God's original design. Easter is the beginning of the "laughter of the redeemed ... God's protest against death." A person without future faith may assume from the suffering on this planet that God is neither all-good nor all-powerful. Future faith allows me to believe that God is not satisfied with this world either, and intends to make all things new.

In a single sentence Jürgen Moltmann expresses the great span from Good Friday to Easter: "God weeps with us so that we may someday laugh with him."

"Back Page" column, *Christianity Today*,
September 2005 (120)

¡Ha Resucitado!

While training a group of volunteers to build housing for the poor, Bud Ogle nearly severed his hand in two with a power saw. His surgeon took the unusual precaution of ordering a lung X-ray, which revealed a malignant tumor in his chest. The tumor was removed just in time, and Bud then faced the prospect of hand surgery and a long, grueling recovery.

That bad news / good news sequence provides a kind of symbol for Bud's urban ministry. "I wondered what God could possibly have in mind with the accident. Yet, as it turned out, the accident saved my life, a lesson I tried to keep in mind as I kept squeezing a tennis ball to regain strength. Both my salvation and recovery involved excruciating pain."

For those who volunteer to work with him in one of Chicago's poorest neighborhoods, Bud guarantees one spiritual lesson: You will learn how to fail. Nothing goes according to plan. The city shuts down a homeless shelter on technicalities, a promising leader slips back into heroin addiction, arsonists destroy a newly rehabbed building, church windows are broken, gangs shoot two kids outside ministry headquarters. Yet somehow, in the midst of the pain and chaos, the gospel takes root.

"That's what happens in this neighborhood—failure becomes a way to learn God's grace. I see alcoholics and addicts fall off the wagon four, five, six times. Some never climb back up. But others gradually receive God's grace in the midst of failure. In my experience, recovery and transformation depend primarily on whether a person believes he or she is 'forgivable.' Discovering that God forgives us no matter how badly we fail creates the space to be healed."

During an Easter sunrise service seven people told their stories, three of them newly recovering addicts. "I was good as dead," said one. "Now, with Jesus' help and the help of all of you, I feel I'm coming back to life."

Easter took on a new meaning for Bud. Out of the pain, hope; in the midst of the darkness, a bright light. During the bilingual service Bud called out, first in English and then in Spanish, "He is risen!" The answer came back as a shout, "¡Ha resucitado! He is risen indeed!"

"Bud Ogle, Suburban Transplant," *Christianity Today,*
November 17, 1997 (38 – 39)

April

◆

Grace-Starved

I saw in Russia in 1991 a people starved for grace. The economy, indeed the entire society, was in a state of free fall, and everyone had someone to blame. I noted that ordinary Russian citizens had the demeanor of battered children: lowered heads, halting speech, eyes darting this way and that. Whom could they trust?

I will never forget a meeting in which Moscow journalists wept—I had never before seen journalists weep—as Ron Nikkel of Prison Fellowship International told of the underground churches that were now thriving in Russia's penal colonies. For seventy years prisons had been the repository of truth, the one place where you could safely speak the name of God. It was in prison, not church, that people such as Solzhenitsyn found God.

Ron Nikkel also told me of his conversation with a general who headed the Ministry of Internal Affairs. The general had heard of the Bible from the old believers and had admired it, but as a museum piece, not something to be believed. Recent events, though, had made him reconsider. In late 1991 when Boris Yeltsin ordered the closing of all national, regional, and local Communist Party offices, his ministry policed the dismantling. "Not one party official," said the general, "not one person directly affected by the closings protested." He contrasted that to the seventy-year campaign to destroy the church and stamp out belief in God. "The Christians' faith outlasted any ideology. The church is now resurging in a way unlike anything I have witnessed."

In 1983 a group of Youth With A Mission daredevils unfolded a banner on Easter Sunday morning in Red Square: "Christ is Risen!" it read in Russian. Some older Russians fell to their knees and wept. Soldiers soon surrounded the hymn-singing troublemakers, tore up their banner, and hustled them off to jail. Less than a decade later, all over Red Square on Easter Sunday people were greeting each other in the traditional way, "Christ is risen!" ... "He is risen indeed!"

What's So Amazing About Grace? (256–57)

◆

Absentee Landlord

Four parables in Matthew 24 – 25 have a common theme lurking in the background. Consider: an owner who leaves his house vacant, an absentee landlord who puts his servant in charge, a bridegroom who arrives so late the guests fall asleep, a master who distributes talents among his servants and takes off.

In effect, Jesus' four parables anticipated the central question of the modern era, asked by the likes of Nietzsche, Marx, Camus, and Beckett. "Where is God now?" The modern answer is that the landlord has abandoned us. We are free to set our own rules. *Deus absconditus.*

Reading on, I came to one more parable. I knew well the message of the Sheep and the Goats, but I had never noticed its connection with the parables that precede it. This last parable answers the question raised by the others, the issue of the absentee landlord, in two ways.

First, it gives a glimpse of the landlord's return, on judgment day, when there will be hell to pay — literally.

Second, the parable gives an insight into the meantime, the mean time, the centuries-long interval when God seems absent. Matthew 25's answer is at once profound and shocking. God has not absconded at all, but instead has taken on a most unlikely disguise of the stranger, the poor, the hungry, the prisoner, the sick, the ragged ones of earth. "I tell you the truth, whatever you did for one of the least of these brothers of mine, you did it for me."

Jesus' final parable leaves the church with a heavy burden, yet one that offers the only lasting solution for the world. We must oppose anarchy by insisting that there is a leader, a landlord for the entire planet who, unlike some policemen, will dispense perfect justice. Furthermore, until the landlord's return it is up to us to demonstrate God's presence. We reach out to needy places not out of paternalism, but out of love. By serving the needy, we serve God in disguise.

"Back Page" column, *Christianity Today,*
July 20, 1992 (64)

Free Partners

No one can reduce to a formula the secret to close communion with God. The English bishop Hugh Latimer wrote to a fellow martyr, "I am sometimes so fearful, that I would creep into a mouse-hole; sometimes God doth visit me again with his comfort. So he cometh and goeth." We may experience a spiritual high one day and spend the next month wandering in the desert. "The wind blows wherever it pleases," Jesus told Nicodemus. So he cometh and goeth.

On the hill behind my mountain home, each spring a pair of red foxes raises a litter of kits. When I whistle a greeting, sometimes the young ones poke their faces out the crevice in the rock, sniffing the air and staring at me with alert, shiny eyes. Sometimes I hear them scrabbling around inside. Sometimes I hear nothing and assume them asleep. Once, when a visitor from New Zealand stopped by, I took him to the den, warning him that he may see and hear nothing at all. "They are wild animals, you know," I said. "We're not in charge. It's up to them whether they make an appearance or not."

A bold young fox did poke his nose out of the den that day, thrilling my visitor, and a few weeks later I received a letter from him, now back home in New Zealand. As he reflected on it, oddly enough, my comment about foxes helped him understand God. He had just gone through a long season of depression. Sometimes God seemed as close as his wife or children. Sometimes he had no sense of God's presence, no faith to lean on. "God is wild, you know," he wrote. "We're not in charge."

"Come near to God and he will come near to you," wrote James, in words that sound formulaic. James does not put a time parameter on the second clause, however. He reminds me that keeping company with God involves two parties, and I have an important role to play in the relationship. As James suggests, I can purify my heart and humble my spirit. I am learning to take responsibility for my part and then leave the rest to God.

Prayer: Does It Make Any Difference? (207 – 8)

Unanswered Prayer

As I was writing on unanswered prayer, my wife recommended that I interview some senior citizens about prayer. "Most of them pray, and they've been at it a long time," she said. "Surely they'll have some wisdom for you."

She was right. I accompanied her to the retirement center where she assists as a chaplain, and I heard one miracle story after another. One woman had felt a sudden urge to leave a card game and go home. As she walked in the door she saw that a candle had burned to the nub, igniting a bouquet of plastic roses — a fire she was able to smother with a pillow just in time. Another told of remarkable survival stories from World War II. Another told of her husband choking on a homemade cinnamon roll, just as two paramedics walked past who saved his life by performing the Heimlich maneuver.

I heard, too, of prayers for world peace and against injustice. One African-American senior reminisced about praying while growing up as a second-class citizen in the South. Who could imagine then the changes she would live through?

Although I probed for accounts of unanswered prayers, most of the seniors preferred to talk about answered prayers. All could tell of family tragedies and health breakdowns, but somehow these events did not shake their faith in prayer.

After our meeting, however, I wandered through a portion of the facility that cares for seniors who need more assistance. They lay in beds or sat in wheelchairs. I tried talking to these seniors too, but the lights in their minds had gone out. Any secrets they had learned about prayer lay hidden beyond retrieval.

I drove away from the facility more convinced than ever that the only final solution to unanswered prayer is Paul's explanation to the Corinthians: "For now we see through a glass, darkly; but then face to face: now I know in part; but then shall I know even as also I am known." No human being, no matter how wise or how spiritual, can interpret the ways of God, explain why one miracle and not another, why an apparent intervention here and not there. Along with the apostle Paul, we can only wait, and trust.

Prayer: Does It Make Any Difference? (247)

◆

Prayers from the Heart

I have learned to tell God exactly what I want regardless of how impossible it may sound. I pray for peace in the Middle East, for justice in Africa, for religious freedom in China and other countries, for an end to homelessness and racism in the U.S., because I earnestly desire those things—and moreover, I believe God does too.

A friend of mine in Chicago tried to recruit some colleagues in urban ministry to join him in a season of prayer for an end to poverty in that city. Almost everyone he asked balked. "Why pray for something so idealistic and impossible?" they objected. My friend had a different view. What is the point of prayer if not to express our heart's desire, especially when it matches what we know to be God's will on earth? Who knows what will happen when we pray what we know God desires? Remember the many prayers of Christians behind the Iron Curtain and in an apartheid South Africa, prayers that also seemed impossible and idealistic.

God invites us to ask plainly for what we need. We will not be scolded any more than a child who climbs into her parent's lap and presents a Christmas wish list. Dr. Vernon Grounds says that when he hears of someone in need of healing, he prays like this: "God, I know you have your own purposes and undoubtedly have a plan for this person, but I'll tell you straight out what I would like to see happen."

If diagnosed with a serious illness, I would ask directly for physical healing. We are commanded to pray for healing, Jesus decisively demonstrated God's desire for human health and wholeness, and dozens of studies have borne out the effectiveness of prayer in the healing process. Faith works. It aligns body, mind, and spirit, and galvanizes the healing processes built into our bodies.

Sometimes Jesus asked a person, "Do you want to be healed?" That was no idle question: as doctors testify, some patients can hardly imagine an identity apart from their unwell condition. In prayers for healing, as in all prayers of request, we should honestly present the problem and tell God our heart's desire.

Prayer: Does It Make Any Difference? (267 – 68)

◆

Touching the Void

I take some comfort in the fact that virtually all the masters of spirituality recount a dark night of the soul. Sometimes it passes quickly and sometimes it persists for months, even years. I have yet to find a single witness, though, who does not tell of going through a dry period. Teresa of Avila spent twenty years in a nearly prayerless state before breaking through to emerge as a master of prayer. William Cowper had prayer times in which he thought he would die from excess of joy; but later he described himself as "banished to a remoteness from God's presence, in comparison with which the distance from the East to the West is vicinity."

Religious radio and television, as well as certain books and magazines, say little of God's silence. By their accounts God seems to speak volubly, commanding this minister to build a new sanctuary and that housewife to launch a new Web-based company. God represents success, good feelings, a sense of peace, a warm glow. To an audience regaled by such inspiring stories, an encounter with the silence of God hits like a shocking exception and stirs up feelings of inadequacy.

The exception, in fact, is the cheery optimism of modern consumer-oriented faith. For centuries Christians learned what to expect on the spiritual journey from the bumbling pilgrim in *Pilgrim's Progress*, from John of the Cross's *Dark Night of the Soul*, from Thomas à Kempis's challenging *Imitation of Christ*. The one mentor who wrote most openly about the presence of God, Brother Lawrence, composed his thoughts while washing dishes and cleaning toilets.

If I suffer a time of spiritual aridity, of darkness and blankness, should I stop praying until new life enters my prayer? Every one of the spiritual masters insists, No. If I stop praying, how will I know when prayer does become alive again? And, as many Christians have discovered, the habit of not praying is far more difficult to break than the habit of praying.

Prayer: Does It Make Any Difference? (201 – 2)

◆

Scent of Scandal

Grace, like water, always flows downward, to the lowest place. I know no one who embodies this principle better than John Newton, author of perhaps the best-loved hymn of all time. Against all odds "Amazing Grace," written some 230 years ago, still endures.

Pressed into service in the Royal Navy, John Newton was dismissed for insubordination and turned to a career trafficking in slaves. Notorious for cursing and blasphemy even among his fellow degenerates, Newton served on a slave ship during the darkest and cruelest days of trans-Atlantic slavery, finally working his way up to captain.

A dramatic conversion on the high seas set him on the path to grace. After he studied theology, the Church of England appointed him to a parish. He never forgot, nor did he ever deny, the sense of *undeservedness* that marked all that followed. As he wrote in his diary soon after moving to Olney, England, "Thou hast given an apostate a name and a place among Thy children—called an infidel to the ministry of the gospel."

Under the tutelage of such luminaries as John Wesley and George Whitefield, Newton became a rousing evangelical preacher and eventually a leader in the abolitionist movement. He befriended a haunted young poet named William Cowper and ministered to him throughout Cowper's suicidal episodes of mental illness. Meanwhile, Newton served as a kind of spiritual director to the eminent politician William Wilberforce, urging him not to give up his forty-year fight to abolish slavery in the British Empire. Newton himself appeared before Parliament, giving irrefutable eyewitness testimony to the horror and immorality of the slave trade.

Newton faced opposition, sneers, and second-guessing during his lifetime. Some scorned his evangelical enthusiasm, some charged him with worsening rather than helping the travails of his friend William Cowper, and some scoffed at his abolitionist crusade as an attempt to assuage the guilt of his past. Newton did not try to defend himself, but pointed to any good in himself as an outworking of God's grace. In doing so, he stands squarely in the biblical tradition, for its great heroes include a murderer and adulterer (King David), a traitor (the apostle Peter), and a persecutor of Christians (the apostle Paul). Grace always has about it the scent of scandal.

Foreword to *John Newton: From Disgrace to Amazing Grace* (11 – 13)

Servant in Chief

On the tourist trail in Plains, Georgia, you can still see the public housing apartment where Jimmy Carter once lived. From those humble roots he ascended in 1976 to become the most powerful person in the world.

Jimmy Carter's descent reversed his meteoric rise. After losing the 1980 election to Ronald Reagan, he returned to Plains a broken man, scorned by fellow Democrats and named in some polls as the worst president ever. His family business, held in a blind trust during his term, had accumulated a million-dollar debt.

From that shaky platform, Carter began to rebuild. After writing a book to pay off debts, he established the Jimmy Carter Center in Atlanta to foster programs he believed in. Due mainly to his emphasis on human rights, many developing nations looked to him as a great leader, and Carter responded with visionary projects. A democracy project began monitoring elections all over the world. His support of Habitat for Humanity brought publicity and funding to that fledgling organization. His foundation targeted a handful of major diseases that plague poor nations and mobilized dollars and expert knowledge to address the problems. As a result, both guinea worm and river blindness have nearly been eliminated.

Every weekend he was in town, Carter also taught Sunday school. Turn over the offering plates at Maranatha Baptist, and you'll see the carved initials "J. C." The former president made them in his carpentry shop, just as he made the television cabinet in the Sunday school room. Every other month he took his turn cutting the grass outside the church while Rosalynn cleaned the bathrooms indoors.

Carter's reputation has recovered well. He remains on a first-name basis with world leaders and commands respect and attention wherever he goes. In a stunning reversal, he now makes the list of most admired presidents, and if someone held a contest for best ex-president, he would win hands down. While others leave the White House to enjoy golf or cash in on their celebrity status, the Carters have devoted themselves to service. The result brings to mind Jesus' most-repeated statement in the Gospels: "For whoever wants to save his life will lose it, but whoever loses his life for me and for the gospel will save it."

"Back Page" column, *Christianity Today*,
May 21, 2002 (88)

◆

A Time to Laugh

The human species is distinctive in at least three ways, said poet W. H. Auden. We are the only animals who work, laugh, and pray. I have found that Auden's list provides a neat framework for self-reflection.

At *work*, Christians unabashedly excel. Our forefathers invented the Protestant ethic, after all. We value the work ethic so highly, in fact, that we let it gobble everything in sight. Our churches run like corporations, our quiet times fit into a Day-Timer schedule (ideally on computer software), our pastors maintain the hectic pace of Japanese executives. Work has become for Christians the only sanctioned addiction.

The art of *prayer* we should have mastered by now, but I have my doubts. It is tempting to turn prayer into another form of work, which may explain why prayers in most churches consist mainly of intercession. All too rarely do we get around to listening.

I've noticed that biblical prayers (as seen, for example, in the psalms) tend to be wandering, repetitive, and unstructured—closer in form to the conversation you might hear in a barber shop than a shopping list. I am learning about such prayer from the Catholics, who have a better grasp on prayer as an act of worship. Oddly, for those who do it all day—Thomas Merton, Macrina Wiederkehr, Gerard Manley Hopkins, Teresa of Avila—prayer seems less like a chore and more like a never-ending conversation.

In *laughter*, the third leg of Auden's triad, Christians trail behind the rest of the world. Christians have a great advantage over other people, C. S. Lewis wrote: not by being less fallen than they nor less doomed to live in a fallen world, but by knowing that they are fallen creatures in a fallen world. For this reason, I think, we dare not forget how to laugh at ourselves. One can only parody what one respects, just as one can only blaspheme if one believes.

It occurs to me, in fact, that laughter has much in common with prayer. In both acts, we stand on equal ground, freely acknowledging ourselves as fallen creatures. We take ourselves less seriously. We think of our creatureliness. Work divides and ranks; laughter and prayer unite.

Finding God in Unexpected Places (245 – 49)

◆

In Search of a Both/And Church

Not long ago I attended a conference held on the restored grounds of a century-old utopian community in Indiana. As I ran my fingers over the fine workmanship of the buildings and read the plaques describing the daily lives of the true believers, I marveled at the energy that drove this movement, one of dozens spawned by American idealism and religious fervor.

It occurred to me, though, that in recent times the perfectionist urge has virtually disappeared. Nowadays we tilt in the opposite direction, toward a kind of anti-utopianism. Many churches have formed twelve-step groups that by definition center on members' *inability* to be perfect.

I confess my preference for this modern trend. I observe far more human fallibility than perfectibility, and I have cast my lot with a gospel based on grace. Most utopian communities—like the one I was standing in—survive only as museums. Perfectionism keeps running aground on the barrier reef of original sin.

How can we in the church uphold the ideal of holiness, the proper striving for Life on the Highest Plane, while avoiding the consequences of disillusionment, pettiness, abuse of authority, spiritual pride, and exclusivism?

Or, to ask the opposite question, how can we moderns who emphasize community support (never judgment), vulnerability, and introspection keep from aiming too low? An individualistic society, America is in constant danger of freedom abuse; its churches are in danger of grace abuse.

With these questions in mind, I read the New Testament epistles. I took some comfort in the fact that the church in the first century was already on a seesaw, tilting now toward perfectionistic legalism and now toward raucous antinomianism. James wrote to one extreme; Paul often addressed the other. Each letter had a strong correcting emphasis, but all stressed the dual message of the gospel. The church, in other words, should be both: a people who strive toward holiness and yet relax in grace, a people who condemn themselves but not others, a people who depend on God and not themselves.

The seesaw is still lurching back and forth. Some churches tilt one way, some another. My reading of the epistles left me yearning for a both/and church. I have seen too many either/or congregations.

Finding God in Unexpected Places (254–57)

◆

Hope from a Jewish Extremist

We need hopeful stories. How easily we pass judgment on the church that launched the Crusades or on the Muslim restrictions on women. Yet are we doing any better at making good and just decisions today?

Of the books I've read recently on the "clash of civilizations," one gives me hope: *At the Entrance to the Garden of Eden: A Jew's Search for God with Christians and Muslims in the Land,* by Yossi Klein Halevi.

At first glance, Halevi seems an unlikely candidate to light a candle of hope. Raised in an Orthodox Jewish community of Holocaust survivors in Brooklyn (his own father had survived detention in Hungary), he grew up dreading Christians.

Emboldened by a move to Israel, Halevi began to consider the two main minorities in Israel, Christians and Muslims. Acting both as a journalist and as a spiritual seeker, he began to make inquiries into his neighbors.

Halevi learned early on that Jews and Muslims had more in common with each other than with Christians. (A not-too-well-informed sheik told him, "We both have religious law; the Christians don't. We have fast days; they don't. We forbid the use of images; they pray to images. We believe in one God; they have three gods.")

Halevi gives a model of a person of distinct faith learning to honor people who see the world very differently, without yielding to a mushy "anything goes" attitude of omnitolerance. He reflects on Jesus:

> Jews need to make their peace with Jesus. We're still angry and afraid of him. My father used to blame Jesus for all our troubles. But until we welcome him back as a brother, we'll continue to treat Christianity as inauthentic. Jesus was the divine instrument for fulfilling the Jewish goal of spreading the word of God through the world. Thanks to Jesus, I have a common spiritual language with half of humanity.

Halevi goes on to say that he finds himself wishing for someone in Israel today like Jesus, a Jewish visionary who would take on the religious bureaucrats, a fervent believer who would nevertheless preach love and forgiveness. If a self-confessed "Jewish extremist" could arrive at such a place, maybe there's hope for the Middle East yet.

"A Conversation on Books about Islam and the Middle East" by Philip Yancey and John Wilson, *Books and Culture,* July/August 2002 (25 – 26)

◆

A Healthy Start

When I visited India, I accompanied a true lover of the country, Dr. Paul Brand, who had spent nearly half his life there. He led me on an unforgettable tour of Indian medical work.

In some respects, medicine in India differs little from that in the U.S. and Europe. But out beyond the cities, in India's million villages, medicine can be downright adventuresome. How does an Indian doctor rehydrate cholera victims when no sterile water is available? Why, he hangs a fresh coconut on the IV stand, of course: the glucose mixture in the airtight coconut is as sterile, and nearly as nutritious, as any product from a medical supply house. Still, it is a bit jarring to see a long rubber tube snaking up from a patient's arm to a shiny green coconut.

Christian Medical College Hospital in Vellore has had a reputation as being one of the very best medical institutions in Asia. To counteract a trend in overtraining students, however, the school erected a separate hospital, featuring open-air, mud-wall-and-thatch construction, to duplicate conditions at the village level. Now CMC students must supplement their training at that hospital, using only the medical resources common to India's remote villages.

In addition, CMC sponsors regular excursions to outlying villages. On a given day a month, a CMC van transports young doctors and assistants, who pile out, set up examining tables, and begin their routines of injections, bonesplints, and minor surgery. Thousands of patients receive care each month in their own villages.

One telling statistic reveals the fruit of two centuries of faithful mission work: of India's billion people, less than 3 percent call themselves Christian, and yet Christians are responsible for more than 18 percent of the nation's health care.

Despite the many bumbling errors of paternalistic missionaries, the Christians have given India an inspired legacy of education and medicine. If you say the word "Christian" to an Indian peasant — who may never have heard of Jesus Christ — the first image to pop into his or her mind may well be that of a hospital, or of a medical van that stops by the village once a month to provide free, personal care in Christ's name. It's certainly not the whole of the gospel, but it's not a bad place to start.

I Was Just Wondering (51 – 55)

◇

God's Face

Much of my career as a writer has revolved around the problem of pain. I return again and again to the same questions, as if fingering an old wound that never quite heals. I hear from readers of my books, and their anguished stories give human faces to my doubts.

I remember when two people called in the same week to talk about their experiences of disappointment with God. One was a youth pastor in Colorado who had just learned his wife and baby daughter were dying of AIDS. "How can I talk to my youth group about a loving God?" he asked. Another was a blind man who, several months before, had invited a recovering drug addict into his home as an act of mercy. He had just learned the recovering addict was carrying on an affair with his wife, under his own roof. "It's like God is punishing me for trying to serve him," he said. Just then he ran out of quarters, the pay phone went dead, and I never heard from the man again.

I have learned not even to attempt an answer to the why questions. Why did the youth pastor's wife happen to get the one tainted bottle of blood? Why does a tornado hit one town in Oklahoma and skip over another? Why did one particular woman's child get hit by a skateboard on Boston Common? Why do so few of the millions of prayers for physical healing get answered?

One question, however, no longer gnaws at me as it once did: the question "Does God care?" I know of only one way to answer that question, and for me it has proved decisive: Jesus is the answer. In Jesus, God gave us a face. If you wonder how God feels about the suffering on this groaning planet, look at that face. By no means did Jesus solve the problem of pain—he healed only a few in one small corner of the globe—but he did signify an answer to the question *Does God care?*

"Do I Matter? Does God Care?" *Christianity Today,*
November 22, 1993 (22)

◇

The Wager

Is it absurd to believe that one human being, a tiny dot on a tiny planet, can make a difference in the history of the universe? It certainly seemed so to Job's friends. The opening and closing chapters of Job, however, prove that God was greatly affected by the response of one man and that cosmic issues were at stake. (Later, in a message to the prophet Ezekiel, God would point with pride to Job—along with Daniel and Noah—as one of his three favorites.)

Job's example, drawn in sharp relief, shows how life on earth affects the universe. I have come to believe that The Wager scene in chapter 1 [in which Satan charges that if times get tough people will quickly abandon God; God accepts the challenge and allows Job to be tested] offers a message of great hope to all of us—perhaps the most powerful and enduring lesson from Job. In the end, The Wager resolved decisively that the faith of a single human being counts for very much indeed. Job affirms that our response to testing *matters*. The history of mankind—and, in fact, my own individual history of faith—is enclosed within the great drama of the history of the universe.

The Bible rustles with hints that something like The Wager is played out in other believers as well. We are God's Exhibit A, his demonstration piece to the powers in the unseen world. The apostle Paul pictured himself on public display: "We have been made a spectacle to the whole universe, to angels as well as to men." And he commented, in an astonishing aside, "Do you not know that we will judge angels?"

We humans inhabit a mere speck of a planet in the outer suburbs of a spiral galaxy that is only one of about a million million such galaxies in the observable universe, but the New Testament insists that what happens among us here will, in fact, help determine the future of that universe. Paul is emphatic: "The whole creation is on tiptoe to see the wonderful sight of the sons of God coming into their own." Natural creation, "groaning" in travail and decay, can only be set free by the transformation of human beings.

Disappointment with God (169 – 71)

◆

Out of Time

Recognizing our incurable time-boundedness may help us understand why God did not answer Job's "Why?" Instead, God replied by reeling off a few fundamental facts of the universe that Job could barely comprehend, and warning, "Leave the rest to me." Perhaps God keeps us ignorant because neither Job, nor Einstein, nor you or I could possibly understand the view "from above."

We cannot understand what "rules" apply to a God who lives outside of time, as we perceive it, and yet sometimes steps into time. Consider all the confusion that surrounds the word "foreknowledge." Did God know in advance whether Job would stay faithful to him and thus win The Wager? If God did, how was it a real wager? Or what about natural disasters on earth? If God knows about them in advance, isn't God to blame?

But—and this may be the main message underlying God's vigorous speech to Job—we cannot apply our simplistic rules to God. The very word *fore*knowledge betrays the problem. Strictly speaking, God does not "foresee" us doing things. God simply *sees* us doing them, in an eternal present. And whenever we try to figure out God's role in any given event, we necessarily see things "from below," judging God's behavior by the frail standards of a time-contingent morality. One day we may see such problems as "Did God cause that airplane to crash?" in a very different light.

The church's long arguments over *fore*knowledge and *pre*destination illustrate our awkward attempts to comprehend what, to us, only makes sense as it enters time. In another dimension, we will undoubtedly view such matters very differently. The Bible says that Christ "was chosen before the creation of the world," which means before Adam and before the Fall and thus before the need for redemption at all. It says grace and eternal life were "given us in Christ Jesus before the beginning of time." How could anything be said to occur "*before* the beginning of time"? Before creating time, God made provision to redeem a fallen planet that did not yet even exist! But when he "stepped into" time, God's Son had to live, and die, by the rules of our world, trapped within time.

Disappointment with God (198 – 99)

Tragic Lessons

To the students at Virginia Tech:

I wish I could say that the pain you feel will disappear, vanish, never to return. Yet what happened on April 16, 2007, will stay with you forever. You are a different person because of that day, because of one troubled young man's actions.

So I cannot say what I want to say, that this too shall pass. Instead, I point to the pain you feel, and will continue to feel, as a sign of life and love. I'm wearing a neck brace because I broke my neck in an auto accident. As I lay strapped to a body board, for the first few hours they refused to give me any pain medication because they needed my response. The doctor kept probing, moving my limbs, asking, "Does this hurt? Do you feel that?" The correct answer, the answer both he and I desperately wanted, was, "Yes. It hurts! I can feel it." Each sensation gave proof that my spinal cord had not been severed. Pain offered proof of life, of connection, a sign that my body remained whole.

In grief, love and pain converge. The young man Cho felt no grief as he gunned down your classmates because he felt no love for them. You feel that grief because you did have a connection. Those who died belonged to a body to which you too belong. When that body suffers, you suffer. Remember that as you cope with the pain. Don't simply try to numb it. Acknowledge it as a perception of life, of love.

My challenge to you is to trust a God who can redeem what now seems unredeemable. Ten days before the shootings on this campus, Christians around the world remembered the darkest day of all human history, a day in which evil human beings violently rose up against God's own Son and murdered the only truly innocent human being who has ever lived. We remember that day not as Dark Friday, Tragic Friday, Disaster Friday — rather, Good Friday. That awful day led to the salvation of the world and also led to Easter.

"Where Is God When It Hurts: A Sermon Given on the
Virginia Tech Campus Two Weeks after the Shootings,"
Christianity Today, June 2007 (55, 59)

◆

Keeping Faith

The last few paragraphs of Hebrews 10 reveal much about the original readers of Hebrews. Converting to Christ has brought them abuse: confiscation of property, public insult, and even imprisonment. In the early days they accepted such persecution gladly, even joyfully. But as time has gone on, and the trials continue, some are beginning to lose heart.

To these discouraged people, Hebrews 11 presents a stirring reminder of what constitutes "true faith." It's tempting to think of faith as a kind of magic formula: if you muster up enough of it, you'll get rich, stay healthy, and live a contented life, with automatic answers to all your prayers. But the readers of Hebrews are discovering that life does not work according to such neat formulas. As proof, the author painstakingly reviews the lives of some Old Testament giants of faith. (Some have dubbed Hebrews 11 the "Faith Hall of Fame.")

"Without faith," Hebrews says bluntly, "it is impossible to please God." But the author uses rather pointed words in describing that faith: "persevere," "endure," "don't lose heart." As a result of their faith, some heroes triumphed: they routed armies, escaped the sword, survived lions. But others met less happy ends: they were flogged, chained, stoned, sawed in two. The chapter concludes, "These were all commended for their faith, yet none of them received what had been promised."

The picture of faith that emerges from this chapter does not fit into an easy formula. Sometimes faith leads to victory and triumph. Sometimes it requires a gritty determination to "hang on at any cost." Hebrews 11 does not hold up one kind of faith as superior to the other. Both rest on the belief that God is in ultimate control and will indeed keep promises — whether that happens in this life or in the next. Of such people, Hebrews says, "God is not ashamed to be called their God, for he has prepared a city for them."

Meet the Bible (646 – 47)

Better

A re religions all that different?" skeptics ask. "Isn't the most important thing to be sincere in whatever you believe?" Such "modern" questions have in fact been debated for thousands of years. The book of Hebrews is written in response to people of the early church torn between the Jewish religion and the new faith of Christianity.

Some favor sticking with the familiar routine of Judaism, which has centuries-old traditions behind it. Another advantage: the Jews of the day enjoy Rome's official protection, while Christians are subject to persecution. Is faith in Christ worth the risk?

Hebrews insists there are decisive reasons to choose Christ. The whole book revolves around the word *better*. Jesus is better than the angels or Moses or the Old Testament way—better than anything the world has to offer.

Even so, after recording a gust of grand theology from the Psalms, the author of Hebrews (whose identity we don't know) seems to pause and reconsider. "At present we do not see everything subject to him." Could a world in which Christians are being arrested, tortured, and tossed into jail really be subject to Christ?

From there, the author explains why it matters that God descended to the world and became a human being. He did not magically remove all human problems but rather subjected himself to the same hardships that any of us face. Hebrews goes further than any other New Testament book in explaining Jesus' human nature.

Chapter 2 gives two powerful reasons why Jesus came to earth. First, by dying, he freed us from the power of death and won for us eternal life. And second, by experiencing normal human temptations, he can better help us with our own temptations.

No angel, and no God in distant heaven, could have accomplished those things. Jesus came, in effect, on a rescue mission to free humanity from slavery. Apart from Christ, we live in constant fear of death and in constant bondage to our failures, or sins. Only Jesus can set us free. That's why he's worth the risk.

Meet the Bible (642 – 43)

◆

Weight of a Nation

On a trip to Japan I found myself late at night in a pastor's study in one of the largest churches in Tokyo. I had flown in that morning and had already endured a rigorous day of meetings. I wanted to check into my hotel room and go to sleep, but Japanese hospitality required this courtesy visit.

The pastor pulled out a sheaf of papers and, through an interpreter, told me that during his entire career he had worried over this one issue but was afraid of speaking to anyone about it.

For the next twenty minutes without interruption the pastor poured out the agony he felt over the 99 percent of Japanese who had not accepted Jesus. Would they all burn in hell because of their ignorance? He had heard of theologians who believed in people having a second chance after death and knew the mysterious passage in 1 Peter about Jesus preaching to those in Hades. Some theologians he had read seemed to believe in universal salvation although certain passages in the Bible indicated otherwise. Could I offer him any hope?

Thinking aloud, I mentioned that God causes the sun to rise on the just and unjust and has no desire that anyone should perish. God's Son on earth spent his last strength praying for his enemies. We discussed the view of hell presented in C. S. Lewis's intriguing fantasy *The Great Divorce*, which shows people like Napoleon who have a second chance after death but opt against it. "*Thy* will be done," says God reluctantly to those who make a final rejection.

"I do not know the answer to your questions," I said at last. "But I believe strongly that at the end of time no one will be able to stand before God and say 'You were unfair!' However history settles out, it will settle on the side of justice tempered by mercy."

Like Job, I reached that conclusion not through observation or argument but through encounter. "Surely God will be able to understand my doubts in a world like this, won't He?" asked the Dutch prisoner Etty Hillesum from a Nazi concentration camp. I believe God will, in part because God's revelation to us includes eloquent expressions of those very doubts.

Prayer: Does It Make Any Difference? (38 – 40)

Jolt of Tragedy

Lord, to whom shall we go?" asked the apostle Peter in a moment of confusion. For many, it takes the jolt of tragedy to provoke such a question. It happened in Littleton, Colorado, at Columbine High School near my home.

Ministers, parents, school administrators, and everyone touched by the event still ask "Why?" and no one has an answer. The element of evil looms so large in this particular tragedy—hate-filled, racist teenagers spraying their classmates with automatic weapons—that no one publicly links God to the event.

You would have to live in Colorado to appreciate the answer to the other question posed by the tragedy: Can any good come out of such horror? Can it be redeemed? You would have to visit Clement Park and read for yourself the handwritten notes from all over the world. You would have to attend the churches that filled with grieving worshipers the days and weeks following the event. You would have to watch *The Today Show* as Craig Scott, brother of one of the victims, put his hand on the shoulder of the parent of the one African-American student killed and comforted him, even as Katie Couric broke down on the air. You would have to hear Cassie Bernall's friends describe her bravery as a gunman pointed his weapon at her head and demanded, "Do you believe in God?" "Yes," she replied, "and you need to follow along God's path"—her last words on earth. You would have to listen to the girlfriend of another victim who said, with the innocence of hope and the hope of innocence, "I take great comfort knowing I will see him again." You would have to attend a fifth-grade classroom in a public school where a teacher had her students kneel on the floor, hold hands, and pray aloud. (At such a time, the ACLU was keeping a low profile.) In other Denver schools, teachers apologized to their classes for not having identified themselves as Christians, and invited students to meet them after school to help process the tragedy.

Out of evil, good may come.

"Back Page" column, *Christianity Today*,
June 14, 1999 (104)

◆

Happy Ending

In its "plot," the Bible ends up very much where it began. The broken relationship between God and human beings has healed over at last, and the curse of Genesis 3 is lifted. Borrowing images from Eden, Revelation pictures a river and a tree of life. But this time a great city replaces the garden setting—a city filled with worshipers of God. No death or sadness will ever darken that scene.

John sees heaven as the fulfillment of every Jewish dream: Jerusalem restored, with walls of jasper and streets of gleaming gold. For someone else—say, a refugee in the developing world today—heaven may represent a family reunited, a home abundant with food and fresh drinking water. Heaven stands for the fulfillment of every true longing.

Revelation promises that our longings are not mere fantasies. They will come true. When we awake in the new heaven and new earth, we will have at last whatever we have longed for. Somehow, from out of all the bad news in a book like Revelation, good news emerges—spectacular Good News. A promise of goodness without a catch in it somewhere. There is a happy ending after all.

In the Bible, heaven is not an afterthought or optional belief. It is the final justification of all creation. The Bible never belittles human tragedy and disappointment—is any book more painfully honest?—but it does add one key word: *temporary*. What we feel now, we will not always feel. The time for re-creation will come.

For people who feel trapped in pain or in a broken home, in economic misery or in fear—for all those people, for all of us, heaven promises a future time, far longer and more substantial than the time we spend on earth, a time of health and wholeness and pleasure and peace. The Bible began with that promise, in the book of Genesis. And the Bible ends with that same promise, a guarantee of future reality. The end will be a beginning.

Meet the Bible (684 – 85)

◆

New Moon in the Moral Universe

Using the Torah as a starting point, Jesus pushed the law in the same direction, further than any Pharisee had dared push it, further than any monk has dared live it. The Sermon on the Mount introduced a new moon in the moral universe that has exerted its own force of gravity ever since.

Jesus made the law impossible for anyone to keep and then charged us to keep it. Consider some examples.

Every human society in history has had a law against murder. But no society has come up with anything like Jesus' expanded definition of murder: "I tell you that anyone who is angry with his brother will be subject to judgment ... anyone who says 'You fool!' will be in danger of the fire of hell."

Every society also has taboos against sexual promiscuity. But no society has ever proposed a rule as strict as Jesus': "I tell you that anyone who looks at a woman lustfully has already committed adultery with her in his heart. If your right eye causes you to sin, gouge it out and throw it away. It is better for you to lose one part of your body than for your whole body to be thrown into hell."

I have heard calls for castration of serial rapists, but never have I heard a proposal for facial mutilation on account of lust. Indeed, lust in America is an established national pastime, celebrated in ads for blue jeans and beer, in the annual *Sports Illustrated* swimming suit issue, and in the twenty million copies of pornographic magazines sold each month. "How strangely on modern ears," said John Updike, "falls the notion that lust—sexual desire that wells up in us as involuntarily as saliva—in itself is wicked!"

I stare at these and the other strict commands of the Sermon on the Mount and ask myself how to respond. Does Jesus really expect me to give to every panhandler who crosses my path? Should I abandon all insistence on consumer rights? Cancel my insurance policies and trust God for the future? Discard my television to avoid temptations to lust? How can I possibly translate such ethical ideals into my everyday life?

The Jesus I Never Knew (132 – 33)

The Flame of Ideals

From Russian novelist Leo Tolstoy I learned a deep respect for God's inflexible, absolute Ideal. The ethical ideals Tolstoy encountered in the Gospels attracted him like a flame, though his failure to live up to those ideals ultimately consumed him. Tolstoy strove to follow the Sermon on the Mount literally, and his intensity soon caused his family to feel like victims of his quest for holiness. For instance, after reading Jesus' command to the rich man to give away everything, Tolstoy decided to free serfs, give away his copyrights, and dispose of his vast estate. He wore peasant clothes, made his own shoes, and began working in the fields. His wife, Sonya, seeing the family's financial security about to vaporize, protested petulantly until he made some concessions.

As I read Tolstoy's diaries, I see flashbacks of my own lunges toward perfectionism. The diaries record many struggles between Tolstoy and his family, but many more between Tolstoy and himself. In an attempt to reach perfection he kept devising new lists of rules. He gave up hunting, smoking, drinking, and meat. He drafted "Rules for developing the emotional will. Rules for developing lofty feelings and eliminating base ones." Yet he could never achieve the self-discipline necessary to keep the rules. More than once, Tolstoy took a public vow of chastity and asked for separate bedrooms. He could never keep the vow for long, and much to his shame, Sonya's sixteen pregnancies broadcast to the world that inability.

Sometimes Tolstoy managed to accomplish great good. For example, after a long hiatus he wrote one last novel, *Resurrection*, at the age of seventy-one, in support of the Doukhobors—an Anabaptist group undergoing persecution by the tsar—donating all proceeds to finance their emigration to Canada. Also, Tolstoy's philosophy of nonviolence, lifted directly from the Sermon on the Mount, had an impact that long outlived him, in ideological descendants like Gandhi and Martin Luther King Jr.

[Continued on April 24]

The Jesus I Never Knew (137)

◆

An Unhappy Life

[Continued from April 23]

By any measure Tolstoy's quest for holiness ended in disappointment. In short, he failed to practice what he preached. His wife put it well (in an obviously biased account):

> There is so little genuine warmth about him; his kindness does not come from his heart, but merely from his principles. His biographies will tell of how he helped the laborers to carry buckets of water, but no one will ever know that he never gave his wife a rest and never — in all these thirty-two years — gave his child a drink of water or spent five minutes by his bedside to give me a chance to rest a little from all my labors.

Tolstoy's ardent strides toward perfection never resulted in any semblance of peace or serenity. Up to the moment of his death the diaries and letters kept circling back to the rueful theme of failure, exposing the vast gap between the high ideals of the gospel and the sad actuality of his own life.

Leo Tolstoy was a deeply unhappy man. He fulminated against the Russian Orthodox Church of his day and earned their excommunication. His schemes for self-improvement all foundered. At times he had to hide the ropes on his estate and put away his guns in order to resist the temptation toward suicide. In the end, Tolstoy fled from his fame, his family, his estate, his identity; he died like a vagrant in a rural railroad station.

In view of such failures, what can I possibly learn from the tragic life of Leo Tolstoy? I have read many of his religious writings, and without fail I come away inspired by his reverence for God's absolute Ideal. Tolstoy reminds us that, contrary to those who say the gospel solves our problems, in many areas — justice issues, money issues, race issues, personal issues of pride and ambition — the gospel actually adds to our burdens. Tolstoy took as dead-serious Jesus' question, "What shall it profit a man to gain the whole world and lose his soul?"

A man willing to liberate his serfs and give away his possessions in simple obedience to Christ's command is not easy to dismiss. If only Tolstoy could live up to those ideals — if only I could live up to them.

[Continued on April 25]

Soul Survivor (127 – 28)

◆

Staggering on the Path

[Continued from April 24]

To his critics Tolstoy replied, Don't judge God's holy ideals by my inability to meet them. Don't judge Christ by those of us who imperfectly bear his name. One passage especially, taken from a personal letter, shows how Tolstoy responded to such critics toward the end of his life. It stands as a summary of his spiritual pilgrimage, at once a ringing affirmation of the truth that he believed with all his heart and a plangent appeal for grace that he never fully realized.

"What about you, Lev Nikolayevich, you preach very well, but do you carry out what you preach?" This is the most natural of questions and one that is always asked of me; it is usually asked victoriously, as though it were a way of stopping my mouth. "You preach, but how do you live?" And I answer that I do not preach, that I am not able to preach, although I passionately wish to. I can preach only through my actions, and my actions are vile.... And I answer that I am guilty, and vile, and worthy of contempt for my failure to carry them out....

Attack me, I do this myself, but attack *me* rather than the path I follow and which I point out to anyone who asks me where I think it lies. If I know the way home and am walking along it drunkenly, is it any less the right way because I am staggering from side to side! If it is not the right way, then show me another way; but if I stagger and lose the way, you must help me, you must keep me on the true path, just as I am ready to support you. Do not mislead me, do not be glad that I have got lost, do not shout out joyfully: "Look at him! He said he was going home, but there he is crawling into a bog!" No, do not gloat, but give me your help and support.

[Continued on April 26]

Soul Survivor (129 – 31). Quote from
A. N. Wilson, *The Lion and the Honeycomb:
The Religious Writings of Tolstoy* (147 – 48)

◇

Truth Minus Grace

[Continued from April 25]

I feel sad as I read Tolstoy's religious writings. The X-ray vision into the human heart that made him a great novelist also made him a tortured Christian. Like a spawning salmon, he fought upstream all his life, in the end collapsing from moral exhaustion.

Yet I also feel grateful to Tolstoy, for his relentless pursuit of authentic faith has made an indelible impression upon me. I first came across his novels during a period when I was suffering the delayed effects of "church abuse." The churches I grew up in contained too many frauds, or at least that is how I saw it in the arrogance of youth. When I noted the rift between the ideals of the gospel and the flaws of its followers, I was sorely tempted to abandon those ideals as hopelessly unattainable.

Then I discovered Tolstoy. He was the first author who, for me, accomplished that most difficult of tasks: to make good as believable and appealing as evil. I found in his novels, fables, and short stories a source of moral power.

A. N. Wilson, a biographer of Tolstoy, remarks that "his religion was ultimately a thing of Law rather than of Grace, a scheme for human betterment rather than a vision of God penetrating a fallen world." With crystalline clarity Tolstoy could see his own inadequacy in the light of God's Ideal. But he could not take the further step of trusting God's grace to overcome that inadequacy.

Shortly after reading Tolstoy I discovered his countryman Fyodor Dostoevsky. These two, the most famous and accomplished of all Russian writers, lived and worked during the same period of history. Though they read each other's work with admiration, they never met, and perhaps it was just as well — they were opposites in every way. Where Tolstoy wrote bright, sunny novels, Dostoevsky wrote brooding, interior ones. Where Tolstoy worked out ascetic schemes for self-improvement, Dostoevsky periodically squandered his health and fortune on alcohol and gambling.

Dostoevsky made many mistakes in life, but achieved an amazing feat in art. His novels communicate grace and forgiveness, the heart of the Christian gospel, with a Tolstoyan force.

[Continued on April 27]

Soul Survivor (131 – 34)

Second Chance

[Continued from April 26]

Early in his life, Dostoevsky underwent a virtual resurrection. He had been arrested for belonging to a group judged treasonous by Tsar Nicholas I, who, to impress upon the young parlor radicals the gravity of their errors, sentenced them to death and staged a mock execution. A firing squad stood at the ready. Bareheaded, robed in white burial shrouds, hands bound tightly behind them, they were paraded through the snow before a gawking crowd. At the very last instant, as the order, "Ready, aim!" was heard and rifles were cocked and lifted, a horseman galloped up with a message from the tsar: he would mercifully commute their sentences to hard labor.

Dostoevsky never recovered from this experience. He had peered into the maw of death, and from that moment life became for him precious beyond all calculation. "Now my life will change," he said; "I shall be born again in a new form." As he boarded the convict train toward Siberia, a devout woman handed him a New Testament, the only book allowed in prison. Believing that God had given him a second chance to fulfill his calling, Dostoevsky pored over that New Testament during his confinement. After ten years he emerged from exile with unshakable Christian convictions, as expressed in a letter to the woman who had given him the New Testament, "If anyone proved to me that Christ was outside the truth ... then I would prefer to remain with Christ than with the truth."

Prison offered Dostoevsky another opportunity, which at first seemed a curse: it forced him to live at close quarters with thieves, murderers, and drunken peasants. His shared life with these prisoners later led to unmatched characterizations in his novels, such as that of the murderer Raskolnikov in *Crime and Punishment*. Dostoevsky's liberal view of the inherent goodness in humanity could not account for the pure evil he found in his cell mates, and his theology had to adjust to this new reality. Over time, though, he also glimpsed the image of God in the lowest of prisoners. He came to believe that only through being loved is a human being capable of love.

[Continued on April 28]

Soul Survivor (134 – 38)

◇
Two Spiritual Guides

[Continued from April 27]

I encountered grace in the novels of Dostoevsky. Although *Crime and Punishment* portrays a despicable human being who commits a despicable crime, the soothing balm of grace enters Raskolnikov's life through a converted prostitute, Sonia, who follows him to Siberia and leads him to redemption. In *The Idiot*, Dostoevsky presents a Christ figure in the form of an epileptic prince. Quietly, mysteriously, Prince Myshkin moves among the circles of Russia's upper class, exposing their hypocrisy while also illuminating their lives with goodness and truth.

The Brothers Karamazov, one of the greatest novels ever written, draws a contrast between Ivan, the brilliant agnostic, and his devout brother, Alyosha. Ivan can critique the failures of humankind and every political system designed to deal with those failures, but he can offer no solutions. Alyosha has no solutions for the intellectual problems Ivan raises, but he has a solution for humanity: love. "I do not know the answer to the problem of evil," said Alyosha, "but I do know love."

Today, I claim these two Russians as my spiritual guides. From Tolstoy I learn the need to look inside, to the kingdom of God that is within me. I see how miserably I fall short of the high ideals of the gospel. But from Dostoevsky I learn the full extent of grace. Not only the kingdom of God is within me; God's own self dwells there. "Where sin increased, grace increased all the more," is how the apostle Paul expressed it in Romans.

There is only one way for any of us to resolve the tension between the high ideals of the gospel and the grim reality of ourselves: to accept that we will never measure up, but that we do not have to. Tolstoy got it halfway right: anything that makes me feel comfort with God's moral standard, anything that makes me feel, "At last I have arrived," is a cruel deception. Dostoevsky got the other half right: anything that makes me feel discomfort with God's forgiving love is also a cruel deception. "There is now no condemnation to those who are in Christ Jesus," Paul insisted.

Soul Survivor (139 – 45)

◇

Grace for All

Absolute ideals and absolute grace: after learning that dual message from Russian novelists, I returned to Jesus and found that it suffuses his teaching throughout the Gospels and especially in the Sermon on the Mount. In his response to the rich young ruler, in the parable of the good Samaritan, in his comments about divorce, money, or any other moral issue, Jesus never lowered God's Ideal. "Be perfect, as your heavenly Father is perfect," he said. "Love the Lord your God with all your heart and with all your soul and with all your mind." Not Tolstoy, not Francis of Assisi, not anyone has completely fulfilled those commands.

Yet the same Jesus tenderly offered absolute grace. Jesus forgave an adulteress, a thief on the cross, a disciple who had denied ever knowing him. He tapped that traitorous disciple, Peter, to found his church and for the next advance turned to a man named Saul, who had made his mark persecuting Christians. Grace is absolute, inflexible, all-encompassing. It extends even to the people who nailed Jesus to the cross: "Father, forgive them, for they do not know what they are doing" were among the last words he spoke on earth.

For years I had felt so unworthy before the absolute ideals of the Sermon on the Mount that I had missed in it any notion of grace. Once I understood the dual message, however, I went back and found that the message of grace gusts through the entire speech. It begins with the Beatitudes — Blessed are the poor in spirit, those who mourn, the meek; blessed are the desperate — and it moves toward the Lord's Prayer: "Forgive us our debts ... deliver us from the evil one." Jesus began this great sermon with gentle words for those in need, and continued on with a prayer that has formed a model for all twelve-step groups.

"One day at a time," say the alcoholics in AA; "Give us this day our daily bread," say the Christians. Grace is for the desperate, the needy, the broken, those who cannot make it on their own. Grace is for all of us.

The Jesus I Never Knew (142 – 43)

Safety Net

For years I had thought of the Sermon on the Mount as a blueprint for human behavior, a pattern that no one could possibly meet. Reading it again, I found that Jesus gave these words not to cumber us, but to tell us what *God* is like. The character of God is the urtext of the Sermon on the Mount.

Why should we love our enemies? Because our clement Father causes his sun to rise on the evil and the good. Why be perfect? Because God is perfect. Why store up treasures in heaven? Because the Father lives there and will lavishly reward us. Why live without fear and worry? Because the same God who clothes the lilies and the grass of the field has promised to take care of us. Why pray? If an earthly father gives his son bread or fish, how much more will the Father in heaven give good gifts to those who ask.

How could I have missed it? Jesus did not proclaim the Sermon on the Mount so that we would, Tolstoy-like, furrow our brows in despair over our failure to achieve perfection. He gave it to impart to us God's Ideal toward which we should never stop striving, but also to show that none of us will ever reach that Ideal. The Sermon on the Mount forces us to recognize the great distance between God and us, and any attempt to reduce that distance by somehow moderating its demands misses the point altogether.

The worst tragedy would be to turn the Sermon on the Mount into another form of legalism; it should rather put an end to all legalism. Legalism like the Pharisees' will always fail, not because it is too strict but because it is not strict enough. Thunderously, inarguably, the Sermon on the Mount proves that before God we all stand on level ground: murderers and tantrum-throwers, adulterers and lusters, thieves and coveters. We are all desperate, and that is, in fact, the only state appropriate to a human being who wants to know God. Having fallen from the absolute Ideal, we have nowhere to land but in the safety net of absolute grace.

The Jesus I Never Knew (143 – 44)

May

Life in Part

Søren Kierkegaard told a parable about a rich man riding in a lighted carriage driven by a peasant who sat behind the horse in the cold and dark outside. Precisely because he sat near the artificial light inside, the rich man missed the panorama of stars outside, a view gloriously manifest to the peasant. In modern times, it seems, as science casts more light on the created world, its shadows further obscure the invisible world beyond.

I am no Luddite who opposes technological change. My laptop computer allows me to access the text of every book I have written in the past twenty years, as well as thousands of notes I have made during that time. Though I am holed up in a mountain retreat, using this same computer I have sent messages to friends in Europe and Asia. I pay my monthly bills electronically. In these and other ways I gratefully enjoy the benefits of technology and science.

Yet I also see dangers in our modern point of view. For one thing, reductionism, the spirit of our age, has the unfortunate effect of, well, reducing things. Science offers a map of the world, something like a topographical map, with colors marking the vegetation zones and squiggly lines tracing the contours of cliffs and hills. When I hike the mountains of Colorado, I rely on such maps. Yet no map of two dimensions, or even three dimensions, can give the full picture. And none can possibly capture the experience of the hike: thin mountain air, a carpet of wildflowers, a ptarmigan's nest, rivulets of frothy water, a triumphant lunch at the summit. Encounter trumps reduction.

More importantly, the reducers' approach allows no place for an invisible world. It takes for granted that the world of matter is the sum total of existence.

Of course, an invisible God cannot be examined or tested. Most definitely, God cannot be quantified or reduced. As a result, many people in societies advanced in technology go about their daily lives assuming God does not exist. They stop short at the world that can be reduced and analyzed, their ears sealed against rumors of another world. As Tolstoy said, materialists mistake what limits life for life itself.

Rumors of Another World (18 – 19)

◆

Beyond Belief

I have a neighbor who is obsessively neat. He lives on ten forested acres, and every time he drove up his long, winding driveway, the disorderly dead branches on the Ponderosa pine trees bothered him. One day he called a tree-trimming service and learned it would cost him five thousand dollars to trim all those trees. Appalled at the price, he rented a chain saw and spent several weekends perched precariously on a ladder cutting back all the branches he could reach.

He then called the service for a new estimate and got an unwelcome surprise. "Mr. Rodrigues, it will probably cost you twice as much. You see, we were planning to use those lower branches to reach the higher ones. Now we have to bring in an expensive truck and work from a bucket."

In some ways, modern society reminds me of that story. We have sawed off the lower branches on which Western civilization was built, and the higher branches now seem dangerously out of reach. "We have drained the light from the boughs in the sacred grove and snuffed it in the high places and along the banks of sacred streams," writes Annie Dillard.

No society in history has attempted to live without a belief in the sacred, not until the modern West. Such a leap has consequences that we are only beginning to recognize. We now live in a state of confusion about the big questions that have always engaged the human race, questions of meaning, purpose, and morality. A skeptical friend of mine used to ask himself the question, "What would an atheist do?" in deliberate mockery of the What Would Jesus Do (WWJD) slogan. He finally stopped asking because he found no reliable answers.

Eliminating the sacred changes the story of our lives. In times of greater faith, people saw themselves as individual creations of a loving God who, regardless of how it may look at any given moment, has final control over a world destined for restoration. Now, people with no faith find themselves lost and alone, with no overarching story, or meta-narrative, to give promise to the future and meaning to the present.

Rumors of Another World (19 – 20)

❖

World without God

Václav Havel, former president of the Czech Republic, a survivor of a Communist culture that earnestly tried to live without God, stated the problem:

> I believe that with the loss of God, man has lost a kind of absolute and universal system of coordinates, to which he could always relate everything, chiefly himself. His world and his personality gradually began to break up into separate, incoherent fragments corresponding to different, relative coordinates.

Havel saw the Marxist rape of his land as a direct outgrowth of atheism. "I come from a country where forests are dying, where rivers look like sewers, and where in some places the citizens are sometimes recommended not to open their windows," he said, tracing the cause to the "arrogance of new age human beings who enthroned themselves as lords of all nature and of all the world." Such people lack a metaphysical anchor: "I mean, a humble respect for the whole of creation and awareness of our obligations to it. . . . If the parents believe in God, their children will not have to wear gas masks on their way to school and their eyes will not be blinded with pus."

We live in dangerous times and face urgent questions not only about the environment but also about terrorism, war, sexuality, world poverty, and definitions of life and death. Society badly needs a moral tether, or "system of coordinates," in Havel's phrase. We need to know our place in the universe and our obligations to each other and to the earth. Can we answer those questions without God?

Modern literature exalts as a hero the rebel who defiantly stands his ground in a meaningless universe. Evolutionary philosophy holds up Homo sapiens, a species much like any other, destined to live out the script of selfish genes. What if both views of the world are missing something large, important, and portentous for our future — like the natives of South America who simply ignored Magellan's ships sailing past?

Rumors of Another World (25 – 26)

Heaven's Shadow

Rumors of another world sneak in even among those who restrict their view to the world of matter. Scientists who dare not mention God or a Designer speak instead of an "anthropic principle" evident in creation. Nature is exquisitely tuned for the possibility of life on planet Earth: adjust the laws of gravity up or down by one percent, and the universe would not form; a tiny change in electromagnetic force, and organic molecules will not adhere. It appears that, in physicist Freeman Dyson's words, "The universe knew we were coming." To those who know it best, the universe does not seem like a random crapshoot. It seems downright purposeful — but what purpose, and whose?

I find more of a spirit of reverence among secular science writers than in some theologians. The wisest among them admit that all our widening knowledge merely exposes our more-widening pool of ignorance. Things that used to seem clear and rational, such as Newtonian physics, have given way to gigantic puzzles. In my lifetime, astronomers have "discovered" seventy billion more galaxies, admitted they may have overlooked 96 percent of the makeup of the universe ("dark energy" and "dark matter"), and adjusted the time of the Big Bang by four to five billion years. Biologists who gaze through microscopes have discovered unfathomable complexity in the simplest cells.

The process of reducing has, ironically, made the world more complex, not less. The DNA molecule inside each cell contains a three-billion-letter software code capable of overseeing and regulating all the anatomy in the human body. Increasingly, we are learning to read the code. But who wrote it? And why? Can anyone guide us in reading not only the microcode inside each cell but the macrocode governing the entire planet, the universe?

Rumors of another world seep into art as well. Poets, painters, novelists, and playwrights — those who know a little about creating a universe — feel stirrings even when they cannot detect their source. To an artist, the world presents itself as a creation, akin to Beethoven's quartets and Shakespeare's *Hamlet*. If we are in fact God's music and God's words, what tune should we be playing, what words reciting? Milton's question echoes across time: "What if earth be but the shadow of heaven?"

Rumors of Another World (29 – 30)

Body Parts

How can we sense God's love now that Jesus has ascended to the Father? One New Testament answer centers around "the body of Christ," a mysterious phrase used more than thirty times. Paul, especially, settled on that phrase as a summary image of the church. When Jesus left, he turned over his mission to flawed and bumbling men and women. He assumed the role of head of the church, leaving the tasks of arms, legs, ears, eyes, and voice to the erratic disciples — and to you and me.

A careful reading of the four gospels shows that this new arrangement was what Jesus had in mind all along. He knew his time on earth was short, and he proclaimed a mission that went beyond even his death and resurrection. "I will build my church," he declared, "and the gates of hell will not prevail against it" (Matthew 16:18 KJV).

Jesus' decision to operate as the invisible head of a large body with many members affects our view of suffering. It means that he often relies on us to help one another cope. The phrase "the body of Christ," expresses well what we are called to do: to represent in flesh what Christ is like, especially to those in need.

The apostle Paul must have had something like that process in mind when he wrote these words: "[God] comforts us in all our troubles, so that we can comfort those in any trouble with the comfort we ourselves have received from God. For just as the sufferings of Christ flow over into our lives, so also through Christ our comfort overflows" (2 Corinthians 1:4 – 5). And all through his ministry Paul put that principle into practice, taking up collections for famine victims, dispatching assistants to go to troubled areas, acknowledging believers' gifts as gifts from God himself.

Where Is God When It Hurts? (235 – 37)

Turning It Over

The "disadvantage" of knowing God through the Holy Spirit is that, when God turned over the mission to the church, God truly turned it over. As a result, many people who reject God are rejecting not God but a caricature presented by the church. Yes, the church has led the way in issues of justice, literacy, medicine, education, and civil rights. But to our everlasting shame, the watching world judges God by a church whose history also includes the Crusades, the Inquisition, anti-Semitism, suppression of women, and support of the slave trade.

I find it much easier to accept the fact of God dwelling in Jesus of Nazareth than in the people who attend my local church and in me. Yet the New Testament insists this pattern fulfills God's plan from the beginning: not a continuing series of spectacular interventions but a gradual delegation of the mission to flawed human beings. All along, Jesus planned to die so that we, his church, could take his place. What Jesus brought to a few—healing, grace, hope, the good-news message of God's love—his followers could now bring to all. "Unless a kernel of wheat falls to the ground and dies," he explained, "it remains only a single seed. But if it dies, it produces many seeds."

God's withdrawal behind human skin, a condescension to live inside common foot soldiers, guarantees that all will sometimes doubt and many will reject God altogether. The plan also guarantees that the kingdom will advance at a slow, tedious pace, which God, showing remarkable restraint, does not overrule. It took eighteen centuries for the church to rally against slavery, and even then many resisted. Poverty still abounds, as do war and discrimination, and in some places the church does little to help.

The questions we ask, God often turns back on us. We plead for God to "come down" and only reluctantly acknowledge that God is already here, within us, and that what God does on earth closely resembles what the church does. In short, the chief "disadvantage" to knowing God as Spirit is the history of the church—and the spiritual biography of you and me.

Reaching for the Invisible God (154–57)

◆

Beauty Test

I have seen evidence of God's presence in the most unexpected places. During a trip to Nepal, a therapist gave my wife and me a tour of the Green Pastures Hospital, which specializes in leprosy rehabilitation. As we walked along an outdoor corridor, I noticed in a courtyard one of the ugliest human beings I have ever seen. Her hands were bandaged in gauze and she had deformed stumps for feet. Her nose had shrunken away so that, looking at her, I could see into her sinus cavity. Her eyes, mottled and covered with callus, let in no light; she was totally blind. Scars covered patches of skin on her arms.

Later we returned along the same corridor. This creature had crawled to the very edge of the walkway, pulling herself along the ground by planting her elbows and dragging her body. Without hesitation my wife bent and put her arm around the woman, who rested her head against Janet's shoulder and began singing a song in Nepali, a tune that we all instantly recognized: "Jesus Loves Me."

"Dahnmaya is one of our most devoted church members," the physical therapist later told us. "Most of our patients are Hindus, but we have a little Christian chapel here, and Dahnmaya comes every time the door opens. She's a prayer warrior. She loves to greet and welcome every visitor who comes to Green Pastures, and no doubt she heard us talking as we walked along the corridor."

A few months later we heard that Dahnmaya had died. Close to my desk I keep a photo that I snapped just as she was singing to Janet. Whenever I feel polluted by the beauty-obsessed culture I live in—where people pay exorbitant sums to achieve some impossible ideal of beauty while hospitals like Green Pastures scrape by on charity crumbs—I pull out that photo. I see two beautiful women: my wife, smiling sweetly, wearing a brightly colored Nepali outfit she had bought the day before, holding in her arms an old crone who would flunk any beauty test ever devised except the one that matters most. Out of that deformed, hollow shell of a body, the light of God's presence shines out. The Holy Spirit found a home.

Prayer: Does It Make Any Difference? (273–74)

◆

Holy Inefficiency

I once visited Henri Nouwen at L'Arche, a home for the seriously disabled near Toronto. We shared lunch in his small room. A renowned psychologist and theologian who had taught in Ivy League universities, Nouwen had become highly successful as an author and conference speaker, yet here the church "industry" seemed very far away.

After lunch we celebrated a special Eucharist service for Adam, the young man Nouwen looked after. He led the liturgy in honor of Adam's twenty-sixth birthday. Unable to talk, walk, or dress himself, profoundly retarded, Adam gave no sign of comprehension. He seemed to recognize, at least, that his family had come. He drooled throughout and grunted loudly a few times.

Later Nouwen told me it took him two hours to prepare Adam each day: bathing and shaving him, brushing his teeth, combing his hair, guiding his hand as he tried to eat breakfast. I must admit I had a fleeting doubt as to whether this was the best use of the busy priest's time. "I am not giving up anything," Nouwen insisted. "It is I, not Adam, who gets the main benefit from our friendship."

It had been difficult for him at first, he said. Yet in the process he had learned what it must be like for God to love us—spiritually uncoordinated, retarded, able to respond with what must seem to God like inarticulate grunts and groans.

Nouwen has said that all his life two voices competed inside him. One encouraged him to succeed and achieve, while the other called him simply to rest in the comfort that he was "the beloved" of God. Only in the last decade of his life did he truly listen to that second voice. Ultimately Nouwen concluded that "the goal of education and formation for the ministry is continually to recognize the Lord's voice, his face, and his touch in every person we meet."

I will miss Henri Nouwen. For me a single image captures him best: the energetic priest, hair in disarray, using his restless hands as if to fashion a homily out of thin air, celebrating an eloquent birthday Eucharist for an unresponsive child-man so damaged that most parents would have had him aborted. A better symbol of the incarnation, I can hardly imagine.

"Back Page" column, *Christianity Today*,
December 9, 1996 (80)

❖

Disarming Fear

For years I labored under a huge *apparent* fear: the image of a stern, judgmental God as a sort of cosmic Enforcer. Who would want to pray to that God? With such a fearsome partner, how could I pursue an intimate relationship? My defenses lowered over time as I experienced grace, as I met trustworthy guides, and then supremely as I got to know Jesus.

For a recovering fundamentalist, it takes courage to trust that the gospel truly is good news from a God who is love. I sought out guides who believed this most fundamental and yet seldom-realized fact of faith. For ten years I followed around Dr. Paul Brand, who brought healing and grace to some of the lowest people on the planet, low-caste Hindus afflicted with leprosy. Sometimes we prayed together and always I marveled at his simple faith. He showed a spirit of thanksgiving even as he worked for near-poverty wages in trying conditions. He faced into old age with anticipation, not fear. Even at the end, he saw death as a true homecoming, not an interruption but a culmination.

Henri Nouwen proved another trustworthy guide, one who demonstrated that a true image of God calms, rather than provokes, fear. Despite his own inner fears, Nouwen put his trust in the character of God. He learned about fear that "you do not run away from it but feel it through and stand up in it and look it right in the face.... So I am praying while not knowing how to pray."

I marvel that many of the exalted prayers of the apostle Paul appear in the prison epistles, composed in a dungeon. Prayer served as a way for Paul to rise above the fears of the present circumstances into a radical trust in God's tender care. In the same way, ministers and civil rights protestors in the 1960s used their prison time to pray aloud and sing hymns. A skeptic could see those prayers as reality-denial of the worst kind. A believer sees them as faith in a reality that transcends circumstances and disarms fear.

Prayer: Does It Make Any Difference? (291–92)

◇

Failsafe

As I reconsider my own assumptions about relating to God, I now see them as misguided and simplistic. From childhood I inherited an image of God as a stern teacher passing out grades. I had the same goal as everyone else: to get a perfect score and earn the teacher's approval. Cut up in class and you'll be sent to the back of the room to stand in the corner or to a vacant room down the hall.

Almost everything about that analogy, I have learned, contradicts the Bible and distorts the relationship. In the first place, God's approval depends not on my "good conduct" but on God's grace. I could never earn grades high enough to pass a teacher's perfect standards—and, thankfully, I do not have to.

In addition, a relationship with God does not switch on or off depending on my behavior. God does not send me to a vacant room down the hall when I disobey. Quite the opposite. The times when I feel most estranged from God can bring on a sense of desperation, which presents a new starting point for grace. Sulking in a cave in flight from God, Elijah heard a gentle whisper that brought comfort, not a scolding. Jonah tried his best to run from God and failed. And it was at Peter's lowest point that Jesus lovingly restored him.

I tend to project onto God my understanding of how human relationships work, including the assumption that betrayal permanently destroys relationship. God, however, seems undeterred by betrayal (or perhaps has grown used to it): "Upon this *rock*," Jesus said to unstable Peter, "I will build my church." As Luther remarked, we are always at the same time sinners, righteous, and penitent. The halting, stuttered expressions of love we offer may not measure up to what God wants, but like any parent God accepts what the children offer.

Reaching for the Invisible God (192–93)

Prayer as Therapy

I recall a time in our marriage when Janet and I were at loggerheads about, well, almost everything. We were still sorting out power issues, and neither of us was giving much ground. Every decision, major or minor, escalated into a tug-of-war. Stymied, we agreed to try something that had never before worked for us: we would pray together. Each day we sat down and spilled out our inner selves to God. We prayed about those decisions, about the people we would contact that day, about our friends and family members. Our own power issues took on an entirely new light as we subjected ourselves to a Higher Power. We were now side by side before God, not facing each other in opposition. Twenty-five years later we keep up the practice.

I wrote a book on the Old Testament, *The Bible Jesus Read*, in which I discussed the cursing psalms that called for revenge on enemies. I described a practice of taking a weekly "anger walk" on the hill behind my home, during which I would present to God the resentment I felt toward people who had wronged me. Forcing myself to open up deep feelings to God had a therapeutic effect. "Usually I come away feeling as if I have just released a huge burden," I wrote in that book. "The unfairness no longer sticks like a thorn inside me, as it once did; I have expressed it aloud to someone — to God. Sometimes I find that in the process of expression, I grow in compassion. God's Spirit speaks to me of my own selfishness, my judgmental spirit, my own flaws that others have treated with grace and forgiveness, my pitifully limited viewpoint."

I came across that passage just today and had the startling feeling that someone else had written it. You see, it has been several years since I have taken an anger walk. I still stroll on that hill. I check the fox den, look for signs of beetle damage on the Ponderosa pines, follow animal tracks in the snow. And I still pray, though now it would be more accurate to call them "praise walks." In time, the anger melted away. Healing took place, even without my conscious awareness.

Prayer: Does It Make Any Difference? (289–90)

◆

Weeds and Flowers

When I moved to Colorado I soon learned about noxious weeds. Unwelcome species such as dandelion, oxeye daisy, Russian thistle, and toadflax are spreading like botanical viruses in my part of the state, threatening the survival of native species. Wanting to be a good citizen, I bought a hardy weed-puller and began a routine I have kept up through each spring and summer. I take an afternoon walk on the hill behind my home in search of the noxious invaders. As it happens, that walk presents an ideal opportunity for prayer. For a few minutes in the middle of the day I am alone in the beauty of nature, away from the distractions of my home office.

One day when my wife accompanied me I had an epiphany about my weed walks and also my prayers. Her keen eyes helped in the process of spotting weeds, yes, but more importantly she changed the entire nature of the walk by pointing out more than twenty species of wildflowers. I had been so intent on finding the weeds that my eyes had skipped right past the wildflowers adorning the hills—the very flowers my weed-pulling endeavored to protect!

It occurred to me that I do something similar in my prayer practice. I tend to bring a tangled mess of problems to God, not unlike the snarl of weeds I carry home in my collection bag, while overlooking opportunities for praise and thanksgiving. My prayers are essentially selfish, an effort to employ God to help me accomplish my ends. I look on God as a problem-solver (a weed-puller) while overlooking the striking evidence of God's work all around me. And when nothing much seems to happen, I grow impatient.

There is a cure for impatience in prayer, I have found: Keep praying. You will likely grow so frustrated that you will either give up the practice or change your approach to prayer. Jean Nicolas Grou, a mystic from the eighteenth century, prescribed that healthy prayer should be humble, reverent, loving, confident, and persevering—in other words, the exact opposite of impatient.

Prayer: Does It Make Any Difference? (296)

◆

Peacock Praise

On a trip to Australia I tried to experience wildlife with the eyes of worship. I spent three days on Phillip Island, a showcase of God's creation. In the morning I jogged alongside kangaroos and wallabies while cockatoos wheeled overhead and koalas slept in eucalyptus forests. At night I watched the spectacle of shearwaters and fairy penguins.

A million short-tailed shearwaters return to Phillip Island each year on September 24. Each night they swoop toward shore in waves, skimming the surface of the sea ("shearing the water") to pluck off tiny fish. Awkward birds, they crash-land, take a few tumbles, and stagger indignant to their nests. They migrate nine thousand miles from Alaska and the Aleutian Islands. Most remarkable are their child-rearing habits. They fatten their babies, but then the parents take off en masse, leaving the inexperienced nestlings to figure out how to fly, fish, and navigate to Alaska. Amazingly, almost half survive the ordeal.

For sheer entertainment, nothing compares to the nightly parade of the fairy penguins, who return to their nests after a day's fishing. At dusk they float shoreward in "rafts" of ten or twenty. Less than a foot high, these midget penguins assemble along the beach in formation, waiting for courage to cross the expanse of sand. One feints, a few follow, then fear strikes and they all dash back into the sea.

C. S. Lewis suggests that observing God's creation is a holy calling:

> For the beasts can't appreciate it and the angels are, I suppose, pure intelligences. They *understand* colours and tastes better then our greatest scientists; but have they retinas or palates? I fancy the "beauties of nature" are a secret God has shared with us alone. That may be one of the reasons why we were made.

Flannery O'Connor once wrote an essay about her peacocks and the reactions they would get as they unfurled their feathers to present "a galaxy of gazing, haloed suns." One truck driver yelled, "Get a load of that!" and braked to a halt. Most people would fall silent. Her favorite response came from an old black woman who simply cried, "Amen! Amen!"

I think the Artist who designed the peacock rather enjoyed that response. It's certainly what I felt on Phillip Island.

"Back Page" column, *Christianity Today*,
April 7, 1997 (72)

◆

Endangered Wildness

God makes most plain how he feels about the animal kingdom in a magnificent address found at the end of Job. Look closely and you will notice a common thread in the specimens held up for Job's edification: a lioness, a mountain goat, a rogue donkey, an ostrich, a stallion, a hawk, an eagle, a raven, and a behemoth.

Wildness is God's underlying message to Job, the one trait this menagerie all share. God is celebrating those members of the created world who will never be domesticated by human beings. Evidently, wild animals serve an essential function in "the world as God sees it." They bring us down a notch, reminding us of something we'd prefer to forget: our creatureliness. And they also announce to our senses the splendor of an invisible, untamable God.

It is hard to avoid a sermonic tone when writing about wild animals, for our sins against them are very great. In some African nations the elephant population has been reduced by half and rhinoceroses nearly made extinct, thanks mainly to poachers and rambunctious soldiers with machine guns. And every year we are destroying an area of rain forest—and all its animal residents—equal in size to all of New England.

Most wildlife writing focuses on these vanishing animals themselves, but I find myself wondering about the ultimate impact on us. What else, besides that innate appreciation for wildness, have we lost? Could distaste for authority, or even a loss of God-awareness, derive in part from this atrophied sense? God's mere mention of the animals struck a chord of awe in Job; what about us, who grow up tossing peanuts across the moat to the behemoths and leviathans?

Naturalist John Muir concluded sadly, "It is a great comfort ... that vast multitudes of creatures, great and small and infinite in number, lived and had a good time in God's love before man was created."

The heavens declare the glory of God; and so do breaching whales and pronking springboks. Fortunately, in some corners of the world vast multitudes of creatures can still live and have a good time in God's love. The least we could do is make room for them—for our sakes as well as theirs.

I Was Just Wondering (10 – 13)

◇

Power Sharing

I used to feel spiritually inferior because I had not experienced the more spectacular manifestations of the Spirit and could not point to any bona fide "miracles" in my life. Increasingly, though, I have come to see that what I value may differ greatly from what God values. Jesus, often reluctant to perform miracles, considered it progress when he departed earth and entrusted the mission to his flawed disciples. Like a proud parent, God seems to take more delight as a spectator of the bumbling achievements of stripling children than in any self-display of omnipotence.

From God's perspective, if I may speculate, the great advance in human history may be what happened at Pentecost, which restored the direct correspondence of spirit to Spirit that had been lost in Eden. I want God to act in direct, impressive, irrefutable ways. God wants to "share power" with the likes of me, accomplishing his work through people, not despite them.

"Take me seriously! Treat me like an adult, not a child!" is the cry of every teenager. God honors that request, making me a partner for kingdom work, granting me freedom in full knowledge that I will abuse it. God does this out of desire for a mature lover as a partner, not a puppy-love adolescent.

In marriage two partners can achieve a unity while preserving their freedom and independence. Even so, as every couple learns, combining two genders in a marriage introduces differences that may take a lifetime to work out.

I will never be able to reduce life with God to a formula for the same reason I cannot reduce my marriage to a formula. It is a living, growing relationship with another free being. No relationship has proved more challenging than marriage. I am tempted sometimes to wish for an "old-fashioned" marriage, in which roles and expectations are more clearly spelled out and need not always be negotiated. I sometimes yearn for an intervention from outside that would decisively change one of the characteristics that bring my wife and me pain. So far, this has not happened. We wake up each day and continue the journey on ground that grows incrementally more solid with each step.

Love works that way, with partners visible or invisible.

Reaching for the Invisible God (182 – 84)

◇

God's Voices

Think of God's plan as a series of Voices. The first Voice, thunderingly loud, had certain advantages. When the Voice spoke from the trembling mountain at Sinai, or when fire licked up the altar on Mount Carmel, no one could deny it. Yet, amazingly, even those who heard the Voice and feared it—the Israelites at Sinai and at Carmel, for example—soon learned to ignore it. Its very volume got in the way. Few of them sought out that Voice; fewer still persevered when the Voice fell silent.

The Voice modulated with Jesus, the *Word* made flesh. For a few decades the Voice of God took on the timbre and volume and rural accent of a country Jew in Palestine. It was a normal human voice, and though it spoke with authority, it did not cause people to flee. Jesus' voice was soft enough to debate against, soft enough to kill.

After Jesus departed, the Voice took on new forms. On the day of Pentecost, tongues—*tongues*—of fire fell on the faithful, and the church, God's body, began to take shape. That last Voice is as close as breath, as gentle as a whisper. It is the most vulnerable Voice of all, and the easiest to ignore. The Bible says the Spirit can be "quenched" or "grieved"—try quenching Moses' burning bush or the molten rocks of Sinai! Yet the Spirit is also the most intimate Voice. In our moments of weakness, when we do not know what to pray, the Spirit within intercedes for us with groans that words cannot express. Those groans are the early pangs of birth, the labor pains of the new creation.

The Spirit will not remove all disappointment with God. The very titles given to the Spirit—Intercessor, Helper, Counselor, Comforter—imply there will be problems. But the Spirit is also "a deposit, guaranteeing what is to come," Paul said, drawing on an earthy metaphor from the financial world. The Spirit reminds us that such disappointments are temporary, a prelude to an eternal life with God.

Disappointment with God (151–52)

Holy Fools

God often does his work through "holy fools," dreamers who strike out in ridiculous faith, whereas I approach my own decisions with calculation and restraint. In fact, a curious law of reversal seems to apply in matters of faith. The modern world honors intelligence, good looks, confidence, and sophistication. God, apparently, does not. Instead God often relies on simple, uneducated people who don't know any better than to trust God, and through them wonders happen. The least gifted person can become a master in prayer, because prayer requires only an intense desire to spend time with God.

My church in Chicago, a delightful mixture of races and economic groups, once scheduled an all-night vigil of prayer during a major crisis. Several people voiced concern. Was it safe, given our inner-city neighborhood? Should we hire guards or escorts for the parking lot? What if no one showed up? At length we discussed the practicality of the event.

The poorest members of the congregation, a group of senior citizens from a housing project, responded the most enthusiastically to the prayer vigil. I could not help wondering how many of their prayers had gone unanswered over the years—they lived in the projects, after all, amid crime, poverty, and suffering—yet still they showed a childlike trust in the power of prayer. "How long do you want to stay—an hour or two?" we asked, thinking of the logistics of van shuttles. "Oh, we'll stay all night," they replied.

One African-American woman in her nineties, who walked with a cane and could barely see, explained to a staff member why she wanted to spend the night sitting on the hard pews of a church in an unsafe neighborhood. "You see, they's lots of things we can't do in this church. We ain't so educated, and we ain't got as much energy as some of you younger folks. But we can pray. We got time, and we got faith. Some of us don't sleep much anyway. We can pray all night if needs be."

And so they did. Meanwhile, a bunch of yuppies in a downtown church learned an important lesson: faith appears where least expected and falters where it should be thriving.

Reaching for the Invisible God (38 – 39)

◇

Extreme Makeover

Rarely do I wake up in the morning full of faith. Instead, I feel a bit like a tropical fish I used to keep in a saltwater aquarium. This fish would excrete a poisonous sac around its body at night, then sleep in peace, free from harassment by its neighbors. Each morning, however, the fish woke up in a milky cloud of poison. So often my faith disappears overnight and I wake up in a cloud of poisonous doubt.

"Don't you know that you yourselves are God's temple and that God's Spirit lives in you?" Paul asked the Corinthians. If God himself lives inside me, shouldn't I wake up with that knowledge and live in constant awareness all day long? Alas, I do not.

Paul says elsewhere that God "set his seal of ownership on us, and put his Spirit in our hearts as a deposit, guaranteeing what is to come." After an organ transplant, doctors must use antirejection drugs to suppress the immune system or else the body will throw off the newly grafted member. I have come to see the Holy Spirit as a power living inside me that keeps me from throwing off the new identity God has implanted. My spiritual immune system needs daily reminders that God's presence *belongs* within me and is no foreign object.

Absorbing a new identity requires an act of will. Take off your old self and put on your new self, Paul advises, as if we "clothe our minds" in the way we make daily selections from a wardrobe. I have found that the process requires a determined effort.

Rather than rushing from one task to the next, pause for a moment and recognize the time between times. Before dialing the phone, pause and think about the person on the other end. After reading from a book, pause and think back through how you were moved. After watching a television show, pause and ask what it contributed to your life. Before reading the Bible, pause and ask for a spirit of attention.

Reaching for the Invisible God (167 – 69)

◆

A Lost Gift?

I heard a story from a friend who works with the down-and-out in Chicago:

A prostitute came to me in wretched straits, homeless, sick, unable to buy food for her two-year-old daughter. Through sobs and tears, she told me she had been renting out her daughter — two years old! — to men interested in kinky sex. She made more renting out her daughter for an hour than she could earn on her own in a night. She had to do it, she said, to support her own drug habit. I could hardly bear hearing her sordid story. For one thing, it made me legally liable — I'm required to report cases of child abuse. I had no idea what to say to this woman.

At last I asked if she had ever thought of going to a church for help. I will never forget the look of pure, naive shock that crossed her face. "Church!" she cried. "Why would I ever go there? I was already feeling terrible about myself. They'd just make me feel worse."

What struck me about my friend's story is that women much like this prostitute fled toward Jesus, not away from him. The worse a person felt about herself, the more likely she saw Jesus as a refuge. Has the church lost that gift? Evidently the down-and-out, who flocked to Jesus when he lived on earth, no longer feel welcome among his followers. What has happened?

The more I pondered this question, the more I felt drawn to one word as the key: Grace.

Author Stephen Brown notes that a veterinarian can learn a lot about a dog owner he has never met just by observing the dog. What does the world learn about God by watching God's followers on earth? Trace the roots of *grace*, or *charis* in Greek, and you will find a verb that means "I rejoice, I am glad." In my experience, rejoicing and gladness are not the first images that come to mind when people think of the church. They think of holier-than-thous. They think of church as a place to go after you have cleaned up your act, not before. They think of morality, not grace.

What's So Amazing About Grace? (11 – 12, 14)

❖

The Last Best Word

As a writer, I play with words all day long. I toy with them, listen for their overtones, crack them open, and try to stuff my thoughts inside. I've found that words tend to spoil over the years, like old meat. Their meaning rots away. Consider the word *charity*, for instance. When King James translators contemplated the highest form of love they settled on the word *charity* to convey it. Nowadays we hear the scornful protest, "I don't want your charity!"

Perhaps I keep circling back to *grace* because it is one grand theological word that has not spoiled. I call it "the last best word" because every English usage I can find retains some of the glory of the original. Like a vast aquifer, the word underlies our proud civilization, reminding us that good things come not from our own efforts, rather by the grace of God.

Grace is indeed amazing—truly our last best word. It contains the essence of the gospel as a drop of water can contain the image of the sun. The world thirsts for grace in ways it does not even recognize; little wonder the hymn "Amazing Grace" edged its way onto the Top Ten charts two hundred years after composition. For a society that seems adrift, without moorings, I know of no better place to drop an anchor of faith.

Like grace notes in music, though, the state of grace proves fleeting. The Berlin Wall falls in a night of euphoria; South African blacks queue up in long, exuberant lines to cast their first votes ever; Yitzhak Rabin and Yasser Arafat shake hands in the Rose Garden—for a moment, grace descends. And then Eastern Europe sullenly settles into the long task of rebuilding, South Africa tries to figure out how to run a country, Arafat dodges bullets and Rabin is felled by one. Like a dying star, grace dissipates in a final burst of pale light, and is then engulfed by the black hole of "ungrace."

What's So Amazing About Grace? (12 – 13)

◆

A Fall to Grace

Grace did not come to me initially in the forms or the words of faith. I grew up in a church that often used the word but meant something else. Grace, like many religious words, had been leached of meaning so that I could no longer trust it.

I first experienced grace through music. At the Bible college I was attending, I was viewed as a deviant. People would publicly pray for me and ask me if I needed exorcism. I felt harassed, disordered, confused. I began to climb out the window of my dorm room and sneak into the chapel, which contained a nine-foot Steinway grand piano. In a chapel dark but for a small light by which to read music, I would sit for an hour or so each night and play Beethoven's sonatas, Chopin's preludes, and Schubert's impromptus. My own fingers pressed a kind of tactile order onto the world. My mind was confused, my body was confused, the world was confused—but here I sensed a hidden world of beauty, grace, and wonder light as a cloud and startling as a butterfly wing.

Something similar happened in the world of nature. To get away from the crush of ideas and people, I would take long walks in the pine forests splashed with dogwood. I followed the zigzag paths of dragonflies along the river, watched flocks of birds wheeling overhead, and picked apart logs to find the iridescent beetles inside. I liked the sure, inevitable way of nature giving form and place to all living things. I saw evidence that the world contains grandeur, great goodness, and, yes, traces of joy.

About the same time, I fell in love. It felt exactly like a fall, a head-over-heels tumble into a state of unbearable lightness. The earth tilted on its axis. I was as unprepared for love as I had been for goodness and beauty. Suddenly, my heart seemed swollen, too large for my chest.

I was experiencing "common grace," to use the theologians' term. It is a terrible thing, I found, to be grateful and have no one to thank, to be awed and have no one to worship. Gradually, very gradually, I came back to the cast-off faith of my childhood.

What's So Amazing About Grace? (41 – 42)

❖

Why I Don't Attend a Megachurch

I resist the trend toward megachurches, preferring smaller places out of the spotlight. I never fully understood why until I came across this paradoxical observation in G. K. Chesterton's *Heretics*:

> The man who lives in a small community lives in a much larger world.... The reason is obvious. In a large community we can choose our companions. In a small community our companions are chosen for us.

Precisely! Given a choice, I tend to hang out with folks like me: people who have college degrees, drink only Starbucks dark roast coffee, listen to classical music, and buy their cars based on EPA gas mileage ratings. Yet after a short while I get bored with people like me. Smaller groups (and smaller churches) force me to rub shoulders with everybody else.

Henri Nouwen defines "community" as the place where the person you least want to live with always lives. Often we surround ourselves with the people we *most* want to live with, which forms a club or a clique, not a community. Anyone can form a club; it takes grace, shared vision, and hard work to form a community.

The Christian church was the first institution in history to bring together on equal footing Jews and Gentiles, men and women, slaves and free. The apostle Paul waxed eloquent on this "mystery, which for ages past was kept hidden in God." By forming a community out of diverse members, Paul said, we have the opportunity to capture the attention of the world and even the supernatural world beyond (Ephesians 3:9–10).

In some ways the church has sadly failed in this assignment. (Yes, Billy Graham, eleven o'clock Sunday is still the most segregated hour in America.) Still, even all-white or all-black churches show diversity in age, education, and economic class. Church is the one place I visit that brings together generations: infants still held at their mothers' breasts, children who squirm and giggle at all the wrong times, responsible adults who know how to act appropriately at all times, and senior citizens who may drift asleep if the preacher drones on too long.

I deliberately seek a congregation comprising people *not* like me, and I find such people less avoidable in smaller churches.

"Back Page" column, *Christianity Today*,
May 20, 1996 (80)

Quiet Care

How do I help someone else in need? Specifically, what can I do to alleviate their fear? I have learned that simple availability is the most powerful force we can contribute to help calm the fears of others.

We rightly disparage Job's three friends for their insensitive response to his suffering. But read the account again: when they came, they sat in silence beside Job for seven days and seven nights before opening their mouths. As it turned out, those were the most eloquent moments they spent with him.

Instinctively, I shrink back from people who are in pain. Who can know whether they want to talk about their predicament or not? Do they want to be consoled, or cheered up? What good can my presence possibly do? My mind spins out these rationalizations and as a result I end up doing the worst thing possible: I stay away.

Tony Campolo tells the story of going to a funeral home to pay his respects to the family of an acquaintance. By mistake he ended up in the wrong parlor. It held the body of an elderly man, and his widow was the only mourner present. She seemed so lonely that Campolo decided to stay for the funeral. He even drove with her to the cemetery.

At the end of the grave-side service, as he and the woman were driving away, Campolo finally confessed that he had not known her husband. "I thought as much," said the widow. "I didn't recognize you. But it doesn't really matter." She squeezed his arm so hard it hurt. "You'll never, ever, know what this means to me."

No one offers the name of a philosopher when I ask the question, "Who helped you most?" Most often they answer by describing a quiet, unassuming person. Someone who was there whenever needed, who listened more than talked, who didn't keep glancing down at a watch, who hugged and touched, and cried. In short, someone who was available, and came on the sufferer's terms and not their own.

Where Is God When It Hurts? (176–77)

◆

Touch Love

I received a copy of a letter from a woman who experienced the healing touch of the body of Christ. For seven years she ministered to her husband, a well-known church musician afflicted with ALS, or Lou Gehrig's disease. He died, and on the first anniversary of his death, the widow sent out a letter of gratitude to her many friends at church. It read, in part:

> Ever since the first symptoms of ALS appeared, you have surrounded us with love and support. You have cheered us with innumerable notes and letters and cards.
>
> You visited and phoned, often from faraway places.... You brought marvelous food. You ran errands for us and repaired our broken things while yours waited. You shoveled our walks, brought our mail, dumped our trash. And you brought gifts of love to brighten our hours.
>
> You "doctored" ... and even repaired a tooth right here in our home. You did ingenious things that made life easier for both of us, like the "coughing jacket" and signal switch that Norm was able to use until the last few days of his life. You shared Scripture verses with us and some of you made it your ministry to pray for those who came to our home regularly to give respiratory treatments. You made him feel like he was still a vital part of the music ministry.
>
> And how you prayed!!! Day after day, month after month, even year after year! Those prayers buoyed us up, lifted us through particularly hard places, gave us strength that would have been humanly impossible to have, and helped us to reach out on our own for God's resources. Someday we'll understand why Norm's perfect healing did not take place here. But we do know that he was with us much longer and in much better condition than is the norm for an ALS victim. Love is not a strong enough word to tell you how we feel about you!

This widow's fellow church members had became the presence of God for her. Because of their loving concern, she was not tormented by doubts over whether God loved her. She could sense his love in the human touch of Christ's body, her local church.

Where Is God When It Hurts? (240 – 41)

◆

Jungle Trails

When I begin a book, I take up a machete and start hacking my way through the jungle, not to clear a trail for others, rather to find a path through for myself. Will anyone follow? Have I lost my way? I never know the answers to those questions as I write; I just keep swinging the machete.

That image is not quite accurate, however. In carving my path I am following a map laid out by many others, the "great cloud of witnesses" who have preceded me. My struggles with faith have at least this in their favor: they come from a long, distinguished line. I find kindred expressions of doubt and confusion in the Bible itself. Sigmund Freud accused the church of teaching only questions that it can answer. Some churches may do that, but God surely does not. In books like Job, Ecclesiastes, and Habakkuk, the Bible poses blunt questions that have no answers.

As I investigate, I find that great saints also encountered many of the same roadblocks, detours, and dead ends that I experience and that my correspondents express. Modern churches tend to feature testimonies of spiritual successes, never failures, which only makes the strugglers in the pew feel worse. Yet delve a bit deeper into church history and you will find a different story, of those who strain to swim upstream like spawning fish.

I mention this not to dampen anyone's faith but to add a dose of realism to spiritual propaganda that promises more than it can deliver. In an odd way the very failures of the church prove its doctrine. Grace, like water, flows to the lowest part. We in the church have humility and contrition to offer the world, not a formula for success. Almost alone in our success-oriented society, we admit that we have failed, are failing, and always will fail. That is why we turn to God so desperately.

Reaching for the Invisible God (18 – 20)

Doubt Companions

Over time, I have grown more comfortable with mystery rather than certainty. God does not twist arms and never forces us into a corner with faith as the only exit. We will always, with Pascal, see "too much to deny and too little to be sure."

I look to Jesus, God laid bare to human view, for proof of God's refusal to twist arms. Jesus often made it harder, not easier, for people to believe. He never violated an individual's freedom to decide, even to decide against him.

The church environment I grew up in had no room for doubt. "Just believe!" they told us. Anyone who strayed risked punishment as a deviant. In Bible college my brother received an F on a speech that, in the 1960s, had the effrontery to suggest that rock music is not inherently immoral. Although my brother was a classical musician who in fact had no taste for rock music, he could find no biblical support for the arguments about rock music made at that school.

I have heard my brother speak many times — he was a competitive debater — and saw the notes for his presentation, and have no doubt that he received an F for one reason: the teacher disagreed with his conclusion. More, the teacher concluded that *God* disagreed with his conclusion. My brother left the school. He also left the faith, and has never returned — in large part, I believe, because he did not observe truth setting people free and never found a church that makes room for prodigals.

I had a very different experience from my brother's. In my pilgrimage I found a grace-filled church and Christians who formed a safe place for my doubts. I note in the Gospels that Jesus' disciple Thomas kept company with the other disciples even though he could not believe their accounts of Jesus' resurrection, and it was amid that community that Jesus appeared in order to strengthen Thomas's faith. In a similar way, my friends and colleagues at *Campus Life* magazine, then *Christianity Today*, and LaSalle Street Church in Chicago created a haven of acceptance that carried me along when my faith wavered. I feel sad for lonely doubters; we all need trustworthy doubt companions.

Reaching for the Invisible God (45 – 46)

◆

Room for Doubt

Having said so many laudatory things about doubt, I need also acknowledge that doubt may lead a person away from faith rather than toward it. In my case, doubt has prompted me to question many things that need questioning and also to investigate alternatives to faith, none of which measure up. I remain a Christian today due to my doubts. For many others, though, doubt has had the opposite effect, working like a nerve disease to cause a slow and painful spiritual paralysis. Nearly every week I answer a letter from someone tormented by doubts. Their suffering is as acute and debilitating as any suffering I know.

Although we cannot control doubt, we can learn to channel it in ways that make doubt more likely to be nourishing than toxic. For starters, I try to approach my doubts with the humility appropriate to my creaturely status.

Our approach to difficult issues should befit our status as finite creatures. Take the doctrine of God's sovereignty, taught in the Bible in such a way that it stands in unresolved tension with human freedom. God's perspective as an all-powerful being who sees all of history at once, rather than unfolding second by second, will always baffle theologians simply because that point of view is unattainable to us, even unimaginable by us. The best physicists in the world struggle to explain the multidirectional arrows of time. A humble approach accepts that difference in perspective and worships a God who transcends our limitations.

Of course, we must and should investigate some of the issues occupying the margins of doctrine. I have found consolation, for example, in the depiction in *The Great Divorce* of hell as a place that people choose, and continue to choose even when they end up there. As Milton's Satan put it, "Better to reign in Hell than serve in Heaven." Still, I must insist that the most important questions about heaven and hell—who goes where, whether there are second chances, what form the judgments and rewards take, intermediate states after death—are opaque to us at best. More and more, I am grateful for that ignorance, and grateful that the God revealed in Jesus is the one who determines the answers.

Reaching for the Invisible God (43 – 45)

◆

Lack of Alternatives

I must exercise faith simply to believe that God exists, a basic requirement for any relationship. And yet when I wish to explore how faith works, I usually sneak in by the back door of doubt, for I best learn about my own need for faith during its absence. God's invisibility guarantees I will experience times of doubt.

Everyone dangles on a pendulum that swings from belief to unbelief, back to belief, and ends—where? Some never find faith.

I feel kinship with those who find it impossible to believe or find it impossible to keep on believing in the face of apparent betrayal. I have been in a similar place at times, and I marvel that God bestowed on me an unexpected gift of faith. Examining my own periods of faithlessness, I see in them all manner of unbelief. Sometimes I shy away for lack of evidence, sometimes I slink away in hurt or disillusionment, and sometimes I turn aside in willful disobedience. Something, though, keeps drawing me back to God. What? I ask myself.

"This is a hard teaching. Who can accept it?" said Jesus' disciples in words that resonate in every doubter. Jesus' listeners found themselves simultaneously attracted and repelled, like a compass needle brought close to a magnet. As his words sank in, one by one the crowd of onlookers and followers slouched away, leaving only the twelve. "You do not want to leave too, do you?" Jesus asked them in a tone somewhere between plaintiveness and resignation. As usual, Simon Peter spoke up: "Lord, to whom shall we go?"

That, for me, is the bottom-line answer to why I stick around. To my shame, I admit that one of the strongest reasons I stay in the fold is the lack of good alternatives, many of which I have tried. *Lord, to whom shall I go?* The only thing more difficult than having a relationship with an invisible God is having no such relationship.

Reaching for the Invisible God (37 – 38)

Marked by Passion

So which is it, fullness or dryness, light or darkness, victory or failure? If pressed to answer, I would suggest, "Both." Chart out a course that guarantees a successful prayer life, the active presence of God, and constant victory over temptation, and you will probably run aground. A relationship with an invisible God will always include uncertainty and variability.

I prefer to dodge the question, however, because I believe it is the wrong question. As I look back over the giants of faith, all had one thing in common: neither victory nor success, but *passion*. An emphasis on spiritual technique may lead us away from the passionate relationship that God values above all. More than a doctrinal system, more than a mystical experience, the Bible emphasizes a relationship with a Person, and personal relationships are never steady-state.

God's favorites responded with passion in kind. Moses argued with God so fervently that several times he persuaded God to change plans. Jacob wrestled all night and used trickery to grab hold of God's blessing. Job lashed out in rage against God. David broke at least half the Ten Commandments. Yet never did they wholly give up on God, and never did God give up on them. God can handle anger, blame, and even willful disobedience. One thing, however, blocks relationship: indifference. "They turned their backs to me and not their faces," God told Jeremiah, in a damning indictment of Israel.

From the spiritual giants of the Bible, I learn this crucial lesson about relating to an invisible God: Whatever you do, don't ignore God. Invite God into every aspect of life.

For some Christians, the times of Job-like crisis will represent the greatest danger. How can they cling to faith in a God who appears unconcerned and even hostile? Others, and I count myself among them, face a more subtle danger. An accumulation of distractions—a malfunctioning computer, bills to pay, an upcoming trip, a friend's wedding, the general busyness of life—gradually edges God away from the center of my life. Some days I meet people, eat, work, make decisions, all without giving God a single thought. And that void is far more serious than what Job experienced, for not once did Job stop thinking about God.

Reaching for the Invisible God (188–89)

◇

Belly of the Beast

Zagorsk Prison, oldest in Russia, was constructed in 1832. The builders set its stone walls below ground to cut down the need for heating. To reach the prisoners' quarters, we went through four steel gates, down, down, down worn stone steps that led progressively toward the source of an oppressive stench, the prisoners' cells on the bottom level.

The first cell we entered was about the size of my bedroom in Chicago. Eight teenage boys—the youngest was actually twelve—jumped to attention when the door opened. The room held only four beds, so two boys shared each bed. There was a rickety table, but no other furniture. A thin, soiled blanket covered each bed, but there were no sheets or pillowcases.

In one corner of the room was a ceramic-lined hole in the ground, with two footpads marked out for squatting. This hole, open to view on all sides, functioned as both toilet and "shower," although the only water came from a single cold water spigot an arm's length away. The basement cell had a single six-inch window, which was frosted over and did not open, at the very top of one wall. A bare bulb hung on a wire from the ceiling.

I saw no board games, no television or radio sets, no diversions of any kind. For security, Zagorsk observes a permanent twenty-four-hour lockdown. All day every day for a year, two years, maybe five, these boys will sit in their tiny dungeon cell like animals and wait for freedom. Most of them, I learned, are serving time for petty thievery.

The warden of the worst prison in the Soviet Union turned out to be a dedicated, even courageous man. Two years before, when the government cut off his supplies of food, this warden approached the monks at the famous Zagorsk monastery for help. Out of their own storehouses, the monks supplied enough bread and vegetables to feed the prisoners throughout the winter. Their selfless response impressed the warden, a Communist at the time. In 1989 he authorized the monks to rebuild a chapel in the prison basement—an act of remarkable boldness for a Communist functionary in the atheistic state prevailing then.

[Continued on May 31]

Praying with the KGB (55 – 58)

Oasis in a Dungeon

[Continued from May 30]

Located on the lowest subterranean level, the chapel was an oasis of beauty in an otherwise grim dungeon. The priests had installed a marble floor and mounted finely wrought candle sconces on the walls. Each week priests traveled from the monastery to conduct a service, and for this occasion prisoners were allowed out of their cells, which naturally guaranteed excellent attendance.

My companion, Ron Nikkel, asked Brother Bonifato Peter if he would say a prayer for the prisoners. The priest looked puzzled. "A prayer? You want a prayer?" We nodded.

He looked thoughtful, then disappeared behind the altar at the end of the room. He brought out an icon. Then he retrieved two candle holders and two incense bowls, which he laboriously hung in place and lit. Next he removed his headpiece and robe. He meticulously laced gold cuffs over his black sleeves. He placed a droopy gold stole around his neck, and then a gold crucifix. Finally, he was ready to pray.

Brother Bonifato did not say prayers; he sang them, from a liturgy book propped on another stand. Finally, twenty minutes after Ron had requested a prayer for the prisoners, Brother Bonifato said "Amen," and we exited the prison into the bracing fresh air outside.

Watching the procedure in the chapel brought back for me the inner conflict I had felt while standing in the magnificent cathedrals of Russia. Reverence, submission, awe, *mysterium tremendum* — the Orthodox Church conveyed these qualities superbly in worship. But God remained far away, approachable only after much preparation and only through intermediaries such as priests and icons. I thought of the teenagers back in their basement cell. If one of them asked for prayer, for the strength to endure or for a sick family member outside, would Brother Bonifato have followed the same ritual? Would the boys in the cell dare to think of approaching God themselves, praying in the casual and everyday language that Jesus used?

Yet when a need arose, the monks had responded: with bread, with their incarnational presence, with the reinstitution of worship in the unlikeliest of places. I had seen the best and worst of Russia in one morning in Zagorsk, and for just a moment they had come together.

Praying with the KGB (58 – 60)

June

Atrocious Mathematics

It was altogether in character for the scrupulous apostle Peter to pursue some mathematical formula of grace. "How many times shall I forgive my brother when he sins against me?" he asked Jesus. "Up to seven times?" Peter was erring on the side of magnanimity, for the rabbis in his day had suggested three as the maximum number of times one might be expected to forgive.

"Not seven times, but seventy-seven times," replied Jesus in a flash.

Peter's question prompted another of Jesus' trenchant stories, about a servant who somehow piles up a debt of several million dollars. The fact that realistically no servant could accumulate a debt so huge underscores Jesus' point: confiscating the man's family, children, and all his property would not make a dent in repaying the debt. It is unforgivable. Nevertheless the king, touched with pity, abruptly cancels the debt and lets the servant off scot-free.

The more I reflect on Jesus' parables, the more tempted I am to use the word "atrocious" to describe the mathematics of the gospel. I believe Jesus gave us these stories about grace in order to call us to step completely outside our tit-for-tat world of ungrace and enter into God's realm of infinite grace. As Miroslav Volf puts it, "The economy of undeserved grace has primacy over the economy of moral deserts."

From nursery school onward we are taught how to succeed in the world of ungrace. The early bird gets the worm. No pain, no gain. There is no such thing as a free lunch. Demand your rights. Get what you pay for. I know these rules well because I live by them. I work for what I earn; I like to win; I insist on my rights. I want people to get what they deserve — nothing more, nothing less.

Yet if I care to listen, I hear a loud whisper from the gospel that I did not get what I deserved. I deserved punishment and got forgiveness. I deserved wrath and got love. I deserved debtor's prison and got instead a clean credit history. I deserved stern lectures and crawl-on-your-knees repentance; I got a banquet spread for me.

What's So Amazing About Grace? (63 – 64)

◆

Defining Grace

God exists outside of time, the theologians tell us. God created time as an artist chooses a medium to work with, and is unbound by it. God sees the future and the past in a kind of eternal present. If right about this property of God, the theologians have helped explain how God can possibly call "beloved" a person as inconstant, fickle, and temperamental as I am. When God looks upon my life graph, he sees not jagged swerves toward good and bad but rather a steady line of good: the goodness of God's Son captured in a moment of time and applied for all eternity.

I grew up with the image of a mathematical God who weighed my good and bad deeds on a set of scales and always found me wanting. Somehow I missed the God of the Gospels, a God of mercy and generosity who keeps finding ways to shatter the relentless laws of ungrace. God tears up the mathematical tables and introduces the new math of grace, the most surprising, twisting, unexpected-ending word in the English language.

Grace makes its appearance in so many forms that I have trouble defining it. I am ready, though, to attempt something like a definition of grace in relation to God. *Grace means there is nothing we can do to make God love us more*—no amount of spiritual calisthenics and renunciations, no amount of knowledge gained from seminaries and divinity schools, no amount of crusading on behalf of righteous causes. *And grace means there is nothing we can do to make God love us less*—no amount of racism or pride or pornography or adultery or even murder. Grace means that God already loves us as much as an infinite God can possibly love.

Brennan Manning tells the story of an Irish priest who, on a walking tour of a rural parish, sees an old peasant kneeling by the side of the road, praying. Impressed, the priest says to the man, "You must be very close to God." The peasant looks up from his prayers, thinks a moment, and then smiles, "Yes, he's very fond of me."

What's So Amazing About Grace? (69 – 70)

◆

Unnatural Act

In the heat of an argument my wife came up with an acute theological formulation. We were discussing my shortcomings in a rather spirited way when she said, "I think it's pretty amazing that I forgive you for some of the dastardly things you've done!"

Since I'm writing about forgiveness, not sin, I will omit the juicy details of those dastardly things. What struck me about her comment, rather, was its sharp insight into the nature of forgiveness. It is no sweet platonic ideal to be dispersed in the world like air-freshener sprayed from a can. Forgiveness is achingly difficult, and long after you've forgiven, the wound—my dastardly deeds—lives on in memory. Forgiveness is an unnatural act, and my wife was protesting its blatant unfairness.

A story from Genesis captures much the same sentiment in the account of Joseph's reconciliation with his brothers. One moment Joseph acted harshly, throwing his brothers in jail; the next moment he seemed overcome with sorrow, leaving the room to blubber like a drunk. He played tricks on his brothers, hiding money in their grain sacks, seizing one as a hostage, accusing another of stealing his silver cup. Finally Joseph could restrain himself no longer. He summoned his brothers and dramatically forgave them.

I now see that story as a realistic depiction of the unnatural act of forgiveness. The brothers Joseph struggled to forgive were the very ones who had bullied him, had cooked up schemes to murder him, had sold him into slavery. Because of them he had spent the best years of his youth moldering in an Egyptian dungeon. Though he went on to triumph over adversity and though with all his heart he now wanted to forgive these brothers, he could not bring himself to that point, not yet. The wound still hurt too much.

I view Genesis 42–45 as Joseph's way of saying, "I think it's pretty amazing that I forgive you for the dastardly things you've done!" When grace finally broke through to Joseph, the sound of his grief and love echoed throughout the palace. *What is that wail? Is the king's minister sick?* No, Joseph's health was fine. It was the sound of a man forgiving.

What's So Amazing About Grace? (84–85)

◆

Nonviolent Weapons

Richard Attenborough's movie *Gandhi* contains a fine scene in which Gandhi tries to explain his philosophy to the Presbyterian missionary Charlie Andrews. Walking together in a South African city, the two suddenly find their way blocked by young thugs. Reverend Andrews takes one look at the menacing gangsters and decides to run for it. Gandhi stops him. "Doesn't the New Testament say if an enemy strikes you on the right cheek you should offer him the left?" Andrews mumbles that he thought the phrase was used metaphorically.

"I'm not so sure," Gandhi replies. "I suspect he meant you must show courage —be willing to take a blow, several blows, to show you will not strike back nor will you be turned aside. And when you do that it calls on something in human nature, something that makes his hatred decrease and his respect increase. I think Christ grasped that and I have seen it work."

Gandhi's deeply felt sensibility gradually took shape as a firm doctrine. Violence against another human being—even against a soldier firing into an unarmed crowd—contradicted everything he believed about universal human dignity. You cannot change a person's conviction through violence, he believed. Violence brutalizes and divides; it does not reconcile. If his supporters ever turned violent during one of his campaigns, Gandhi would call it off. No cause, no matter how just, merited bloodshed. "I would die for the cause," he concluded, "but there is no cause I'm prepared to kill for."

Since Gandhi, other political leaders have adopted his tactics. Martin Luther King Jr., who considered himself a spiritual successor, visited India and imported the methods to the United States. He and others proved that nonviolence can move mountains in relatively open societies, but what about in places like Nazi Germany, or modern China and Myanmar/Burma, where military regimes quash all protest? (Ironically, some Hindu leaders, Gandhi's own religious heirs, suggest that this principle grew out of his Christian influences and has no place in Hinduism.)

Ethicists, politicians, and theologians will continue to disagree on whether and when armed force is justified. But after Gandhi, no one can deny the power of nonviolence in effecting change. It did, after all, bring freedom to the second most populous nation on earth.

Soul Survivor (153 – 54)

The End of Protest

Martin Luther King Jr. had some weaknesses, but one thing he got right. He stayed true to the principle of peacemaking. He did not strike back. Where others called for revenge, he called for love. The civil rights marchers put their bodies on the line before sheriffs with nightsticks and fire hoses and snarling German shepherds. That, in fact, was what brought them the victory. Historians point to one event as the single moment in which the movement attained a critical mass of public support for its cause. It occurred on a bridge outside Selma, Alabama, when Sheriff Jim Clark turned his policemen loose on unarmed black demonstrators. The American public, horrified by the scene of violent injustice, at last gave assent to passage of a civil rights bill.

I grew up in Atlanta, across town from Martin Luther King Jr., and I confess with some shame that while he was leading marches in places like Selma and Montgomery and Memphis, I was on the side of the white sheriffs with the nightsticks and German shepherds. I was quick to pounce on his moral flaws and slow to recognize my own blind sin. But because he stayed faithful, by offering his body as a target but never as a weapon, he broke through my moral calluses.

The real goal, King used to say, was not to defeat the white man, but "to awaken a sense of shame within the oppressor and challenge his false sense of superiority.... The end is reconciliation; the end is redemption; the end is the creation of the beloved community." And that is what Martin Luther King Jr. finally set into motion, even in racists like me.

King, like Gandhi before him, died a martyr. After his death, more and more people began adopting the principle of nonviolent protest as a way to demand justice. In the Philippines, Poland, Hungary, Czechoslovakia, East Germany, Bulgaria, Yugoslavia, Mongolia, Albania, the Soviet Union, and Chile, more than half a billion people threw off the yoke of oppression through nonviolent means. In many of these places, the Christian church led the way. Protesters marched through the streets carrying candles, singing hymns, and praying. As in Joshua's day, the walls came tumbling down.

The Jesus I Never Knew (122 – 23)

Those Who Mourn

Because I have written books with titles like *Where Is God When It Hurts?* and *Disappointment with God*, I have spent time among mourners. They intimidated me at first. I had few answers for the questions they were asking, and I felt awkward in the presence of their grief. I remember especially one year when, at the invitation of a neighbor, I joined a therapy group at a nearby hospital. This group, called Make Today Count, consisted of people who were dying, and I accompanied my neighbor to their meetings for a year.

Certainly I cannot say that I "enjoyed" the gatherings; that would be the wrong word. Yet the meetings became for me some of the most meaningful events of each month. In contrast to a party, where participants try to impress each other with signs of status and power, in this group no one was trying to impress. Clothes, fashions, apartment furnishings, job titles, new cars — what do these things mean to people who are preparing to die? More than any other people I had met, the Make Today Count group members concentrated on ultimate issues. I found myself wishing that some of my shallow, hedonistic friends would attend a meeting.

Later, when I wrote about what I had learned from grieving and suffering people, I began hearing from strangers. I have three folders, each one several inches thick, filled with these letters. They are among my most precious possessions. One letter, twenty-six pages long, was written on blue-lined note paper by a mother sitting in a lounge outside a room where surgeons were operating on her four-year-old daughter's brain tumor. Another came from a quadriplegic who "wrote" by making puffs of air into a tube, which a computer translated into letters on a printer.

Many of the people who have written me have no happy endings to their stories. Some still feel abandoned by God. Few have found answers to the "Why?" questions. But I have seen enough grief that I have gained faith in Jesus' promise that those who mourn will be comforted.

The Jesus I Never Knew (123 – 24)

◆

Suffering for the Wrong Reasons

I have come to believe that the chief contribution Christians can make is to keep people from suffering for the wrong reasons. We can "honor" pain. In the most important sense, all pain is pain; it does not matter whether the pain comes from migraine headaches or strep throat or acute depression. The first step in helping a suffering person (or in accepting our own pain) is to acknowledge that pain is valid, and worthy of a sympathetic response. In this way, we can begin to ascribe meaning to pain.

At a different level, Christians apply a further set of values to suffering. Visitors to a hospital bedside can heap coals of fire on the suffering. We can add guilt: "Haven't you prayed? Have you no faith that God will heal you?" Or confusion: "Is Satan causing this pain? Just natural providence? Or has God specially selected you as an example to others?" Pain is a foolproof producer of guilt, I have learned. We all do things we shouldn't, and when pain strikes, it's easy to blame ourselves for what has happened.

In a context of intense suffering, even well-intended comments may produce a harmful effect. "God must have loved your daughter very much to take her home so soon," we may be tempted to say, leaving the bereaved parents to wish that God had loved their daughter less. "God won't give you a burden heavier than you can bear"; the suffering person may wish for weaker faith that might merit a lighter burden.

I have interviewed enough suffering people to know that the pain caused by this kind of bedside response can exceed the pain of the illness itself. One woman well known in Christian circles poignantly described the agony caused by TMJ (temporomandibular joint dysfunction). The pain dominates her entire life. Yet, she says, it hurts far worse when Christians write her with judgmental comments based on their pet formulas of why God allows suffering. Perhaps the chief contribution a Christian can make is to keep people from suffering for the wrong reasons.

Where Is God When It Hurts? (198–99)

Mining Diamonds

Frankly, to me much suffering would remain meaningless if we spent all our efforts on the unanswerable "Why?" questions. Why did Solzhenitsyn have to spend eight years in a hard labor camp just for making a casual criticism of Stalin in a letter to a friend? Why did millions of Jews have to die to fulfill the whims of a crazed dictator? Such suffering is meaningless in itself, and will remain so unless the sufferer, like a miner searching for diamonds in a vein of coal, finds in it a meaning.

Viktor Frankl, who spent time in one of Hitler's camps, said, "Despair is suffering without meaning." Frankl and Bruno Bettelheim extracted meaning from the senseless suffering of the Holocaust: observing the behavior of human beings in the extreme conditions of the camps gave them insights that formed the basis for all their later work. For Elie Wiesel and others, "bearing witness" became the meaning. They now devote themselves to honoring those who did not survive.

In prison Dostoevsky pored over the New Testament and the lives of the saints. Prison became, for him and later for his countryman Solzhenitsyn, a crucible of religious faith. Both describe a process in which, first, the blunt reality of human evil convinced them of the need for redemption. Then, through the living witness of believers in the camps, they saw the possibility of transformation. As Solzhenitsyn elegantly expressed it in his classic *One Day in the Life of Ivan Denisovich*, faith in God may not get you out of the camp, but it is enough to see you through each day.

Although my own suffering seems trivial in comparison with these pioneers, I too strive to extract meaning from it. I begin with the biblical promise that suffering can produce something worthwhile in me. I go through a list like that in Romans 5, where Paul mentions perseverance, character, hope, and confidence. "How does suffering accomplish these?" I ask myself. It produces perseverance, or steadiness, by slowing me down and forcing me to turn to God; it produces character by calling on my reserves of inner strength. I continue through the list, asking how God can be involved in bringing meaning to the suffering process.

Where Is God When It Hurts? (199 – 200)

Shared Suffering

Sometimes the only meaning we can offer a suffering person is the assurance that their suffering, which has no apparent meaning for them, has a meaning for us.

My wife worked with some of the poorest people in the city of Chicago, directing a program of LaSalle Street Church that intentionally seeks out lonely and abandoned senior citizens no one else cares for. Many times I have seen her pour herself into a senior citizen's life, trying to convince the senior that it *matters* whether he or she lives or dies. In such a way she "graces" their suffering.

One man Janet worked with, ninety-year-old Mr. Kruider, refused cataract surgery for twenty years. At age seventy he had decided that nothing much was worth looking at and, anyhow, God must have wanted him blind if he made him that way. Maybe it was God's punishment for looking at girls as a youngster, he said.

It took my wife two years of cajoling, arguing, persisting, and loving to convince Mr. Kruider to have cataract surgery. Finally, Mr. Kruider agreed, for one reason only: Janet impressed on him that it mattered to her, Janet, that he regain his sight. Mr. Kruider had given up on life; it held no meaning for him. But Janet transferred a meaning. It made a difference to someone that even at age ninety-two Mr. Kruider not give up. At long last the old man agreed to the surgery.

In a literal sense, Janet shared Mr. Kruider's suffering. By visiting so often she convinced him that someone cared, and that it mattered whether he lived or died or had sight or not. That principle of shared suffering is the thesis of Henri Nouwen's book on the *wounded* healer, and perhaps the only sure contribution we can make to the meaning of suffering. In doing so, we follow God's pattern, who also took on pain. God joined us and lived a life of more suffering and poverty than most of us will ever know. Suffering can never ultimately be meaningless, because God has shared it.

Where Is God When It Hurts? (203 – 4)

◆

Lessons from the Camps

In the spring of 1978, while the TV series *The Holocaust* was being shown, my church introduced a service of identification for the Jews who had suffered, a Yom HaShoah liturgy for Christians. Various members of the congregation, including children, read us voices from the survivors: Chaim Kaplan's diary in the Warsaw ghetto, a child's poem about the lack of butterflies in the ghetto, Viktor Frankl's observations as a prison doctor, Elie Wiesel's poignant tales, Nelly Sach's poem about the crematorium chimneys, and a selection called "Why Do the Christians Hate Us?" from Andre Schwarz-Bart's novel *The Last of the Just*.

The congregation sat quietly during each of the readings. A few people had to leave when the descriptions became too graphic. A friend thoughtfully absorbed all that was said, and after the service gave me this reaction: "Something pains me more than all the agony and guilt I feel hearing those voices of the Jews. All I can do for them is empathize and feel sorry. What really bothers me is how many situations like that we are ignoring now. It's easy to blame the Christians in World War II for not acting quicker, more decisively. But are we reacting today—what about recent situations such as in Cambodia and Uganda? Should we be having services about those places instead?"

The facts of the Jewish concentration camps were published in great detail in advertisements in the *New York Times* as early as 1939. Yet few believed them, no one responded, and the United States did not enter the war until two years later, after a direct attack by the Japanese.

Outside of Auschwitz, there is a field covered with several inches of fine bone loam, the remains of Jews burned there. Yet millions of Cambodians and Rwandans were killed in recent times, and many are still dying in places like Darfur and Congo. How have we responded?

One lesson seems more important than all others: justice must come from the outside. All victims of a camp are apocalyptic—they can only wait for relief from an outside force. No amount of morality or courage, no sense of beauty or infection of hope, will assure their survival apart from the outside force. For the overwhelming majority, survival depends on the destruction of the concentration camp world.

Open Windows (28–30)

Faith Under Fire

Paradoxically, difficult times may help nourish faith and strengthen bonds. I see this in human relationships, which tend to solidify in times of crisis. My wife and I both have grandmothers who have lived past a hundred. Talking with them and their friends, I detect a trend that seems almost universal in the reminiscences of older people: they recall difficult, tumultuous times with a touch of nostalgia. The elderly swap stories about World War II and the Great Depression; they speak fondly of hardships such as blizzards, the childhood outhouse, and the time in college when they ate canned soup and stale bread three weeks in a row.

Ask a strong, stable family where they got such strength, and you may very well hear a story of crisis. Seeing this principle lived out among people, I can better understand one of the mysteries of relating to God. Faith boils down to a question of trust in a given relationship. Do I have confidence in my loved ones—or in God? If I do stand on a bedrock of trust, the worst of circumstances will not destroy the relationship.

One Christian thinker, Søren Kierkegaard, spent a lifetime exploring the tests of faith that call into question God's trustworthiness. A strange man with a difficult personality, Kierkegaard lived with constant inner torment. Again and again he turned to biblical characters like Job and Abraham, who survived excruciating trials of faith. During their times of testing, it appeared to both Job and Abraham that God was contradicting himself. *God surely would not act in such a way—yet clearly God is.* Kierkegaard ultimately concluded that the purest faith emerges from just such an ordeal. Even though I do not understand, I will trust God regardless.

For the believer, faith revolves around a crisis in personal relationship more than intellectual doubts. Does God deserve our trust, no matter how things appear at the time?

Reaching for the Invisible God (53 – 55)

◆

Two-Handed Faith

I am learning that mature faith, which encompasses both simple faith and fidelity, works the opposite of paranoia. It reassembles all the events of life around trust in a loving God. When good things happen, I accept them as gifts from God. When bad things happen, I do not take them as necessarily sent by God—I see evidence in the Bible to the contrary—and I find in them no reason to divorce God. Rather, I trust that God can use even those bad things for my benefit. That, at least, is the goal toward which I strive.

A faithful person sees life from the perspective of trust, not fear. Bedrock faith allows me to believe that, despite the chaos of the present moment, God does reign; that regardless of how worthless I may feel, I truly matter to a God of love; that no pain lasts forever and no evil triumphs in the end. Faith sees even the darkest deed of all history, the death of God's Son, as a necessary prelude to the brightest.

Many things happen in this world that are clearly against God's will. Read the prophets, God's designated spokesmen, who thunder against idolatry, injustice, violence, and sin and rebellion. Read the Gospel accounts, where Jesus upsets the religious establishment by freeing people from disabilities the divines had deemed "God's will." I find no justification for blaming God for what God so clearly opposes.

The skeptic's question does not melt away, though. How can I praise God for the good things in life without censuring God for the bad? I can do so only by establishing an attitude of trust—paranoia in reverse—based on what I have learned in relationship with God.

God's style often baffles me: God moves at a slow pace, prefers rebels and prodigals, restrains power, and speaks in whispers and silence. Yet even in these qualities I see evidence of God's longsuffering, mercy, and desire to woo rather than compel. When in doubt, I focus on Jesus, the most unfiltered revelation of God's own self. I have learned to trust God, and when some tragedy or evil occurs that I cannot synthesize with the God I have come to know and love, then I look to other explanations.

Reaching for the Invisible God (65 – 67)

Sweet Poison

A society that denies the supernatural usually ends up elevating the natural to supernatural status. Annie Dillard tells of experiments in which entomologists entice male butterflies with a painted cardboard replica larger and more enticing than the females of their species. Excited, the male butterfly mounts the piece of cardboard; again and again he mounts it. "Nearby, the real, living female butterfly opens and closes her wings in vain."

C. S. Lewis uses the phrase "sweet poison of the false infinite" to describe this same tendency in the human species. We allow substitute sacreds, or false infinites, to fill the vacuum of our disenchanted world.

Sex seems the most blatant of the false infinites today. I remember with a start the first glimpse I got of a *Playboy* centerfold, just a few years into its publication. The sight pulled back a veil of mystery and beckoned me, an adolescent, to a new, unexplored world charged with seduction and promise. Now *Playboy* is something of a relic, long since overtaken (outstripped?) in its audacity.

I do not mean to pick on sex nor flinch like a middle-aged moralist. I am merely suggesting that the modern West has raised it almost to divine status. Tellingly, *Sports Illustrated* refers to its bathing beauties as "goddesses" and Victoria's Secret dresses its supermodels in angel outfits. Previous generations honored virginity and celibacy. Now we present sex as the highest good, the magical lure that advertisers use to sell us convertibles, Coke, and toothpaste.

A priest I know mentioned that he has come to suspect the transcendent power of sex as portrayed in ads and rock music videos. According to the surveys, one out of three or four of the people he sees on the commuter train each day has had sex the previous night. But he can't see any difference as he studies their faces. They look no happier, no more fulfilled, no more transformed. "Shouldn't something as powerful as sex is promised to be — I speak as a celibate priest — have a more lasting effect?" he asks.

Rumors of Another World (31 – 33)

Why Be Pure?

During a period of my life when I was battling sexual temptation, I came across an article that referred me to a thin book, *What I Believe*, by the French Catholic writer François Mauriac, who had won the Nobel Prize in Literature for his earlier novels. It surprised me that Mauriac, an old man, devoted considerable space to a discussion of his own lust. He explained, "Old age risks being a period of redoubled testing because the imagination in an old man is substituted in a horrible way for what nature refuses him."

Mauriac dismissed most of the arguments in favor of sexual purity he had heard in his Catholic upbringing.

"Marriage will cure lust": it did not for Mauriac, as it has not for so many others, because sex involves the attraction of unknown creatures and the taste for adventure and chance meetings.

"With self-discipline you can master lust": Mauriac found that sexual desire is like a tidal wave powerful enough to bear away all the best intentions.

"True fulfillment can only be found in monogamy": this may be true, but it certainly does not *seem* true to someone who finds no slackening of sexual urges even in monogamy.

Thus he weighed the traditional arguments for purity and found them wanting. Mauriac concluded that in the end, he could find only one reason to be pure, and that is what Jesus presented in the Beatitudes: "Blessed are the pure in heart, for they will see God." In Mauriac's words, "Impurity separates us from God. The spiritual life obeys laws as verifiable as those of the physical world.... Purity is the condition for a higher love—for a possession superior to all possessions: that of God. Yes, this is what is at stake, and nothing less."

Reading François Mauriac's words did not end my struggle with lust. But I must say beyond all doubt that I have found his analysis to be true. The love God holds out to us requires that our faculties be cleansed and purified before we can receive a higher love, one attainable in no other way. That is the motive to stay pure. By harboring lust, I limit my own intimacy with God.

The Jesus I Never Knew (118 – 19)

Advance Echoes

I learned a healthy approach to lifestyle from C. S. Lewis, who had awakened to the reality of another world through such pleasures as Nordic myths, nature, and Wagnerian music. He sensed in our longings not just rumors but "advance echoes" of that world. Flashes of beauty and pangs of aching sweetness, he said, "are not the thing itself; they are only the scent of a flower we have not found, the echo of a tune we have not heard, news from a country we have never yet visited."

I realized I needed to smell some flowers and listen to some melodies in order to recognize what clues I might be missing on earth. My attention turned from dividing life into natural and supernatural, or spiritual and unspiritual, and instead I sought a way to combine the two, to bring about the unity that, as I increasingly believed, God intended.

What pleasures do I enjoy? I asked myself. I find a strange thrill in wildness. Dashing down to the safety of timberline over slippery mountain rock as the thunder clouds roll in and lightning bolts strike closer. Coming face to face with a grizzly bear on a trail and realizing that not a single decision I make matters; the bear controls the options. Visiting exotic cultures where I can identify nothing that I eat, smell, or hear. Oh, I enjoy domesticated pleasures also: gourmet coffee, high-fat ice cream, peaches and blueberries picked at the orchards. And now that I live in the country, I miss the cultural fare of the city: foreign movies, fine music, theater productions that stay with me for days.

I began to listen to my own longings as rumors of another world, a bright clue to the nature of the Creator. Somehow I had fallen for the deception of judging the natural world as unspiritual and God as anti-pleasure. But God invented matter, after all, including all the sensors in the body through which I feel pleasure. Nature and supernature are not two separate worlds, but different expressions of the same reality.

Rumors of Another World (35 – 36)

Pitfalls of Christian Writing

Too often today Christian writers tiptoe around God's creation; it is simply "matter," unworthy of the attention granted supernatural issues. (Similarly, says Jacques Ellul, science avoids questions of supernature to such an extent that it puts on blinders and severely restricts intellectual thought.) It is time for Christian writers to rediscover our natural environment and the characteristics of true humanity.

By avoiding nature we divorce ourselves from the greatest images and carriers of supernature, and our writing loses its chief advantage, the ability to mimic creation. When Tolstoy describes spring, the wonder of tiny flowers poking up through the thawing tundra, he invests in it the same exuberance and significance that he gives to a description of Christian conversion. It too is an expression of God's world. As a result, both passages stir up the feeling of longing in a sensitive reader. People live in the world of nature; we must first affirm that and plumb its meaning before leading them on to supernature.

Recently some fine authors have led the way in attempting to reveal nature as a carrier for supernature. Annie Dillard's *Pilgrim at Tinker Creek* was a landmark in that genre. Lewis Thomas applies the same approach but from a less explicitly religious viewpoint. Response to these two authors demonstrates the hunger in readers for a more holistic approach to the world. Nature and supernature are not two separate worlds but different expressions of the same reality, and effective writing must deal with both.

Creativity is, at heart, a Christian concept. That thought did not exist among the Greeks, who instead used the word *techna*, from which we derive our word "technological." The great Greek poets and playwrights thought in terms of arranging or manufacturing their works; they had no model of divine *creatio ex nihilo* to mimic. It staggers me that we Christians so blithely forfeit our opportunity to explore that magnificently created world. We fly instead to a supernatural world so far removed from our fringe readers that they cannot possibly make the leap.

Open Windows (164 – 66)

Every Good Thing

God lavished good gifts on the world, and how we use those gifts determines whether or not they remain good and satisfying. Living a balanced life is like riding a horse, in that falling poses equal dangers on the left side or the right. Only if you stay in the saddle can you experience the thrill of riding.

The churches I knew while growing up showed no balance in handling God's good gifts. They looked upon pleasure and desire with a frowning face. It took years for me to trust God as the smiling source of every good thing on this planet. "The thief comes only to steal and kill and destroy; I have come that they may have life, and have it to the full," said Jesus (pointedly, he was addressing the religious establishment). From another world, he came to show us how best to live in this one.

Over time, Christians have gotten the reputation of being antipleasure. The more we deny natural desires, the more "spiritual" we are. The apostle Paul had stern words against such purveyors of super-spirituality who, in effect, were slandering God's good gifts. "Hypocritical liars," he called them. "They forbid people to marry and order them to abstain from certain foods, which God created to be received with thanksgiving by those who believe and who know the truth. For everything God created is good, and nothing is to be rejected if it is received with thanksgiving."

Clearly, God did not create us with desires simply so that we would renounce them. As Paul insisted, this world is God's creation. Like a loving parent, the God who created us wants for us the best, most satisfying life possible.

Christianity does not promise the ultimate in personal pleasure, a life oriented around hedonism. Rather, it promises an ordering of life—a putting together, not a reduction—so that we realize pleasures as they were intended by our Creator. Otherwise, we risk indulging to our own destruction, like an alcoholic who determines how much to drink. Abuses arise from regarding pleasure as an end in itself rather than a pointer to something more. "Perfect are the good desires you have given me," prayed Pascal; "Be their End, as you have been their Beginning."

Rumors of Another World (61 – 63)

The Music of God

Born in the shadow of the Wartburg castle where Luther translated the Bible into German, Johann Sebastian Bach became the single composer most identified with the church. He wrote as though, not a wealthy patron, but God himself was scrutinizing every note and phrase, beginning most manuscripts with the abbreviation *JJ* ("Jesus, help") and ending with *SDG* (*Soli Deo Gloria*, "To God alone the glory").

Of Bach's works, *The Passion According to St. Matthew* is generally acclaimed as the greatest choral work ever written in German. It received one performance in Bach's day, caused little stir, and lay unperformed for exactly one hundred years. Then in 1829 Felix Mendelssohn obtained a copy from his teacher, who had allegedly bought the original from a cheese merchant using worthless manuscript pages to wrap cheese. Mendelssohn staged a revival of *The Passion*, unleashing a tidal wave of enthusiasm for Bach that has never ebbed.

I heard that great work in a summer concert by the Chicago Symphony Orchestra and Chorus at Ravinia Park near Chicago. Three thousand people gathered for the four-hour performance. I was struck by the irony of that crowd: upper-class patrons balanced by a strong contingent of the scruffy blue-jean set, with Chicago's North Shore Jewish population liberally sprinkled throughout. All these listened enraptured to a forthright retelling of Jesus' crucifixion adapted from Matthew's gospel.

The scene was as far removed from that dusty, bloody night on Calvary as any I can imagine. Yet somehow the master had woven his spell. Paid performers rendered the agony and horror of that dark day, as well as its profound significance for all mankind, far better than any heavy-breathing Southern evangelist macabrely describing nail prints and thorn marks.

Who knows what impact the performance had? I know of no church revivals sparked by classical music. But in me, a believer, the painstaking care invested by music's greatest mind in expressing the one event that split history in two found reward. If great art represents the "drippings of grace" that can awaken in us a thirst for the true Object, under the right master those drippings can become a flood of God's presence. *SDG*.

Open Windows (154–56)

Paying Attention

I learned a lesson about paying attention from an eccentric orchestra conductor, a year when the Romanian musician Sergiu Celibidache paid a visit to Chicago with his Munich Philharmonic. Few orchestras would work with Celibidache because he demands twelve to eighteen rehearsals before every performance, compared with four for most orchestras. He insists on an Eastern approach to music: striving not so much to recapitulate an "ideal" performance by some other conductor and orchestra, but rather to create an engrossing encounter with music at the moment.

Celibidache made his first trip to the U.S. at age seventy-one, and when I heard him, five years later, he needed assistance mounting the podium. He chose familiar pieces for the concert, but, oh, what a difference. He ignored the tempo markings by the composer, stretching out Mussorgsky's *Pictures at an Exhibition* to twice its normal length. Considering one phrase and the next, he seemed far more interested in drawing out the tonal quality of a given passage than incorporating that passage in the onward march of the piece. He approached the music more like meditation than performance.

Our very bodies react when we pay attention. At Orchestra Hall I leaned forward, moved my head from one side to the other, cupped my hands behind my ears, closed my eyes. Simone Weil says a poet encounters beauty by intensely fixing attention on something real. So does a lover. Can I do something similar in the inner life, with God? I need not always search for new insights, new truths: "The most commonplace truth when it floods the *whole* soul, is like a revelation."

I realized, on reflection, that I tend to approach life as a sequence rather than as a series of moments. I schedule my time, set goals, and march onward toward their achievement. Phone calls, or any unscheduled event, I view as a jarring interruption. How different from the style of Jesus, who often let other people — interruptions — determine his daily schedule. He gave full attention to the person before him, whether it be a Roman officer or a nameless woman with a hemorrhage of blood. And he drew lasting spiritual lessons from the most ordinary things: wildflowers, wheat crops, vineyards, sheep, weddings, families.

Rumors of Another World (54 – 55)

◇

Serenity Source

I have visited Calcutta, India, a place of poverty, death, and irremediable human problems. There, the nuns trained by Mother Teresa serve the poorest, most miserable people on the planet: half-dead bodies picked up from the streets of Calcutta. The world stands in awe at the Sisters' dedication and the results of their ministry, but something about these nuns impresses me even more: their serenity. If I tackled such a daunting project, I would likely be scurrying about, faxing press releases to donors, begging for more resources, gulping tranquilizers, grasping at ways to cope with my mounting desperation. Not these nuns.

Their serenity traces back to what takes place before their day's work begins. At four o'clock in the morning, long before the sun, the Sisters rise, awakened by a bell and the call, "Let us bless the Lord." "Thanks be to God," they reply. Dressed in spotless white saris, they file into the chapel, where they sit on the floor, Indian-style, and pray and sing together. On the wall of the plain chapel hangs a crucifix with the words, "I thirst." Before meeting their first "client," they immerse themselves in worship and in the love of God.

I sense no panic in the Sisters who run the Home for the Dying and Destitute in Calcutta. I see concern and compassion, yes, but no obsession over what did not get done. In fact, early on in their work Mother Teresa instituted a rule that her Sisters take Thursdays off for prayer and rest. "The work will always be here but if we do not rest and pray, we will not have the presence to do our work," she explained.

I pray that some day I will attain something like the holy simplicity these nuns embody. In the morning I ask for the grace to live for God alone, and yet when the phone rings with a message that strokes my ego, or when I open a letter from an irate reader, I find myself slipping back — no, tumbling back — to a self-consciousness in which other people, or circumstances, determine my worth and my serenity. I sense my need for transformation and keep going only because that sense is the one sure basis for potential change.

Reaching for the Invisible God (83 – 84)

◇

Faith at Work

As a form of truth in advertising, I feel obligated to explore how faith works in actual daily practice. My own life of faith has included many surprises. Of course, if the journey did not include a few unexpected detours, we would hardly need faith.

Some monastics describe an integrated life in which spiritual strength flows outward to bathe every activity. Then again, most of them live in spiritual communities with scheduled prayer and worship times and have no cell phones and televisions to interrupt their days. What about the rest of us, who face to-do lists that never get done and live in a culture that conspires to drown out silence and fill all pauses?

When I begin the morning by intentionally centering on God, from that still point I hope that serenity and peace will expand to affect the rest of my day. Yet I have found that even if I get *only* that half-hour of calmness in an otherwise jumbled day, the effort still proves worthwhile. I used to think that everything important in my life — marriage, work, close friends, relationship with God — needed to be in order. One defective area, like one malfunctioning program on my computer, would cause the entire system to crash. I have since learned to pursue God and lean heavily on God's grace even when, especially when, one of the other areas is plummeting toward disaster.

As one who writes and speaks publicly about my faith, I have also learned to accept that I am a "clay vessel" whom God may use at a time when I feel unworthy or hypocritical. I can give a speech or preach a sermon that was authentic and alive to me when I composed it, even though as I deliver it my mind is replaying an argument I just had or nursing an injury I received from a friend. I can write what I believe to be true even while painfully aware of my own inability to attain what I urge others toward.

Exercising faith in the present means trusting God to work through the encounter before me despite the background clutter of the rest of my life. As the recovery movement has taught us, our very helplessness drives us to God.

Reaching for the Invisible God (85 – 86)

◆

God Loveth Adverbs

The Puritans had a saying, "God loveth adverbs," implying that God cares more about the spirit in which we live than the concrete results. They sought to connect all of life to its source in God, bringing the two worlds together rather than dividing them into sacred and secular.

Pleasing God does not mean that we must busy ourselves with a new set of "spiritual" activities. As the Puritans said, whether cleaning house or preaching sermons, shoeing horses or translating the Bible for the Indians, any human activity may constitute an offering to God. In that spirit, Thomas Merton would later remark, "You can tell more about a monk by the way he uses a broom than by anything he says."

I find it relatively easy to "hallow" God in nature and much harder to hallow the ordinary events of my life. How can I see the mundane tasks that comprise my day as forming any sort of meaningful pattern? How can I bring the two worlds together, reading God into the course of my day?

Martin Luther saw a potential calling in any kind of work. "Even dirty and unpleasant work, such as shoveling manure or washing diapers, is pure and holy work if it comes from a pure heart," he said. Luther urged ordinary folk — farmers, milkmaids, butchers, and cobblers — to perform their work as if God was personally watching.

Caring for an elderly parent. Cleaning up after a child. Sitting on a porch with a neighbor. Fielding a customer's complaint. Laying fiber-optic cable. Filling out charts at a nurses station. Sitting in traffic. Sawing lumber. Reporting waitress tips. Shopping for groceries. We spend much of our time, if not most, immersed in the mundane. It takes faith to believe that these things matter.

"We have the mind of Christ," Paul writes to the Corinthian church, which of all his churches shows least evidence of that mind. What does it mean to exercise "the mind of Christ" in the midst of the mundane?

A Benedictine writer, Joan Chittister, summarizes spirituality as "living the ordinary life extraordinarily well ... if we are not spiritual where we are and as we are, we are not spiritual at all."

Rumors of Another World (63 – 67)

Act As If

My teaching is not my own," Jesus said. "It comes from him who sent me. If anyone chooses to do God's will, he will find out whether my teaching comes from God or whether I speak on my own." Note the sequence: Choose to do God's will, and the confidence will later follow. Jesus presents the journey of faith as a personal pilgrimage begun in uncertainty and fragile trust.

Some psychologists practice a school of behavior therapy that encourages the client to "act as if" a certain state is true, no matter how unreasonable it seems. We change behavior, says this school, not by delving into the past or by trying to align motives with actions but rather by "acting as if" the change should happen. It's much easier to act your way into feelings than to feel your way into actions.

If you want to preserve your marriage but are not sure you really love your wife, start acting as if you love her: surprise her, show affection, give gifts, be attentive. You may find that feelings of love materialize as you act out the behavior. If you want to forgive your father but find yourself unable, act as if he is forgiven. Say the words, "I forgive you," or "I love you," even though you are not entirely convinced you mean them. Often the change in behavior in the one party brings about a remarkable change in the other.

Something similar works in my relationship with God. I wish all obedience sprang from an instinctive desire to please God—alas, it does not. For me, the life of faith sometimes consists of *acting as if* the whole thing is true. I assume that God loves me infinitely, that good will conquer evil, that any adversity can be redeemed, though I have no sure confirmation and only rare epiphanies to spur me along the way. I act as if God is a loving Father; I treat my neighbors as if they truly bear God's image; I forgive those who wrong me as if God has forgiven me first.

Reaching for the Invisible God (88 – 89)

◇

Now and When

According to Stanley Hauerwas, the life of faith consists of patience and hope. When something comes along to test our relationship with God, we rely on those two virtues: patience formed by a long memory, and hope that our faithfulness will prove worth the risk. Jews and Christians have always emphasized these virtues, Hauerwas notes, for we believe that a God who is both good and faithful controls the universe; patience and hope keep faith alive during times that cast doubt on that belief.

I would paraphrase Hauerwas by saying the life of faith consists of living in the past and in the future. I live in the past in order to ground myself in what God has already done, as a way of gaining confidence in what God might do again. Relating to an invisible God involves certain handicaps: with no sensory evidence in the present, we must look backward to remind ourselves of who it is we are relating to. The phrase "the God of Abraham, Isaac, and Jacob," reminded the chosen people of God's history with them—a history that for all three forebears included seasons of testing and doubt.

New Testament letters advise the same: study the Scriptures diligently, as necessary road maps for contests of faith. Beyond the Bible, the testimony of the entire church bears witness of God's faithfulness. Where would my own faith be, I wonder, without Augustine, Donne, Chesterton, Dostoevsky, Jürgen Moltmann, Thomas Merton? Many times I have leaned on their words as an exhausted traveler might lean against a roadside monument.

Although I do not keep a formal journal, my writings accomplish something similar. I pick up an article I wrote twenty-five years ago and marvel at the passion I felt over an issue I have hardly thought about since. Mainly, from the past I gain perspective that what I feel and believe right now I will not always feel and believe.

Reaching for the Invisible God (74 – 76)

◆

A Writer's Life

During the years we lived in Chicago, my wife directed a senior citizens' program among the very poor. A typical dinner-table conversation in our house went like this:

"How was your day, Janet?"

"Rough. I met a homeless family who'd been living in Lincoln Park and hadn't eaten in three days. After taking care of them I learned that eighty-nine-year-old Peg Martin had died. And then I discovered some gang members had broken into the church van and spray-painted graffiti all over it."

After filling in the details of those adventures, Janet would ask about my day. A mild sense of panic set in. "Uh, let me think. What did happen today? I stared at a computer screen all day. A UPS package came. Oh yeah — around 2:30 this afternoon I found a very good adverb!"

Our daily routines, not to mention our personalities, could hardly differ more. Janet, vivacious, outgoing, gregarious, worked out of an office on Hill Street, the seamy locale made famous by the TV show "Hill Street Blues." Her days were full of adventure, and full of people: often she served meals to seventy people at a time, and nearly every day she dealt with several dozen clients.

After we moved to Colorado, she began working in a hospice. The average patient admitted there dies within ten days. Janet now came home with stories of families who had differing responses of courage, rage, or despair, but all marked by the passion that grief compels.

Meanwhile, whether in Chicago or Colorado, I sit at home in my basement office staring at a flickering computer screen in search of the perfect word. The main "event" in my day occurs around noon, when the mailman arrives. Occasionally the telephone rings. And once a week or so I may meet someone for lunch. The daily regimen of a writer is not what you'd call glamorous.

Finding God in Unexpected Places (41 – 42)

◆

Who Only Sit and Click

I listen to Janet's stories of working with low-income senior citizens and hospice patients and think to myself, *If I could have her job, I'd never experience writer's block again.* But then sober reality sets in to correct my fantasies. *There are two problems, Philip: First, you'd be terrible at Janet's job, and second, you'd have no time left over to write.* And so the next morning after eating my cereal I head downstairs to spend another day making the sound of insect clicks on my computer keyboard.

Over time, I have come to see that the very differences between us — in personality, outlook, and daily routine — actually represent a great strength. Janet provides me with a new set of eyes into a world I barely know about. I find challenge there, and stimulation. My own faith is tested as I hear of her attempts to bring hope to the lives of those who have so little. Sometimes, like now, her experiences even edge their way into my writing.

I no longer view Janet's work with a sense of competition. Rather, I marvel at the difference in temperament and spiritual gifts that allows her to spend her day dealing with situations that would probably drive me crazy. I have learned to take pride in her work, to see it as a part of my own service to God. By serving her, and offering a listening ear, I can strengthen her and thus help assure that her vital work will continue.

On good days, I remember this principle, pray for Janet, and look for ways to help equip her for her demanding and wonderful work. As for bad days — well, you'll probably find me sitting in front of a computer screen, looking a little cross-eyed, daydreaming of the great novels I could write if I spent my time on Hill Street instead of in my basement.

Finding God in Unexpected Places (43 – 44)

Soft Power

I grew up in a Southern fundamentalist church that taught blatant racism, apocalyptic fear of communism, and America-first patriotism.

For me, reading opened a chink of light that became a window to another world. I remember the impact of a mild book like *To Kill A Mockingbird*, which called into question the apartheid assumptions of my friends and neighbors. Later, reading books like *Black Like Me*, *The Autobiography of Malcolm X*, and Martin Luther King Jr.'s *Letter from Birmingham City Jail*, I felt my whole world shatter. I experienced the power that allowed one human mind to penetrate another with no intermediary but a piece of flattened wood pulp.

I especially came to value the freedom-enhancing aspect of writing. Speakers in the churches I attended could RAISE THEIR VOICES! and play emotions like musical instruments. But alone in my room, voting with every turn of the page, I met other representatives of the kingdom—C. S. Lewis, G. K. Chesterton, Saint Augustine—whose calmer voices leapt across time to convince me that somewhere Christians lived who knew grace as well as law, love as well as judgment, reason as well as passion.

I became a writer, I believe, because of my own experience of the power of words. I saw that spoiled words, their original meaning wrung out, could be reclaimed. I saw that writing could penetrate into the crevices, bringing spiritual oxygen to people trapped in airtight boxes. I saw that when God conveyed to us the essence of self-expression, God called it the Word. The Word comes in the most freedom-enhancing way imaginable.

We may be entering a different kind of Dark Ages, a time when the Devil owns the airwaves and when words seem gray and dull compared to the dazzle of virtual reality and multimedia DVDs. I have hope, though. Despite the waves of hysteria and authoritarianism in church history, words of truth have survived and emerged later as living forces to change individuals and entire cultures. I have experienced their power. I pray that the church, in increasingly oppressive times, will remember that words have their greatest impact when they enhance freedom, when they liberate.

Finding God in Unexpected Places (55 – 56)

◇

Art and Propaganda

Like a bipolar magnet, the Christian writer today feels the pull of two forces: a fervent desire to communicate what gives life meaning counteracted by an artistic inclination toward self-expression, form, and structure that any "message" might interrupt. The result: a constant, dichotomous pull toward both propaganda and art.

Propaganda is a word currently out of favor, implying unfair manipulation or distortion of means to an end. I use it in a more acceptable sense, the original sense of the word as coined by Pope Urban VIII. He formed the College of Propaganda in the seventeenth century in order to disseminate the Christian faith. As a Christian writer, I readily admit that I do strive for propaganda in this sense. Much of what I write is designed to cause others to consider a viewpoint I hold to be true.

Counterbalancing the literary tug away from propaganda, many Christian writers feel an insidious tug away from art. Is this not fiddling while Rome burns? Novels written by evangelicals, especially, tend toward the propagandistic (even to the extent of fictionalizing Bible stories and foretelling the second coming) and away from the artful.

Somewhere in this magnetic field between art and propaganda the Christian writer (or painter or musician) works. One force tempts us to lower artistic standards and preach an unadorned message; another tempts us to submerge or even alter the message for the sake of artistic sensibilities. Having lived in the midst of this tension, I have come to recognize it as a healthy tension that should be affirmed.

Success often lies with the extremes: an author may succeed in the Christian world by erring on the side of propaganda. But ever so slowly, the fissure between the Christian and secular worlds will yawn wider. If we continue tilting toward propaganda, we will soon find ourselves writing and selling books to ourselves alone. On the other hand, the Christian writer cannot simply absorb the literary standards of the larger world. Our ultimate goal cannot be a self-expression, but rather a God-expression.

Open Windows (173 – 74)

◇

Television Church

For the mainline Christian, religious television shows offer an infusion of excitement about personal faith that is often lacking in the local church. Some viewers who strongly disagree with the philosophy of a show are nevertheless inspired by the fresh example of people who can articulate their faith in Christ.

The danger comes when viewers confuse the excitement of Christian television with the message and the work of the church incarnate. Compared to television glitter, the average local church is lackluster. Services are boring by contrast; the message seems complex and confusing. And perhaps most dangerous of all is the latent effect of television to create a dependence on vicarious experiences. The church on television is experienced, after all, not in a room that includes sniffling children, restless teenagers, hard-of-hearing grandparents, and sleepy parishioners. It occurs in a much safer, more sterile environment: your own living room.

When you watch a television church, no one asks you to participate in a visitation program. No one challenges you to hold the attention of a junior high Sunday school class. No one asks you to make meals for shut-ins. The only response solicited is a monthly check of gratitude. What better way is there to reach the world for God? A member of the electronic church may easily conclude the answer is his cash contribution to the newest satellite, never questioning whether his own personal involvement is of greater value. What can one solitary person's service accomplish, he may wonder, when dwarfed by the marvels of electronic evangelism.

The Bible presents a realistic picture of the Christian life, including long, dull marches through the wilderness, humiliating failures, pain, struggle. These don't come off well on television—unless they're told as a quick, summarized prelude to the victorious conclusion. The resulting picture of the Christian life as being one of incessant joy and constant success can actually backfire. The viewer, whose experience is different, can begin to feel distressingly inferior, as if somehow he or she is missing out on the magic of faith. In essence, the electronic church is the mouth of the body, but without the other parts.

Open Windows (200–201)

A Different Mountain

Dear Janet,

Now that we live in Colorado, we climb mountains. Over time we have learned that climbing mainly consists of picking up one foot and putting it in front of the next. No matter how hard you breathe and how much your legs ache, eventually you reach the top.

For some, marriage may seem like a chairlift ride; you and I, however, have climbed a mountain. Indeed, we've learned that marriage lives on love, but it is the kind of love that parenthood demands, or Christian discipleship: a gritty decision to go forward, step-by-step, one foot in front of the other. Perhaps that is why I feel so good about this day commemorating three hundred months of marriage.

At times we have both considered the prospect of life apart. We have gone to marriage counseling. We have paid our dues. But today, what strikes me above all—I speak with humility and gratitude to God—is that from the struggle, great good has come.

Wherever we have gone together—away from the provincial South, a scary move into downtown Chicago, travels to other continents—you have adjusted, and grown larger. Yet here is what I love about you: as you grow larger you make no one else grow smaller.

For twelve years in Chicago you headed a program that served senior citizens. The woman who slipped and lay in the tub three days before help came. The aging prostitutes who faced death with no one but you to mourn them. The family of five who lived in an old car. They became your children, and you fussed over them with inexhaustible care.

Now you work in a hospice. Unresolved tensions, sibling wars, unforgiven hurts bubble to the surface as the patient lies comatose, waiting to die. You counsel these people, listen, and pray with them.

I marvel at your skills, yet I marvel far more that you choose to devote them to the forgotten and the suffering. Because I write in a public setting, I get more accolades. But I believe that at the end of my life nothing will surpass in holy significance the role I have played in providing an environment that helps you do what you do. Together we have climbed a mountain, you and I.

[Continued on July 1]

"Back Page" column, *Christianity Today,*
April 8, 1996 (104)

July

◆

View from the Top

[Continued from June 30]

Last year I was in Portland, Oregon. I debated how to spend my free time. I could drive along the Columbia River Gorge and gawk at the waterfalls. I could ride the light-rail train downtown and eat oyster stew. I could stroll along a pedestrian mall to a cappuccino stand.

Instead I sat in my room, ordered room service, and worked on a manuscript. This is what twenty-five years together has done: it has made it difficult for me to experience pleasure on my own. I would rather toil like a workaholic when we are apart, saving those sensory moments to share with the one who awakened my senses.

It was you, after all, who taught me to truly notice the roses and rhododendrons in Portland. Not once in twenty-five years have we stopped by a stream or a waterfall without you rushing over to the water, removing your shoes, and testing its temperature with your toes. You make us stop at roadside stands for fresh peaches or raspberries. To experience such delights apart from the one who awakened me to them seems a kind of betrayal.

Before marriage, each by instinct strives to be what the other wants. The young woman desires to look sexy, and takes up interest in sports. The young man notices plants and flowers, and works at asking questions instead of just answering monosyllabically. After marriage, the process slows and somewhat reverses. Each insists on his or her rights. Each resists bending to the other's will.

After years, though, that process may subtly begin to reverse again. I sense a new willingness to bend back toward what the other wants—maturely, this time, not out of a desire to catch a mate but out of a desire to please a mate who has shared a quarter-century of life. I grieve for those couples who give up before reaching this stage.

It has crept up on us, as it always does, yet this middle age is not so bad. We have less to prove to the world and to each other. We have surveyed what we want in life, and part of the conclusion we have reached is this: we want each other. The view from the mountaintop looks good, very good.

"Back Page" column, *Christianity Today*,
April 8, 1996 (104)

A Long, Warm Glow

I met with Vernon Grounds the morning after his sixty-fifth wedding anniversary and the day he would join dignitaries in breaking ground for Denver Seminary's new campus. For twenty-three years Grounds served as the seminary's president before retiring into the chancellor role. He was a pioneer in Christian counseling as well as social activism.

Through the windows we watched a cluster of students walk from classroom to library, bundled against the wind on a cold, drizzly day. "So many of these students seem concerned about sensing the presence of God. They expect to live in perpetual sunshine. When a student tells me about an unsatisfying spiritual life, I point them to others, such as Henri Nouwen, who struggled with the same problem. Or Lewis Smedes, who never really felt he was God's friend.

"We shouldn't expect a relationship with God to be on a constant plane all the time. Believe me, over sixty-five years of marriage you don't stay on a plane of ecstasy all the time. Romance started for me as a blazing bonfire—you know, 'You light up my life.' After a few decades it settled into something more like a heap of glowing coals. Sure, some of the heat dissipated, but coals are good, too: you can roast marshmallows, warm your feet. A different level of companionship opens up."

A few times, Grounds says, he has felt twinges of spiritual ecstasy. But these were rare. Mostly he persisted because he valued the relationship with God, just as he valued the marriage relationship: "I warm my feet by the fire." When he passed sixty he began reflecting more often on old age, praying in words borrowed from Robert Frost "how to make the most of a diminished thing." Little did he know a third of his life lay ahead.

In nine decades Grounds has seen his share of trials. "I have unquestioning confidence in God's ability to accomplish whatever God wants—the resurrection proves that—but I also believe that other spiritual forces are trying to frustrate the forces of good. I accept mystery and paradox. When you've been around as long as I have, you have to. Like the Chinese philosopher riding backwards on a donkey, we only understand life looking back."

"Back Page" column, *Christianity Today,*
May 2006 (88)

◇

Believing in Advance

Going through a stack of old *Time* magazines recently, I was astonished at how different the world looks now compared to thirty years ago. Back then *Time* was running cover stories on "The Coming Ice Age"; now we hear about global warming. World maps showed a large red stain of communism spreading across Indochina and Africa. Economists predicted the end of American dominance and a new global parity among the U.S., Russia, China, Japan, and Europe.

In a more recent magazine, from August 2001, I searched in vain for the words al-Qaeda and Osama bin Laden. Somehow prognosticators missed all the defining events in my own lifetime, including the war on terrorism and the end of the cold war.

As I reflected on our poor record at predicting the future, it struck me that the Bible often centers on the act of waiting. Abraham waiting for just one child. The Israelites waiting four centuries for deliverance from Egypt. David waiting in caves for his promised coronation. Prophets waiting for the fulfillment of their own strange predictions. The disciples waiting impatiently for Jesus to act like the power-messiah they longed for.

Jesus' final words at the end of Revelation are "I am coming soon," followed by an urgent, echoing prayer, "Amen. Come, Lord Jesus." That prayer remains unanswered.

In a German prison camp in World War II, unbeknownst to the guards, the Americans built a homemade radio. One day news came that the German high command had surrendered, ending the war, a fact that, because of a communications breakdown, the German guards did not yet know. As word spread a loud celebration broke out.

For three days the prisoners were hardly recognizable. They sang, waved at guards, laughed at the German shepherd dogs, and shared jokes over meals. On the fourth day, they awoke to find that all Germans had fled, leaving the gates unlocked. The time of waiting had come to an end.

Here is the question I ask myself: As we Christians face contemporary crises, why do we respond with such fear and anxiety? Why don't we, like the Allied prisoners, act on the good news we say we believe? What is faith, after all, but believing in advance what will only make sense in reverse?

"Back Page" column, *Christianity Today,*
March 2005 (120)

What Politics Can't Do

Three months before the 2008 Democratic National Convention in Denver, I spoke at a state prayer luncheon. Inside the same hall where now we were focusing on prayer, politicians would soon take turns promising to turn the nation in a new direction and right its wrongs.

Thinking about what to say to the leaders gathered before me, I recalled a line from the contemporary German philosopher Jürgen Habermas: Democracy requires of its citizens qualities that it cannot provide. Politicians can conjure an exalted vision of a prosperous, healthy, and free society, but no government can supply the qualities of honesty, compassion, and personal responsibility that must underlie it.

Fortunately, politicians of both parties in the U.S. still recognize that faith plays a vital role in a healthy society. People of faith are charged to uphold a different kind of vision. That this is God's planet, not ours, and as we scar it beyond repair, God weeps. That a person's worth is determined not by appearance or income, or ethnic background, or even citizenship status, but rather is bestowed as a sacred, inviolable gift of God. That compassion and justice—our care for "the least of these my brothers," in Jesus' words—are not arbitrary values agreed on by politicians and sociologists but holy commands from the One who created us as a species.

I freely admit that we Christians don't always live out that vision. We find it difficult to maintain a commitment both to this world and the next, to this life and the next. We do well to remember that the Bible has far more to say about how to live during the journey than about the ultimate destination.

The world needs people devoted to God's creatures and God's children as well as to God, and as committed to this life as to the afterlife, to this city as to the heavenly city. For, as Jürgen Habermas says, a democracy of free people must look elsewhere for the qualities its citizens need.

"Back Page" column, *Christianity Today,*
September 2008 (102)

Grace-Healed Eyes

In his own social interactions Jesus was putting into practice "the great reversal" heralded in the Beatitudes. Normally in this world we look up to the rich, the beautiful, the successful. Grace, however, introduces a world of new logic. Because God loves the poor, the suffering, the persecuted, so should we. Because God sees no undesirables, neither should we. By his own example, Jesus challenged us to look at the world through what Irenaeus would call "grace-healed eyes."

Jesus' parables underscored that mission, for often he made the poor and oppressed the heroes of his stories. One such story featured a poor man, Lazarus—the only named person in Jesus' parables—who was being exploited by a rich man. At first the rich man enjoyed sumptuous clothes and food while the beggar Lazarus, covered with scars, lay outside his gate with the dogs. Death, though, stunningly reversed their fortunes. The rich man heard from Abraham, "Son, remember that in your lifetime you received your good things, while Lazarus received bad things, but now he is comforted here and you are in agony."

That trenchant story sank deep into the consciousness of early Christians, many of whom belonged to lower economic classes. For a while, the church worked hard to follow this new logic. Within the Roman Empire, early Christians were renowned for their support of the poor and suffering. The Christians, unlike their pagan neighbors, readily ransomed their friends from barbarian captors, and when plague hit, the Christians tended their sufferers whereas the pagans abandoned the sick at the first symptoms. For the first few centuries, at least, the church took literally Christ's commands to receive strangers, clothe the naked, feed the hungry, and visit those in prison.

According to church historians, this good work continued until the triumph of Constantine, who legalized the faith and established an official imperial church. From that point on the church tended to spiritualize poverty and leave "welfare" to the emperor. Over time the church itself became part of the wealthy establishment.

The Jesus I Never Knew (155 – 56)

◆

The Gospel through Third World Eyes

As I read the stories of Jesus and study the history of the early church, I feel both inspired and troubled. In view of Jesus' clear example, how is it that the church has now become a community of respectability, where the down-and-out no longer feel welcome?

I presently live in Colorado, where I attend a church in which most people come from the same race (white) and the same social class (middle). It startles me to open the New Testament and see in what mixed soil the early church took root. The middle-class church many of us know today bears little resemblance to the diverse group of social rejects described in the Gospels and the book of Acts.

Projecting myself back into Jesus' time, I try to picture the scene. The poor, the sick, the tax collectors, sinners, and prostitutes crowd around Jesus, stirred by his message of healing and forgiveness. The rich and powerful stand on the sidelines, testing him, spying, trying to entrap him. I know these facts about Jesus' time, and yet, from the comfort of a middle-class church in a wealthy country like the U.S., I easily lose sight of the radical core of Jesus' message.

To help correct my vision, I have read sermons that come out of the Christian base communities in the Third World. The gospel through Third World eyes looks very different from the gospel as preached in many U.S. churches. The poor and the unlearned cannot always identify Jesus' mission statement ("he has anointed me to preach good news to the poor ... to proclaim freedom for the prisoners and recovery of sight for the blind, to release the oppressed") as a quotation from Isaiah, but they hear it as good news indeed. They understand the great reversal not as an abstraction but as God's promise of defiant hope and Jesus' challenge to his followers. Regardless of how the world treats them, the poor and the sick have assurance, because of Jesus, that God knows no undesirables.

The Jesus I Never Knew (156–57)

✦

Sermon of Offense

A friend of mine named Virginia Stem Owens assigned the Sermon on the Mount to her composition class at Texas A&M University, asking the students to write a short essay. She had expected them to have a basic respect for the text, since the Bible Belt extends right across Texas, but her students' reactions soon disabused her of that notion. "In my opinion religion is one big hoax," wrote one. "There is an old saying that 'you shouldn't believe everything you read' and it applies in this case," wrote another.

Virginia recalled her own introduction to the Sermon on the Mount in Sunday school, where pastel poster illustrations showed Jesus sitting on a green hillside surrounded by eager, pink children. It never occurred to her to react with anger or disgust. Her students thought otherwise:

> The stuff the churches preach is extremely strict and allows for almost no fun without thinking it is a sin or not.

> I did not like the essay "Sermon on the Mount." It was hard to read and made me feel like I had to be perfect and no one is.

> The things asked in this sermon are absurd. To look at a woman is adultery. That is the most extreme, stupid, unhuman statement that I have ever heard.

"At this point," Virginia wrote about the experience, "I began to be encouraged. There is something exquisitely innocent about not realizing you shouldn't call Jesus stupid.... This was the real thing, a pristine response to the gospel, unfiltered through a two-millennia cultural haze.... I find it strangely heartening that the Bible remains offensive to honest, ignorant ears, just as it was in the first century. For me, that somehow validates its significance. Whereas the Scriptures almost lost their characteristically astringent flavor during the past century, the current widespread biblical illiteracy should catapult us into a situation more nearly approximating that of their original, first-century audience."

The Jesus I Never Knew (130)

◆

Designer Sex

Why does sex play so much larger in modern cities than, say, in the villages of the Amazon? Clothing fashions, billboards, and ads on the sides of city buses give human sexuality a prominence it never attains in the naked jungle. The French sociologist Jacques Ellul sees our modern fixation with sex as the symptom of a breakdown in intimacy. Having detached the physical act of sex from relationship, we can only work at perfecting the "technique"—hence the proliferation of sex studies, sex manuals, and sex videos, none of which address the real source of our pain.

I would suggest that the rumor of another world also enters in. Many sophisticated moderns have little transcendence in their lives. They avoid church and believe science has figured out most of the mysteries of the universe. Sex, though, poses a mystery to which normal principles of reductionism do not apply. Feed it, and the appetite increases. No amount of knowledge diminishes its magic: even a nudist gets turned on when his wife greets him in Victoria's Secret underwear.

When a society loses faith in its gods, or God, lesser powers arise to take their place. Blocked longings seek new routes. "Every man who knocks on the door of a brothel is looking for God," said G. K. Chesterton. In modern Europe and the U.S., sex has a near-sacred quality of mythic, numinous power. We select our sexiest individuals and accord them the status of gods and goddesses, fawning over the details of their lives, broadcasting their bodily statistics, surrounding them with paparazzi, rewarding them with money and status. Sex no longer points to something beyond; it becomes the thing itself, the substitute sacred.

Perhaps worse, though, the church in its prudery has silenced a powerful rumor of transcendence that could point to the Creator and originator of human sexuality, who invested in it far more meaning than most modern people can imagine. We have desacralized it, in effect, by suppression and denial, and along the way our clumsy attempts at repression helped empower a false infinite. Sexual power lives on, but few see in that power a pointer to the One who designed it.

Rumors of Another World (78–79, 81)

◆

The Good Life

For a time I resisted thinking of God as an authority figure; harsh images from childhood had scarred too deep. Like many people, I saw religion mainly as a set of rules, a moral code handed down from an invisible world that we on this planet were somehow obligated to obey. Why it might matter to God whether puny creatures on a tiny planet kept the rules, I had no clue. I only heard the dire warnings that if I broke the rules, I would pay.

More recently, however, I have come to recognize that sometimes I submit gladly to authority. When my computer software acts up, I call technical support and scrupulously follow the technician's orders. When I want to master a difficult sport, such as golf, I pay for lessons. And when I get hurt or sick, I see a doctor.

A doctor is probably the most helpful image for me to keep in mind while thinking about God and sin. Why should I seek out God's view on how to live my life? For the same reason I seek my doctor's opinion. I defer to my doctor, trusting that we share the same goal, my physical health, but that he brings to the process greater wisdom and expertise. And I am learning to view sins as spiritual dangers — much like carcinogens, bacteria, viruses, and injuries — that must be avoided. I am learning to trust that God wants the *best* life for me in this world, not some diminished, repressed life.

At the traveling Body Worlds exhibit of preserved human bodies, I bought a catalog of the organs I had seen on display. I cannot comprehend how any doctor who has seen healthy lungs and the lungs of a chain smoker, side by side, could ever smoke again. If I feel a temptation toward tobacco, I turn to page 66 of the catalog. So many of the displays in Body Worlds show how human behavior brings disorder to the body, subjecting its organs to stresses they were not designed to bear. I remind myself of the two sets of lungs when I think about sin: it too retards growth, ravages health, and chokes off the supply of new life.

Rumors of Another World (128 – 29)

Twisted Interests

In my childhood, thinking about sin terrified me. In adolescence it repulsed me. But as I learn to envision God more accurately, as a physician or a loving parent, my defenses crumble. I once had a caricature of God as a cranky old codger who concocted an arbitrary list of rules for the express purpose of making sure no one had a good time. I now see the true object of those rules.

Every parent knows the difference between rules designed primarily for the benefit of the parent ("Don't talk while I'm on the telephone!" "Clean up your room—your grandmother's coming!") and those designed for the benefit of the child ("Wear mittens and a hat—it's below freezing outside. But don't skate on the pond yet!"). God's rules primarily fall into the latter category. As Creator of the human race, God knew how human society would work best.

I began to look at the Ten Commandments in this light, as rules designed primarily for the benefit of the people themselves. Jesus underscored this principle when he said, "The Sabbath was made for man, not man for the Sabbath." The Bible is a most realistic book, and it assumes human beings will at times be tempted to lust after a neighbor or covet someone else's property, to work too hard, to strike out in anger at those who wrong them. In short, it assumes humanity will bring disorder to whatever we touch.

Each of the Ten Commandments offers a shield of protection against that disorder, stated negatively. Unlike the animals, we have the freedom to say no to our base instincts. By doing so, we avoid certain harm.

Taken together, the Ten Commandments weave life on this planet into some kind of meaningful whole, the purpose of which is to allow us to live as a peaceful, healthy community under God. Three hundred years ago the biblical commentator Matthew Henry observed, "God has been pleased therein to twist interests with us, so that in seeking his glory we really and effectually seek our own true interests."

Rumors of Another World (133–34)

◇

Doctor's Orders

I once had an encounter with masked men bearing scalpels. A surgeon operated on my foot, and the horizontal recovery time gave me a chance to reflect on pain that we choose voluntarily, sometimes for our own good and sometimes to our peril.

On one visit to my doctor I tried to talk him into a premature golf match. "Some friends get together once a year. It's important to me. I've been practicing my swing, and if I use only my upper body, and keep my legs and hips very still, could I join them?"

Without a flicker of hesitation, my doctor replied, "It would make me very unhappy if you played golf within the next two months."

Later, I told my wife about his strange way of expressing disapproval. "Why should I care if my doctor is unhappy?" I joked. "I'm not his psychiatrist."

The point was obvious. My doctor has nothing against my playing golf; a fellow-golfer, he sympathizes with me. But he has my best interests at heart. It will indeed make him unhappy if I do something prematurely that might damage my long-term recovery. He wants me to play golf next year, and the next, and the rest of my life, and for that reason he could not sanction a match too soon after my surgery.

As we talked, I began to appreciate my doctor's odd choice of words. If he had issued an edict, "No golf!" I might have stubbornly rebelled. He left me the free choice and expressed the consequences in a most personal way: disobedience would grieve him, for his job was to restore my health.

The role of a doctor may be the most revealing image in thinking about God and sin. What a doctor does for me physically — guide me toward health — God does for me spiritually. I am learning to view sins not as an arbitrary list of rules drawn up by a cranky Judge, but rather as a list of dangers that must be avoided at all costs — *for our own sakes.*

"Back Page" column, *Christianity Today,*
December 6, 1999 (104)

Jesus and Pain

The fact that Jesus came to earth where he suffered and died does not remove pain from our lives. But it does show that God did not sit idly by and watch us suffer in isolation. God became one of us. Thus, in Jesus, God gives us an up-close and personal look at the divine response to human suffering. All our questions about God and suffering should, in fact, be filtered through what we know about Jesus.

How did God-on-earth respond to pain? When he met a person in pain, he was deeply moved with compassion (from the Latin words *pati* and *cum*, "to suffer with"). Not once did he say, "Endure your hunger! Swallow your grief!" Very often, every time he was directly asked, he healed the pain.

Sometimes he broke deep-rooted customs to do so, as when he touched a woman with a hemorrhage of blood, or when he touched outcasts, ignoring their cries of "Unclean!"

The pattern of Jesus' response should convince us that God is not a God who enjoys seeing us suffer. I doubt that Jesus' disciples tormented themselves with questions like "Does God care?" They had visible evidence of God's concern every day: they simply looked at Jesus' face.

And when Jesus himself faced suffering, he reacted much as any of us would. He recoiled from it, asking three times if there was any other way. There was no other way, and then Jesus experienced, perhaps for the first time, that most human sense of abandonment. In the Gospel accounts of Jesus' last night on earth, I detect a fierce struggle with fear, helplessness, and hope — the same frontiers all of us confront in our suffering.

The record of Jesus' life on earth should forever answer the question, How does God feel about our pain? In reply, God did not give us words or theories on the problem of pain. God gave us himself. A philosophy may explain difficult things, but has no power to change them. The gospel, the story of Jesus' life, promises change.

Where Is God When It Hurts? (225 – 26)

◆

What No One Could Teach

At times, despite our best efforts to honor others' pain, we encounter suffering that seems utterly devoid of meaning. I am thinking specifically of a man with Alzheimer's disease; the daughter tries to tend to his needs, but every day her heart is broken by the sad shell of what used to be her father. Or I think of a severely disabled child with an IQ in the 30–40 range. The child may live a long life lying motionless in a crib, unable to talk, unable to comprehend, soaking up hours of expensive professional care.

"What is the point of their lives? Do their lives have any meaning?" asked Dr. Jürgen Trogisch, a pediatrician who works among the severely mentally handicapped.

For many years Dr. Trogisch could not answer the question of meaning. Then he ran an introductory course to train new helpers, and at the end of the one-year training period, he asked the young helpers to fill out a survey. Among the questions was this one, "What changes have taken place in your life since you became totally involved with disabled people?"

Here is a sampling of their answers:

- For the first time in my life I feel I am doing something really significant.
- I feel I can now do things I wouldn't have thought myself capable of before.
- During my time here I have won the affection of Sabine. Having had the opportunity to involve myself with a disabled person, I no longer think of her as disabled at all.
- I am more responsive now to human suffering and it arouses in me the desire to help.
- It's made me question what is really important in life.
- I've become more tolerant. My own little problems don't seem so important any longer, and I've learned to accept myself with all my inadequacies. Above all I've learned to appreciate the little pleasures of life.

As Dr. Trogisch read over these and other responses, he realized with a start the answer to his question. The meaning of the suffering of those children was being worked out in the lives of others, his helpers, who were learning lessons that no sophisticated educational system could teach.

Where Is God When It Hurts? (204–6)

◇

Why Persevere?

There is an inherent difference between relating to another human and relating to God. I go to the grocery store and run into a neighbor. *Judy just went through a divorce,* I say to myself. Seeing Judy prods me to act. I ask about her life, check on her children, maybe invite her to church. "We must get together with Judy and the kids," I tell my wife later that day.

With God, the sequence reverses. I never "see" God. I seldom run into visual clues that remind me of God *unless I am looking.* The act of looking, the pursuit itself, makes possible the encounter. For this reason, Christianity has always insisted that trust and obedience come first, and knowledge follows.

Because of that difference, I persevere at spiritual disciplines no matter how I feel. I want to know God. And in pursuing a relationship, we must come on God's terms, not our own.

Old Testament prophets set out the preconditions for knowing God, as in this verse from Micah: "And what does the Lord require of you? To act justly and to love mercy and to walk humbly with your God." The New Testament epistles tell us that acting in loving ways toward God nurtures the relationship and leads toward growth. I do not get to know God, then do God's will; I get to know God *by* doing that will. I enter into an active relationship, which means spending time with God, caring about the people God cares about, and following God's commands — whether I spontaneously feel like it or not.

"How shall we begin to know You Who are if we do not begin ourselves to be something of what You are?" asked Thomas Merton. God is holy, Other. I can no more get to know God apart from some common ground than I can get to know a Hungarian person apart from common language. Merton adds:

> We receive enlightenment only in proportion as we give ourselves more and more completely to God by humble submission and love. We do not first see, then act: we act, then see.... And that is why the man who waits to see clearly, before he will believe, never starts on the journey.

Reaching for the Invisible God (89 – 90)

◇

Mastery of the Ordinary

Faith gets tested when a sense of God's presence fades or when the very ordinariness of life makes us question whether our responses even matter. We wonder, "What can one person do? What difference will my small effort make?"

I once watched a series based on interviews with survivors from World War II. The soldiers recalled how they spent a particular day. One sat in a foxhole all day; once or twice, a German tank drove by, and he shot at it. Others played cards and frittered away the time. A few got involved in furious firefights. Mostly, the day passed like any other day for an infantryman on the front. Later, they learned they had just participated in one of the largest, most decisive engagements of the war, the Battle of the Bulge. It did not *feel* decisive to any of them at the time, because none had the big picture of what was happening elsewhere.

Great victories are won when ordinary people execute their assigned tasks— and a faithful person does not debate each day whether he or she is in the mood to follow the sergeant's orders or show up at a boring job. We exercise faith by responding to the task that lies before us. I sometimes wish the gospel writers had included details about Jesus' life before he turned to ministry. Did he ever question the value of the time he was spending as a carpenter on such repetitious tasks?

More often than I would care to admit, doubts gnaw away at me. I wonder about apparent conflicts in the Bible, about suffering and injustice, about the huge gap between the ideals and reality of the Christian life. At such times, I plod on, "acting as if" it is true, relying on the habit of belief, praying for the assurance that eventually comes yet never shields me against the doubts' return.

Reaching for the Invisible God (90 – 91)

◇

Furious Opposites

As Andrew Greeley said, "If one wishes to eliminate uncertainty, tension, confusion and disorder from one's life, there is no point in getting mixed up either with Yahweh or with Jesus of Nazareth." I grew up expecting that a relationship with God would bring order and a calm rationality to life. Instead, I have discovered that living in faith involves much dynamic tension.

Throughout church history, Christian leaders have shown an impulse to pin everything down, to reduce behavior and doctrine to absolutes that could be answered on a true-false test. Significantly, I do not find this tendency in the Bible. I find instead the mystery and uncertainty that characterize any relationship, especially a relationship between a perfect God and fallible human beings.

In a phrase that became the cornerstone of his theology, G. K. Chesterton said, "Christianity got over the difficulty of combining furious opposites, by keeping them both, and keeping them both furious." Most heresies come from espousing one opposite at the expense of the other.

A church uncomfortable with paradox tends to tilt in one direction or the other, usually with disastrous consequences. Read the theologians of the first few centuries as they try to fathom Jesus, the center of our faith, who was somehow fully God and fully man. Read the theologians of the Reformation as they discover the majestic implications of God's sovereignty, then strive to keep their followers from settling into a resigned fatalism.

The first shall be last; find your life by losing it; no achievement matters apart from love; work out your salvation with fear and trembling for it is God who works in you; God's kingdom has come but not fully; enter the kingdom of heaven like a child; he who serves is greatest; measure self-worth not by what others think of you but by what you think of them; where sin abounds grace abounds more; we are saved by faith alone but faith without works is dead—all these profound principles of life appear in the New Testament, and none easily reduces to logical consistency.

"Truth is not in the middle, and not in one extreme, but in both extremes," the British pastor Charles Simeon remarked. With some reluctance, I have come to agree.

Reaching for the Invisible God (92–93)

◆

Changed by Contact

I conceive of the spiritual life as a capacity built into the human person, but one that can only develop in relationship with God. "I call you into my soul," said Augustine, "which you prepare to accept by the longing that you breathe into it." Although we all have the capacity, our spiritual longing will remain unfulfilled until we make contact, and then develop the skills of spiritual "correspondence." Considered in this way, Jesus' striking image of being born again makes perfect sense. Conversion, the process of connecting to spiritual reality, awakens the potential of brand new life. And as God's children we become who we are through relationship with God and God's people.

I think of the person who has influenced my Christian life more than any other: the missionary surgeon Paul Brand. Over a fifteen-year period of time, I wrote three books with Dr. Brand. I accompanied him on trips to India and England where together we retraced the main events in his life. I spent hundreds of hours asking him about his experiences with medicine, life, and God. I interviewed his former patients, his colleagues, his family, his operating-room scrub nurses. Dr. Brand is both a good and a great man, and I have everlasting gratitude for the time we spent together. At a stage in my spiritual development when I had little confidence to write about my own faith, I had absolute confidence writing about his.

I changed because of my relationship with Dr. Brand. I now view justice, lifestyle, and money issues largely through his eyes; I see the natural environment differently; I look at the human body, and especially pain, in a very different light. My relationship with Dr. Brand affected me deeply, in my core, on the inside. Yet as I look back, I can think of no instance in which he manipulatively sought to change me. I changed willingly, gladly, as my world and my self encountered his.

A similar process works, I believe, with God. I become who I am as a Christian by relating to God. In ways mysterious and often hard to describe — yet never coercive or manipulative — I have changed over time because of my contact with God.

Reaching for the Invisible God (107 – 8)

◆

An Audience of One

When I worked as a young journalist for *Campus Life* magazine, my assistant kept a plaque on her desk with this two-line poem:

> Only one life, 'twill soon be past
> Only what's done for Christ will last.

Reading that plaque brought me up short every time. Although I believed its truth, how could I put it into practice? Getting the oil changed in my car, watching the Chicago Bears football game on television, swapping funny stories at coffee break downstairs, planning an outing on Lake Michigan, marking up a manuscript with typesetting codes—were these acts done for Christ? How *should* my faith in the invisible world affect day-to-day life in the visible world?

According to Jesus, what other people think of me matters very little. What God thinks matters far more. Pray in a closed room, Jesus said, where no one but your Father can see you, rather than in a public place where you might get credit for being spiritual. In other words, live for God and not other people. I keep clamoring for attention and achievement. Jesus invites me to let go of that competitive struggle, to trust that God's opinion of me is the only one that counts, ultimately.

"There are but two principles of moral life in the universe," said the mystic Madame Guyon: "one which makes ourselves, or the most limited private good, the center; the other, which makes God, who may be called the universal good, the center." I could summarize my entire spiritual pilgrimage as an effort to move the operating center from myself to God.

I ask myself how my life would differ if I truly played to an audience of One, if I continually asked not "What do I want to do?" or "What would bring me approval from others?" but "What would God have me do?" Certainly my sense of ego and rivalry would fade because I would no longer need to worry about proving myself to other people. I could concentrate instead on pleasing God, by living in such a way that would attract people to Jesus' style of life.

Rumors of Another World (68 – 69)

◆

The Scandal of Forgiveness

The scandal of forgiveness confronts anyone who agrees to a moral ceasefire. When I feel wronged, I can contrive a hundred reasons against forgiveness. *He needs to learn a lesson. I don't want to encourage irresponsible behavior. I'll let her stew for a while; it will do her good. She needs to learn that actions have consequences. I was the wronged party—it's not up to me to make the first move. How can I forgive if he's not even sorry?* I marshal my arguments until something happens to wear down my resistance. When I finally soften to the point of granting forgiveness, it seems a capitulation, a leap from hard logic to mushy sentiment.

Why do I make such a leap? One factor that motivates me to forgive is that as a Christian I am commanded to, as the child of a Father who forgives. And I can identify three pragmatic reasons.

First, forgiveness alone can halt the cycle of blame and pain, breaking the chain of ungrace. Without it we remain bound to the people we cannot forgive, held in their vise grip. Second, forgiveness loosens the stranglehold of guilt in the perpetrator. It allows the possibility of transformation in the guilty party, even if a just punishment is still required for the wrong. And third, forgiveness creates a remarkable linkage, placing the forgiver on the same side as the party who did the wrong. Through it we realize we are not as different from the wrongdoer as we would like to think. "I also am other than what I imagine myself to be. To know this is forgiveness," said Simone Weil.

Forgiveness—undeserved, unearned—can cut the cords and let the oppressive burden of guilt roll away. The New Testament shows a resurrected Jesus leading Peter by the hand through a three-fold ritual of forgiveness. Peter need not go through life with the guilty, hangdog look of one who has betrayed the Son of God. Oh, no. On the backs of such transformed sinners Christ would build his church.

What's So Amazing About Grace? (96 – 104)

Enough Blood

In 1987 an IRA bomb went off in a small town west of Belfast, amid a group of Protestants who had gathered to honor the war dead on Veteran's Day. Eleven people died and sixty-three others were wounded. What made this act of terrorism stand out was the response of one of the wounded, Gordon Wilson, a devout Methodist.

The bomb buried Wilson and his twenty-year-old daughter under five feet of concrete and brick. "Daddy, I love you very much," were the last words Marie spoke, grasping her father's hand as they waited for the rescuers.

A newspaper later proclaimed, "No one remembers what the politicians had to say at that time. No one who heard Gordon Wilson will ever forget what he confessed.... His grace towered over the miserable justifications of the bombers." Speaking from his hospital bed, Wilson said, "I have lost my daughter, but I bear no grudge. Bitter talk is not going to bring Marie Wilson back to life. I shall pray, tonight and every night, that God will forgive them."

His daughter's last words were words of love, and Gordon Wilson determined to live out his life on that plane of love. "The world wept," said one report, as Wilson gave a similar interview over the BBC radio that week.

After his release from the hospital, Gordon Wilson led a crusade for Protestant-Catholic reconciliation. Protestant extremists who had planned to avenge the bombing decided, because of the publicity surrounding Wilson, that such behavior would be politically foolish. Wilson wrote a book about his daughter, spoke out against violence, and constantly repeated the refrain, "Love is the bottom line." He met with the IRA, personally forgave them for what they had done, and asked them to lay down their arms. "I know that you've lost loved ones, just like me," he told them. "Surely, enough is enough. Enough blood has been spilled."

The Irish Republic ultimately made Wilson a member of its Senate. When he died in 1995, the Irish Republic, Northern Ireland, and all of Great Britain honored this ordinary Christian citizen who had gained fame for his uncommon spirit of grace and forgiveness.

What's So Amazing About Grace? (117 – 18)

◆

Political Repentance

In 1990 the world watched a drama of forgiveness enacted on the stage of world politics. After East Germany chose a parliament in its first free elections, the representatives convened to take up the reins of government. The Communist bloc was changing daily, West Germany was proposing the radical step of reunification, and the new parliament had many weighty matters of state to consider. For their first official act, however, they decided to vote on this extraordinary statement, drafted in the language of theology, not politics:

> We, the first freely elected parliamentarians of the GDR ... on behalf of the citizens of this land, admit responsibility for the humiliation, expulsion and murder of Jewish men, women and children. We feel sorrow and shame, and acknowledge this burden of German history.... Immeasurable suffering was inflicted on the peoples of the world during the era of national socialism.... We ask all the Jews of the world to forgive us. We ask the people of Israel to forgive us for the hypocrisy and hostility of official East German policies toward Israel and for the persecution and humiliation of Jewish citizens in our country after 1945 as well.

East Germany's parliament passed the statement unanimously. Members rose to their feet for a long ovation and then paused for a moment of silence in memory of the Jews who had died in the Holocaust.

What did such an act of parliament accomplish? Certainly it did not bring the murdered Jews back to life or undo the monstrous deeds of Nazism. No, but it helped loosen the stranglehold of guilt that had been choking East Germans for nearly half a century—five decades in which their government had steadfastly denied any need for forgiveness.

For its part, West Germany had already repented officially for the abominations. In addition, West Germany has paid out sixty billion dollars in reparations to Jews. The fact that a relationship exists at all between Germany and Israel is a stunning demonstration of transnational forgiveness. Grace has its own power, even in international politics.

What's So Amazing About Grace? (124–25)

◆

Breaking the Chains

Recent times have seen public dramas of forgiveness play out in nations formerly controlled by Communists.

In 1983, before the Iron Curtain lifted and during the period of martial law, Pope John Paul II visited Poland, where he conducted a huge open-air mass. Throngs of people, organized in orderly groups by their parishes, marched over the Poniatowski Bridge and streamed toward the stadium. Just before the bridge, the route crossed directly in front of the Communist Party's Central Committee Building, and hour after hour the platoons of marchers chanted in unison, "We forgive you, we forgive you!" as they passed the building. Some said the slogan with heartfelt sincerity. Others shouted it almost with contempt, as if to say, "You're nothing—we don't even hate you."

A few years later Jerry Popieluszko, a thirty-five-year-old priest whose sermons had electrified Poland, was found floating in the Vistula River with his eyes gouged out and his fingernails torn off. Once again the Catholics took to the streets, marching with banners that read "We forgive. We forgive." Popieluszko had preached the same message Sunday after Sunday to the multitude who filled the square in front of his church: "Defend the truth. Overcome evil with good." After his death they continued to obey him, and in the end it was exactly this spirit of prevailing grace that caused the regime to collapse.

All over Eastern Europe the struggle of forgiveness is still being waged. Should a pastor in Russia forgive the KGB officers who imprisoned him and razed his church? Should Romanians forgive the doctors and nurses who chained sick orphans to their beds? Should citizens of Eastern Germany forgive the stool pigeons—including seminary professors, pastors, and treacherous spouses—who spied on them? When human rights activist Vera Wollenberger learned that it was her husband who had betrayed her to the secret police, resulting in her arrest and exile, she ran to the bathroom and vomited.

Paul Tillich once defined forgiveness as remembering the past in order that it might be forgotten—a principle that applies to nations as well as individuals. Though forgiveness is never easy, and may take generations, what else can break the chains that enslave people to their historical past?

What's So Amazing About Grace? (125 – 26)

◆

His Own Body

God miraculously provided food for the Israelites wandering through the Sinai desert, and even made sure their shoes would not wear out. Jesus too fed hungry people and ministered directly to their needs. Many Christians who read those thrilling stories look back with a sense of nostalgia or even disappointment. "Why doesn't God act like that now?" they wonder. "Why doesn't God miraculously provide for my needs?"

But the New Testament letters seem to show a different pattern at work. Locked in a cold dungeon, Paul turned to his longtime friend Timothy to meet his physical needs. "Bring my cloak and my scrolls," he wrote, "and also bring Mark, who has always been so helpful." In other straits, Paul received "God's comfort" in the form of a visit from Titus. And when a famine broke out in Jerusalem, Paul himself led a fund-raising effort among all the churches he had founded. God was meeting the needs of the young church as surely as he had met the needs of the Israelites, but indirectly, through fellow members of Christ's body. Paul made no such distinction as "the church did this, but God did that." Such a division would miss the point he had made so often. The church is Christ's body; therefore if the church did it, God did it.

Paul's insistence on this truth may trace back to his first, dramatic personal encounter with God. At the time, he was a fierce persecutor of Christians, a notorious bounty hunter. But on the road to Damascus he saw a light bright enough to blind him for three days, and heard a voice from heaven: "Saul, Saul, why do you persecute me?"

Persecute you? Persecute who? I'm only after those heretics the Christians.

"Who are you, Lord?" asked Saul at last, knocked flat on the ground.

"I am Jesus, whom you are persecuting," came the reply.

That sentence summarizes as well as anything the change brought about by the Holy Spirit. Jesus had been executed months before. It was the Christians Saul was after, not Jesus. But Jesus, alive again, informed Saul that those people were in fact his own body. What hurt them, hurt him. It was a lesson the apostle Paul would never forget.

Disappointment with God (141 – 42)

◆

Why I Believe

In my own days of skepticism, I wanted a dramatic interruption from above. I wanted proof of an unseen reality. In my days of faith, such supernatural irruptions seem far less important, in part because I find the materialistic explanations of life inadequate to explain reality. I have learned to attend to fainter contacts between the seen and unseen worlds. I sense in romantic love something insufficiently explained by mere biochemical attraction. I sense in beauty and in nature marks of a genius Creator for which the natural response is worship. Like Jacob, I have at times awoken from a dream to realize, "Surely the Lord is in this place, and I was not aware of it."

I sense in desire, including sexual desire, marks of a holy yearning for connection. I sense in pain and suffering a terrible disruption that omnipotent love surely cannot abide forever. I sense in compassion, generosity, justice, and forgiveness a quality of grace that speaks to me of another world, especially when I visit places, like Russia, marred by their absence. I sense in Jesus a person who lived those qualities so consistently that the world could not tolerate him and had to silence and dispose of him. In short, I believe not so much because the invisible world impinges on this one but because the visible world hints at a lack of completion.

I once heard a woman give a remarkable account of achievement. An early feminist, she gained renown in the male-dominated field of endocrinology. At the end of her story she said simply, "As I look back, this is what matters. I have loved and been loved, and all the rest is just background music."

Love, too, is why I believe. At the end of life, what else matters? "Love never fails," Paul wrote. "It always protects, always trusts, always hopes, always perseveres." He could only be describing God's love, for no human love meets that standard of perfection. What I have tasted of love convinces me that a perfect love will not be satisfied with the sad tale of this planet, will not rest until evil is conquered and good reigns, will not allow its object to pass from existence. Perfect love perseveres until it perfects.

Rumors of Another World (171–72)

Homecoming

My wife, Janet, worked with senior citizens near a Chicago housing project judged the poorest community in the United States. About half her clients were white, half were black. All of them had lived through harsh times—two world wars, the Great Depression, social upheavals—and all of them, in their seventies and eighties, lived in awareness of death. Yet Janet noted a striking difference in the way the whites and the blacks faced death. There were exceptions, of course, but the trend was this: many of the whites became increasingly fearful and anxious. They complained about their lives, their families, and their deteriorating health. The blacks, in contrast, maintained a good humor and triumphant spirit even though they had more apparent reason for bitterness and despair.

What caused the difference in outlooks? Janet concluded the answer was hope, a hope that traced directly to the blacks' bedrock belief in heaven. If you want to hear contemporary images of heaven, attend a few African-American funerals. With characteristic eloquence, the preachers paint word pictures of a life so serene and sensuous that everyone in the congregation starts fidgeting to go there. The mourners feel grief, naturally, but in its proper place—as an interruption, a temporary setback in a battle whose end has already been determined.

I am convinced that for these neglected saints, who learned to anticipate and enjoy God in spite of the difficulties of their lives on earth, heaven will seem more like a long-awaited homecoming than a visit to a new place. In their lives, the Beatitudes have become true. To people who are trapped in pain, in broken homes, in economic chaos, in hatred and fear, in violence—to these, Jesus offers a promise of a time, far longer and more substantial than this time on earth, of health and wholeness and pleasure and peace. A time of reward.

The Jesus I Never Knew (112 – 13)

◆

Personality Change

During high school years I tried desperately to deconstruct and then reconstruct my personality. For starters, I hated being Southern. Television programs like "The Beverly Hillbillies" and "Hee Haw" embarrassed me, and I cringed every time I heard President Lyndon Johnson open his mouth: "Mah fella Amuricuns . . ." Since the rest of the nation in the 1960s seemed to judge Southerners as backward, ignorant, and racist, I wanted to disassociate myself from my region.

Vowel by vowel I worked on my accent, succeeding so well that people ever since have reacted with surprise when they hear I grew up in the Deep South. I began a campaign to read great books in order to remove provincial blinders. I shunned any behavior that conformed to "appropriate" or "proper" Southern etiquette, and sought only the "authentic." I worked to gain control of my emotions so that they were my servant, never my master. I even changed my handwriting, forcing myself to form each letter in a different way than I had before.

By and large the makeover worked, giving me a personality that has fit comfortably in the decades since. I became less vulnerable and more open-minded and flexible—traits not cultivated in my upbringing but useful in my profession as a journalist. It was only years later that I realized the limits to a self-constructed personality. In most ways important to God, I had failed miserably. I was selfish, joyless, loveless, and lacked compassion. With the exception of self-control, I lacked all nine of the fruits of the Spirit listed in Galatians 5. These qualities, I came to realize, cannot be constructed. They must be grown, under the direction of an inner power, the Spirit.

I have since made it a regular practice to pray through the list in Galatians: love, joy, peace, patience, kindness, goodness, faithfulness, gentleness, and self-control. Do I show love, experience joy, feel peace, exhibit patience? I am humbly aware that any progress in those qualities comes as a result of the Spirit's work. I agree with J. Heinrich Arnold that Christian discipleship "is not a question of our own doing; it is a matter of making room for God so that he can live in us."

"Back Page" column, *Christianity Today*,
October 25, 1999 (104)

More Ourselves

Mark van Doren, the former literature professor of Thomas Merton (and subject of the movie *Quiz Show*), visited his ex-student at the Kentucky monastery after a thirteen-year absence. Van Doren and other friends of Merton still could not comprehend the change that had come over Merton. What power could have transformed him from a New York party animal into a monk who cherished solitude and silence? Van Doren reported, "Of course he looked a little older; but as we sat and talked I could see no important difference in him. 'Tom,' I said, 'you haven't changed at all.' 'Why would I? Here,' he said, 'our duty is to be more ourselves not less.' It was a searching remark and I stood happily corrected."

The New Testament presents the realm of the Spirit as the culmination of God's work on earth, and as I compare it to what went before, I catch a glimpse why. An Israelite in the Old Testament approached God with fear and trembling, through an elaborate series of rituals under the auspices of professional priests. Jesus' disciples had a much more personal connection, though even so they seemed to grasp only a portion of what he said, and until the end badly misconstrued his mission. The Holy Spirit, though, "personalizes" God's presence in a way uniquely tailored to my own soul.

Henri Nouwen said toward the end of his life that prayer had become for him primarily a time of "listening to the blessing." "The real 'work' of prayer," he said, "is to become silent and listen to the voice that says good things about me." That may sound self-indulgent, he admitted, but not if it meant seeing himself as the Beloved, a temple in which God chose to dwell. The more he listened to that voice, the less likely he was to judge his worth by how others responded to him, or by how much he achieved. He prayed for that inner presence to express itself in his daily life, in such things as eating and drinking, talking and loving, playing and working. He sought true freedom in an identity that was anchored in a place "beyond all human praise and blame."

"Back Page" column, *Christianity Today*,
October 25, 1999 (104)

◇

Frank Confession

One issue comes up in virtually every one of Paul's letters: What good is the law? To most of Paul's readers, the word *law* stands for the huge collection of rules and rituals codified from the Old Testament. Thanks to his earlier days as a Pharisee, Paul knows those rules well. And whenever he starts talking about "the new covenant" or "freedom in Christ," the Jews want to know what he now thinks about that law.

Romans 7, the most personal and autobiographical chapter in Romans, discloses exactly what Paul thinks.

Paul never recommends throwing out the law entirely. He sees that it reveals a basic code of morality, an ideal of the kind of behavior that pleases God. The law is good for one thing: it exposes sin. "Indeed I would not have known what sin was except through the law." To Paul, such rules as the Ten Commandments are helpful, righteous, and good.

The law has one major problem, however: although it proves how bad you are, it doesn't make you any better. As a heritage of his days of legalism, Paul has developed a very sensitive conscience, but, as he poignantly recounts, it mainly makes him feel guilty all the time. "What a wretched man I am!" he confesses. The law bares his weaknesses but cannot provide the power needed to overcome them. The law—or *any* set of rules—leads ultimately to a dead end.

Romans 7 gives a striking illustration of the struggle that ensues when an imperfect person commits himself to a perfect God. Any Christian who wonders, *How can I ever get rid of my nagging sins?* will find comfort in Paul's frank confession. In the face of God's standards, every one of us feels helpless, and that is Paul's point precisely. No set of rules can break the terrible cycle of guilt and failure. We need outside help to "serve in the new way of the Spirit, and not in the old way of the written code." Paul celebrates that help in Romans 8.

Meet the Bible (594)

The God Within

The Holy Spirit is the theme of Romans 8, and in this chapter Paul gives a panoramic survey of how the Spirit can make a difference in a person's life.

First in Romans 8, Paul sets to rest the nagging problem of sin he has just raised so forcefully. "There is now no condemnation," he announces. Jesus Christ, through his life and death, took care of "the sin problem" for all time.

Elsewhere (Romans 4), Paul borrows a word from banking to explain the process. God "credits" Jesus' own perfection to our accounts, so that we are judged not by our behavior but by his. Similarly, God has transferred all the punishment we deserve onto Jesus, through his death on the cross. In this transaction, human beings come out the clear winners, set free at last from the curse of sin.

And, as always, Paul insists on the best news of all: that Jesus Christ did not stay dead. Paul marvels that the very same power that raised Christ from the dead can also "enliven" us. The Spirit is a life-giver who alone can break the gloomy, deathlike pattern described in Romans 7.

To be sure, the Spirit does not remove all problems. But "the God within" can do for us what we could never do for ourselves. The Spirit works alongside us as we relate to God, helping us in our weakness, even praying for us when we don't know what to ask.

The way Paul tells it, what happens inside individual believers is the central drama of history: "The creation waits in eager expectation for the sons of God to be revealed." Somehow, spiritual victories within us will help bring about the liberation and healing of a "groaning" creation. The apostle can hardly contain himself as he contemplates these matters. Romans 8 ends with a ringing declaration that nothing—*absolutely, positively nothing*—can ever separate us from God's love.

Meet the Bible (596)

Cranking Up the Volume

Ironically, some of the brightest, most hopeful books of the Bible—the letters to the Philippians, Colossians, and Ephesians—come out of Paul's term of house arrest in Rome. There's a good reason: prison offers him the precious commodity of time. Paul is no longer journeying from town to town, stamping out fires set by his enemies. Settled into passably comfortable surroundings, he can devote attention to lofty thoughts about the meaning of life.

A prisoner who survived fourteen years in a Cuban jail told how he kept his spirits up: "The worst part was the monotony. I had no window in my cell, and so I mentally constructed one on the door. I 'saw' in my mind a beautiful scene from the mountains, with water tumbling down a ravine over rocks. It became so real to me that I would visualize it without effort every time I looked at the cell door."

The letter to the Ephesians gives a hint as to what the apostle Paul "sees" when he lets his mind wander beyond the monotony of his place of confinement. First he visualizes the spiritual growth in the churches he has left behind. This passage opens with a burst of thanksgiving for the vitality of the Ephesian church. Then he seeks to open "the eyes of their hearts" to even more exalted sights: the "incomparable riches" of God's grace.

Ephesians is full of staggering good news. In it, Paul asks the grandest question of all: What is God's overall purpose for this world? He raises the sights far above his own circumstances to bigger issues, cosmic issues. And when he cranks up the volume to express God's plan of love, not one low, mournful note sneaks in.

If you feel discouraged, or wonder if God really cares, or question whether the Christian life is worth the effort, Ephesians provides a great tonic. It prescribes the "riches in Christ" available to all.

Meet the Bible (613 – 14)

The Human Cycle

Observing the modern world, the French sociologist Jacques Ellul noted a striking trend: as the Christian gospel permeates society, it tends to produce values that, paradoxically, contradict the gospel. What accounts for this strange development?

I found a clue in the writings of Gordon Cosby, the founding pastor of Church of the Savior in Washington, D.C. Cosby noted that high-commitment Christian communities begin with a strong sense of devotion, which expresses itself in a life of discipline. Groups organized around devotion and discipline tend to produce abundance, but ultimately that very success breaks down discipline and leads to indulgence and decadence.

Cosby termed this pattern the "monastic cycle." Early Benedictines worked hard to clear forests and cultivate land, investing their surplus in drainage, livestock, and seed. Six centuries later, according to historian Paul Johnson, "Benedictine abbeys had virtually ceased to be spiritual institutions. They had become collegiate sinecures reserved very largely for members of the upper classes." The abbots now absorbed about half the order's revenue in order to maintain their luxurious lifestyles. Johnson judges most Benedictines of the era as "unenterprising, upper-class parasites."

Dominicans, Jesuits, and Franciscans duplicated the cycle: an initial burst of devotion and discipline, a resulting period of abundance, then a drift toward indulgence until some reformer came along to revive the ideals of the founder. And Protestant reformers faced the same challenge.

As the Old Testament shows, entire nations can fall into a similar pattern. Perhaps we should call this trend the "human cycle" rather than the "monastic cycle." Beginning with Adam and Eve's brief sojourn in Paradise, human beings have shown a remarkable inability to handle prosperity and success. We turn to God out of need and forget God when things go well.

Observing this trend in numerous countries, I better understand why Jesus warned against wealth and called the poor and persecuted "blessed." Out of sheer desperation, the needy may turn to God. Meanwhile I worry about my own society, which relies mainly on its wealth and power and fills every vacant space with entertainment options. Can we, in a time of abundance, find a way to break the "monastic cycle"? On the answer to that question, our future health may hinge.

"Back Page" column, *Christianity Today,* September 2004 (104)

August

"¡O, Evangelicos!"

When I return from trips abroad and read profiles in *Time* and *Newsweek* about American evangelicals, I feel sad. In the United States, everything eventually boils down to politics, and usually that means polarization. Many Americans view evangelicals as a monolithic voting bloc obsessed with a few moral issues. They miss the vibrancy and enthusiasm, the *good-newsness* that the word represents in much of the world.

Evangelicals in Africa bring food to prisoners, care for AIDS orphans, and operate mission schools that train many of that continent's leaders. There, and in Asia and Latin America, evangelicals also manage microenterprise loan programs that allow families to buy a sewing machine or a flock of chickens. In the last fifty years, the percentage of American missionaries sponsored by evangelical agencies has risen from 40 percent to 90 percent.

A friend of mine visiting a barrio in Sao Paulo, Brazil, began to feel anxious as he noticed the minions of drug lords patrolling the neighborhood with automatic weapons. The streets narrowed to dirt paths; plastic water pipes dangled overhead; and a snarl of wires tapped power from high-voltage lines. The stench of sewage was everywhere. Anxiety increased as he noticed that people inside the tin shacks were glowering at him, a suspicious gringo invading their turf. Was he a narc? An undercover cop? Then the chief drug lord of that neighborhood noticed on the back of his T-shirt the logo of a local Pentecostal church. He broke out in a big smile, "¡O, evangelicos!" he called out, and the scowls turned to smiles. Over the years, that church had extended practical help to the barrio, and now the foreign visitors were joyfully welcomed.

In the United States too, evangelicals are thriving even as mainline Protestant churches decline. Evangelicals staff many of the five hundred Christian agencies that have sprung up since World War II to combat social problems. Megachurches based on the 23,000-member Willow Creek Community Church near Chicago and Saddleback Community Church in Southern California are replicating in major cities. A new, hard-to-classify "emergent church" has evolved to minister to the postmodern generation. In fact, one recent survey revealed that ninety-three of the top one hundred rapidly growing churches in the U.S. identify themselves with evangelicals.

"A Quirky and Vibrant Mosaic," *Christianity Today,*
June 3, 2005 (38)

◆

Word on the Street

If you're writing a book about prayer, you should hang around the homeless for a while," said my wife, a veteran of inner-city ministry. "Street people pray as a necessity, not a luxury."

Her advice made sense, and when I visited a coffee house for the homeless in Denver I was struck by the down-to-earth quality of the prayers—indeed, their resemblance to the Lord's Prayer. "Give us this day our daily bread": they all had stories about running out of food, praying, and then finding a burrito or uneaten pizza. "Deliver us from evil": living on mean streets, believers prayed that daily. "Forgive us our trespasses": deep down lay buried secrets of shame and regret.

"You'd be surprised by how many street people are fundamentalists," said John, a trained counselor. "Little wonder. Visit a rescue mission and you'll hear a steady diet of hellfire and brimstone sermons. They get a constant dose of sin and worthlessness."

After twenty years of ministry, John has a theory that street people have in common with fundamentalists a major "attachment disorder." In childhood they never learned to bond with parents or other people, and never learned to bond with God either. They find it difficult to commit, to open up to another, to trust, and they see the world as an unsafe, alien place.

From my time with the homeless, I learned a new meaning to prayer: a safe place to bear secrets. Those of us fortunate enough to have a spouse or a trustworthy friend can share our secrets. If not, at least we have God. (The fact that we're still alive, and loved, shows that God has more tolerance for whatever those secrets represent than we may give God credit for.)

"If I'm right about the attachment disorders," John said, "the best ministry I can offer is a long-term relationship. I hope that over months and years street people learn to trust me as someone who can handle their secrets. I hope that gradually they can learn to trust God. And I tell people who confront the homeless that eye contact may be more important than food or money. They need to connect in some small way with another human being, someone who sees them as a person of worth."

"Back Page" column, *Christianity Today*,
January 2006 (80)

The Unwanted Disease

Jesus knew all about the social stigma that accompanies a disease like AIDS or leprosy. Levitical laws decreed that a person with leprosy live outside the town, keep a six-foot distance from everyone else, and wear the clothes of a mourner going to a burial service. I can easily imagine indignation rippling through the crowd when one such outcast walked through them, no doubt given a wide berth, and threw himself at the feet of Jesus. "Lord, if you are willing, you can make me clean," he said.

Matthew, Mark, and Luke all include the same explosive sentence: "Jesus reached out his hand and touched the man." The crowd must have gasped—had not Moses' law forbidden such an act? The leprosy victim may have flinched. For how many months or years had he been deprived of the sensation of warm human flesh against his own? Because of that one touch from Jesus, his state of dis-ease came to an end. Shalom was restored.

Jesus' response to dis-ease set a pattern for the church that formed around him, and Christians proceeded to follow his example of caring for the sick, the poor, and the outcast. In the case of leprosy, although the church sometimes added to the misery with its "curse of God" message, at the same time individuals rose up to lead the way in treatment. Religious orders dedicated themselves to the care of leprosy, and scientific breakthroughs on the disease tended to come from missionaries because they were the only ones willing to work with leprosy patients.

Mother Teresa, whose sisters in Calcutta run both a hospice and a clinic for leprosy patients, once said, "We have drugs for people with diseases like leprosy. But these drugs do not treat the main problem, the disease of being *unwanted*. That's what my sisters hope to provide." The sick and the poor, she said, suffer even more from rejection than material want. "An alcoholic in Australia told me that when he is walking along the street he hears the footsteps of everyone coming toward him or passing him becoming faster. Loneliness and the feeling of being unwanted is the most terrible poverty." One need not be a doctor or a miracle worker to meet that need.

The Jesus I Never Knew (172 – 73)

Which Is Easier?

The Gospels tell of a paralytic who wanted so desperately to meet Jesus that he talked four friends into digging up a roof and lowering him through the hole! The man who had spent his life horizontal would have one moment of vertical fame.

Apparently, Jesus rather enjoyed the interruption. Outstanding faith never failed to impress him, and certainly the four-man demolition crew had demonstrated that. Yet his response baffled the observers. When Jesus saw *their* faith —plural, emphasizing the four friends' role in the healing—he said, "Take heart, son; your sins are forgiven."

Who said anything about sins? And who was Jesus to forgive them?

Jesus hushed the debate with enigmatic words that seem to sum up his general attitude toward physical healing: "Which is easier, to say to the paralytic, 'Your sins are forgiven,' or to say, 'Get up, take your mat and walk'?" As if to prove the point, Jesus merely gave a word and the paralyzed man stood to his feet, rolled up his mat, and walked home.

Jesus never met a disease he could not cure, a birth defect he could not reverse, a demon he could not exorcize. But forgiveness of sins requires an act of will on the receiver's part, and some who heard Jesus' strongest words about grace and forgiveness turned away unrepentant.

"But that you may know that the Son of Man has authority on earth to forgive sins ...," Jesus announced to the skeptics as he healed the man, a clear illustration of the "lower" serving the "higher." Jesus knew that spiritual dis-ease has a more devastating effect than any mere physical ailment. Every healed person ultimately dies—then what? He had not come primarily to heal the world's cells, but to heal its souls.

How easily do we who live in material bodies devalue the world of spirit. It occurs to me that although Jesus spent much time on issues such as hypocrisy, legalism, and pride, I know of no television ministries devoted to healing those "spiritual" problems; yet I know of many that center on physical ailments. Just as I begin feeling smug, however, I remember how easily I feel tormented by the slightest bout with physical suffering, and how seldom I feel tormented by sin.

The Jesus I Never Knew (173 – 75)

Overheard on Tour

I spent last fall chasing a suitcase from city to city on tours in the U.K. and U.S., introducing a new book on prayer. Along the way I got a bird's-eye view of the church:

Christians in Great Britain seem more serious about their faith than their counterparts in the U.S. British audiences still hunger for content whereas in America content goes over best enwrapped in entertainment.

If you drew your conclusions from CNN, you would view Christians, and especially evangelicals, as a voting bloc to be manipulated by politicians. Yet I met countless ordinary Christians who devote themselves to causes as disparate as the homeless in Pennsylvania and school dropouts in inner-city New Jersey to Asian students at Harvard and Silicon Valley executives, not to mention mission trips to less-developed countries.

The world is full of pain. For all its faults and failures, the church offers a place to bring wounds and to seek meaning in times of brokenness and struggle. An older man who walked with a shuffle mumbled to me, "God gave me Parkinson's disease. How can I possibly think he listens to what I have to say in prayer?" A woman told of praying with desperation during her nineteen years in an abusive marriage. I heard of suicides, of birth defects, of children hit by trucks and teenagers raped. One woman, now an ordained pastor, told of a dark period after her son died when for eighteen months she could not bring herself to pray. She cried out one day, "God, I don't want to die like this, with all communication cut off!" Even so, it took her six more months before she could pray again.

In one meeting a twenty-year-old came to the microphone and chided me for not taking literally the Bible's promises about faith that could move mountains. I agreed I needed a larger dose of such childlike faith, yet at the same time I could not dishonor the pain of suffering people by telling them their faith is somehow defective. From such souls I learn that life is not a problem to be solved but a mystery to be lived. Prayer offers no ironclad guarantee, but the certain promise that we need not live that mystery alone.

"Back Page" column, *Christianity Today,*
March 2007 (120)

◆

Traveling with Wesley

During my tour of Great Britain, for my morning reading I brought along *The Journal of John Wesley*, a day-by-day account of the indefatigable evangelist. As it happened, some mornings I would read of Wesley's journey to a town that I would visit that very evening.

Oh, what a difference, though! I rode in a comfortable car between cities and spoke at ticketed evening events before friendly audiences. John Wesley rode a horse through rain and snow, spoke four or five times a day to huge crowds in open fields, and faced angry opponents.

I finished Wesley's *Journal* impressed with his physical endurance, his austere lifestyle, and his absolute devotion to the clusters of believers springing up all over Britain. On the other hand, I could not help noting Wesley's lack of appreciation for the surrounding beauties and cultural riches. Gazing at a flower garden, he quickly demurred, "What can delight always, but the knowledge and love of God." He toured one of England's historic great houses and noted, "How little a time will it be before the house itself, yea, the earth, shall be burned up!"

How do we cherish this life with its gifts of art, beauty, music, and love, even while serving the poor and storing up treasures of the kingdom?

Wesley once articulated the danger of wealth: "I do not see how it is possible, in the nature of things, for any revival of religion to continue long. For religion must necessarily produce both industry and frugality, and these cannot but produce riches. But as riches increase, so will pride, anger, and love of the world in all its branches."

I learned that if present trends continue there will be no more Methodists in England in thirty years. My thoughts turned to my own country, the wealthiest in the world and yet, for now at least, one of the most religious. What will historians learn about the present American church two hundred years from now? A quote from G. K. Chesterton came to mind: "It is always simple to fall: there are an infinity of angles at which one falls, only one at which one stands."

"Back Page" column, *Christianity Today,*
November 2007 (104)

Shameful Past

I grew up a racist. I remember well when the South practiced a perfectly legal form of apartheid. Stores in downtown Atlanta had three rest rooms: White Men, White Women, and Colored. Gas stations had two drinking fountains, one for Whites and one for Colored. Motels and restaurants served white patrons only, and when the Civil Rights Act made such discrimination illegal, many owners shuttered their establishments.

Lester Maddox, later elected governor of Georgia, was one of the protesting restaurateurs. After closing his fried chicken outlets, he opened a memorial to the death of freedom, featuring a copy of the Bill of Rights resting in a black-draped coffin. To support himself he sold clubs and ax handles in three different sizes—Daddy, Mama, and Junior—replicas of the clubs used to beat black civil rights demonstrators. I bought one of those ax handles with money earned from my paper route. Lester Maddox sometimes attended my church (his sister was a member), and it was there I learned a twisted theological basis for my racism.

In the 1960s the church deacon board mobilized lookout squads, and on Sundays these took turns patrolling the entrances lest any black "troublemakers" try to integrate us.

When Congress passed the Civil Rights Act, our church founded a private school as a haven for whites, expressly barring all black students. A few "liberal" members left the church in protest when the kindergarten turned down the daughter of a black Bible professor, but most of us approved of the decision. A year later the church board rejected a Carver Bible Institute student for membership (his name was Tony Evans and he went on to become a prominent pastor and speaker).

We used to call Martin Luther King Jr. "Martin Lucifer Coon." We said that King was a card-carrying Communist, a Marxist agent who merely posed as a minister. Not until much later was I able to appreciate the moral strength of the man who, perhaps more than any other person, kept the South from outright racial war.

What's So Amazing About Grace? (130 – 31)

Soul Force

Martin Luther King Jr. recorded his struggle with forgiveness in *Letter from Birmingham City Jail*. Outside the jail Southern pastors were denouncing him as a Communist, mobs were yelling "Hang the nigger!" and policemen were swinging nightsticks at his unarmed supporters. King writes that he had to fast for several days in order to achieve the spiritual discipline necessary for him to forgive his enemies.

By forcing evil out into the open, King was attempting to tap into a national reservoir of moral outrage. After Selma, Alabama, that outrage flooded its banks. There, mounted troopers spurred their horses at a run into the crowd of marchers, flailing away with their nightsticks, cracking heads and driving bodies to the ground. As whites on the sidelines cheered, the troopers shot tear gas into the hysterical marchers.

Most Americans got their first glimpse of the scene when ABC interrupted its Sunday movie, *Judgment at Nuremberg*, to show footage. What the viewers saw broadcast live from Alabama bore a horrifying resemblance to what they were watching on film from Nazi Germany. Eight days later President Lyndon Johnson submitted the Voting Rights Act of 1965 to the U.S. Congress.

King had developed a sophisticated strategy of war fought with grace, not gunpowder. He never refused to meet with his adversaries. He opposed policies but not personalities. Most importantly, he countered violence with nonviolence, and hatred with love. "Let us not seek to satisfy our thirst for freedom by drinking from the cup of bitterness and hatred," he exhorted his followers. "We must not allow our creative protest to degenerate into physical violence. Again and again, we must rise to the majestic heights of meeting physical force with soul force."

What's So Amazing About Grace? (132 – 33)

Time to Repent

On November 4, 2008, I boarded a plane for Memphis just before polling places closed in the East. When I landed, I learned the U.S. had elected its first African-American president.

The next day I toured the Civil Rights Museum built around the motel where Martin Luther King Jr. was assassinated. For several hours I studied displays of the scenes I had known so well as a teenager. The brave college students in Greensboro, NC, who sat at a lunch counter as goons stamped out cigarettes in their hair, squirted mustard and ketchup in their faces, then knocked them off the stools and kicked them while white policemen looked on, laughing. The Freedom Ride bus burned in Alabama, the corpses unburied in Mississippi. Looking back, it seems incredible to imagine such ferocity directed against people who were seeking the basic ingredients of human dignity: the right to vote, to eat in restaurants and stay in motels, to attend college.

Outside the museum, words from King's final "I have been to the mountaintop" speech are forged in steel, words that caught in my throat on a sunny day mere hours after Barack Obama got elected: "I may not get there with you, but I want you to know that we, as a people, will get to the Promised Land." The next day King died in a pool of blood on the very spot where I was standing.

In no way do I discount the important policy differences between Obama and many Christians. But at the least can we use this moment as a time of reflection and, yes, repentance over our share in the sin of racism that has marked this nation since its founding? It took Southern Baptists 150 years to apologize for their support of slavery, and not until 2008 did Bob Jones University admit their error in barring black students before 1971. Their words of apology — "We failed to accurately represent the Lord and to fulfill the commandment to love others as ourselves" — apply to us, for many evangelicals vigorously opposed the civil rights movement. Can we now respond to a leader's call for racial healing and reconciliation?

"Back Page" column, *Christianity Today*,
March 2009 (96)

◆

Backsliding Closer

I visited two friends who work in inner-city ministry and asked each of them the same question. "Typically, church folks tell us that when we sin, or 'backslide,' we disrupt our relationship with God. You work with people who live with failure every day. Have you found that 'backsliding' draws them further from God or presses them toward God?"

Bud, who works among drug addicts, had an immediate answer. "Without question, it pushes them toward God. I could tell you story after story of addicts who give in to their addiction, knowing what a terrible thing they are doing to themselves and their families. Watching them, I understand the power of evil in this world, evil they want above all else to resist but cannot. Yet those moments of weakness are the very moments when they are most likely to turn to God, to cry out in desperation. They have failed, terribly. Now what? Can they get up and walk again, or will they stay paralyzed? Through the grace of God, some of them do get up. In fact, I've decided there is one key in determining whether individual drug addicts can be cured: if they deeply believe they are a *forgivable* child of God. Not a failure-free child of God, a forgivable one."

David, who directs a hospice for AIDS patients, agreed. "I have met no more spiritual people than the men in this house who face death and know that in some ways they brought the disease on themselves. Most got the HIV virus through drug use and sexual promiscuity. Their lives are defined by failure. I cannot explain it, but these men have a spirituality, a connection with God, that I've seen nowhere else."

Francis de Sales wrote, "Now the greater our knowledge of our own misery, the more profound will be our confidence in the goodness and mercy of God, for mercy and misery are so closely connected that the one cannot be exercised without the other." De Sales decried those who stumbled and then wallowed in their wretchedness: "How miserable I am! I am fit for nothing!" True followers of God quietly humble themselves and rise again courageously.

Reaching for the Invisible God (193 – 94)

◆

Serve or Die

Dr. Paul Brand told me of his most memorable visitor to Vellore, India, where he directed a leprosy hospital. One day a French friar named Pierre showed up. Over the next few weeks he stayed with the Brands and told them his life's story. Born into a noble family, he had served in the French Parliament until he became disillusioned with the slow pace of political change. After World War II, thousands of homeless beggars lived in the streets. Pierre could not tolerate the endless debates by noblemen and politicians while so many street people starved outside.

During an unusually harsh winter, many of the Parisian beggars froze to death. Pierre resigned his post and became a Catholic friar to work among them. He concluded his only recourse was to organize the beggars themselves. He taught them to do menial tasks better. They divided into teams to scour the city for bottles and rags. Next, he led them to build a warehouse from discarded bricks and then start a business in which they sorted and processed vast quantities of used bottles from hotels and businesses. Finally, Pierre inspired each beggar by giving him responsibility to help another beggar poorer than himself. The project caught fire, and in a few years an organization called Emmaus was founded.

But now the organization was facing a point of crisis. After years of this work, there were no beggars left in Paris. "I must find somebody for my beggars to help!" he declared. "If I don't find people worse off than my beggars, this movement could turn inward. They'll become a powerful, rich organization, and the whole spiritual impact will be lost. They'll have no one to serve."

At a leprosy colony in India, five thousand miles away, Abbé Pierre found at last the solution. He met hundreds of leprosy patients, many from the Untouchable caste, worse off in every way than his former beggars. As he met them, his face would break into a huge grin. Returning to his beggars in France, he mobilized them to build a ward at the hospital in Vellore. "No, no, it is you who have saved us," he told the grateful recipients of his gift in India. "We must serve or we die."

Reaching for the Invisible God (239 – 40)

◇

Downward Surrender

W hoever tries to keep his life will lose it, and whoever loses his life will preserve it," Jesus said, in a statement repeated six times in the Gospels. Jesus' own life bears out that principle, for he experienced the loss as soon as he committed himself to public ministry. Crowds stalked him with ever-increasing demands. Opposition arose. Ultimately he lost his life.

Bernard of Clairveaux set forth four stages of spiritual growth: (1) Loving ourselves for our own sake; (2) Loving God for our own sake, in view of what God does for us; (3) Loving God for God's sake, unselfishly; and (4) Loving ourselves for God's sake, in awareness of God's great love for us. I would add one more, representing the Parent stage of spiritual maturity: Loving others for God's sake.

Christians best influence the world by sacrificial love, the most effective way truly to change a world. Parents express love by staying up all night with sick children, working two jobs to pay school expenses, sacrificing their own desires for the sake of their children's. And every person who follows Jesus learns a similar pattern. God's kingdom gives itself away, in love, for that is precisely what God did for us.

Jesus did not disparage self-love: Love your neighbor *as yourself*, he commanded. Rather, he proposed that the highest fulfillment results from service to others, not narcissism. We develop or "actualize" ourselves in order that we may share those gifts with others less blessed.

Some college students strike out for the wilderness or take up meditation in order to "discover themselves." Jesus suggests that we discover that self not by staring inward but by gazing outward, not through introspection but through acts of love. In the end, Jesus' prediction—"Whoever loses his life will preserve it"—proves true, for the downward surrender leads upward.

Reaching for the Invisible God (244 – 46)

Longsuffering Love

People who struggle with long-term suffering report that a fatigue factor sets in. At first, no matter what the illness, they get a spurt of attention. Cards fill their mailboxes, and flowers fight for space on the countertops. But over time, attention fades.

We are embarrassed and troubled by problems that do not go away. In a book on her own experience, Betsy Burnham reports that with each successive reappearance of her cancer, fewer visitors came to see her. As the illness stretched out, she felt even more vulnerable and afraid, and she also felt more alone. Some Christians seemed resentful that their prayers for healing had gone unanswered, almost as if they blamed her. They lost faith and stayed away, leaving Betsy with guilt and self-hatred to cope with in addition to her pain.

Parents of children with genetic defects echo Betsy's account. A flurry of sympathetic response follows the birth but soon fades. As the parents' needs and emotional difficulties increase, offers of help tend to decrease.

In his list of fruits of the Spirit, Paul included one that we translate with the ancient-sounding word "longsuffering." We would do well to revive that word, and concept, in its most literal form to apply to the problem of long-term pain.

Let me say this carefully, but say it nevertheless. I believe we in the body of Christ are called to show love *when God seems not to*. People in pain, especially those with long-term pain, often have the sensation that God has left them. No one expressed this better than C. S. Lewis in the poignant journal he kept about his wife's death (*A Grief Observed*). He recorded that at the moment of his most profound need, God, who had seemed always available to him, suddenly seemed distant and absent, as if God had slammed a door shut and double-bolted it from the inside.

Sometimes we must voice prayers that the suffering person cannot voice. And in moments of extreme pain or grief, very often God's love can only be perceived through the flesh of ordinary people like you and me. In such a way we can, indeed, function as the body of Jesus Christ.

Helping the Hurting booklet (10 – 11)

◆

Ordinary Healers

Not even God attempted a rationale for suffering in his reply to Job. The great king David, the righteous man Job, and finally even the Son of God reacted to pain much the same as we do. They recoiled from it, thought it horrible, did their best to alleviate it, and finally cried out to God in despair because of it. Personally, I find it discouraging that we can come up with no final, satisfying answer for people in pain.

And yet viewed in another way that nonanswer is surprisingly good news. When I have asked suffering people, "Who helped you?" not one person has mentioned a Ph.D. from Yale Divinity School or a famous philosopher. The kingdom of suffering is a democracy, and we all stand in it or alongside it with nothing but our naked humanity. All of us have the same capacity to help, and that is good news.

No one can package or bottle "the appropriate response to suffering." And words intended for everyone will almost always prove worthless for one individual person. If you go to the sufferers themselves and ask for helpful words, you may find discord. Some recall a friend who cheerily helped distract them from the illness, while others think such an approach insulting. Some want honest, straightforward confrontation; others find such discussion unbearably depressing.

Mainly, such a person needs love, for love instinctively detects what is needed. Jean Vanier, founder of L'Arche movement, says it well: "Wounded people who have been broken by suffering and sickness ask for only one thing: a heart that loves and commits itself to them, a heart full of hope for them."

In fact, the answer to the question, "How do I help those who hurt?" is exactly the same as the answer to the question, "How do I love?" If you asked me for a Bible passage to teach you how to help suffering people, I would point to 1 Corinthians 13 and its eloquent depiction of love. That is what a suffering person needs: love, and not knowledge and wisdom. As is so often his pattern, God uses very ordinary people to bring about healing.

Where Is God When It Hurts? (168)

A Sense of Place

People in a hospital group I visited referred to a process they called "premortem dying." It occurs when well-intentioned relatives and friends look for ways to make the suffering person's last months trouble-free. *Oh, you mustn't do that! I know you've always taken out the garbage, but really, not in your condition. Let me do it.* And then, *Don't burden yourself with balancing the checkbook. It would just create an unnecessary worry for you. I'll take care of it from now on.*

Gradually, inexorably, everything that gives a person a sense of place or a role in life is taken away. A mother encourages her sick single daughter to sell her house and move back home. She does so, and discovers that in the process she has also lost her individual identity. Feelings of worth and value, already precarious because of the illness, slip further away.

Obviously, a very sick person needs to depend on others to cope with practical matters of life. But too easily we can fall into a pattern of removing everything that gives dignity.

Suffering people already question their place in the world. Often they cannot continue working, and the fatigue brought on by illness or treatment makes every action harder. Yet they, like all of us, need to cling to something to remind them that they have a place, that life would not go on without a bump if they simply disappeared, that the checkbook would go unbalanced except for their expert attention. Wise friends and relatives sense the delicate balance between offering help and offering too much help.

We live in a culture that has no natural "place" for sick people. We put them out of sight, behind the walls of hospitals and nursing homes. We make them lie in beds, with nothing to occupy their time but the remote control devices that operate the television sets. We even give them the telling label "invalid" (try pronouncing it a different way: in-*val*-id).

We who are friends and loved ones of sick people must look for ways to help them preserve a sense of place. For some, the answer will consist of very practical acts of service; for others, a structured way of helping other sick people through the same stages.

Helping the Hurting booklet (11 – 14)

◆

Angel to the Dying

Since opening St. Christopher's Hospice in 1967, Cicely Saunders — now *Dame* Cicely, after being so honored by Queen Elizabeth II — has made it possible for 15,000 people to die in the way they choose, without high-tech, artificial postponements. The design of her sixty-two-bed hospice incorporates everything she has learned about care for the dying. "Every person deserves a good death," says Dame Cicely, and she devotes her boundless energy to providing that right for her patients.

Early on Saunders trained in nursing and patient advocacy. Her work in a cancer ward with dying patents supplied a vantage point no nursing school could teach. Cicely found that in crowded, busy modern hospitals, terminal patients died very much alone. She began to sense an inner tug, a vocation to spend her life among the terminally ill.

Saunders qualified as a doctor in 1957, at nearly thirty-nine years of age. Two years later, while reading the devotional book *Daily Light*, she came across the familiar verse from Psalm 37: "Commit thy way unto the Lord; trust also in him; and he shall bring it to pass." It was time to act on her calling. After a full day of meditation in a chapel, she emerged to write up a prospectus on what had been taking shape in her mind for many years. She divided her thoughts into "The Need" and "The Scheme," and with that paper the modern hospice movement was born.

As Cicely Saunders sees it, the community of the dying both receives and gives back benefits. Dying people need the comfort and strength of the church. But the church needs the community of the dying as well: to summon up eternal issues, to teach us to listen, to provide a way of serving Christ by serving others in his name.

"My own hospice vision," she says, "is of a God who shares the journey more deeply than we ever can, with all the solidarity of his sacrificial and forgiving love and the strength of his powerlessness; a God who does not prevent the hard things that happen in this free and dangerous world but who instead shares them with us all."

"Angel to the Dying," *Christianity Today*,
December 17, 1990 (22 – 24)

◇

Our Real Struggle

I had a conversation with Bob Seiple, then president of the relief agency World Vision, after he returned from Rwanda at the time of the massacres there in 1994. Standing on a bridge, he had watched thousands of bodies float beneath him on a river scarlet with their blood. Hutu tribesmen had hacked to death with machetes almost a million Tutsis—their neighbors, their fellow parishioners, their school classmates—for reasons no one could begin to explain.

Seiple seemed badly shaken. "It was a crisis of faith for me," he said. "There are no categories to express such horror. Someone used the word *bestiality*—no, that dishonors the beasts. Animals kill for food, not for pleasure. They kill one or two prey at a time, not a million of their own species for no reason at all."

As I listened to Seiple, I too could think of no force in nature to explain what was happening in Rwanda, only a malevolent force from supernature—the same kind of inexplicable force that caused Hitler to divert badly needed resources during wartime in order to carry out genocide against the Jews.

We in the U.S. have recently seen another spiritual power at work, the force of greed, which impelled the directors of companies to siphon off millions of dollars in profits while allowing the companies to go bankrupt, wiping out the retirement savings of thousands of hardworking employees. When Jesus encountered a similar power, which drove people to build beautiful palaces and vast barns while some in Palestine lived as slaves—in other words, when Jesus encountered the first-century equivalent of greedy CEOs—he recognized it as a spiritual power and gave it the name of the god Mammon.

I have not changed my belief in spiritual powers because I learned anything new about this world. I simply learned to recast what I already knew in the language of the Bible. I came to accept the apostle Paul's assertion that our real struggle is waged against forces we cannot see. Much more is happening on this planet than is visible to the human eye.

Rumors of Another World (183–84)

◆

Profaning Money

Jesus saw money as something to guard against, not desire. "Where your treasure is, there your heart will be also," he said—an alarming thought to those of us who live in societies loaded with tangible treasure. He portrayed money as a negative spiritual force, a god named Mammon that pits itself against the kingdom of heaven. "You cannot serve both God and Money," he said bluntly.

As a defense, Jesus challenged us to do whatever it takes to break free of money's power, even to the extent of giving it all away. I remember reading *Money and Power*, Jacques Ellul's provocative book about money, and being shocked by some of his suggestions. We must find ways to profane money, he said, to demagnetize its spiritual force, even if that means handing wads of bills to strangers or throwing them into the air on a busy street. Such a notion seemed to me preposterous and almost obscene—which gave me a clue that I had succumbed to the spiritual force of Mammon. I considered its waste a form of desecration.

At the time, I thought I was using money to serve the kingdom of heaven. I came to see that I had missed the point of giving. I worried about exactly how much I should give, and to whom. I sought out the charities that offered the best return, the most result per dollar invested, and of course I expected a tax-deductible receipt and a thank you note for my efforts. That kind of uptight, calculated giving is the opposite of what the Bible teaches. The apostle Paul mentions a hilarious, or cheerful, giver, and the hilarity comes because the act of giving is at its core irrational. It destroys the aura of worth surrounding money. By instinct we hoard money in steel vaults and secret caches; giving flagrantly sets it free, turning grace loose in a world of competition and balance sheets.

Rumors of Another World (210 – 11)

Loosening the Grip

Living in downtown Chicago, I became aware of needs around me that fit no rational giving scheme. My wife, who was working among the low-income elderly, often came home with heartrending stories of senior citizens who were about to be evicted or have their electricity turned off. A hundred dollars or so would see them through another month—but try to get a government bureaucracy or even a closely audited charity to respond quickly to such a need. We began putting fifty- and hundred-dollar bills in envelopes and slipping them under the door, with an anonymous note that said simply, "From someone who cares."

It seemed like sacrilege the first few times, to give with no assurance the money would be well used and with no tax receipt making it worth our while. Those feelings betrayed the real sacrilege, I soon realized. I had adopted a rational economic viewpoint that exalted money as the supreme value, and I needed to profane it and break its hold over me, as Jacques Ellul had suggested in his book on money. I needed to see money for what it is, a loan that God has entrusted to me for the purpose of investing in the kingdom of heaven, the only kingdom that pays eternal dividends. Give to the needy in secret, said Jesus. "Then your Father, who sees what is done in secret, will reward you."

I also needed to learn to laugh at the somber actors on television who warn me what may happen if I don't choose the right mutual fund or buy the right insurance policy. I needed to treat *Fortune* magazine and the money programs on CNN as if they were pornographic, for I recognized they had that effect on me. Money works on me much like lust and pride: it holds me in a pythonic grip and attracts me to fantasies it can never fulfill. And, like lust and pride, money presents an arena of personal struggle that I will never "get over." It is a force with a personality. It is, in truth, a god, and Jesus called it that.

Rumors of Another World (211)

◆

Vast Silence

We need look no further than the Bible for examples of God's absence. "You have hidden your face from us," said Isaiah. "Why are you like a stranger in the land, like a traveler who stays only a night?" demanded Jeremiah. Any relationship involves times of closeness and times of distance, and in a relationship with God, no matter how intimate, the pendulum will swing from one side to the other.

I experienced the sense of abandonment just as I was making progress spiritually, advancing beyond childish faith to the point where I felt I could help others. Suddenly, the darkness descended. For an entire year, my prayers seemed to go nowhere; I had no confidence that God was listening. No one had prepared me with "the ministry of absence." I found myself turning for comfort to poets like George Herbert, frank about his times of spiritual desolation, and also Gerard Manley Hopkins, who wrote:

> God, though to Thee our psalm we raise
> No answering voice comes from the skies;
> To Thee the trembling sinner prays
> But no forgiving voice replies;
> Our prayer seems lost in desert ways,
> Our hymn in the vast silence dies.

My prayers too seemed lost, my hymns dead in the vast silence. When no "techniques" or spiritual disciplines seemed to work for me, in desperation I bought a book of hours used in high-church liturgy. Throughout that year I simply read the prayers and Bible passages, offering them to God as my prayers. "I have no words of my own," I told God. "Maybe I have no faith. Please accept these prayers of others as the only ones I can offer right now. Accept their words in place of my own."

I now look back on that period of absence as an important growth time, for in some ways I had pursued God more earnestly than ever before. I came away with renewed faith and an appreciation of God's presence as gift rather than entitlement.

Reaching for the Invisible God (242 – 43)

◆

Waiting

I like to see the results of my labors. I work on an article and several months later it appears in print. I climb a mountain and reach the summit. Prayer operates by different rules, God's rules. We do it in secret, so that no one notices the effort, and the results — God's results, not ours — come in surprising ways, often long after we expected them. Prayer means opening myself to God and not limiting God through my own preconceptions. In sum, prayer means letting God be God.

Many prayers in the Bible come out of the act of waiting. Jacob waiting seven years for a wife and then seven more years after being tricked by her father. The Israelites waiting four centuries for deliverance, and Moses waiting four decades for the call to lead them, then four more decades for a Promised Land he would not enter. Mary and Joseph, Elizabeth and Zechariah, Anna, Simeon waiting like most Jews for a Messiah.

God, who is timeless, requires of us a mature faith that may, as it did for many of these, involve delays that seem like trials. Patience is one sign of that maturity, a quality that can develop only through the passage of time.

Children want things *now*: "Are we there yet?" ... "But I want dessert now!" ... "Now can we open our presents?" ... "Is my time-out over?" In contrast, lovers learn to wait. Medical students wait through training. Parents wait in hopes that the prodigal will return. We wait for what is worth waiting for, and in the process learn patience.

"My soul waits for the Lord more than watchmen wait for the morning," wrote one of the psalmists. The picture comes to mind of a watchman counting the minutes for his shift to be over. I pray for the patience to endure times of trial, to keep anticipating, keep hoping, keep believing. I pray for the patience to be patient.

Prayer: Does It Make Any Difference? (296 – 97)

◆

Without Ceasing

I met with one of the few people I know personally who takes prayer as seriously as did Martin Luther, George Müller, and other giants of prayer. Marcia has a designated prayer closet in which she follows the interior-castle model set forth by Teresa of Avila. Yet when I asked her about prayer, to my surprise she talked about all the other hours in her day:

"Conversation can be a prayer. Think of the Samaritan woman at the well, talking with Jesus about water and mountains and Jerusalem—wasn't that a prayer? I like to think of my conversations with people as prayer. I speak to Jesus within a person. I ask, Lord, let this lunch or tea or whatever be a prayer. When I read the Bible, that's a prayer. I don't read Psalm 73, I *pray* Psalm 73. I willingly refer my actions to God, and in so doing they become a prayer.

"I'm a painter. I pray as I paint, and my painting becomes a kind of prayer. If someone asks me for help in prayer, I tell them to find what they most *enjoy* and do that, only do it for the glory of God. For you it may be writing or climbing a mountain. Ask God to remind you, as you do it, that you're doing it for him. Often as I'm doing what I enjoy, specific requests come to mind. I pray instantly, as soon as something comes to mind, and I trust God to bring it to mind.

"Spending time with God is what's important. We spend the time anyway. Why not recognize that we spend it with God, and then act like it?"

Listening to Marcia, I realized how easily I compartmentalize my life. I had the notion of prayer as a spiritual act oddly unrelated to the rest of my life. Out of a sense of duty I would put in the time, sometimes gladly and sometimes not, then get on with the real business of the day. I have since come to see prayer as something like a warm-up exercise, not an end in itself but a means to an end: to increase awareness of God at all other times.

Prayer: Does It Make Any Difference? (314 – 15)

Inappropriate Prayers

The New Testament emphasizes God's intimate involvement with every detail of our lives. "Even the very hairs of your head are all numbered," Jesus assured his listeners. Frankly, I find it hard to comprehend such sweeping claims of God's personal interest, let alone apply them to prayer. As one friend said to me, "I cannot imagine *anyone*, much less God, caring that much about my life. God has far more to worry about than my petty concerns."

Some people, like my friend, muzzle their prayers because of a poor self-image, while others do so out of a sense of piety. The mystic Meister Eckhart refused to "pray the rich and loving God for such trifles" as recovery from an illness. Catherine of Genoa took pride in never asking anything for herself in thirty-five years of constant prayer. Sometimes I feel tempted to follow their example, to squelch all prayers that might seem selfish or inappropriate. Then I turn again to prayers in the Bible.

The Bible records with approval all sorts of "selfish" prayers: an infertile woman who wants a baby, a widow who needs more cooking oil, a soldier who begs for victory in battle. People pray for rain during a drought, for vengeance on their enemies. The Lord's Prayer itself includes a plea for daily bread. Paul prays about safe travels, prosperous work, relief from a physical ailment, and boldness in preaching. James urges prayers for wisdom and physical healing.

After reviewing the prayers contained in the Bible, I have stopped worrying about inappropriate prayers. If God counts on prayer as a primary way to relate to me, I may block potential intimacy by devising a test for appropriateness and filtering out prayers that may not meet the criteria. According to Jesus, nothing is too trivial. Everything about me — my thoughts, my motives, my choices, my moods — attracts God's interest.

Prayer: Does It Make Any Difference? (317 – 18)

Closing the Gulf

Jesus saw like no one else the anguish and injustice, the terror, of this planet. Shouldn't such awareness have filled his every waking hour and robbed him of sleep at night? Shouldn't it have shaken his very soul?

No, Jesus left the global concerns in the care of his Father and spent his time instead among nobodies: tax collectors, fishermen, widows, prostitutes, outcasts. Speaking to the Father—praying—notes Helmut Thielicke, was more important to Jesus than speaking to crowds. "And that's why he has time for persons; for all time is in the hands of his Father. And that too is why peace and not unrest goes out from him. For God's faithfulness already spans the world like a rainbow: he does not need to build it; he needs only to walk beneath it."

Those of us who follow Jesus also believe that God's faithfulness spans the world like a rainbow, with Jesus himself offering one of the best proofs of that faithfulness. Times will come that test such belief to the limit. When I face those times, I cry a prayer of desperation, a thrust in the dark in hopes of regaining trust in the big picture, a renewed glimpse of God's point of view. And when things are going well, ironically, I have to work even harder to keep the conversation going, to believe that God cares about the details of my life.

I pray in astonished belief that God desires an ongoing relationship. I pray in trust that the act of prayer is God's designated way of closing the vast gulf between infinity and me. I pray in order to put myself in the stream of God's healing work on earth. I pray as I breathe—because I can't help it. Prayer is hardly a perfect form of communication, for I, an imperfect, material being who lives on an imperfect, material planet am reaching out for a perfect, spiritual Being. Some prayers go unanswered, a sense of God's presence ebbs and flows, and often I sense more mystery than resolution. Nevertheless I keep at it, believing with Paul that "now I know in part; then I shall know fully, even as I am fully known."

Prayer: Does It Make Any Difference? (326 – 27)

Grace in Action

Grace means that no mistake we make in life disqualifies us from God's love. It means that no person is beyond redemption, no human stain beyond cleansing. We live in a world that judges people by their behavior and requires criminals, debtors, and moral failures to live with the consequences. Even the church finds it difficult to forgive those who fall short.

Grace is irrational, unfair, unjust, and only makes sense if I believe in another world governed by a merciful God who always offers another chance. "Amazing Grace," a rare hymn that in recent times climbed the charts of popular music, holds out the promise that God judges people not for what they have been but what they could be, not by their past but by their future. John Newton, a gruff and bawdy slave trader, "a wretch like me," wrote that hymn after being transformed by the power of amazing grace.

When the world sees grace in action, it falls silent. Nelson Mandela taught the world a lesson in grace when, after emerging from prison after twenty-seven years and being elected president of South Africa, he asked his jailer to join him on the inauguration platform. He then appointed Archbishop Desmond Tutu to head an official government panel with a daunting name, the Truth and Reconciliation Commission. Mandela sought to defuse the natural pattern of revenge that he had seen in so many countries where one oppressed race or tribe took control from another.

For the next two-and-a-half years, South Africans listened to reports of atrocities coming out of the TRC hearings. The rules were simple: if a white policeman or army officer voluntarily faced his accusers, confessed his crime, and fully acknowledged his guilt, he could not be tried and punished for that crime. Hard-liners grumbled about the obvious injustice of letting criminals go free, but Mandela insisted that the country needed healing even more than it needed justice.

[Continued on August 26]

Rumors of Another World (222–23)

◆

Beyond Justice

[Continued from August 25]

At one TRC hearing, a policeman named van de Broek recounted an incident when he and other officers shot an eighteen-year-old boy and burned the body. Eight years later van de Broek returned to the same house and seized the boy's father. The wife was forced to watch as policemen bound her husband on a woodpile, poured gasoline over his body, and ignited it.

The courtroom grew hushed as the elderly woman who had lost first her son and then her husband was given a chance to respond. "What do you want from Mr. van de Broek?" the judge asked. She said she wanted van de Broek to go to the place where they burned her husband's body and gather up the dust so she could give him a decent burial. His head down, the policeman nodded agreement.

Then she added a further request, "Mr. van de Broek took all my family away from me, and I still have a lot of love to give. Twice a month, I would like for him to come to the ghetto and spend a day with me so I can be a mother to him. And I would like Mr. van de Broek to know that he is forgiven by God, and that I forgive him too. I would like to embrace him so he can know my forgiveness is real."

Spontaneously, some in the courtroom began singing "Amazing Grace" as the elderly woman made her way to the witness stand, but van de Broek did not hear the hymn. He had fainted, overwhelmed.

Justice was not done in South Africa that day, nor in the entire country during months of agonizing procedures by the TRC. Something beyond justice took place. "Do not be overcome by evil, but overcome evil with good," said Paul. Nelson Mandela and Desmond Tutu understood that when evil is done, one response alone can overcome the evil. Revenge perpetuates the evil. Justice punishes it. Evil is overcome by good only if the injured party absorbs it, refusing to allow it to go any further. And that is the pattern of otherworldly grace that Jesus showed in his life and death.

Rumors of Another World (223 – 24)

◆

Widening the Circle

On a trip to Russia in 1991 I participated with a group of Christians who actually prayed with officers in the KGB. "We invited you because we need to learn the meaning of the word *repentance*," said the presiding colonel. After we left, he proceeded to distribute two million copies of the New Testament to Russian army troops. With shame I realized that during the Cold War not once had I prayed for Russian leaders. Perceiving them as mere enemies, I never took the step of bringing them before God and asking for God's point of view.

What about Islamist radicals who now oppose the West with violence? What effect might it have if every Christian church adopted the name of one al-Qaeda member and prayed faithfully for that person?

More, should we be searching our souls prayerfully for the very symptoms in our society that arouse such opposition in the first place? The evening of September 11, 2001, my church filled with members who spontaneously assembled with no prior announcement of a service. For a brief time Americans turned inward. Prayer in awareness of enemies, not to mention prayer *for* enemies, offers an opportunity for self-reflection; in a strange way, our enemies help to define us as much as our friends do.

In a letter to his brother, C. S. Lewis mentioned that he prayed every night for the people he was most tempted to hate, with Hitler, Stalin, and Mussolini heading the list. In another letter he wrote that as he prayed for them, he meditated on how his own cruelty might have blossomed into something like theirs. He remembered that Christ died for them as much as for him, and that he himself was not "so different from these ghastly creatures."

Almost everyone has an enemies list. For some in the United States it may include fundamentalists and right-wing Republicans; for others, secular humanists and the ACLU. Elsewhere, Christians face outright persecution from governments and religions. True followers of Jesus, however, hold in common his stunning command to love our enemies and pray for those who mistreat us. In so doing, we join together to extend the widening circle of God's love to those who may experience it in no other way.

Prayer: Does It Make Any Difference? (309 – 12)

◆

Three Questions

Is God unfair? Is God silent? Is God withdrawn? Exodus and Numbers taught me that quick solutions to those three questions may not solve the underlying problems of disappointment with God. The Israelites, though exposed to the bright, unshaded light of God's presence, were as fickle a people as have ever lived. Ten different times on the melancholy pathless plains of the Sinai they rose up against God. Even at the very border of the Promised Land, with all its bounty stretching out before them, they were still keening for the "good old days" of slavery in Egypt.

These dismal results may provide insight into why God does not intervene more directly today. Some Christians long for a world well-stocked with miracles and spectacular signs of God's presence. I hear wistful sermons on the parting of the Red Sea and the ten plagues and the daily manna in the wilderness, as if the speakers yearn for God to unleash power like that today. But the follow-the-dots journey of the Israelites should give us pause. Would a burst of miracles nourish faith? Not the kind of faith God seems interested in, evidently. The Israelites give ample proof that signs may only addict us to signs, not to God.

True, the Israelites were a primitive people emerging out of slavery. But the biblical accounts have a disturbingly familiar ring to them. The Israelites tended to behave, in Frederick Buechner's phrase, "just like everybody else, only more so."

I came away from my study of them both surprised and confused: surprised to learn how little difference it made in people's lives when three major reasons for disappointment with God—unfairness, silence, and hiddenness—were removed; confused by the questions stirred up about God's actions on earth. Has God changed, by pulling back, withdrawing?

Disappointment with God (48)

◆

Unfiltered Sunlight

I have often longed for God to act in a direct, closeup manner. But in the Israelites' dreary stories of failure I can perceive certain "disadvantages" to God acting so directly. One problem they encountered immediately was the lack of personal freedom. For the Israelites to live in proximity to a holy God, nothing — not sex, menstruation, the content of clothing fabric, or dietary habits — could fall outside the purview of God's laws. Being a "chosen people" had a cost. Just as God found it nearly impossible to live among sinful people, the Israelites found it nearly impossible to live with a holy God in their midst.

Listen to the words of the worshipers themselves: "We will die! We are lost, we are all lost! Anyone who even comes near the tabernacle of the Lord will die." And again, "Let us not hear the voice of the Lord our God nor see this great fire anymore, or we will die."

Once, as an experiment, the great scientist Isaac Newton stared at the image of the sun reflected in a mirror. The brightness burned into his retina, and he suffered temporary blindness. Even after he hid for three days behind closed shutters, still the bright spot would not fade from his vision. "I used all means to divert my imagination from the sun," he writes, "but if I thought upon him I presently saw his picture though I was in the dark." If he had stared a few minutes longer, Newton might have permanently lost all vision. The chemical receptors that govern eyesight cannot withstand the full force of unfiltered sunlight.

There is a parable in Isaac Newton's experiment, and it helps illustrate what the Israelites ultimately learned from the wilderness wanderings. They had attempted to live with the Lord of the Universe visibly present in their midst; but, in the end, out of all the thousands who had so gladly fled Egypt, only two survived God's presence. If you can barely endure candlelight, how can you gaze at the sun?

"Who of us can dwell with the consuming fire?" asked the prophet Isaiah. Is it possible that we should be grateful for God's hiddenness, rather than disappointed?

Disappointment with God (73 – 75)

◇

Ancient Prophets, Modern Questions

I had always misread the prophets—when I bothered to read them at all. I had seen them as finger-wagging, fusty old men who, like Elijah, called down judgment on the pagans. I discovered to my surprise that the ancient prophets' writings actually sound the most "modern" of any part of the Bible. They deal with the very same themes that hang like a cloud over our century: the silence of God, the seeming sovereignty of evil, the unrelieved suffering in the world. The prophets' questions are, in fact, modern questions: God's unfairness, silence, hiddenness.

More passionately than anyone in history, the prophets of Israel gave voice to the feeling of disappointment with God. Why do godless nations flourish? they asked. Why is there such poverty and depravity in the world? Why so few miracles? Where are you, God? Why do you always forget us? Why do you forsake us so long? Show yourself; break your silence. For God's sake, literally, ACT!

There was the urbane voice of Isaiah, an aristocrat and adviser to kings, in personal style as far removed from Elijah as Winston Churchill was from Gandhi. "Truly you are a God who hides himself," Isaiah said.

Jeremiah loudly protested the failure of "success theology." In his day, prophets were being tossed in dungeons and wells, and even sawed in half. Jeremiah compared God to a weakling, "a man taken by surprise ... a warrior powerless to save."

Like all Israelites, the prophets had been raised on victory stories. As children they had learned how God freed people from slavery, descended to live among them, and carried them into the Promised Land. But now in visions of the future they saw, in slow-motion detail, all those victories being undone. In a stark reversal of the unforgettable scene from Solomon's day, the prophet Ezekiel watched God's glory rise, hover above the temple for a moment, and then vanish.

What Ezekiel saw in a vision, Jeremiah saw in stark reality. Babylonian soldiers entered the temple, looted it, then burned it to the ground. Jeremiah wandered the deserted streets of Jerusalem in a state of shock, like a survivor of Hiroshima staggering through the rubble.

Disappointment with God (85 – 87)

Too Good Not to Be True

No summary of the prophets would be complete apart from one last message: their loud insistence that the world will not end in "universal final defeat," but in joy. Always, the prophets of the Old Testament got around to a word of hope.

Their voices soar like songbirds' when the prophets turn at last to describe the joy beyond the walls of the world. In that final day, God will roll up the earth like a carpet and weave it anew. Wolves and lambs will feed together in the same field, and a lion graze in peace beside an ox.

One day, says Malachi, we will leap like calves released from the stall. There will be no fear then, and no pain. No infants will die; no tears will fall. Among the nations, peace will flow like a river, and armies will melt their weapons into farm tools. No one will complain about the hiddenness of God in that day. God's glory will fill the earth, and the sun will seem dim by contrast.

For the prophets, human history is not an end in itself but a transition time, a parenthesis between Eden and the new heaven and new earth still to be formed by God. Even when everything seems out of control, God remains firmly in control.

Some people find no comfort in the prophets' vision of a future world. "The church has used that line for centuries to justify slavery, oppression, and all manner of injustice," they say. The criticism sticks because the church has abused the prophets' vision. But you will never find that "pie in the sky" rationale in the prophets themselves. They have scathing words about the need to care for widows and orphans and aliens, and to clean up corrupt courts and religious systems. The people of God are not merely to mark time, waiting for God to step in and set right all that is wrong. Rather, they are to model the new heaven and new earth, and by so doing awaken longings for what God will someday bring to pass.

Disappointment with God (98–99)

September

Grace Dispensers

One way in which Jesus' revolution affects me centers on how we are to view "different" people. Jesus' example convicts me today because I sense a subtle shift in the reverse direction. As society unravels and immorality increases, I hear calls from some Christians that we show less mercy and more morality, calls that hark back to the style of the Old Testament.

A phrase used by both Peter and Paul has become one of my favorite images from the New Testament. We are to administer, or "dispense," God's grace, say the two apostles. The image brings to mind one of the old-fashioned "atomizers" women used before the perfection of spray technology. Squeeze a rubber bulb, and droplets of perfume come shooting out of the fine holes at the other end. A few drops suffice for a whole body; a few pumps change the atmosphere in a room. That is how grace should work, I think. It does not convert the entire world or an entire society, but it does enrich the atmosphere.

Now I worry that the prevailing image of Christians has changed from that of a perfume atomizer to a different spray apparatus: the kind used by insect exterminators. *There's a roach!* Pump, spray, pump, spray. *There's a spot of evil!* Pump, spray, pump, spray. Some Christians I know have taken on the task of "moral exterminator" for the evil-infested society around them.

I share a deep concern for our society. I am struck, though, by the alternative power of mercy as demonstrated by Jesus, who came for the sick and not the well, for the sinners and not the righteous. Jesus never countenanced evil, but he did stand ready to forgive it. Somehow, he gained the reputation as a lover of sinners, a reputation that his followers are in danger of losing today. As Dorothy Day put it, "I really only love God as much as I love the person I love the least."

What's So Amazing About Grace? (157 – 58)

◆

Politics of Polarization

People who looked to Jesus as their political savior were constantly befuddled by his choice of companions. He became known as a friend of tax collectors, a group clearly identified with the foreign exploiters, not the exploited. Though he denounced the religious system of his day, he treated a leader like Nicodemus with respect, and though he spoke against the dangers of money and of violence, he showed love and compassion toward a rich young ruler and a Roman centurion.

In short, Jesus honored the dignity of every person, whether he agreed with them or not. He would not found his kingdom on the basis of race or class or other such divisions. Anyone, even a half-breed with five husbands or a thief dying on a cross, was welcome to join his kingdom. The person was more important than any category or label.

I feel convicted by this quality of Jesus every time I get involved in a cause I strongly believe in. How easy it is to join the politics of polarization, to find myself shouting across the picket lines at the "enemy" on the other side. How hard it is to remember that the kingdom of God calls me to love the woman who has just emerged from the abortion clinic (and, yes, even her doctor), the promiscuous person who is dying of AIDS, the wealthy landowner who is exploiting God's creation. If I cannot show love to such people, then I must question whether I have truly understood Jesus' gospel.

A political movement by nature draws lines, makes distinctions, pronounces judgment; in contrast, Jesus' love cuts across lines, transcends distinctions, and dispenses grace. Regardless of the merits of a given issue—whether a pro-life lobby out of the Right or a peace-and-justice lobby out of the Left—political movements risk pulling onto themselves the mantle of power that smothers love. From Jesus I learn that, whatever activism I get involved in, it must not drive out love and humility, or otherwise I betray the kingdom of heaven.

The Jesus I Never Knew (244 – 45)

Shocking Accessibility

My former pastor in Chicago, Bill Leslie, once spoke of the remarkable change of "God drawing near." You need only read the book of Leviticus and then turn to Acts to sense the seismic change. Whereas Old Testament worshipers purified themselves before entering the temple and presented their offerings to God through a priest, in Acts God's followers (good Jews, most of them) were meeting in private homes and addressing God with the informal *Abba*. It was a familiar term of family affection, like "Daddy," and before Jesus no one would have thought of applying such a word to Yahweh, the Sovereign Lord of the Universe. After him, it became the standard word used by early Christians to address God in prayer.

During John F. Kennedy's administration, photographers sometimes captured a winsome scene. Seated around the president's desk in gray suits, cabinet members are debating matters of world consequence, such as the Cuban missile crisis. Meanwhile, a toddler, the two-year-old John-John, crawls atop the huge presidential desk, oblivious to White House protocol and the weighty matters of state. John-John was simply visiting his daddy, and sometimes to his father's delight he would wander into the Oval Office with nary a knock.

That is the kind of shocking accessibility conveyed in Jesus' word *Abba*. God may be the Sovereign Lord of the Universe, but through his Son, God became as approachable as any doting human father. In Romans 8, Paul brings the image of intimacy even closer. God's Spirit lives inside us, he says, and when we do not know what we ought to pray "the Spirit himself intercedes for us with groans that words cannot express."

We need not approach God by a ladder of hierarchy, anxious about cleanliness issues. If God's kingdom had a "No Oddballs Allowed" sign posted, none of us could get in. Jesus came to demonstrate that a perfect and holy God welcomes pleas for help from a widow with two mites and from a Roman centurion and a miserable publican and a thief on a cross. We need only call out "Abba" or, failing that, simply groan. God has come that close.

What's So Amazing About Grace? (156–57)

◆

Why Pray?

As a journalist, I have had occasion to spend time with famous people who make me feel very small. I have interviewed two presidents of the United States, members of the rock band U2, Nobel laureates, television stars, and Olympic athletes. Although I prepare my questions thoroughly in advance, I rarely sleep well the night before and have to fight a case of nerves. I hardly think of these people as mutual friends.

In prayer I am approaching the Creator of all that is, Someone who makes me feel immeasurably small. How can I do anything but fall silent in such presence? More, how can I believe that whatever I say matters to God? If I step back and look at the big picture, I even wonder why such a magnificent, incomprehensible God would bother with a paltry experiment like planet Earth.

A God unbound by our rules of time has the ability to invest in every person on earth. God has, quite literally, all the time in the world for each one of us. The common question, "How can God listen to millions of prayers at once?" betrays an inability to think outside time. Trapped in time, I cannot conceive of infinity. The distance between God and humanity—a distance that no one can grasp—is, ironically, what allows the intimacy.

Jesus, who accepted the constraints of time while living on this planet, understood better than anyone the vast difference between God and human beings. Obviously, he knew of the Father's greatness and at times reflected nostalgically on the big picture, "the glory I had with you before the world began." Yet Jesus did not question the personal concern of God who watches over sparrows and counts the hairs on our heads.

More to the point, Jesus valued prayer enough to spend many hours at the task. If I had to answer the question "Why pray?" in one sentence, it would be, "Because Jesus did." He bridged the chasm between God and human beings. While on earth he became vulnerable, as we are vulnerable; rejected, as we are rejected; and tested, as we are tested. In every case his response was prayer.

Prayer: Does It Make Any Difference? (48 – 50)

Subversive Act

Etty Hillesum, the Jewish girl who kept a journal while at Auschwitz, wrote of an "uninterrupted dialogue" with God. She had epiphanies even in that morally barren place. "Sometimes when I stand in some corner of the camp, my feet planted on Your earth, my eyes raised towards Your Heaven, tears sometimes run down my face, tears of deep emotion and gratitude." She knew the horror. "And I want to be there right in the thick of what people call horror and still be able to say: life is beautiful. Yes, I lie here in a corner, parched and dizzy and feverish and unable to do a thing. Yet I am also with the jasmine and the piece of sky beyond my window."

Prayer is a subversive act performed in a world that constantly calls faith into question. I may have a sense of estrangement, yet by faith I continue to pray and to look for other signs of God's presence. If God were not present at some submolecular level in all of creation, I believe, the world would simply cease to exist. God is present in the beauties and oddities of creation, most of which go undetected by any human observer. God is present in his Son Jesus, who visited the planet and now serves as advocate for those left behind. God is present in the hungry, the homeless, the sick, and the imprisoned, as Jesus claimed in Matthew 25, and we serve God when we serve them. God is present in base communities in Latin America and in house churches that meet surreptitiously in barns in China, as well as in cathedrals and buildings constructed to God's glory. God is present in the Spirit, who groans wordlessly on our behalf and who speaks in a soft voice to all attuned consciences.

I have learned to see prayer not as my way of establishing God's presence, rather as my way of responding to God's presence that is a fact whether or not I can detect it. Whenever I fixate on techniques, or sink into guilt over my inadequate prayers, or turn away in disappointment when a prayer goes unanswered, I remind myself that prayer means keeping company with God who is already present.

Prayer: Does It Make Any Difference? (51 – 53)

Looking Up

I saw the Milky Way in full glory once, while visiting a refugee camp in Somalia, just below the equator. Our galaxy stretched across the canopy of darkness like a highway paved with diamond dust. Since that night, when I lay with warm sand at my back far from the nearest streetlight, the sky has never seemed as empty and the earth never as large.

I had spent all day interviewing relief workers about the megadisaster of the moment. Kurdistan, Rwanda, Sudan, Ethiopia—place-names change, but the spectacle of suffering has a dreary sameness: mothers with shriveled, milkless breasts, babies crying and dying, fathers foraging for firewood in a treeless terrain.

After three days hearing tales of human misery, I could not lift my sights beyond that refugee camp situated in an obscure corner of an obscure country on the Horn of Africa. Until I saw the Milky Way. It abruptly reminded me that the present moment did not comprise all of life. History would go on. Tribes, governments, whole civilizations may rise and fall, trailing disaster in their wake, but I dared not confine my field of vision to the scenes of suffering around me. I needed to look up, to the stars.

"Can you bind the beautiful Pleiades? Can you loose the cords of Orion? Can you bring forth the constellations in the seasons or lead out the Bear with its cubs? Do you know the laws of the heavens? Can you set up God's dominion over the earth?" These questions God asked a man named Job, who, obsessed with his own great pain, had confined his vision to the borders of his itchy skin. Remarkably, God's reminder seemed to help Job. His skin still itched, but Job got a glimpse of other matters God must attend to in a universe of a hundred billion galaxies.

To me, God's speech in the book of Job conveys a tone of gruffness. But perhaps that is its most important message: the Lord of the Universe has a right to gruffness when assailed by one tiny human being, notwithstanding the merits of his complaint. We descendants of Job dare not lose sight of The Big Picture, a sight best glimpsed on moonless, starry nights.

Finding God in Unexpected Places (22 – 23)

◇

Genesis in the Wild

After thirteen years in downtown Chicago, it took a while for me to adjust to our new setting in the Rocky Mountains. I find myself missing the characters in our old neighborhood: the can-collector who called himself Tut Uncommon, the mental patient who sat in a coffee shop all day pretending to smoke an unlit cigarette, the eccentric who roamed Clark Street with a sign that read, "I NEED A WIFE!"

In our new location, we see more animals than people. Elk graze on the hill behind our house, woodpeckers pound on the siding, and a red fox we've named Foster drops by every evening in search of handouts. The other day Foster sat outside the screen door and listened to Garrison Keillor's radio program as I wallpapered my office. He cocked his head quizzically during the bluegrass music, but all in all seemed to enjoy the show.

Not long after the move I began reading through the Bible, starting with Genesis, and soon discovered that the Bible takes on a different tone in new surroundings. I read the creation account during snow season. Mountains gleamed in the morning sunlight, and every Ponderosa pine wore a mantle of pure, crystalline white. It was easy to imagine the joy of original creation, a time when, as God later described to Job, "the morning stars sang together and all the angels shouted for joy."

That same week, however, a loud thump interrupted my reading. A small bird, a pine siskin with a notched tail and yellow chevron stripes on each wing, had crashed into the window. It lay stomach-down on a clump of snow, gasping for breath, with bright red drops of blood spilling from its beak. For twenty minutes it lay there, its head nodding as if in drowsiness, until finally it made one last fluttering effort to rise, then dropped its head into the snow and died.

As tragedies go, I had witnessed a minor one. On the noon news I heard of slaughter in the Middle East and bloodshed in Africa. Somehow, though, a single bird's death, enacted just across the windowpane, brought home the gravity of my reading for that day: it captured in miniature the chasmic change between Genesis 2 and 3, between paradise and fallen creation.

Finding God in Unexpected Places (30 – 31)

◇

After the Fall

Genesis 2 includes an editorial comment, one I had never before noticed. In a remarkable scene, God parades the many animals before Adam "to see what he would name them." What a strange new sensation for omnipotence! The Creator of the universe in all its vast array assumes the role of spectator, waiting "to see" what Adam would do.

We humans have been granted "the dignity of causation," said Blaise Pascal, and the next few chapters of Genesis prove causation to be both dignity and burden. In short order, human beings master the basics of family life, agriculture, music, and tool making. But they also master the art of murder, fornication, and other deeds drearily characteristic of the species. Before long, God "regrets" his decision to create: "The Lord was grieved that he had made man on the earth, and his heart was filled with pain" (6:6).

Throughout the Old Testament, God seems to alternate between Spectator and Participant. At times, when blood cries out from the ground, when injustice grows intolerable, when evil overruns all constraints, God acts—decisively, even violently. Mountains smoke, the ground yawns open, people die. The New Testament, though, shows the God who selflessly shared the dignity of causation by descending to become its Victim. The One who had the right to destroy the world—and had nearly done so once in Noah's day—chose instead to love the world, at any cost.

I sometimes wonder how hard it has been for God *not* to act in history. How must it feel to see the glories of creation—the rain forests, the whales, the elephants—obliterated one by one? How must it feel to see the Jews themselves nearly annihilated? To lose a Son? What is the cost of God's self-restraint?

I had always thought of the Fall in terms of its effect on us humans, namely, the penalties outlined in Genesis 3. This time I was struck by its effect on God. The Bible devotes only two chapters to the glories of original creation. All that follows describes the agonizing course of re-creation.

Finding God in Unexpected Places (31 – 32)

The Great Divide

In an irony of history, Islam has now co-opted the word *martyr*. Early Christians prevailed over Rome because they opted for eternal rewards instead of mere physical survival. They refused to renounce their faith, and the blood of the martyrs became the seed of the church. (A key difference: the Christians were dying at the hands of Rome, not killing anyone else.)

Nowadays you hear very little talk in the West about eternal rewards and much talk about techniques to keep death at bay. Young Arabs who study here come away impressed with, and often scandalized by, how much energy we invest in the physical life. Scout the magazine racks at a local drug store sometime, counting the titles devoted to body-building, diet, fashion, and naked women—all emblems of the prominence we give to materiality.

Puritanical is another Christian word co-opted by Islamic societies. While fighting in the two gulf wars, for the first time in recent memory U.S. soldiers had to get by without alcohol and *Playboy*, in deference to the strict Islamic code in the staging nations. Few of them realized, however, that the difference in moral standards between Islam and the West is philosophical, not just cultural.

In determining morality, American society tends to apply the bottom-line principle, "Does it hurt anyone else?" Thus pornography is legal, but not if it involves explicit violence or child molestation. You can get legally drunk as long as you do not break a neighbor's window or drive a car, endangering others. Violence on television is okay because everyone knows the characters are just acting.

This yardstick of morality betrays our implicit materialism. Whereas we define "hurt" in the most physical terms, Islamic societies see it in more spiritual terms. In that deeper sense, what could be more harmful than pornography, or violence-as-entertainment, or even the cynical depiction of banal evil on television soap operas? It is from this vantage point that the U.S. has gained its reputation as "The Great Satan."

Finding God in Unexpected Places (87–88)

Learning from the Clash

Lamin Sanneh is a rarity: a native of Gambia, West Africa, he grew up Muslim and then as a teenager decided to convert to Christianity. Ironically, the liberal Methodist missionary to whom he announced his decision reacted with embarrassment, not joy, and asked the young man to reconsider. Sanneh did reconsider, felt "inexorably driven" to the gospel, and talked the missionary into baptizing him.

To compound the ironies, Sanneh proceeded to earn a doctorate in Islamic history even as he studied Christian theology. Throughout his spiritual pilgrimage he kept up close ties with his Muslim family. A professor first at Harvard, then at Yale, Sanneh brings singular qualifications to interfaith dialogue between Christians and Muslims.

Sanneh urges Western Christians to move past the guilt of colonialism and the Crusades. The global picture has changed, after all. Seventy-five thousand people a day become Christians, two-thirds of whom live in Africa. These buoyant new believers experience the gospel as good news.

At the same time, Christians in Africa and Asia are confronting a newly resurgent and sometimes militant Islam. Repulsed by the decadence and rampant secularism of the West, Muslims have their own evangelism agenda. In Iran, Egypt, and Palestine, moderates are losing out to religious zealots who want to impose a harsh version of Shari'ah law.

When he addresses Muslims, Sanneh cautions them to consider lessons learned by the medieval Christian church. Ally religion too closely to the state, and you open your faith to corruption and abuse of power. Christian experiments with church-state blending, whether in Geneva under Calvin, Britain under Cromwell, or Spain and Latin America under the Inquisition, may have worked for a time but inevitably provoked a backlash.

Christians and Muslims face opposite challenges. We in the West have something to learn from cultures that do not push religion to the margins, that see faith as affecting all of life, that look to religious leaders for guidance on societal and ethical issues.

Meanwhile, Islamic nations have something to learn from the Christian West, which has found liberal democracy to be the best way to protect minorities' rights in a world that is becoming increasingly multicultural. Not to learn those lessons leads to disaster, as is playing out in the "clash of civilizations" right now.

"Back Page" column, *Christianity Today,* July 2007 (64)

❖

Fueling Relief

When we finally got the clearance to drive through the checkpoints, two weeks after the World Trade Center attacks, the street was lined with New Yorkers—*New Yorkers!*—waving banners with simple messages. "We love you. You're our heroes. God bless you. Thank you." The workers were running on that support as their vehicles ran on fuel. They had so little good news in a day. They faced a mountainously depressing task of removing tons and tons of twisted steel, compacted dirt, smashed equipment, broken glass. But every time they drove past the barricades, they faced a line of fans cheering them on, like the tunnel of cheerleaders that football players run through, reminding them that an entire nation appreciated their service. In a Salvation Army van with lights flashing, we attracted some of the loudest cheers of all.

Moises Serrano, the Salvation Army officer leading us, was Incident Director for the city. He had been on the job barely a month when the planes hit. He worked thirty-six straight hours and slept four, forty hours and slept six, forty more hours and slept six. Then he took a day off. His assistant had an emotional breakdown early on, in the same van I was riding in, and may never recover.

Many of the Salvationists I met hailed from Florida, the hurricane crews who keep fully stocked canteens and trucks full of basic supplies. When the Manhattan buildings fell, they mobilized all those trucks and drove them to New York. The crew director told me, "To tell you the truth, I came up here expecting to deal with Yankees, if you know what I mean. Instead, it's all smiles and thank yous."

I came to appreciate the cheerful toughness of the Salvation Army. These soldiers worked in the morgue and served on the front lines. Over the years, though, they had developed an inner strength based on discipline, on community, and above all on a clear vision of whom they were serving. The Salvation Army may have a hierarchy of command, but every soldier knows he or she is performing for an audience of One. As one told me, Salvationists serve in order to earn the ultimate accolade from God himself: "Well done, thy good and faithful servant."

Finding God in Unexpected Places (69 – 71)

Oasis at Ground Zero

Salvation Army representatives would certainly counsel you and pray with you if you wanted, and at Ground Zero the Salvationists in the shiny red "Chaplain" jackets were sought after for just that reason. Mainly, though, they were there to assist with more basic human needs: to wash out eyes stinging from smoke, and provide Blistex for parched lips and foot inserts for boots walking across hot metal. They operated hydration stations and snack canteens. They offered a place to rest, and freshly cooked chicken courtesy of Tyson's. The day I arrived, they distributed 1500 phone cards for the workers to use in calling home. Every day they served 7500 meals. They offered an oasis of compassion in a wilderness of rubble.

I had studied the maps in newspapers, but no two-dimensional representation could capture the scale of destruction. For about eight square blocks, buildings were deserted, their windows broken, jagged pieces of steel jutting out from floors high above the street. Thousands of offices equipped with faxes, phones, and computers, sat vacant, coated in debris. On September 11, people were sitting there punching keys, making phone calls, grabbing a cup of coffee to start the day, and suddenly it must have seemed like the world was coming to an end.

I studied the faces of the workers, uniformly grim. I didn't see a single smile at Ground Zero. How could you smile in such a place? It had nothing to offer but death and destruction, a monument to the worst that human beings can do to each other.

I saw three booths set up in a vacant building across from the WTC site: Police Officers for Christ, Firemen for Christ, and Sanitation Workers for Christ. (That last one is a charity I'd like to support.) Salvation Army chaplains had told me that the police and fire had asked for two prayer services a day, conducted on the site. The Red Cross, a nonsectarian organization, had asked if the Salvationists would mind staffing it. "Are you kidding? That's what we're here for!"

Finding God in Unexpected Places (71 – 72)

◇

The Rejected One

Japanese novelist Shusaku Endo's story reads like the plot of one of his novels. As a child in Manchuria he had lived as an alien, a despised Japanese occupier. Returning to Japan and converting to Catholicism along with his mother, he suffered once again the anguish of an alien. The Christian church comprised less than one percent of the population. Classmates bullied him for his association with a Western religion. World War II intensified this sense of estrangement: Endo had always looked to the West as his spiritual homeland, but these were the people now vaporizing the cities of Japan.

After the war he traveled to France to study French Catholic novelists such as François Mauriac and George Bernanos. Yet as one of the first Japanese overseas exchange students, and the only one in Lyons, he was spurned this time on account of race, not religion. The Allies had cranked out a steady stream of anti-Japanese propaganda, and Endo found himself the target of racial abuse from fellow Christians. "Slanty-eyed gook," some called him.

Before returning to Japan from his studies in Europe, Endo visited Palestine in order to research the life of Jesus, and while there he made a transforming discovery: Jesus too knew rejection. More, Jesus' life was defined by rejection. His neighbors laughed at him, his family questioned his sanity, his closest friends betrayed him, and his fellow citizens traded his life for that of a common criminal. Throughout his ministry, Jesus purposely moved among the rejected.

This new insight into Jesus hit Endo with the force of revelation. From the faraway vantage point of Japan he had viewed Christianity as a triumphant, Constantinian faith. He had studied the Holy Roman Empire and the glittering Crusades, had admired the grand cathedrals of Europe, had dreamed of living in a nation where one could be a Christian without disgrace. Now, studying the Bible in its homeland, he saw that Jesus himself had not avoided "dis-grace." Jesus himself came as the Suffering Servant, as depicted by the prophet Isaiah: "Despised and rejected by men, a man of sorrows, and familiar with suffering. Like one from whom men hide their faces." Surely this Jesus, if anyone, could understand the rejection Endo himself was going through.

Soul Survivor (278 – 79)

◆

Mother-Love

Therapist Erich Fromm says that a child from a balanced family receives two kinds of love. Mother-love tends to be unconditional, accepting the child no matter what. Father-love tends to be more provisional, bestowing approval as the child meets certain standards of behavior. Ideally, says Fromm, a child should receive and internalize both kinds of love. According to novelist Shusaku Endo, Japan, a nation of authoritarian fathers, has understood the father-love of God, but not the mother-love.

For Christianity to have any appeal to the Japanese, Endo concludes, it must stress instead the mother-love of God, the love that forgives wrongs and binds wounds and draws, rather than forces, others to itself ("O Jerusalem, Jerusalem, you who kill the prophets and stone those sent to you, how often I have longed to gather your children together, as a hen gathers her chicks under her wings, but you were not willing!").

"In 'maternal religion' Christ comes to prostitutes, worthless people, misshapen people and forgives them," says Endo. As he sees it, Jesus brought the message of mother-love to balance the father-love of the Old Testament. A mother's love will not desert even a child who commits a crime; it forgives any weakness. To Endo, what really impressed the disciples was their realization that Christ still loved them even after they had betrayed him. To be proven wrong was nothing new; to be proven wrong and still loved—that was new.

Endo's *A Life of Jesus* fills in the portrait of the mother-love of Jesus:

> He was thin; he wasn't much. One thing about him, however—he was never known to desert other people if they had trouble. When women were in tears, he stayed by their side. When old folks were lonely, he sat with them quietly. It was nothing miraculous, but the sunken eyes overflowed with love more profound than a miracle. And regarding those who deserted him, those who betrayed him, not a word of resentment came to his lips. No matter what happened, he was the man of sorrows, and he prayed for nothing but their salvation.
>
> That's the whole life of Jesus. It stands out clean and simple, like a single Chinese ideograph brushed on a blank sheet of paper.

Soul Survivor (287 – 89)

Journalists in Moscow

The inordinately polite reception we were receiving in Moscow was making me nervous. Changes were happening at lightning speed in the Soviet Union in 1991. Yet I knew that an entire atheistic state had not warmed to Christianity overnight, and I longed for a dialogue of true substance. I wanted our group of nineteen Christian leaders from the U.S. to be challenged with hard questions about what difference Christianity could make in a country coming apart at the seams. I could count on cynical, hard-bitten journalists to render such a challenge, I thought.

I thought wrong. This is what happened at the Journalists' Club of Moscow. First we North American Christians, seated on a spotlighted stage in a small theater, introduced ourselves. Ron Nikkel of Prison Fellowship International, normally taciturn, was feeling rather expansive. "Winston Churchill said you can judge a society by its prisons," he began. "By that standard, both the USSR and the U.S. are tragedies. Our prisons are awful.

"I have been in prisons all over the world, and have talked to sociologists, behaviorists, and criminal justice experts. None of them know how to get prisoners to change. But we believe—and I have seen abundant proof—that Christ can transform a person from the inside out. Jesus, himself a prisoner, was executed, but he rose again. Now many prisoners are rising again, thanks to him."

Ron then mentioned a prisoner in India who had returned to jail scores of times over a twenty-one-year span. The criminal simply could not break the cycle, until he found Christ. Puzzled by his absence in court, the local magistrate visited the man's home and asked what had happened. "For the first time in my life, someone forgave me," the ex-prisoner answered.

The room fell silent, and then these "cynical, hard-bitten journalists" did something I would not have predicted in a thousand years. They broke into loud, prolonged applause. These are the probing questions they tossed at Ron: "What is this forgiveness? How can we find it? How do you get to know God?" Later, one of the journalists told us that in the USSR his profession had a special affinity for prisoners, since many had served time themselves.

Praying with the KGB (44–45)

◆

Goodness without God

The editors of *Pravda* remarked wistfully that Christianity and communism have many of the same ideals. Some have even called communism a "Christian heresy" because of its emphasis on equality, sharing, justice, and racial harmony. But "seventy-four years on the road to nowhere," which is how Russians derisively refer to their Marxist past, have taught that the grandest social experiment in human history was terribly flawed.

Classical Marxists preached atheism and fought fiercely against religion for a shrewd reason: in order to inspire workers to rise up violently against their oppressors, Marxists had to kill off any hope in a heavenly life beyond this one, and any fear of divine punishment.

A Romanian pastor named Josif Ton once wrote of the contradiction that lies at the heart of a Marxist view of humanity.

[They teach] their pupils that life is the product of chance combinations of matter, that it is governed by Darwinian laws of adaptation and survival. There is no afterlife, no "savior" to reward self-sacrifice or to punish egoism or rapacity. After the pupils have been thus taught, I am sent in to teach them to be noble and honorable men and women, expending all their energies on doing good for the benefit of society. But they lack motivation for goodness. They see that in a purely material world only he who grabs for himself possesses anything. Why should they be self-denying and honest? What motive can be offered them to live lives of usefulness to others?

The *Pravda* editors conceded that they were having a hard time motivating people to show compassion. "How do you reform, change, motivate people?" the editors asked us. The whole country seemed in a state of depression and despair.

"Everyone is looking for a society so perfect that people don't have to be good," said T. S. Eliot, who saw many of his friends embrace the dream of Marxism. What we were hearing from Soviet leaders, and the KGB, and now *Pravda*, was that the Soviet Union ended up with the worst of both: a society far from perfect, and a people who had forgotten how to be good.

Praying with the KGB (74–75)

◆

When God Wrote

One day as I was wallowing in a writer's funk I found myself wondering whether God knew something of the process I was going through. God spoke, of course, but did God write?

The Ten Commandments came immediately to mind. God gave Moses two "tablets of stone inscribed by the finger of God" (Exodus 31:18). By the time Moses descended from Mount Sinai, however, the Israelites had already broken the first two commandments. Enraged, Moses dashed the tablets to pieces —which led to the first divine rewrite.

The next scene of supernatural writing occurred in Babylon (modern-day Iraq) during a banquet, when King Belshazzar profaned gold goblets from the temple in Jerusalem. Suddenly the fingers of a hand appeared and wrote four words on the plaster wall. That night the mighty Babylonian empire fell to the Persians (modern-day Iran).

The Gospels record a single occurrence of Jesus writing. Religious authorities had caught a woman in adultery. She deserved a death sentence according to Mosaic law. Yet the Romans forbade Jews to exercise capital punishment. Jesus said nothing, but instead bent down and wrote on the ground. When he spoke, he said, "If any one of you is without sin, let him be the first to throw a stone at her." The trap sprang, but back on the accusers. The reign of grace was underway.

Paul later spoke of laws being written on the heart. He said of the Corinthians, "You show that you are a letter from Christ,... written not with ink but with the Spirit of the living God, not on tablets of stone but on tablets of human hearts" (2 Corinthians 3:3).

Taken together, these scenes provide a progression from law toward grace, and, significantly, they involve each member of the Trinity. Three of the media—stone tablets, a plaster wall, and sand in the temple courts—did not survive the ravages of history. Instead, God's literature gets passed down generation by generation in transformed lives. "For we are God's [work of art]," Paul wrote, using the Greek word *poiema*, or *poem* (Ephesians 2:10).

After surveying scenes of God writing, I no longer felt so burdened. Composing words on paper is one thing; creating sacred works of art out of fickle human beings is quite another.

"Back Page" column, *Christianity Today,*
September 2007 (112)

The Art Within

The Czech-born author Milan Kundera once wrote that he had always objected to Goethe's notion that "a life should resemble a work of art." Instead, Kundera wondered if perhaps art arose because life is so shapeless and unpredictable, art thus supplying the structure and interpretation that life lacks. But he had to make an exception, he admitted, in the case of his friend Václav Havel, who began as a writer like Kundera and went on to become president of the Czech Republic and one of the strong moral voices of our time. Havel's life, to Kundera, showed a thematic unity, a gradual, continuous progression toward a goal.

Having read some of both authors, I wonder if the difference lies in their underlying point of view. For Kundera, as for most postmodern thinkers, life has no "metanarrative," no structure of meaning to explain where it comes from and where it is going. For Havel, it does. He laments, "I have become increasingly convinced that the crisis of the much-needed global responsibility is in principle due to the fact that we have lost the certainty that the Universe, nature, existence and our lives are the work of creation guided by a definite intention, that it has a definite meaning and follows a definite purpose."

The Christian — and Havel has never fully described himself as such — sees not just all of life but every individual life as a potential work of art. We are participating with God to fashion from raw materials something of enduring beauty. We are writing a small story with our lives, part of a larger story whose plot line we know in the sketchiest of details.

"It is not up to you to finish the work, but neither are you free not to take it up," goes an old Talmudic saying. The work is God's work, the work of reclaiming and redeeming a planet badly damaged. For the Jew and Christian both, that work means bringing a touch of peace, justice, hope, healing, *shalom* wherever our hands touch. For the Christian it means doing so as a follower of Jesus, who made possible the redemption we could never accomplish on our own.

Reaching for the Invisible God (276 – 77)

❖

Rift in My Routine

Be still and know that I am God." I read in this familiar verse from Psalm 46 two commands of equal importance. First, I must be still, something that modern life conspires against. Ten years ago I responded to letters within a couple of weeks and kept my correspondents happy. Five years ago I faxed a response in a couple of days and they seemed content. Now they want email responses the same day and berate me for not using instant messaging or a mobile phone.

Mystery, awareness of another world, an emphasis on being rather than doing, even a few moments of quiet do not come naturally to me in this hectic, buzzing world. I must carve out time and allow God to nourish my inner life.

On a walking pilgrimage to Assisi in Italy, the writer Patricia Hampl began to make a list in answer to the question, What is prayer? She wrote down a few words. Praise. Gratitude. Begging/pleading/cutting deals. Fruitless whining and puling. Focus. And then the list broke off, for she discovered that prayer only seems like an act of language: "Fundamentally it is a position, a placement of oneself." She went on to discover that "prayer as focus is not a way of limiting what can be seen; it is a habit of attention brought to bear on all that is."

Ah, a habit of attention. Be still. In that focus, all else comes into focus. In that rift in my routine, the universe falls into alignment.

Stillness prepares me for the second command: "Know that I am God; I will be exalted among the nations, I will be exalted in the earth." Only through prayer can I believe that truth in the midst of a world that colludes to suppress, not exalt, God.

Prayer: Does It Make Any Difference? (24 – 25)

◆

Uncreating My World

Psalm 2 depicts God laughing in the heavens, scoffing at the kings and rulers arrayed in revolt. For the African prisoner, or a pastor harassed in China, or believers persecuted in North Korea, it requires a great leap to attain that sublime faith, to believe that God is indeed exalted among the nations. I think of Paul *singing* in a Philippian jail and of Jesus correcting Pilate with the plain truth, "You would have no power over me if it were not given to you from above." Even at that moment of crisis, Jesus had the long view, the view from a time antedating the solar system.

"Be still and know that *I* am God": the Latin imperative for "be still" is *vacate*. As Simon Tugwell explains, "God invites us to take a holiday [*vacation*], to stop being God for a while, and let him be God." Too often we think of prayer as a serious chore, something that must be scheduled around other appointments, shoehorned in among other pressing activities. We miss the point, says Tugwell: "God is inviting us to take a break, to play truant. We can stop doing all those important things we have to do in our capacity as God, and leave it to him to be God." Prayer allows me to admit my failures, weaknesses, and limitations to one who responds to human vulnerability with infinite mercy.

To let God be God, of course, means climbing down from my own executive chair of control. I must uncreate the world I have so carefully fashioned to further my ends and advance my cause. Adam and Eve, the builders of Babel, Nebuchadnezzar, the prison guards, not to mention all who struggle with addictions or even ego, know well what is at stake. If original sin traces back to two people striving to become like God, the first step in prayer is to acknowledge or "remember" God—to restore the truth of the universe. "That Man may know he dwells not in his own," said Milton.

Prayer: Does It Make Any Difference? (25 – 27)

Starting Upstream

My home sits in a canyon in the shadow of a large mountain along a stream named Bear Creek. During the spring snowmelt and after heavy rains the stream swells, tumbles frothily over rocks, and acts more like a river than a creek. People have drowned in it. Once I traced the origin of Bear Creek to its very source, atop the mountain. I stood on a snowfield marked by "sun cups," the bowl-shaped indentations that form as snow melts. Underneath I could hear a soft gurgling sound, and at the edge of the snow, runnels of water leaked out. These collected into a pool, then a small alpine pond, then spilled over to begin the long journey down the mountain, joining other rivulets to take shape as the creek below my house.

It occurs to me, thinking about prayer, that most of the time I get the direction wrong. I start downstream with my own concerns and bring them to God. I inform God, as if God did not already know. I plead with God, as if hoping to change God's mind and overcome divine reluctance. Instead, I should start upstream where the flow begins.

When I shift direction, I realize that God already cares about my concerns—my uncle's cancer, world peace, a broken family, a rebellious teenager—more than I do. Grace, like water, descends to the lowest part. Streams of mercy flow. I begin with God, who bears primary responsibility for what happens on earth, and ask what part I can play in God's work on earth. "Let justice roll on like a river, righteousness like a never-failing stream!" cried the prophet. Will I stand by the bank or jump in the stream?

With this new starting point for prayer, my perceptions change. I look at nature and see not only wildflowers and golden aspen trees but the signature of a grand artist. I look at human beings and see not only a "poor, bare, forked animal" but a person of eternal destiny made in God's image. Thanksgiving and praise surge up as a natural response, not an obligation.

Prayer: Does It Make Any Difference? (23 – 24)

Pursuing the Way

I am the way, the truth, and the life," Jesus said. Truth and life may supply the motives for following, yet in the end a relationship with God, like any relationship, boils down to the "way," the daily process of inviting God into the details of my existence. Søren Kierkegaard likened some Christians to schoolboys who want to look up solutions to the math problems in the back of the book. Only by doing the math, step-by-step, can you learn the math. Or in John Bunyan's analogy, only by pursuing the way, progressing through its joys, hardships, and apparent detours, can the pilgrim arrive at the destination.

I have an unmarried friend who prays earnestly for God to lessen or even remove his sexual drive. It causes him constant temptation, he says. Pornography distracts him, plunges him into a failure spiral, and ruins his devotional life. As gently as I can, I tell him that I doubt God will answer the prayer as he wants, by recalibrating his testosterone level. More likely, he will learn fidelity the way anyone learns it, relying on discipline, community, and constant pleas of dependence.

For whatever reason, God has let this broken world endure in its fallen state for a very long time. For those of us who live in that broken world, God seems to value character more than our comfort, often using the very elements that cause us most discomfort as the tools in fashioning that character.

In my own spiritual life, I am trying to remain open to new realities, not blaming God when my expectations go unmet but trusting God to lead me through failures toward renewal and growth. I am also seeking a trust that "the Father knows best" in how this world is run. Reflecting on Old Testament times, I see that the more overt way in which I may want God to act does not achieve the results I might expect. And when God sent the Son — sinless, noncoercive, full of grace and healing — we killed him. God allows personal tragedy to take place in order to achieve some greater goal.

Reaching for the Invisible God (283 – 84)

◆

Hell's Gates

Elton Trueblood notes that the image Jesus used to describe the church's destiny —"the gates of hell will not prevail against it"—is a metaphor of offense, not defense. Christians are storming the gates, and they will prevail. No matter how it looks at any given point in history, the gates guarding the powers of evil will not withstand an assault by grace.

Who can forget the images from the Philippines, when common people knelt before fifty-ton tanks, which lurched to a halt as if colliding with an invisible shield of prayer. The Philippines is the only Christian-majority country in Asia, and it was here that the weapons of grace overcame the weapons of tyranny.

When Benigno Aquino stepped off the plane in Manila, just before his assassination, he had a speech in his hand with this quote from Gandhi: "The willing sacrifice of the innocent is the most powerful answer to insolent tyranny that has yet been conceived by God or man." Aquino never got the chance to deliver that speech, but his life—and his wife's—proved those words prophetic. The Marcos regime suffered a fatal blow.

The Cold War, says former senator Sam Nunn, ended "not in a nuclear inferno, but in a blaze of candles in the churches of Eastern Europe." Candlelight processions in East Germany did not show up well on the evening news, but they helped change the face of the globe. First a few hundred, then a thousand, then thirty thousand, fifty thousand, and finally five hundred thousand—nearly the entire population of the city—turned out in Leipzig for candlelight vigils. After a prayer meeting at St. Nikolai Church, the peaceful protestors would march through the dark streets, singing hymns. Police and soldiers with all their weapons seemed powerless against such a force.

Ultimately, on the night a similar march in East Berlin attracted one million protestors, the hated Berlin Wall came tumbling down without a shot being fired. A huge banner appeared across a Leipzig street: *Wir danken Dir, Kirche* (We thank you, church).

What's So Amazing About Grace? (134–35)

◇

The Arsenal of Grace

Like a gale of pure air driving out stagnant clouds of pollution, peaceful revolution spread across the globe. In 1989 alone ten nations comprising half a billion people experienced nonviolent revolutions. In many of these, the Christian minority played a crucial role. Stalin's mocking question, "How many divisions has the Pope?" got its answer.

Then in 1994 came the most surprising revolution of all, surprising because nearly everyone expected bloodshed. South Africa, though, was also the mother lode of peaceful protest, for it was there that Mohandas Gandhi, studying Tolstoy and the Sermon on the Mount, developed his strategy of nonviolence (which Martin Luther King Jr. later adopted). With much opportunity to practice, South Africans had perfected the use of the weapons of grace. Walter Wink tells of a black woman who was walking on the street with her children when a white man spat in her face. She stopped, and said, "Thank you, and now for the children." Nonplussed, the man was unable to respond.

In one squatters' village, black South African women suddenly found themselves surrounded by soldiers with bulldozers. The soldiers announced through a bullhorn that the residents had two minutes to clear out before their village would be razed. The women had no weapons, and the men of the village were away at work. Knowing the puritanical tendencies of rural Dutch Reformed Afrikaners, the black women stood in front of the bulldozers and stripped off all their clothes. The police fled, and the village remains standing to this day.

News reports barely mentioned the key role that Christian faith played in South Africa's peaceful revolution. After a mediation team led by Henry Kissinger had abandoned all hope of convincing the Inkatha Freedom Party to participate in elections, a Christian diplomat from Kenya met privately with all the principals, prayed with them, and helped change their minds. (A mysteriously malfunctioning compass on an airplane delayed one flight, making this crucial meeting possible.)

What's So Amazing About Grace? (135 – 36)

◆

Complex Forgiveness

Nelson Mandela broke the chain of ungrace in South Africa when he emerged from twenty-seven years of imprisonment with a message of forgiveness and reconciliation, not revenge. F. W. De Klerk himself, elected from the smallest and most strictly Calvinistic of the South African churches, felt what he later described as "a strong sense of calling." He told his congregation that God was calling him to save all the people of South Africa, even though he knew that would mean rejection by his own people.

Black leaders insisted that De Klerk apologize for racial apartheid. He balked, because the people who had started the policy included his own father. But Bishop Desmond Tutu believed it essential that the process of reconciliation in South Africa begin with forgiveness, and he would not relent. According to Tutu, "One lesson we should be able to teach the world, and that we should be able to teach the people of Bosnia, Rwanda, and Burundi, is that we are ready to forgive." Eventually, De Klerk did apologize.

Now that the black majority has political power, they are formally considering issues of forgiveness. The minister of justice sounds downright theological as he formulates a policy. No one can forgive on behalf of victims, he says; victims have to forgive for themselves. And no one can forgive without full disclosure: what happened and who did what must first be revealed. Also, those who committed the atrocities must agree to ask for forgiveness before it can be granted. Step-by-step, South Africans are remembering their past in order to forget it.

Forgiveness is neither easy nor clear-cut, as South Africans are finding out. One may forgive the Germans but put restrictions on the armies, forgive a child abuser but keep him away from his victims, forgive Southern racism but enforce laws to keep it from happening again.

Yet nations that pursue forgiveness, in all its complexity, may at least avoid the awful consequences of the alternative — unforgiveness. Instead of scenes of massacre and civil war, the world was treated to the sight of black South Africans in long, snaking lines that stretched in some cases for more than a mile, *dancing* in jubilation over their first-ever opportunity to vote.

What's So Amazing About Grace? (136 – 37)

The Gift Nobody Wants

Dr. Paul Brand says with utter sincerity, "Thank God for pain!" By definition, pain is unpleasant, enough so to force us to withdraw our fingers from
a stove. Yet that very quality saves us from destruction. Unless the warning
signal demands response, we might not heed it.

Pain is not God's great goof. The sensation of pain is a gift—the gift that
nobody wants. More than anything, pain should be viewed as a communication network. A remarkable network of pain sensors stands guard duty with the
singular purpose of keeping me from injury.

I do not say that all pain is good. Sometimes it flares up and makes life miserable. For someone with crippling arthritis or terminal cancer, pain dominates so
much that any relief, especially a painless world, would seem like heaven itself.
But for the majority of us, the pain network performs daily protective service. It
is effectively designed for surviving life on this sometimes hostile planet.

In Dr. Brand's words, "The one legitimate complaint you can make against
pain is that it cannot be switched off. It can rage out of control, as with a terminal cancer patient, even though its warning has been heard and there is no
more that can be done to treat the cause of pain. But as a physician I'm sure
that less than one percent of pain is in this category that we might call out of
control. Ninety-nine per cent of all the pains that people suffer are short-term
pains: correctable situations that call for medication, rest, or a change in a
person's lifestyle."

Admittedly, the surprising idea of the "gift of pain" does not answer many of
the problems connected with suffering. But it is a beginning point of a realistic
perspective on pain and suffering. Too often the emotional trauma of intense
pain blinds us to its inherent value.

Where Is God When It Hurts? (33 – 35)

Harnessing Pain

I once interviewed Robin Graham, the youngest person ever to sail around the world alone. (His story was told in the book and movie *Dove*.) Robin set sail as an immature sixteen-year-old, not so much seeking his future as delaying it. In the course of the long voyage, he was smashed broadside by a violent ocean storm, had his mast snapped in two by a rogue wave, and barely missed annihilation by a water-spout. He went through such despair in the Doldrums, a windless, currentless portion of the ocean near the equator, that he emptied a can of kerosene in his boat, struck a match, and jumped overboard. (A sudden gust of wind soon caused him to change his mind and he jumped back in to extinguish the blaze and continue the voyage.)

After five years, Robin sailed into the Los Angeles harbor to be greeted by boats, banners, crowds, reporters, honking cars, and blasts from steam whistles. The joy of that moment was on a different level from any other experience he had known. He could never have felt those emotions returning from a pleasure outing off the coast of California. The agony of his round-the-world trip had made possible the exultation of his triumphant return. He left a sixteen-year-old kid and returned a twenty-one-year-old man.

Impressed by the sense of health that self-accomplishment could bring, Robin immediately bought a farm plot in Kalispell, Montana, and built a cabin from hand-cut logs. Publishers and movie agents tried to entice him with round-the-country publicity trips, talk show engagements, and fat expense accounts, but Robin declined them all.

We moderns, in our comfort-controlled environments, have a tendency to blame our unhappiness on pain, which we identify as the great enemy. If we could somehow excise pain from life, ah, then we would be happy. But, as experiences like Robin's show, life does not yield to such easy partitioning. Pain is a part of the seamless fabric of sensations and often a necessary prelude to pleasure and fulfillment. The key to happiness lies not so much in avoiding pain at all costs as in understanding its role as a protective warning system and harnessing it to work on your behalf, not against you.

Where Is God When It Hurts? (54 – 55)

◆

A Surprising Bonus

Jesus captured succinctly the paradoxical nature of life in his one statement most repeated in the Gospels: "Whoever finds his life will lose it, and whoever loses his life for my sake will find it." Such a statement goes against the search for "self-fulfillment" in advanced psychology—which turns out to be not advanced enough. Christianity offers the further insight that true fulfillment comes not through ego satisfaction, but through service to others.

When I think of the great churches I have visited, what comes to mind is not an image of a cathedral in Europe. These are mere museums now. Instead, I think of the chapel at a leprosy hospital, of an inner-city church in Newark with crumbling plaster and a leaky roof, of a mission church in Santiago, Chile, made of concrete block and corrugated iron. In these places, set amidst human misery, I have seen Christian love abound.

The leprosarium in Carville, Louisiana, offers a wonderful example of this principle in action. A government agency bought the property and promised to develop it, but could find no one to clear the roads, repair the plantation's slave cabins, or drain the swamps. The stigma of leprosy kept everyone away.

Finally an order of nuns, the Sisters of Charity, moved to Carville to nurse the leprosy patients. Getting up two hours before daybreak, wearing starched white uniforms in bayou heat, these nuns lived under a more disciplined rule than any Marine boot camp. But they alone proved willing to do the work. They dug ditches, laid foundations for buildings, and made Carville livable, all the while glorifying God and bringing joy to the patients. They learned perhaps the deepest level of pain/pleasure association in life, that of sacrificial service.

If I spend my life searching for happiness through drugs, comfort, and luxury, it will elude me. "Happiness recedes from those who pursue her." Happiness will come upon me unexpectedly as a by-product, a surprising bonus for something I have invested myself in. And, most likely, that investment will include pain. It is hard to imagine pleasure without it.

Where Is God When It Hurts? (57 – 58)

◆

Rainbow Country

In 2006 I went on a multi-city tour of South Africa, speaking on grace. South Africa is one of the best modern examples of grace in action. For example, while countries like North Korea and Iran are desperately seeking nuclear weapons, South Africa dismantled theirs. And everyone speaks of the "miracle" of the changeover that occurred there.

Defying predictions of a civil war and bloodbath, Nelson Mandela and Archbishop Desmond Tutu proposed a new way based not on justice but on reconciliation. In addition to inviting his jailer to sit on his inauguration platform, Mandela hired a white South African policeman, the dreaded enemy of blacks, as his personal bodyguard. Then Desmund Tutu's extraordinary Truth and Reconciliation Commission became a model to the rest of the world.

It didn't take long to experience the variety of this rainbow country. The first night I spoke to an Anglican church, mostly white, comprising English-speaking people of British descent. A few days later I went to the capital, Pretoria, where I spoke to a diehard Afrikaans crowd, Dutch Reformed. They had just moved into a huge new megachurch facility that seats 7,000, a bit of an oxymoron to those who know the starched Dutch Reformed tradition. (No organ, but a great drum set.) The Afrikaans have lost the most in the changeover — power, money, prestige — and they're despised by many as the architects of apartheid. Many fled the country, and the ones who stayed are more humble and open than ever before.

The very next night I spoke at Ray McCauley's 43,000-member Pentecostal church, which is 80 percent black and 10 percent "coloured" or mixed race. No matter what you think of charismatics, I must admit it's a lot more fun to speak to people who clap, yell "Amen!" and nod their heads all the way through. The fact that South African blacks embrace Christianity so widely is astonishing in light of the treatment they endured from those who brought the faith to their country — an observation that has its parallels in the U.S., where African slaves ultimately adopted the faith of their owners.

Unpublished trip notes, South Africa, 2006

◆

Making God Visible

On a 2004 visit to South Africa I met a remarkable woman named Joanna. She is of mixed race, part black and part white, a category known there as "coloured." As a student she agitated for change in apartheid and then saw the miracle that no one had predicted, the peaceful dismantling of that evil system. Afterward, for many hours she sat with her husband and watched live broadcasts of the Truth and Reconciliation Commission hearings.

Instead of simply exulting in her newfound freedoms, Joanna next decided to tackle the most violent prison in South Africa, a prison where Nelson Mandela had spent several years. Tattoo-covered gang members controlled the prison, strictly enforcing a rule that required new members to earn their admittance to the gang by assaulting undesirable prisoners. Prison authorities looked the other way, letting these "animals" beat and even kill each other.

Alone, this attractive young woman started going each day into the bowels of that prison. She brought a simple message of forgiveness and reconciliation, trying to put into practice on smaller scale what Mandela and Bishop Tutu were trying to effect in the nation as a whole. She organized small groups, taught trust games, got the prisoners to open up about the details of their horrific childhoods. The year before she began her visits, the prison had recorded 279 acts of violence; the next year there were two. Joanna's results were so impressive that the BBC sent a camera crew from London to produce two one-hour documentaries on her.

I met Joanna and her husband, who has since joined her in her work, at a restaurant on the waterfront of Cape Town. Ever the journalist, I pressed her for specifics on what had happened to transform that prison. Her fork stopped on the way to her mouth, she looked up and said, almost without thinking, "Well, of course, Philip, God was already present in the prison. I just had to make him visible."

I have often thought of that line from Joanna, which would make a fine mission statement for all of us seeking to know and follow God. God is already present, in the most unexpected places. We just need to make God visible.

Finding God in Unexpected Places (xiii – xiv)

October

Captive Audience

At each meeting on my 2006 tour of South Africa I told the story of Joanna, who embodies grace and reconciliation. When we went to Cape Town she invited us to Pollsmoor Prison, where she works. It's an amazing place, five separate prisons linked by underground tunnels, holding eight thousand prisoners in all, triple the expected number.

Several hundred men crowded into a kind of exercise room, and Joanna led the service. She has a remarkable presence, greets each prisoner by name, and commands respect from inmates and authorities alike. Most days the prisoners are allowed out of their cells for only one hour, so a chance to attend a church service is a welcome relief. I'll not soon forget the sound of several hundred male voices singing lustily, "Soon and very soon we are going to see the King ... No more crying there ... No more dying there ..."

After the meeting we visited one of the three cells that the prison has designated as "Christian cells." Forty-nine men sleep in a room about the size of my living room. They have triple-tiered bunk beds, and a few sleep on pieces of foam on the floor. The "toilet," a plastic garbage bag servicing all forty-nine men, gets emptied once a day, and the resulting stench hit me like a wall.

There, we heard some of the prisoners' own stories: "I'm a murderer in for life plus thirty-eight years ... I'm a rapist ... I killed my wife." One by one they told of how God has changed their lives, and how they seek to live for God even if they never get out. Joanna and her husband, Julian, run a program of restorative justice, which walks the men through stages of confession, repentance, then victim restitution. We sang a few songs and emerged into shockingly fresh air and the beauties of Cape Town.

One scene stayed with me. Instead of pornography or graffiti, the prisoners had decorated their cell with the words of hymns and praise choruses. The most touching to me, in light of what Joanna had said in the restaurant, was "Surely the presence of the Lord is in this place."

Trip notes, South Africa, 2006

◆

Unlikely Champion

I once interviewed Dr. C. Everett Koop, who was then serving as Surgeon General of the United States. Koop's credentials as an evangelical Christian were impeccable. It was he, teamed with Francis Schaeffer, who helped mobilize the conservative Christian community to enter the political fray over pro-life issues.

In his role as "the nation's doctor," Koop visited AIDS patients. Their bodies skeletal, emaciated, and covered with purplish sores, he began to feel for them a deep compassion, both as a doctor and as a Christian. He had vowed to look out for the weak and disenfranchised, and there was no more weak or disenfranchised group in the nation.

For seven weeks Koop addressed only religious groups, including Jerry Falwell's church, the National Religious Broadcasters' convention, conservative groups within Judaism, and Roman Catholics. In those addresses, delivered in full Public Health Service uniform, Koop affirmed the need for abstinence and monogamous marriage. But he added, "I am the Surgeon General of the heterosexuals and the homosexuals, of the young and the old, of the moral and the immoral." He admonished fellow Christians, "You may hate the sin, but you are to love the sinner."

Koop always expressed his personal abhorrence of sexual promiscuity—consistently he used the word "sodomy" when referring to homosexual acts—but as Surgeon General he lobbied on homosexuals' behalf and cared for them. Koop could hardly believe it when he spoke to twelve thousand gay people in Boston and they chanted, Koop! Koop! Koop! Koop! "They give unbelievable support—in spite of what I say about their practices. I guess it's because I'm the person who came out and said, I'm the Surgeon General of all the people and I'll meet them where they are. In addition, I've asked for compassion for them, and for volunteers to go and care for them."

Koop never compromised his beliefs—even now he persists in using the emotionally charged word "sodomy"—but no evangelical Christian gets a warmer reception among homosexuals.

What's So Amazing About Grace? (169 – 70)

◆

Grace Abuse

The potential for "grace abuse" was brought home to me forcefully. Late one night I sat in a restaurant and listened as my friend Daniel confided to me that he had decided to leave his wife of fifteen years. He had found someone who "makes me feel alive, like I haven't felt in years."

A Christian, Daniel knew well the personal and moral consequences of what he was about to do. His decision would inflict permanent damage on his wife and three children. Even so, he said, the force pulling him toward the younger woman, like a powerful magnet, was too strong to resist.

Then he dropped the bombshell: "Philip, you study the Bible. Do you think God can forgive something as awful as I am about to do?"

Daniel's question lay on the table like a live snake. As I drank my coffee I thought long and hard about the repercussions of grace. How can I dissuade my friend from committing a terrible mistake if he knows forgiveness lies just around the corner?

There is one "catch" to grace. St. Augustine says "God gives where He finds empty hands." A person whose hands are full or fists are closed tight can't receive a gift. Grace, in other words, must be received. C. S. Lewis explains that what I have termed "grace abuse" stems from a confusion of condoning and forgiving: "To condone an evil is simply to ignore it, to treat it as if it were good. But forgiveness needs to be accepted as well as offered if it is to be complete: and a man who admits no guilt can accept no forgiveness."

Here is what I told my friend Daniel. "Can God forgive you? Of course. You know the Bible. God uses murderers and adulterers. For goodness' sake, a couple of scoundrels named Peter and Paul led the New Testament church. Forgiveness is *our* problem, not God's. What we have to go through to commit sin distances us from God—we change in the very act of rebellion—and there is no guarantee we will ever come back. You ask me about forgiveness now, but will you even want it later, especially if it involves repentance?"

What's So Amazing About Grace? (179–80)

Loopholes

It is possible, warns the biblical writer Jude, to "change the grace of our God into a license for immorality." At first a devious idea forms in the back of the mind. *It's something I want. Yeah, I know, it's wrong. But why don't I just go ahead anyway? I can always get forgiveness later.* The idea grows into an obsession, and ultimately grace becomes "a license for immorality."

Christians have responded to this danger in various ways. Martin Luther, intoxicated with God's grace, sometimes scoffed at the potential for abuse. "If you are a preacher of grace, do not preach a fictitious, but a true, grace; and if the grace is true, carry a true, and not a fictitious sin," he wrote his friend Melanchthon. "Be a sinner and sin vigorously.... It is sufficient that we recognize through the wealth of God's glory, the lamb who bears the sin of the world; from this, sin does not sever us, even if thousands, thousands of times in one day we should fornicate or murder."

Others, alarmed at the prospect of Christians fornicating or murdering thousands of times in one day, have called Luther to task for his hyperbole. The Bible, after all, presents grace as a healing counterforce to sin. How can the two coexist in the same person? Shouldn't we "grow in grace," as Peter commands? Shouldn't our family likeness to God increase? "Christ accepts us as we are," wrote Walter Trobisch, "but when he accepts us, we cannot remain as we are."

Twentieth-century theologian Dietrich Bonhoeffer coined the phrase "cheap grace" as a way of summarizing grace abuse. Living in Nazi Germany, he was appalled by the cowardly way in which Christians were responding to Hitler's threat. Lutheran pastors preached grace from the pulpit on Sundays, then kept quiet the rest of the week as the Nazis pursued their policies of racism, euthanasia, and finally genocide. Bonhoeffer's book *The Cost of Discipleship* highlights the many New Testament passages commanding Christians to attain holiness. Every call to conversion, he insisted, includes a call to discipleship, to Christlikeness.

What's So Amazing About Grace? (184)

Short-Term Results

One summer I had to learn basic German in order to finish a graduate degree. What a wretched summer! On delightful evenings while my friends sailed on Lake Michigan, rode bikes, and sipped cappuccinos in patio cafés, I was holed up with a Kapomeister tutor, parsing German verbs. Five nights a week, three hours a night I spent memorizing vocabulary and word endings that I would never again use. I endured such torture for one purpose only: to pass the test and get my degree.

What if the school registrar had promised me, "Philip, we want you to study hard, learn German, and take the test, but we promise you in advance that you'll get a passing grade. Your diploma has already been filled out." Do you think I would have spent every delectable summer evening inside a hot, stuffy apartment? Not a chance. In a nutshell, that was the theological dilemma Paul confronts in Romans.

Why learn German? There are noble reasons, to be sure — languages broaden the mind and expand the range of communication — but these had never motivated me to study German before. I studied for selfish reasons, to finish a degree, and only the threat of consequences hanging over me caused me to reorder my summer priorities. Today, I remember very little of the German I crammed into my brain. "The old way of the written code" (Paul's description of the Old Testament law) produces short-term results at best.

What would inspire me to learn German? I can think of one powerful incentive. If my wife, the woman I fell in love with, spoke only German, I would have learned the language in record time. Why? I would have a desperate desire to communicate *mit einer schönen Frau.* I would have stayed up late at night parsing verbs and placing them properly at the ends of my love-letter sentences, treasuring each addition to my vocabulary as a new way of expressing myself to the one I loved. I would have learned German unbegrudgingly, with the relationship itself as my reward.

[Continued on October 6]

What's So Amazing About Grace? (189)

Love Life

[Continued from October 5]

That reality helps me understand Paul's gruff "God forbid!" response to the question "Shall we go on sinning that grace may increase?" Would a groom on his wedding night hold the following conversation with his bride? "Honey, I love you so much, and I'm eager to spend my life with you. But I need to work out a few details. Now that we're married, how far can I go with other women? Can I sleep with them? Kiss them? You don't mind a few affairs now and then, do you? I know it might hurt you, but just think of all the opportunities you'll have to forgive me after I betray you!"

To such a Don Juan the only reasonable response is a slap in the face and a "God forbid!" Obviously, he does not understand the first thing about love.

Similarly, if we approach God with a "What can I get away with?" attitude, it proves we do not grasp what God has in mind for us. God wants something far beyond the relationship I might have with a slave master, who will enforce my obedience with a whip. God is not a boss or a business manager or a magic genie to serve at our command.

Indeed, God wants something more intimate than the closest relationship on earth, the lifetime bond between a man and a woman. What God wants is not a good performance, but my heart. I do "good works" for my wife not in order to earn credit but to express my love for her. Likewise, God wants me to serve "in the new way of the Spirit": not out of compulsion but out of desire. "Discipleship," says Clifford Williams, "simply means the life which springs from grace."

What's So Amazing About Grace? (189 – 90)

◆

Why Be Good?

If I had to summarize the primary New Testament motivation for "being good" in one word, I would choose *gratitude*. Paul begins most of his letters with a summary of the riches we possess in Christ. If we comprehend what Christ has done for us, then surely out of gratitude we will strive to live "worthy" of such great love. We will strive for holiness not to make God love us but because God already does. As Paul told Titus, it is the grace of God that "teaches us to say 'No' to ungodliness and worldly passions, and to live self-controlled, upright and godly lives."

In her memoir *Ordinary Time*, the Catholic writer Nancy Mairs tells of her years of mutiny against childhood images of a "Daddy God," who could only be pleased if she followed a list of onerous prescriptions and prohibitions:

> I was forever on the perilous verge of doing a don't, to atone for which I had to beg forgiveness from the very being who had set me up for trespass, by forbidding behaviors he clearly expected me to commit, in the first place: the God of the Gotcha, you might say.

Mairs broke a lot of those rules, felt constantly guilty, and then, in her words, "learned to thrive in the care of" a God who "asks for the single act that will make transgression impossible: love."

The best reason to be good is to want to be good. Internal change requires relationship. It requires love. "Who can be good, if not made so by loving?" asked Augustine. When Augustine made the famous statement, "If you but love God you may do as you incline," he was perfectly serious. A person who truly loves God will be inclined to please God, which is why Jesus and Paul both summed up the entire law in the simple command, "Love God."

If we truly grasped the wonder of God's love for us, the devious question that prompted Romans 6 and 7 — What can I get away with? — would never even occur to us. We would spend our days trying to fathom, not exploit, God's grace.

What's So Amazing About Grace? (190 – 91)

◆

Tuning Out the Static

The author Brennan Manning, who leads spiritual retreats several times each year, once told me that not one person who has followed his regimen of a silent retreat has failed to hear from God. Intrigued and a bit skeptical, I signed up. We were free to spend most of our five days as we wished, with one requirement: two hours of prayer per day.

I doubt I had devoted more than thirty minutes to prayer at any one session in my life. The first day I wandered to the edge of a meadow and sat down against a tree.

To my great fortune, a herd of 147 elk wandered into the very field where I was sitting. To see one elk is exciting; to watch 147 elk in their natural habitat is enthralling. Yet, as I soon learned, to watch 147 elk for two hours is, to put it mildly, boring.

After a while the very placidity of the scene began to affect me. I no longer thought about the work I had left at home, the deadlines facing me, the reading that Brennan had assigned. My body relaxed. In the leaden silence, my mind fell quiet.

"The quieter the mind," said Meister Eckhart, "the more powerful, the worthier, the deeper, the more telling and more perfect the prayer is."

I never saw the elk again, even though every afternoon I searched the fields and forest for them. Over the next few days I said many words to God. I was turning fifty that year, and I asked for guidance on how I should prepare my soul for the rest of life. I made lists, and many things came to mind that would not have come to mind had I not been sitting in a field for hours at a time. The week became a kind of spiritual checkup that pointed out paths for further growth. I heard no audible voice, and yet at the end of the week I had to agree with Brennan that I had heard from God.

I became more convinced than ever that God finds ways to communicate to those who truly seek God, especially when we lower the volume of the surrounding static.

Prayer: Does It Make Any Difference? (53 – 54)

◆

Unequal Partners

To call God and me unequal partners is a laughable understatement. And yet by inviting us to do kingdom work on earth, God has indeed set up a kind of odd-couple alliance. God delegates work to human beings so that we do history together, so to speak.

Clearly, the partnership has one dominant partner—something like an alliance between the United States and Fiji, perhaps, or between Microsoft and a high school programmer. We know well what happens when human beings form such unequal alliances: the dominant partner throws weight around and the subordinate mostly keeps quiet. God, who has no reason to be threatened by the likes of us, instead invites a steady and honest flow of communication.

I have sometimes wondered why God places such a high value on honesty, even to the extent of enduring unjust outbursts. As I review the prayers recorded in the Bible, I am startled to see how many have a tone of petulance: Jeremiah griping about unfairness; Job conceding, "What profit should we have, if we pray unto him?"; Habakkuk accusing God of deafness. The Bible schools us to pray with blistering honesty.

Walter Brueggemann suggests one obvious reason for candor in the book of Psalms: "because life is like that, and these poems are intended to speak to all of life, not just part of it." Brueggemann finds it jarring to visit upbeat evangelical churches and hear only happy songs, when half of the psalms are "songs of lament, protest, and complaint about the incoherence that is experienced in the world. At least it is clear that a church that goes on singing 'happy songs' in the face of raw reality is doing something very different from what the Bible itself does."

From the Bible's prayers I learn that God wants us to keep it in the alliance, to come in person with our complaints. If I march through life pretending to smile while inside I bleed, I dishonor the relationship.

Prayer: Does It Make Any Difference? (66, 68)

Does Prayer Matter?

After surveying Jesus' practice of prayer, I realize that his example does answer one important question about prayer: Does it matter? When doubts creep in and I wonder whether prayer is a sanctified form of talking to myself, I remind myself that the Son of God, who had spoken worlds into being and sustains all that exists, felt a compelling need to pray. He prayed as if it made a difference, as if the time he devoted to prayer mattered every bit as much as the time he devoted to caring for people.

A physician friend of mine who learned I was investigating prayer told me I would have to start with three rather large assumptions: (1) God exists; (2) God is capable of hearing our prayers; and (3) God cares about our prayers. "None of these three can be proved or disproved," he said. "They must either be believed or disbelieved." He is right, of course, although for me the example of Jesus offers strong evidence in favor of that belief. To discount prayer, to conclude that it does not matter, means to view Jesus as deluded.

Jesus clung to prayer as to a lifeline, for it gave him both the guidance and the energy to know and do the Father's will. Even then he sometimes grew exasperated with his earthly surroundings ("O unbelieving generation, how long shall I stay with you?"), sometimes fought temptation ("Do not put the Lord your God to the test"), and sometimes doubted ("My God, my God, why have you forsaken me?").

Skeptics raise questions about prayer's usefulness: If God knows best, what's the point? To such questions, I have no better answer than the example of Jesus, who knew above any of us the wisdom of the Father and yet who felt a strong need to flood the heavens with requests.

Although Jesus offered no metaphysical proofs of the effectiveness of prayer, the very fact that he did it establishes its worth. "Ask and you will receive," he said frankly, a rebuke to anyone who considers petition a primitive form of prayer. When his disciples failed in their attempts to heal an afflicted boy, Jesus had a simple explanation: lack of prayer.

Prayer: Does It Make Any Difference? (79–81)

Unknown and Unpredictable

It appears that prayer was no simple matter even for Jesus. Like the people who write me letters, Jesus knows the heartbreak of unanswered prayers. His longest prayer, after all, centers in a request for unity, "that all of them may be one, Father." The slightest acquaintance with church history shows how far that prayer remains from being answered.

Another night Jesus sought guidance for choosing the twelve disciples whom he would entrust with his mission. Yet as I read the Gospels I marvel that this dodgy dozen could constitute the answer to any prayer. They included, Luke pointedly notes, "Judas Iscariot, who became a traitor," not to mention the ambitious Sons of Thunder and the hothead Simon, whom Jesus would soon rebuke as "Satan." When Jesus later sighed in exasperation over these twelve, "How long shall I put up with you?" I wonder if he momentarily questioned the Father's guidance back on the mountainside.

In a provocative book, theologian Ray Anderson ponders Jesus' selection of Judas as one of the twelve. Did Jesus foresee Judas's destiny the night he prayed? Did he remind the Father of that prayer as Judas left the Last Supper table to betray him? Anderson draws from the experience of Judas a key principle about prayer: "Prayer is not a means of removing the unknown and unpredictable elements in life, but rather a way of including the unknown and unpredictable in the outworking of the grace of God in our lives."

Jesus' own prayers for his disciples surely did not remove the "unknown and unpredictable elements." The twelve periodically surprised and disappointed Jesus with their petty concerns and their inadequate faith. In the end, all twelve failed him at the hour of his deepest need. Eventually, however, eleven of the twelve underwent a slow but steady transformation, providing a kind of long-term answer to Jesus' original prayer. John softened into "the apostle of Love." Simon Peter later showed how to "follow in his steps" by suffering as Christ did. The one exception, Judas, betrayed Jesus and yet that very act led to the cross and the salvation of the world. In strange and mysterious ways, prayer incorporates the unknown and unpredictable in the outworking of God's grace.

Prayer: Does It Make Any Difference? (81 – 83)

◆

Wrestling Match

I have spoken of the wrestling match that occurred in the garden of Gethsemane, of Jesus struggling with God's will and accepting it only as a last resort since there was no other way. Later, when God chose the least likely person (a notorious human-rights abuser named Saul of Tarsus) to carry his message to Gentiles, a church leader voiced dissent: "I have heard many reports about this man and all the harm he has done to your saints in Jerusalem." God cut this particular argument short: "Go! This man is my chosen instrument." Several years later the same man, now named Paul, was himself bargaining with God, praying repeatedly for the removal of a physical ailment.

Why would God, the all-powerful ruler of the universe, resort to a style of relating to humans that seems like negotiation—or haggling, to put it crudely? Does God require the exercise as part of our spiritual training regimen? Or is it possible that God, if I may use such language, relies on our outbursts as a window onto the world, or as an alarm that might trigger intervention? It was the cry of the Israelites, after all, that prompted God's call of Moses.

I best understand what God wants from us in prayer by analogy to the people closest to me. I think of my brother, who alone knows secrets of shame and pain from our childhood. I think of my wife, who knows more about me than any person on earth, and with whom I negotiate everything from what to order at a restaurant to what state we live in. Or my editor, who holds my hand through each angst-ridden stage of producing a book. With each of these people, my intimate partners, I act in a way reminiscent of the bargaining scenes with God. I make suggestions, back off, accommodate their point of view, reach a compromise, and come away changed.

Like Abraham, I approach God at first in fear and trembling, only to learn that God wants me to stop groveling and start arguing. I dare not meekly accept the state of the world, with all its injustice and unfairness. I must call God to account for God's own promises, God's own character.

Prayer: Does It Make Any Difference? (96 – 97)

Church behind Bars

I am sitting in the midst of a church service with a distinctly Latin and Pentecostal flavor. Except for a few visual reminders, I could easily forget that we are meeting in one of the largest prisons in Chile. I look around at the congregation: all men, wearing a ragtag assortment of handed-down street clothes. A shocking number of their faces are marked with scars.

After the singing a Canadian guest, conspicuous in a white shirt and tie, comes to the platform. The prison chaplain announces that this man, Ron Nikkel, has visited prisons in more than fifty countries. The organization he directs, Prison Fellowship International, brings the message of Jesus to prisoners and works with governments on improving prison conditions. A dozen inmates yell a loud "Amen!"

"I bring you greetings from your brothers and sisters in Christ in prisons around the world," Ron begins, pausing for the translation into Spanish. "I bring you greetings especially from Pascal, who lives in Africa, in a country called Madagascar. Pascal trained as a scientist and took pride in his atheism. One day he was arrested for participating in a student strike. He was thrown into a prison designed for 800 men, but now crowded with 2500 men. They sat elbow to elbow on bare boards, most of them dressed in rags and covered with lice. You can imagine the sanitation there." The Chilean inmates, who have been listening alertly, groan aloud with sympathy.

"Pascal had only one book available in the prison—a Bible provided by his family. He read it daily, and, despite his atheistic beliefs, he began to pray. By the end of three months, Pascal was leading a Bible study every night in that crowded room.

"Much to his surprise, Pascal was released after those three months. But here is an amazing thing: Pascal keeps going back to prison! He visits twice each week to preach and to distribute Bibles. On Fridays he brings in huge pots of vegetable soup, because he found that the prisoners were dying of malnutrition. Many had been jailed for stealing food—they were hungry before they went in!"

When the foreign visitors leave, amid many hugs and handshakes, all the prisoners stay. They are just getting warmed up.

Finding God in Unexpected Places (224–26)

To Sing in Such a Place

I asked Ron Nikkel of Prison Fellowship International to think back to the worst setting he's ever seen. Ron thought for a moment and then told me about the time he and Chuck Colson visited a prison in Zambia. Their "guide," a former prisoner named Nego, brought them to a secret inner prison built inside to hold the very worst offenders.

"We approached a steel cage-like building covered with wire mesh. Cells line the outside of the cage, surrounding a 'courtyard' fifteen by forty feet. Twenty-three hours of each day the prisoners are kept in cells so small that they cannot all lie down at once. For one hour they may walk in the small courtyard. Nego had spent twelve years here.

"When we got near the inner prison, we could see sets of eyes peering at us from a two-inch space under the steel gate. And when the gate swung open, it revealed squalor unlike I have seen anywhere. There were no sanitation facilities — in fact, the prisoners were forced to defecate in their food pans. The blazing African sun had heated up the steel enclosure unbearably. I could hardly breathe in the foul, stifling atmosphere. How could human beings live in such a place, I wondered.

"And yet, here is what happened when Nego told them who we were. Eighty of the 120 prisoners went to the back wall and assembled in rows. They began singing — hymns, Christian hymns, in beautiful four-part harmony. Nego whispered to me that thirty-five of those men had been sentenced to death and would soon face execution.

"I was overwhelmed by the contrast between their peaceful, serene faces and the horror of their surroundings. Just behind them, in the darkness, I could make out an elaborate charcoal sketch drawn on the wall. It showed Jesus, stretched out on a cross. The prisoners must have spent hours working on it. And it struck me with great force that Christ was there with them, sharing their suffering, and giving them joy enough to sing in such a place.

"I was supposed to speak to them, to offer some inspiring words of faith. But I could only mumble a few words of greeting. *They* were the teachers, not I."

Finding God in Unexpected Places (238 – 39)

◆

Pain's Megaphone

We could—some people do—believe that the sole purpose of life is to be comfortable. Gorge yourself, build a nice home, enjoy good food, have sex, live the good life. That's all there is. But the presence of suffering vastly complicates that lifestyle—unless we choose to wear blinders.

It's hard to believe the world is here just so I can party, when a third of its people go to bed starving each night. It's hard to believe the purpose of life is to feel good, when I see teenagers smashed on the freeway. If I try to escape toward hedonism, suffering and death lurk nearby, haunting me, reminding me of how hollow life would be if this world were all I'd ever know.

Sometimes murmuring, sometimes shouting, suffering is a "rumor of transcendence" that the entire human condition is out of whack. Something is wrong with a life of war and violence and human tragedy. He who wants to be satisfied with this world, who wants to believe the only purpose of life is enjoyment, must go around with cotton in his ears, for the megaphone of pain is a loud one.

Of course, I can turn against God for allowing such misery. On the other hand, pain can drive me to God. I can believe God's promise that this world is not all there is, and take the chance that God is making a perfect place for those who follow God on pain-racked earth.

It is hard to be a creature. We think we are big enough to run our own world without such messy matters as pain and suffering to remind us of our dependence. We think we are wise enough to make our own decisions about morality, to live rightly without the megaphone of pain blaring in our ears. We are wrong, as the garden of Eden story proves. Man and woman, in a world without suffering, chose against God.

And so we who have come after Adam and Eve have a choice. We can trust God. Or we can blame God, not ourselves, for the world.

Where Is God When It Hurts? (68–71)

◆

Seeking the Giver

On the surface, the book of Job centers on the problem of suffering. Underneath, a different issue is at stake: the doctrine of human freedom. Job had to endure undeserved suffering in order to demonstrate that God is ultimately interested in freely given love.

The contest posed between Satan and God was no trivial exercise. Satan's accusation that Job loved God only because "you have put a hedge around him," stands as an attack on God's character. It implies that God, alone, is not worthy of love; faithful people like Job follow God only because they are "bribed" to do so. Job's response when all the props of faith were removed would prove or disprove Satan's challenge.

To understand this issue of human freedom, it may help to imagine a world in which everyone truly does get what he or she deserves. That world would be just and consistent, and everyone would clearly know what God expected. Fairness would reign. There is, however, one huge problem with such a tidy world: it's not at all what God wants to accomplish on earth. God wants from us love, freely given love, and we dare not underestimate the premium God places on that love. Freely given love is so important that God allows our planet to be a cancer of evil in the universe — for a time.

If this world ran according to fixed, perfectly fair rules, there would be no true freedom. We would act rightly because of our own immediate gain, and selfish motives would taint every act of goodness. In contrast, the Christian virtues described in the Bible develop when we choose God and God's ways in spite of temptation or impulses to do otherwise.

God wants us to choose to love freely, even when that choice involves pain, because we are committed to God, not to our own good feelings and rewards. God wants us to cleave, as Job did, even when we have every reason to deny God hotly. Job clung to God's justice when he was the best example in history of God's apparent injustice. He did not seek the Giver because of gifts; after all gifts were removed, he still sought the Giver.

Where Is God When It Hurts? (89 – 91)

◆

Dissonant Symphony

Most of us operate on a different scale of values than God. We would rank life as the greatest value (and thus murder as the greatest crime). But clearly God operates from a different perspective. God indeed values human life, so much so as to declare it "sacred," meaning God alone, and no human being, has the right to take life. But in Noah's day, for example, God did not hesitate to exercise that right; numerous times in the Old Testament God took human life in order to halt the spread of evil.

Similarly, many Bible passages show that some things are more awful to God than the pain of God's children. God did not even stay personally exempt from suffering: consider the awesome pain involved in God becoming a man and dying on a cross. Do these show God's lack of compassion? Or do they, rather, demonstrate that some things are more important to God than a suffering-free life for even the most loyal followers?

The Bible consistently changes the questions we bring to the problem of pain. It rarely, or ambiguously, answers the backward-looking question "Why?" Instead, it raises the forward-looking question, "To what end?" We are not put on earth merely to satisfy our desires, to pursue life, liberty, and happiness. We are here to be changed, to be made more like God in order to prepare us for a lifetime with God. And that process may be served by the mysterious pattern of all creation: pleasure sometimes emerges against a background of pain, evil may be transformed into good, and suffering may produce something of value.

Is God speaking to us through our sufferings? It is dangerous and perhaps even unscriptural to torture ourselves by looking for God's message in a specific throb of pain, a specific instance of suffering. The message may simply be that we live in a world with fixed laws, like everyone else. But from the larger view, from the view of all history, yes, God speaks to us through suffering — or perhaps in spite of suffering. The symphony God is composing includes minor chords, dissonance, and tiresome fugal passages. But those of us who follow the conductor through early movements will, with renewed strength, someday burst into song.

Where Is God When It Hurts? (94 – 95)

◆

Pain Transformed

Paul makes a grand, sweeping statement in Romans, "And we know that in all things God works for the good of those who love him." That statement is sometimes twisted and made to imply that "only good things will happen to those who love God." As the rest of the chapter makes clear, Paul meant just the opposite. God used even traumatic events to advance the cause in and through Paul. It would be more accurate to say that God was working *in Paul* through harsh circumstances than to say God was at work in the circumstances themselves.

Does God introduce suffering into our lives so that these good results will come about? Remember the pattern established at the end of Job. Questions about cause lie within God's domain; we cannot expect to understand those answers. We have no right to speculate with pronouncements like "Some relatives came to Christ at the funeral—that must be why God took him home." Instead, *response* is our assignment. Paul and other New Testament authors insist that if we respond with trust God will, without doubt, work in us for good. As Job himself said so presciently, "those who suffer he delivers in their suffering; he speaks to them in their affliction" (36:15).

The notion of suffering as productive brings a new dimension to our experience of pain. Human beings undergo goal-directed suffering quite willingly, as athletes and pregnant women can attest. According to the Bible, a proper Christian response to suffering gives similar hope to the person on the hospital bed. As we rely on God, and trust the Spirit to mold us in God's image, true hope takes shape within us, "a hope that does not disappoint." We can literally become better persons because of suffering. Pain, however meaningless it may seem at the time, can be transformed.

Where is God when it hurts? God is in *us*—not in the things that hurt—helping to transform bad into good. We can safely say that God can bring good out of evil; we cannot say that God brings about the evil in hopes of producing good.

Where Is God When It Hurts? (108–9)

The Good, the Bad, the Redeemed

I was lecturing on writing when out of the blue someone asked a question I had not anticipated. "You've written three books on pain. Bottom line, what have you learned?"

As if by instinct I replied with this simple formula: "Pain is good. Pain is bad. Pain can be redeemed." Later, when I had time to reflect, I concluded that this trilogy of ideas sums up what I have learned not only about pain, but about most everything else in life.

First, pain. My work with leprosy specialist Dr. Paul Brand has taught me that if you take away pain's exquisitely tuned warnings, you get people who destroy themselves—the problem of leprosy, precisely.

Yet pain is also bad, or "fallen." Working in a hospice, my wife saw daily the ravaging effects of pain that no longer has a useful purpose: to the dying patient, pain warnings may seem like the jeers of a cosmic sadist.

Even so, pain can be redeemed. The dying, individual leprosy patients, as well as people like Joni Eareckson Tada who live with permanent afflictions, have demonstrated to me that out of the worst that life offers, great good may come.

This trilogy of belief crops up in so many forms that I have adopted it as the lens through which I view life. I tend to think, though, that for most moderns the notion of redemption has grown as fusty as the word. We err either on the side of Goodness or Fallenness.

Vestigial Marxists, environmentalists, Christian Scientists, liberal Democrats, and health-and-wealth theologians extol the goodness of creation. On the other hand neoconservatives, Calvinists, feminists, UN peacekeepers, human rights lawyers, and newspaper editors remind us daily of the grim reality of human fallenness.

Rather than settling in somewhere along this spectrum, I am striving to complete the cycle and see the world through the third lens of redemption. For me, Romans 8 is the most realistically hopeful passage in all the Bible. It affirms the goodness of creation and also its fallenness. Yet it sounds the ringing affirmation that whatever "things" may come our way—and for Paul these meant manifold hardships—all can be redeemed to work for our ultimate good.

"Back Page" column, *Christianity Today,*
September 11, 1995 (96)

◆

Tremors in China

I interviewed four representatives of the Chinese house-church movement on a trip to Beijing in 2004. The most impressive visitor was Brother Shi, a bright and passionate forty-four-year-old who did not fit the profile of peasant Christianity. Indeed, as a teenager Shi headed up his province's Communist Youth League and later served as a Red Guard. He used to pass by a crowded Three Self Church each day en route to party headquarters.

One day he decided to attend, and the vibrant testimonies of Christians puzzled him further. He bought a Bible and read it through. A few months later he announced to the party chief that he was becoming a Christian. The chief shouted that he was cutting off all chance of advancement in life, throwing away a bright future. As Shi left the room he called the boy's father to report this treachery.

Shi's father met him at the door with oaths. "You have done a very bad thing to us!" he said. "I fought against the Christian Chiang Kai-shek, and I fought against the Christians in Korea, and now I have Jesus in my own house!" He kicked Shi out of the house, throwing his belongings in the dirt outside. For several days, Shi slept in a friend's office. He would see his father on the street and try to speak, but his father always turned his head.

A decade later, after the miraculous healing of his grandson, Shi's father at last began to soften. Today he too is a Christian.

Brother Shi must travel constantly, eluding police through narrow escapes. "I've never been arrested, thanks to the help of churches who hide me," he says. "Once I got away just three minutes before the police came." Due to his leadership skills, Shi now supervises 260,000 Christians in his province. He sees his wife, also a renowned church leader, only once a year.

Before going to China I met with a missionary who had been expelled in 1950. "We felt so sorry for the church we left behind," he said. "They had no one to teach them, no printing presses, no seminaries, no one to run their clinics and orphanages. No resources, really, except the Holy Spirit." It appears the Holy Spirit did just fine.

Finding God in Unexpected Places (178 – 81)

◆

The Paradox of Persecution

In my visits to churches overseas, one difference from North American Christians stands out sharply: their view of hardship and suffering. We who live in unprecedented comfort seem obsessed with the problem of pain. Skeptics mention it as a major roadblock to faith, and believers struggle to come to terms with it. Prayer meetings in the U.S. often focus on illnesses and requests for healing. Not so elsewhere.

I asked a man who visits unregistered house churches in China whether Christians there pray for a change in harsh government policies. After thinking for a moment, he replied that not once had he heard a Chinese Christian pray for relief. "They assume they'll face opposition," he said. "They can't imagine anything else." He then gave some examples.

One pastor had served a term of twenty-two years at hard labor for holding unauthorized church meetings. When he emerged from prison and returned to church, he thanked the congregation for praying. Another imprisoned pastor heard that his wife was going blind. Desperate to rejoin her, he informed the warden that he was renouncing his faith. He was released, but soon felt so guilty that he turned himself in again to the police. He spent the next thirty years in prison.

I found the same pattern in Myanmar (formerly Burma), a dictatorship with brutal policies against religious activities. The person who invited me to the country informed me, "When you speak to pastors, you should remember that probably all of them have spent time in jail because of their faith."

"Then should I talk about one of my book topics like *Where Is God When It Hurts?* or *Disappointment with God?*" I asked.

"Oh, no, that's not really a concern here," he said. "We assume we'll be persecuted for faith. We want you to speak on grace. We need help getting along with each other."

Rumors of Another World (212 – 13)

◇

God at Large

A friend of mine recently returned from a visit to Asian countries where Christians are experiencing persecution. Christians in Malaysia told him, "We're so blessed, because in Indonesia they're killing Christians, but here we just have to put up with discrimination and restrictions on our activities." In Indonesia, where Christians are indeed dying for their faith, they told him, "We're very blessed, because in Malaysia they can't freely publish the gospel. Here, we still can." The church in Indonesia values the power of words.

My job as a writer affords me the opportunity to visit a variety of countries, including some that oppress Christians. I have noticed a striking difference in the wording of prayers. When difficulties come, Christians in affluent countries tend to pray, "Lord, take this trial away from us!" I have heard persecuted Christians and some who live in very poor countries pray instead, "Lord, give us the strength to bear this trial."

Allen Yuan had served a term of twenty-two years at hard labor for holding unauthorized church meetings in China. When he emerged from prison and returned to church, he announced that he had kept a daily count on his dangerous job, and had coupled together one million railroad cars without an injury. "God answered your prayers for my safety!" he rejoiced. Working near the Russian border without warm clothing, he had also avoided serious illness all that time.

According to some estimates, Christians in developed Western countries now represent only 37 percent of believers worldwide. As I travel and also read church history, I have observed a pattern, a strange historical phenomenon of God "moving" geographically from place to place: from the Middle East to Europe to North America to the developing world. My theory is this: God goes where he's wanted.

That's a scary thought in a country like the United States, home to five hundred satellite TV channels for diversion and entertainment.

Finding God in Unexpected Places (57 – 60)

—◆—

True Confession

Psalm 51, a poem of remembrance, may well be the most impressive outcome of David's sordid affair with Bathsheba. It is one thing for a king to confess a moral lapse in private to a prophet. It is quite another for him to compose a detailed account of that confession to be sung throughout the land!

All nations have heroes, but Israel may be alone in making epic literature about its greatest hero's failings. This eloquent psalm, possibly used in worship services as a guide for confession, shows that Israel ultimately remembered David more for his devotion to God than for his political achievements.

Step-by-step, the psalm takes the reader (or singer) through the stages of repentance. It describes the constant mental replays—"Oh, if only I had the chance to do it over"—the gnawing guilt, the shame, and finally the hope for a new beginning that springs from true repentance.

David lives under Old Testament law, which prescribes a harsh punishment for his crimes: death by stoning. But in a remarkable way Psalm 51 reveals the true nature of sin as a broken *relationship* with God. "Against you, you only, have I sinned," David cries out. He sees that no ritual sacrifices or religious ceremonies will cause his guilt to vanish; the sacrifices God wants are "a broken spirit, a broken and contrite heart." Those, David has.

In the midst of his prayer, David looks for possible good that might come out of his tragedy and sees a glimmer of light. He prays for God to use his experience as a moral lesson for others. Perhaps, by reading his story of sin, others might avoid the same pitfalls, or by reading his confession they might gain hope in forgiveness. David's prayer is fully answered and becomes his greatest legacy as king. The best king of Israel has fallen the farthest. But neither he, nor anyone, can fall beyond the reach of God's love and forgiveness.

Meet the Bible (216)

◆

Solomon's Folly

With everything imaginable working in his favor, at first it seemed Solomon would gratefully follow God. His prayer of dedication for the temple in 1 Kings 8 is one of the most majestic ever prayed. Yet by the end of his reign Solomon had squandered away nearly every advantage. The poetic man who had sung of romantic love broke all records for promiscuity: seven hundred wives in all, and three hundred concubines! The wise man who had composed so many commonsense proverbs flouted them with an extravagance that has never been equaled. And to please his foreign-born wives, the devout man who had built the temple of God took a final, terrible step: he introduced idol worship into God's holy city.

In one generation, Solomon took Israel from a fledgling kingdom dependent on God for bare survival to a self-sufficient political power. But along the way he lost sight of the original vision to which God had called them. Ironically, by the time of Solomon's death, Israel resembled the Egypt they had escaped: an imperial state held in place by a bloated bureaucracy and slave labor, with an official state religion under the ruler's command. Success in the kingdom of this world had crowded out interest in the kingdom of God. The brief, shining vision of a covenant nation faded away, and God withdrew sanction. After Solomon's death, Israel split in two and slid toward ruin.

A quotation from Oscar Wilde might provide the best epitaph for Solomon: "In this world there are only two tragedies. One is not getting what one wants, and the other is getting it." Solomon got whatever he wanted, especially when it came to symbols of power and status. Gradually, he depended less on God and more on the props around him: the world's largest harem, a house twice the size of the temple, an army well-stocked with chariots, a strong economy. Success may have eliminated any crises of disappointment with God, but it also seemed to eliminate Solomon's desire for God at all. The more he enjoyed the world's good gifts, the less he thought about the Giver.

Disappointment with God (80 – 81)

Longing for More

People surprised to find a book like Song of Songs in the Bible may be knocked flat by the book of Ecclesiastes. "Meaningless! Meaningless! Everything is meaningless!" cries the author of this bleak capitulation of despair.

Although Ecclesiastes mentions no author by name, it contains broad hints that King Solomon was, if not its author, then at least its inspiration. It tells the story of the richest, wisest, most famous man in the world, who follows every pleasure impulse as far as it can lead him. This man, "the Teacher," finally collapses in regret and despair; he has squandered his life.

Early on, chapter 3 gives a capsule summary of the book, beginning with an elegant poem about time and proceeding from there into musings about life typical of the Teacher's search for meaning. The author concludes that God has laid a "burden" on humanity that keeps us from finding ultimate satisfaction on earth. After a lifetime spent in the pursuit of pleasure, the Teacher asks, "Is that all there is?" Even the rare moments of peace and satisfaction he found were easily spoiled by the onrushing threat of death. According to the Teacher, life doesn't make sense outside of God, and will in fact never fully make sense because we are not God.

But God has also "set eternity in the hearts of men." We feel longings for something more: pleasures that will last forever, love that won't go sour, fulfillment, not boredom, from our work.

The Teacher thus dangles between two states, feeling a steady drag toward despair but also a tug toward something higher. Much like a personal journal, the book of Ecclesiastes records his search for balance. The tension does not resolve in this chapter, and some readers wonder if it resolves at all. But Ecclesiastes ends with one final word of advice, the summation of all the Teacher's wisdom: "Fear God and keep his commandments, for this is the whole duty of man."

Meet the Bible (246)

—————◆—————

A Surprising Prayer

Bible college was for me, initially, a breeding ground of doubt and skepticism. I survived by learning to mimic "spiritual" behavior—a student had to, in fact, just to get good grades. There was the odious matter of "Christian service," for instance. The college required each student to participate in a regular service activity, such as street evangelism, prison ministry, or nursing home visitation. I signed up for "university work."

Every Saturday night I would visit a student center at the University of South Carolina and watch television. I was supposed to be "witnessing," of course, and the next week I would dutifully report on all the people I had approached about personal faith. My embellished stories must have sounded authentic because no one ever questioned them.

I was also required to attend a weekly prayer meeting with four other students involved in university work. Those meetings followed a consistent pattern: Joe would pray, and then Craig, and Chris, and the other Joe, and then all four would pause politely for about ten seconds. I never prayed; and after the brief silence, we would open our eyes and return to our rooms.

But one February night to everyone's surprise, including my own, I did pray. I have no idea why. I had not planned to. But after Joe and Craig and Chris and Joe had finished, I found myself praying aloud. "God," I said, and I could sense the tension level in the room rise.

As I recall it, I said something like this: "God, here we are, supposed to be concerned about those ten thousand students at the University of South Carolina who are going to hell. Well, you know that I don't care if they all go to hell, if there is one. I don't even care if I go to there."

You would have to attend a Bible college to appreciate how these words must have sounded to the others in the room. I may as well have been invoking witchcraft or offering child sacrifices. But no one stirred or tried to stop me, and I continued praying.

[Continued on October 27]

Disappointment with God (249–50)

Role Reversal

[Continued from October 26]

For some reason, as I prayed, I started talking about the parable of the good Samaritan. We Bible college types were supposed to feel the same concern for university students as the Samaritan felt for the bloodied Jew lying in the ditch. But I felt no such concern, I said. I felt nothing for them.

And then it happened. In the middle of my prayer, I saw that story in a new light. I had been visualizing the scene as I spoke: an old-fashioned-looking Samaritan, dressed in robes and a turban, bending over a dirty, blood-crusted form in a ditch. But suddenly, in the internal screen of my brain, those two figures changed. The kindly Samaritan took on the face of Jesus. The Jew, pitiable victim of a highway robbery, took on another face too—a face I recognized with a start as my own.

In a flash I saw Jesus reaching down with a moistened rag to clean my wounds and stanch the flow of blood. And as he bent over, I saw myself, the wounded robbery victim, open my eyes and purse my lips. Then, as if watching in slow motion, I saw myself spit at Jesus, full in the face. I saw all that—I, who did not believe in visions, or in biblical parables, or even in Jesus. It stunned me. Abruptly, I stopped praying, got up, and left the room.

All that evening I thought about what had happened. It wasn't exactly a vision—more like a daydreamed parable with a moral twist. Still, I couldn't put it behind me. What did it mean? Was it genuine? I wasn't sure, but I knew that my cockiness had been shattered. On that campus I had always found security in my agnosticism. No longer. I had caught a new glimpse of myself. Perhaps in all my self-assured and mocking skepticism I was the neediest one of all.

I wrote a brief note to my fiancée that night, saying guardedly, "I want to wait a few days before talking about it, but I may have just had the first authentic religious experience of my life."

Disappointment with God (250–51)

◆

A Crumpled Photo

One holiday I was visiting my mother, who lives seven hundred miles away. We reminisced about times long past, as mothers and sons tend to do. Inevitably, the large box of old photos came down from the closet shelf, spilling out a jumbled pile of thin rectangles that mark my progression through childhood and adolescence: the cowboy-and-Indian getups, the Peter Cottontail suit in the first grade play, my childhood pets, endless piano recitals, the graduations from grade school and high school and finally college.

Among those photos I found one of an infant, with my name written on the back. The portrait itself was not unusual. I looked like any baby: fat-cheeked, half-bald, with a wild, unfocused look to my eyes. But the photo was crumpled and mangled, as if one of those childhood pets had got hold of it. I asked my mother why she had hung onto such an abused photo when she had so many other undamaged ones.

There is something you should know about my family: when I was ten months old, my father contracted spinal lumbar polio. He died three months later, just after my first birthday. My father was totally paralyzed at age twenty-four, his muscles so weakened that he had to live inside a large steel cylinder that did his breathing for him. He had few visitors—people had as much hysteria about polio in 1950 as they do about AIDS today. The one visitor who came faithfully, my mother, would sit in a certain place so that he could see her in a mirror bolted to the side of the iron lung.

My mother explained to me that she had kept the photo as a memento, because during my father's illness it had been fastened to his iron lung. He had asked for pictures of her and of his two sons, and my mother had had to jam the pictures in between some metal knobs. Thus, the crumpled condition of my baby photo.

[Continues on October 29]

Disappointment with God (254)

Someone Is There

[Continued from October 28]

I rarely saw my father after he entered the hospital, since children were not allowed in polio wards. Besides, I was so young that, even if I had been allowed in, I would not now retain those memories.

When my mother told me the story of the crumpled photo, I had a strange and powerful reaction. It seemed odd to imagine someone caring about me whom, in a sense, I had never met. During the last months of his life, my father had spent his waking hours staring at those three images of his family, my family. There was nothing else in his field of view. What did he do all day? Did he pray for us? Yes, surely. Did he love us? Yes. But how can a paralyzed person express his love, especially when his own children are banned from the room?

I have often thought of that crumpled photo, for it is one of the few links connecting me to the stranger who was my father, a stranger who died much younger than I am now. Someone I have no memory of, no sensory knowledge of, spent all day every day thinking of me, devoting himself to me, loving me as well as he could. Perhaps, in some mysterious way, he is doing so now in another dimension. Perhaps I will have time, much time, to renew a relationship that was cruelly ended just as it had begun.

I mention this story because the emotions I felt when my mother showed me the crumpled photo were the very same emotions I felt that February night in a college dorm room when I first believed in a God of love. *Someone is there*, I realized. Someone is watching life as it unfolds on this planet. More, Someone is there who loves me. It was a startling feeling of wild hope, a feeling so new and overwhelming that it seemed fully worth risking my life on.

Disappointment with God (254 – 55)

Handling Disappointment

I know too well my own instinctive response to the hiddenness of God: I retaliate by ignoring God. Like a child who thinks he can hide from adults by holding a chubby hand over his eyes, I try to shut God out of my life. If God won't reveal himself to me, why should I acknowledge God?

The book of Job gives two other responses to such disappointment with God. The first was shown by Job's friends. Job's profound disappointment with God did not match their theology. They saw a clear-cut choice between a man who claimed to be just and a God they knew to be just. Suppress your feelings, they told him. We know for a fact that God is not unjust. Shame on you for the outrageous things you're saying!

The second response, Job's, was a rambling mess, a jarring counterpoint to his friends' relentless logic. "Why then did you bring me out of the womb?" he demanded of God. "I wish I had died before any eye ever saw me." Job lashed out in a protest he knew to be futile, like a bird repeatedly hurling itself against a windowpane.

And which of the two responses does the book endorse? Both parties needed some correction, but after all the windy words had been uttered God ordered the pious friends to crawl repentantly to Job and ask him to pray on their behalf.

One bold message in the book of Job is that you can say anything to God. Throw at God your grief, your anger, your doubt, your bitterness, your betrayal, your disappointment—God can absorb them all. As often as not, spiritual giants of the Bible are shown *contending* with God. They prefer to go away limping, like Jacob, rather than to shut God out. In this respect, the Bible prefigures a tenet of modern psychology: you can't really deny your feelings or make them disappear, so you might as well express them. God can deal with every human response save one. God cannot abide the response I fall back on instinctively: an attempt to ignore God or act as though God does not exist. That response never once occurred to Job.

Disappointment with God (234–35)

Setting Conditions

My friend Richard, who still looks to Job as the most honest part of the Bible, finds its conclusion almost irrelevant. "Job got a personal appearance by God, and I'm happy for him. That's what I've been asking for all these years. But since God hasn't visited me, how does Job help with my struggles?"

I believe that Richard has put his finger on an important dividing line of faith. In a sense, our days on earth resemble Job's *before* God came to him in a whirlwind. We too live among clues and rumors, some of which argue against a powerful, loving God. We too must exercise faith, with no certainty.

Richard lay prone on the wooden floor of his apartment, pleading for God to "reveal" himself, gambling all his faith on God's willingness to step into the seen world as he had done for Job. And Richard lost that gamble. Frankly, I doubt whether God feels any "obligation" to prove something. God did so many times in the Old Testament, and with finality in the person of Jesus. What further incarnations do we require?

I say this with great care, but I wonder if a fierce, insistent desire for a miracle —even a physical healing—sometimes betrays a *lack* of faith rather than an abundance of it. Such prayers may, like Richard's, set conditions for God. When yearning for a miraculous resolution to a problem, do we make our loyalty to God contingent on whether God proves something yet again in the seen world?

If we insist on visible proofs from God, we may well prepare the way for a permanent state of disappointment. True faith does not so much attempt to manipulate God to do our will as it does to position us to do God's will. As I searched the Bible, I was struck by how few saints experienced anything like Job's dramatic encounter with God. The rest responded to God's hiddenness not by demanding that God show himself, but by going ahead and believing a God who stayed hidden. Hebrews 11 pointedly notes that the giants of faith "did not receive the things promised; they only saw them and welcomed them from a distance."

Disappointment with God (240 – 42)

November

Behind the Curtain

An encounter with the hiddenness of God may badly mislead. It may tempt us to see God as the enemy and to interpret God's hiddenness as a lack of concern.

An incident in the life of a famous Bible character makes this point. The prophet Daniel had a mild—mild in comparison with Job's—encounter with the hiddenness of God. Daniel puzzled over an everyday problem of unanswered prayer: why was God ignoring his repeated requests? For twenty-one days Daniel devoted himself to prayer. He mourned. He gave up choice foods. He swore off meat and wine, and used no lotions on his body. All the while he called out to God, but received no answer.

Then one day Daniel got far more than he bargained for. A supernatural being, with eyes like flaming torches and a face like lightning, suddenly showed up on a riverbank beside him. Daniel's companions all fled in terror. When he tried talking to the dazzling being, he could hardly breathe.

The visitor proceeded to explain the reason for the long delay. He had been dispatched to answer Daniel's very first prayer, but had run into strong resistance from "the prince of the Persian kingdom." Finally, after a three-week standoff, reinforcements arrived and Michael, one of the chief angels, helped him break through the opposition.

I will not attempt to interpret this amazing scene of the universe at war, except to point out a parallel to Job. Like Job, Daniel played a decisive role in the warfare between cosmic forces of good and evil, though much of the action took place beyond his range of vision. To him, prayer may have seemed futile, and God indifferent; but a glimpse "behind the curtain" reveals exactly the opposite. Daniel's limited perspective, like Job's, distorted reality.

The big picture, with the whole universe as a backdrop, includes much activity that we never see. When we stubbornly cling to God in a time of hardship, or when we simply pray, more—much more—may be involved than we ever dream. It requires faith to believe that, and faith to trust that we are never abandoned, no matter how distant God seems.

Disappointment with God (235 – 37)

❖

Cross and Swastika

The church's challenge to the state often breaks into open conflict, especially when totalitarian states assert themselves as "Lord." Nazi Germany posed the severest test to Luther's doctrine of two kingdoms, a test that the church mostly failed. Martin Niemöller, one of the leaders of the resistance against Hitler, confessed that the church by and large had lacked the courage to resist Hitler. Practicing an individualistic faith, accustomed to submitting to the state, they waited far too late to protest. Indeed, many Protestant leaders—including Niemöller himself—initially thanked God for the rise of the Nazis, who seemed the only alternative to communism.

Ominously, evangelical Christians were attracted to Hitler's promise to restore morality to government and society. According to Karl Barth, the church "almost unanimously welcomed the Hitler regime, with real confidence, indeed with the highest hopes." German Protestants had no strong tradition of opposing the state. Christians adopted the motto "The Swastika on our breasts, the Cross in our hearts." Their pastors dressed in Nazi uniforms and sang Nazi hymns. Too late did they learn that once again the church had been seduced by the power of the state.

Eventually a minority did wake up to the Nazi threat. Niemöller published a series of sermons with the in-your-face title *Christus ist mein Führer* (Christ [not Hitler] is my Führer). He spent seven years in a concentration camp; Dietrich Bonhoeffer was executed in another. In the end, faithful Christians were the only significant group to oppose Hitler within Germany. Trade unions, Parliament, politicians, doctors, scientists, university professors, lawyers—all these capitulated. Only Christians who understood their loyalty to a higher power resisted.

Thankfully, the church in the United States has never had to face such a stark choice against tyranny. To the contrary, American democracy has historically welcomed religious-based activism. In the words of Robert Bellah, "There has not been a major issue in the history of the United States on which religious bodies did not speak out, publicly and vociferously."

"A State of Ungrace," *Christianity Today,*
February 3, 1997 (35 – 36)

NOVEMBER 3

Fumes of Ungrace

How is it that Christians called to dispense the aroma of grace instead emit the noxious fumes of ungrace? In the modern United States, one answer to that question springs readily to mind. The church has allowed itself to get so swept up in political issues that it plays by the rules of power, which are rules of ungrace. In no other arena is the church at greater risk of losing its calling than in the public square.

I fully support the right, and indeed the responsibility, of Christians to get involved politically: in moral crusades such as abolition, civil rights, and anti-abortion, Christians have led the way. And I believe the media grossly exaggerate the "threat" posed by the religious right. The Christians I know who are involved in politics bear little resemblance to their caricatures. Nevertheless I do worry about the recent tendency for the labels "evangelical Christian" and "religious right" to become interchangeable. Political cartoons show that Christians increasingly are perceived as rigid moralists who want to control others' lives.

I know why some Christians are acting ungraciously: out of fear. We feel under attack in schools, in courts, and sometimes in Congress. Meanwhile we see around us the kind of moral change that marks society's decay. In such categories as crime, divorce, youth suicide, abortion, drug use, children on welfare, and illegitimate births the United States outranks every other industrialized country. Social conservatives feel more and more like an embattled minority, their values under constant attack.

How can Christians uphold moral values in a secular society while at the same time conveying a spirit of grace and love? As the psalmist expressed it, "When the foundations are being destroyed, what can the righteous do?" Behind the gruffness of many Christians with strong opinions, I'm sure, lies a deep and proper concern for a world that has little place for God. Yet I also know that, as Jesus pointed out to the Pharisees, a concern for moral values alone is not nearly enough. Moralism apart from grace solves little.

What's So Amazing About Grace? (229 – 30)

◇

Weapons of Mercy

As should be clear by now, I believe that dispensing God's grace is the Christian's main contribution. As Gordon MacDonald said, the world can do anything the church can do except one thing: it cannot show grace. In my opinion, Christians are not doing a very good job of dispensing grace to the world, and we stumble especially in this field of faith and politics.

Jesus did not let any institution interfere with his love for individuals. Jewish racial and religious policies forbade him to speak with a Samaritan woman, let alone one with a checkered moral background; Jesus selected one as a missionary. His disciples included a tax collector, viewed as a traitor by Israel, and also a Zealot, a member of the super-patriot party. He praised the countercultural John the Baptist. He met with Nicodemus, an observant Pharisee, and also with a Roman centurion. He dined in the home of another Pharisee named Simon and also in the home of an "unclean" man, Simon the Leper. For Jesus, the person was more important than any category or label.

I know how easy it is to get swept away by the politics of polarization, to shout across picket lines at the "enemy" on the other side. But Jesus commanded, "Love your enemies."

Who is *my* enemy? The abortionist? The Hollywood producer polluting our culture? The politician threatening my moral principles? The drug lord ruling my inner city? If my activism, however well-motivated, drives out love, then I have misunderstood Jesus' gospel. I am stuck with law, not the gospel of grace.

The issues facing society are pivotal, and perhaps a culture war is inevitable. But Christians should use different weapons in fighting wars, the "weapons of mercy" in Dorothy Day's wonderful phrase. Jesus declared that we should have one distinguishing mark: not political correctness or moral superiority, but *love*. Paul added that without love nothing we do—no miracle of faith, no theological brilliance, no flaming personal sacrifice—will avail (1 Corinthians 13).

What's So Amazing About Grace? (242)

Watered Down

We dare not forget G. K. Chesterton's aphorism: while a coziness between church and state may be good for the state, it is bad for the church. Herein lies the chief danger to grace: the state, which runs by the rules of un-grace, gradually drowns out the church's sublime message of grace.

Insatiable for power, the state may well decide that the church could prove even more useful if the state controlled it. This happened most dramatically in Nazi Germany when evangelical Christians were attracted to Hitler's promise to restore morality.

The church works best as a force of resistance, a counterbalance to the consuming power of the state. The cozier it gets with government, the more watered-down its message becomes. The gospel itself changes as it devolves into civil religion. The lofty ethics of Aristotle, Alasdair MacIntyre points out, had no place for a good man showing love to a bad man—in other words, had no place for a gospel of grace.

In sum, the state must always water down the absolute quality of Jesus' commands and turn them into a form of external morality—precisely the opposite of the gospel of grace. Jacques Ellul goes so far as to say the New Testament teaches no such thing as a "Judeo-Christian ethic." It commands conversion and then this: "Be perfect ... as your heavenly Father is perfect." Read the Sermon on the Mount and try to imagine any government enacting that set of laws.

A state government can shut down stores and theaters on Sunday, but it cannot compel worship. It can arrest and punish KKK murderers but cannot cure their hatred, much less teach them love. It can pass laws making divorce more difficult but cannot force husbands to love their wives and wives their husbands. It can give subsidies to the poor but cannot force the rich to show them compassion and justice. It can ban adultery but not lust, theft but not covetousness, cheating but not pride. It can encourage virtue but not holiness.

What's So Amazing About Grace? (250–51)

Mirror or Window

Early on, Stalin built a village in Poland called Nowa Huta, or "New Town," to demonstrate the promise of communism. He could not change the entire country at once, he said, but he could construct one new town with a shiny steel factory, spacious apartments, plentiful parks, and broad streets as a token of what would follow. Later, Nowa Huta became one of the hotbeds of Solidarity, demonstrating instead the failure of communism to make just one town work.

What if Christians used that same approach in secular society and succeeded? "In the world the Christians are a colony of the true home," said Bonhoeffer. Perhaps Christians should work harder toward establishing colonies of the kingdom that point to our true home. All too often the church holds up a mirror reflecting back the society around it, rather than a window revealing a different way.

If the world despises a notorious sinner, the church will love her. If the world cuts off aid to the poor and the suffering, the church will offer food and healing. If the world oppresses, the church will raise up the oppressed. If the world shames a social outcast, the church will proclaim God's reconciling love. If the world seeks profit and self-fulfillment, the church seeks sacrifice and service. If the world demands retribution, the church dispenses grace. If the world splinters into factions, the church joins together in unity. If the world destroys its enemies, the church loves them. That, at least, is the vision of the church in the New Testament: a colony of heaven in a hostile world.

Like the dissidents in Communist countries, Christians live by a different set of rules. We are a "peculiar" people, wrote Bonhoeffer, which he defined as extraordinary, unusual, that which is not a matter of course. Jesus was not crucified for being a good citizen, for being just a little nicer than everyone else. The powers of his day correctly saw him and his followers as subversives because they took orders from a higher power than Rome or Jerusalem.

What would a subversive church look like in the modern United States?

What's So Amazing About Grace? (262 – 63)

◆

The Ultimate Protest

Although the Bible usually speaks to broad principles rather than specific guidelines on money, it does present one action open to all of us. We can disarm the power of money, and we do that by giving it away.

It made no sense for a widow to donate her last few pennies to a corrupt and crumbling institution in Jerusalem. But in that woman's act Jesus saw a moving display of the proper spirit of money. It is *best* used when we give it away.

Gordon Cosby of the Church of the Savior in Washington, D.C., tells the story of a widow whose income was barely adequate to feed and clothe her six children. Every week she had been faithfully placing four dollars into the offering plate. A deacon suggested that Cosby go to the widow and assure her that she could put the money to other use for her family's benefit.

Cosby followed the deacon's advice, to his everlasting regret. The widow responded with great sadness. "You are trying to take away the last thing that gives me dignity and meaning," she said. She had learned a key to giving, which she was clinging to at all costs.

The key is this: the main benefit of giving is in its effect on the giver. Yes, people in Africa and India need my financial help, as the fund-raising appeals urgently remind me. But in truth *my need to give is every bit as desperate as their need to receive.*

The act of giving best reminds me of my place on earth. All of us live here by the goodness and grace of God — like the birds in the air and the flowers of the field, Jesus said. Those creations do not worry about future security and safety; neither should we. Giving offers me a way to express my faith and confidence that God will care for me just as God cares for the sparrow and lily.

Money booklet (20 – 21)

Church Hypocrites

Is church really necessary for a believing Christian? Winston Churchill once said that he related to the church rather like a flying buttress: he supported it from the outside. I tried that strategy for a while, after I had come to believe the doctrine sincerely and had committed myself to God. I am not alone. Far fewer people attend church on Sunday than claim to follow Christ. Some of them have stories similar to mine: they feel burned or even betrayed by a former church experience. Others simply "get nothing out of church." Following Jesus is one thing; following other Christians into a sanctuary on Sunday morning is quite another. Why bother? As the poet Anne Sexton put it,

> They pounded nails into his hands.
> After that, well, after that everyone wore hats . . .

As I reflect on my pilgrimage, I can see that several barriers kept me away from church. First was hypocrisy. The atheistic philosopher Friedrich Nietzsche was once asked what made him so negative toward Christians. He replied, "I would believe in their salvation if they looked a little more like people who have been saved."

Scarred by the absolutist fundamentalism of my childhood, I too approached church warily. On Sunday mornings Christians dressed up in fine clothes and smiled at each other, but I knew from personal experience that such a façade could cloak a meaner spirit. I had a knee-jerk reaction against anything that smacked of hypocrisy until one day the question occurred to me, "What would church look like if every member were just like me?" Properly humbled, I began concentrating on my own spirituality, not everyone else's.

God is the ultimate judge of hypocrisy in the church, I decided; I would leave such judgment in God's capable hands. I began to relax and grow softer, more forgiving of others. After all, who has a perfect spouse, or perfect parents or children? We do not give up on the institution of family because of its imperfections —why give up on the church?

Church: Why Bother? (20 – 21)

◆

Cooling Off

What changed my attitude toward church? A skeptic might say that I lowered my expectations somewhere along the way, or perhaps I "got used to" church just as, after numerous false starts, I got used to opera. Yet I sense something else at work: church has filled in me a need that could not be met in any other way. Saint John of the Cross wrote, "The virtuous soul that is alone ... is like the burning coal that is alone. It will grow colder rather than hotter." I believe he is right.

Christianity is not a purely intellectual, internal faith. It can only be lived in community. Perhaps for this reason, I have never entirely given up on church. At a deep level I sense that church contains something I desperately need. Whenever I abandon church for a time, I find that I am the one who suffers. My faith fades, and the crusty shell of lovelessness grows over me again. I grow colder rather than hotter. And so my journeys away from church have always circled back inside.

Nowadays, despite my checkered churchgoing past, I could hardly imagine life without church. How did I move from being a skeptic of the church to an advocate, from a spectator to a participant? Can I identify what rehabilitated my attitude toward church?

I would respond by saying that over the years I have learned what to look for in a church. In childhood I had no more choice over church than I had over what school I attended. Later, I exercised much choice over church, trying first this one and then that one. The process taught me that the key to finding the right church lay inside me. It involved *my way of seeing*. Once I learned how to look, issues such as what denomination a church belonged to mattered far less.

This new way of seeing has helped me to stop merely tolerating the church and instead learn to love it. Once we have a vision of the church, as participants we can help it become the kind of place God intended.

Church: Why Bother? (23 – 24)

◆

Who's the Audience?

I used to approach church with the spirit of a discriminating consumer. I viewed the worship service as a performance. Give me something I like. Entertain me.

Speaking of folks like me, Søren Kierkegaard said that we tend to think of church as a kind of theater: we sit in the audience, attentively watching the actor onstage, who draws every eye to himself. If sufficiently entertained, we show our gratitude with applause and cheers. Church, though, should be the opposite of the theater. In church *God* is the audience for our worship. Far from playing the role of the leading actor, the minister should function as something like a prompter, the inconspicuous helper who sits beside the stage and prompts by whispering.

What matters most takes place within the hearts of the congregation, not among the actors onstage. We should leave a worship service asking ourselves not "What did I get out of it?" but rather "Was God pleased with what happened?" Now I try to look up in a worship service, to direct my gaze beyond the platform, toward God.

The same God who took pains to specify details of animal sacrifice for the ancient Israelites later told them, "I have no need of a bull from your stall or of goats from your pen, for every animal of the forest is mine, and the cattle on a thousand hills." By focusing on the externals of worship, they had missed the point entirely: God was interested in a sacrifice of the heart, an internal attitude of submission and thanksgiving. Now, when I attend church, I try to focus on that internal spirit rather than sitting back in my pew, like a theater critic, making aesthetic judgments.

For many reasons I continue to worship in the Protestant tradition, which places a greater emphasis on the Word spoken from the pulpit. Yet I no longer worry so much about the style of music, the order of worship, the "trappings" of church. By focusing on the trappings and not the goal of worship — to meet God — I had missed the most important message of all.

Church: Why Bother? (24 – 27)

◆

Strange Menagerie

Every family contains some successful individuals and some miserable failures. At Thanksgiving, corporate vice-president Aunt Mary sits next to Uncle Charles, who drinks too much and has never held a job. Although some of the folks gathered around the table are clever and some stupid, some are ugly and some attractive, some healthy and some disabled, in a family these differences become insignificant.

Cousin Johnny seems to try his best to alienate himself from the family, but there is no practical way to drum him out. He belongs, like all of us, because we were born of the same ancestors and the same genes coil inside our cells. Failure does not cancel out membership. A family, said Robert Frost, "is the place where, when you have to go there, they have to take you in."

I sometimes think that God invented the human institution of the family as a training ground to prepare us for how we should relate within other institutions. Families work best not by papering over their differences but rather by celebrating them. A healthy family builds up the weakest members while not tearing down the strong. As John Wesley's mother put it, "Which child of mine do I love best? I love the sick one until he's well, the one away from home until she's back."

Family is the one human institution we have no choice over. We get in simply by being born, and as a result we are involuntarily thrown together with a menagerie of strange and unlike people. Church calls for another step: to voluntarily choose to band together with a strange menagerie because of a common bond in Jesus Christ. I have found that such a community more resembles a family than any other human institution. Henri Nouwen once defined a community as "a place where the person you least want to live with always lives." His definition applies equally to the group that gathers each Thanksgiving and the group that congregates each Sunday morning.

Church: Why Bother? (64 – 65)

◇

A Change Underway

I detect an Old Testament pattern of God as the reluctant intervener in history. God waits, chooses a partner, moves with agonizing slowness, does a few miracles, then waits some more. In the Gospels, supernatural activity again bursts out, with power radiating from Jesus. Yet Jesus too intervened selectively, performing miracles not as a cure-all but as *signs* of God's rule.

Jesus also announced a major change. "A time is coming," he explained, "and has now come when the true worshipers will worship the Father *in spirit and truth*, for they are the kind of worshipers the Father seeks." He dislocated God's presence from its traditional place in a building and relocated it in a most unlikely place: ordinary people.

God did not design this planet as an arena in which to demonstrate natural law-bending skills, much as we humans may crave that at times. Mainly, God wants to relate to creatures personally, to love and be loved. Restoring such a relationship has been painfully slow, fraught with error, and punctuated by fits and starts. Compared to Old Testament stories of miracle and triumph, it often seems like regression. To the contrary, the New Testament presents a long but steady advance in intimacy with God.

I know Christians who yearn for God's older style of a power-worker who topples pharaohs, flattens Jericho's walls, and scorches the priests of Baal. I do not. I believe the kingdom now advances through grace and freedom, God's goal all along. I accept Jesus' assurance that his departure from earth represents progress, by opening a door for the Counselor to enter. We know how counselors work: not by giving orders and imposing changes through external force. A good counselor works on the inside, bringing to the surface dormant health. For a relationship between such unequal partners, prayer provides an ideal medium.

Most of the time the Counselor communicates subtly: feeding ideas into my mind, bringing to awareness a caustic comment I just made, inspiring me to choose better than I would have done otherwise, shedding light on the hidden dangers of temptation, sensitizing me to another's needs. God's Spirit whispers rather than shouts, and brings peace not turmoil.

Prayer: Does It Make Any Difference? (102 – 3)

◇

God-Incidents

In the normal course of providence, God works through and in creation, not despite it. For this reason, most answers to prayer are difficult to prove with any certainty. Trusting God's character, we can see more than coincidence. We see a true partnership, intimate and intertwined.

I remember standing, frantic, in downtown Budapest, after a ten-hour flight. On my laptop computer I had notes to prepare for speeches, and upon checking into my hotel I realized I had left the power cord in an airport somewhere in transit. Stores were closing in an hour, the next day was Sunday, and I had no clue where I might find computer parts in that foreign city, much less get there. I breathed a quick prayer and started searching for anyone who spoke English. Just as I was feeling desperate, a young man and his mother came up to me and said, "Can we help you?" The young man had just completed his English proficiency exam and the two were heading toward a train station adjacent to a computer store — one of two stores in Budapest that carried the particular part I needed. Was that coincidence?

A year later I attended a conference of 1,200 people and had one meal on my own. I chose a seat at random. As conversation unfolded, I learned that the other guests at the table were members of the same family. The father, back home in Michigan, was living through the final stages of esophageal cancer, days from death, and at the last minute two in-laws had come to stay with him. The daughters had driven twenty hours from another state. For six months the mother had not left her husband alone. She came to the conference hoping to talk to me about the topic of suffering because she knew that my wife had worked as a hospice chaplain. She had brought along a list of questions, in faint hope of discussing them. Would I mind?

"When I pray, coincidences happen," said Archbishop William Temple; "when I don't, they don't." Rather than dissecting such incidents, I try to use them as building blocks of faith, to see them as "God-incidents" instead of coincidences.

Prayer: Does It Make Any Difference? (104 – 6)

◆

Kingdom Partners

One busy day, after resurrecting a dead girl and healing a sick woman, then restoring sight to two blind men and voice to a mute, Jesus seemed overwhelmed by the unfinished task. Crowds had gathered, and he felt a surge of compassion "because they were harassed and helpless, like sheep without a shepherd." In the face of such endless human need, Jesus gave one of the few direct commands on what to pray for. "Ask the Lord of the harvest, therefore, to send out workers into his harvest field."

Yes, Jesus made a lasting impact on a small corner of Palestine, but he would need partners to carry the good news of the kingdom to Rome and to continents beyond.

In the late nineteenth century William Carey felt a call to travel to India as one of those workers in the harvest. Pastors around him scoffed: "Young man, if God had wanted to save the heathen in India, he could certainly do it without the likes of you or us." They missed the point of partnership. God does very little on earth without the likes of you and us.

As partners in God's work on earth, we insist that God's will be done while at the same time committing ourselves to whatever that may require of us. "Your kingdom come, your will be done," Jesus taught us to pray. These words are not placid invocations but demands. Give us justice! Set the world aright!

We have different roles to play, we and God. As God made clear to Job, we humans lack the capacity to figure out providence and cosmic justice and answers to the "Why?" questions. It is our role, rather, to follow in Jesus' steps by doing the work of the kingdom both by our deeds and by our prayers. What is God doing in the world? The answer is another question: What are God's people doing? We are Christ's body on earth, to borrow Paul's metaphor. We are "in Christ," a phrase the New Testament repeats 164 times. Those we minister to, Christ ministers to; those we forgive, Christ forgives. When we extend mercy to the broken, we reach out with the hands of Christ himself.

Prayer: Does It Make Any Difference? (110 – 12)

Double Agency

Some people worry that prayer may lead to passivity, that we will retreat to prayer as a substitute for action. Jesus saw no contradiction between the two: he spent long hours in prayer and then long hours meeting human needs. The church in Acts did likewise, acting out a true partnership. They prayed for guidance about caring for widows, then appointed deacons in order to free up other leaders for the vital act of prayer. Stop praying, and they just might stop caring about widows. They prayed together about the cultural controversies between Jews and Gentiles, then convened a council to hammer out a compromise.

The apostle Paul prayed diligently for the early churches, but also wrote and visited them. He prayed and worked with equal abandon. On a sea voyage, after being convinced as a result of his prayers that all passengers would survive an impending shipwreck, he proceeded to take charge of the 276 on board, giving orders and organizing the salvage efforts.

The accounts in Acts present a double agency that makes it impossible to distinguish God's work from the Christians' work—the point, exactly. Recall Paul's paradoxical command to the Philippians: "Continue to work out your salvation with fear and trembling, for it is God who works in you to will and to act according to his good purpose."

In my own frustrations with prayer, I used to focus on the lack of God's intervention. Why won't God do what I ask? My perspective has changed as I understand prayer as partnership, a subtle interplay of human and divine that accomplishes God's work on earth. God asks me to make myself known in prayer and then works my prayers into a master plan for my life—a plan that I can only faintly grasp.

Prayer: Does It Make Any Difference? (113)

◆

Angle of Repose

In the mountains where I live, geologists and miners use the elegant term "angle of repose" to describe the precise angle at which a boulder will rest on the side of a hill, rather than tumble downward. I think of that image as the point at which prayer and action meet. Every so often one of those boulders breaks loose, releasing the potential energy in a crashing rockslide. Something similar happens in an avalanche, when an accumulation of tiny, almost weightless snowflakes breaks loose.

Dietrich Bonhoeffer's secret, said one German theologian, was the creative way in which he combined prayer and earthiness, forging a spirituality that made room for piety as well as activism. While sequestered in a monastery and awaiting orders from the German resistance movement, Bonhoeffer wrote, "A day without morning and evening prayers and personal intercessions is actually a day without meaning or importance." A pastor, he continued to observe regular prayer times even after he went to prison for participating in a plot against Hitler.

Bonhoeffer grasped the nature of prayer as partnership with God's activity on earth. He scolded German Christians who retreated into piety while resigning themselves to the evil around them ("That's just the way things are"). We cannot simply pray and then wait for God to do the rest. At the same time, Bonhoeffer cautioned against an activism that opposed the forces of evil without drawing on the power of prayer. The battle against evil requires both prayer and prayerful action.

During the 1960s and 1970s prayer almost vanished from the campuses of mainline Protestant seminaries, which emphasized the social gospel. Talk about a private life of prayer made a person suspect and might even provoke a lecture on the dangers of pietism. As a result many Protestants began visiting monasteries in search of spiritual direction. They learned from activists such as Dorothy Day and Thomas Merton that social action unsupported by prayer may well lead to exhaustion and despair.

Each of us in our own way will feel the tension between prayer and activism, between action and contemplation. I receive a newsletter from the Center for Action and Contemplation, and together those two words encompass most of what we are called to do in following Jesus.

Prayer: Does It Make Any Difference? (124 – 25)

◆

Light Shed Backward

A Chinese philosopher insisted on riding his donkey backward so that he would not be distracted by where he was going and could instead reflect on where he had been. The Bible works in somewhat the same way. The Epistles shed light backward on the events of the Gospels, so that we understand them in a new way. Epistles and Gospels both shed light backward on the Old Testament.

For centuries the phrase "as predicted by the prophets" was one of the most powerful influences on people coming to faith. Justin the Martyr credited his conversion to the impression made on him by the Old Testament's predictive accuracy. The brilliant French mathematician Blaise Pascal also cited fulfilled prophecies as one of the most important factors in his faith. Nowadays, few Christians read the Prophets except in search of Ouija-board-like clues into the future. We have lost the Reformers' profound sense of unity between the two Testaments.

Understanding our civilization and understanding the Bible may be important reasons for reading the Old Testament, but perhaps the most important reason is that it is the Bible Jesus read. He traced in its passages every important fact about himself and his mission. He quoted from it to settle controversies with opponents such as the Pharisees, Sadducees, and Satan himself. The images—Lamb of God, shepherd, sign of Jonah, stone which the builders rejected—that Jesus used to define himself came straight from the pages of the Old Testament.

Once, a government tried to amputate the Old Testament from Christian Scriptures. The Nazis in Germany forbade study of this "Jewish book" and Old Testament scholarship disappeared from German seminaries and journals. In 1940, Dietrich Bonhoeffer defiantly published a book on Psalms and got slapped with a fine. In letters of appeal he argued convincingly that he was explicating the prayer book of Jesus Christ himself. Jesus quoted often from the Old Testament, Bonhoeffer noted, and never from any other book—even though the Hebrew canon had not been officially closed. Besides, much of the Old Testament explicitly or implicitly points to Jesus.

The Bible Jesus Read (24–25)

◆

Inside Information

According to Elaine Storkey, the question, "Quick, what is God like?" was asked by a small girl who rushed up to her newborn brother in his hospital room. She shrewdly figured that, having just come from Heaven, he might have some inside information.

The Old Testament provides an answer to the little girl's question, a different answer than we might get from the New Testament alone. Apart from the Old Testament we will always have an impoverished view of God. God is not a philosophical construct but a Person who acts in history: the one who created Adam, who gave a promise to Noah, who called Abraham and introduced himself by name to Moses, who deigned to live in a wilderness *tent* in order to live close to his people. From Genesis 1 onward, God has wanted to be known, and the Old Testament is our most complete revelation of what God is like.

The novelist John Updike has said that "our brains are no longer conditioned for reverence and awe." The very words sound old-fashioned, and to the degree that they do, to that degree we have strayed from the picture of God revealed in the Old Testament. We cannot box God in, explain God away. God seems a wild and mysterious Other, not a God we can easily figure out. No one tells God what to do (the main point in God's blistering speech to Job).

I admit that the Old Testament introduces some problems I would rather avoid. "Consider therefore the kindness and sternness of God," wrote Paul. I would rather consider only the kindness of God, but by doing so I would construct my own image of God instead of relying on God's self-revelation. I dare not speak for God without listening to God speak.

It makes an enormous difference how we picture God. Is God an aloof watchmaker who winds up the universe and steps back to watch it wind down on its own? Or is God a caring parent who holds not just the universe but individual men and women in his hands? I cannot conceive of a more important project than restoring a proper notion of what God is like.

The Bible Jesus Read (26 – 27)

Daily Reminders

Like a drumbeat that never stops, in the pages of the Old Testament we hear the consistent message that this world revolves around God, not us. The Hebrews had incessant reminders built into their culture. They dedicated their firstborn livestock and children to God, wore portions of the law on their heads and wrists, posted visible reminders on their doorways, said the word "blessed" a hundred times a day, even wore distinctive hairstyles and sewed tassels on their garments.

A devout Jew could barely make it through an hour, much less an entire day, without running smack into some reminder that he or she lived in God's world. Even the Hebrew calendar marked time by events such as the Passover and Day of Atonement, not merely by the harvest cycle and the moon. The world, they believed, is God's property. And human life is "sacred," which simply means that it belongs to God.

This Old Testament notion sounds very un-American. Do not our founding documents guarantee us the right to life, liberty, and the pursuit of happiness? We rebel against any interference with our personal rights, and anyone who attempts to set boundaries that might encroach on our personal space. In our secularized, industrialized environment, we can go through an entire week, not just a day, without bumping into a reminder that this is God's world.

I remember hearing a chapel message at Wheaton College during the 1970s, when the Death of God movement had reached its peak. Professor Robert Webber chose to speak on the third commandment, "Thou shalt not take the name of the Lord thy God in vain." We usually interpret that commandment in a narrow sense of prohibiting swearing, said Webber, who then proceeded to expand its meaning to "never live as though God does not exist." Or, stated positively, "Always live in awareness of God's existence."

The more I study the commandment in its Old Testament environment, the more I agree with Webber. Any key to living in such awareness must be found in the great Jewish legacy of the Old Testament.

The Bible Jesus Read (28 – 29)

◆

Whitewashed

As I study the life of Jesus, one fact consistently surprises me: the group that made Jesus angriest was the group that, externally at least, he most resembled. Scholars agree that Jesus closely matched the profile of a Pharisee. He obeyed the Torah, or Mosaic law, quoted leading Pharisees, and often took their side in public arguments. Yet Jesus singled out the Pharisees for his strongest attacks. "Snakes!" he called them. "Brood of vipers! Fools! Hypocrites! Blind guides! Whitewashed tombs!"

What provoked such outbursts? The Pharisees had much in common with those whom the press might call Bible-Belt fundamentalists today. They devoted their lives to following God, gave away an exact tithe, obeyed every minute law in the Torah, and sent out missionaries to gain new converts. Rarely involved in sexual sin or violent crime, the Pharisees made model citizens.

Jesus' fierce denunciations of the Pharisees show how seriously he viewed the toxic threat of legalism. Its dangers are elusive, slippery, hard to pin down, and I have scoured the New Testament in search of them—especially Luke 11 and Matthew 23, where Jesus morally dissects the Pharisees. I believe these dangers represent as great a threat in the current century as they did in the first.

Overall, Jesus condemned the legalists' emphasis on externals. "You Pharisees clean the outside of the cup and dish, but inside you are full of greed and wickedness," he said. Expressions of love for God had, over time, evolved into ways of impressing others. In Jesus' day, religious people wore gaunt and hungry looks during a brief fast, prayed grandiosely in public, and wore portions of the Bible strapped to their bodies. In his Sermon on the Mount, Jesus denounced the motives behind such seemingly harmless practices.

Leo Tolstoy, who battled legalism all his life, understood the weaknesses of a religion based on externals. According to Tolstoy, all religious systems tend to promote external rules, or moralism. In contrast, Jesus refused to define a set of rules that his followers could then fulfill with a sense of satisfaction. The proof of spiritual maturity, Tolstoy contended, is not how "pure" you are but awareness of your impurity. That very awareness opens the door to grace.

What's So Amazing About Grace? (195–98)

Smoother than a Billiard Ball

I have written about legalism partly because of my own bruising encounters with it and partly because I believe it represents such a powerful temptation to the church. Legalism stands like a stripper on the sidelines of faith, seducing us toward an easier way. It teases, promising some of the benefits of faith but unable to deliver what matters most. As Paul wrote to the legalists of his day, "For the kingdom of God is not a matter of eating and drinking, but of righteousness, peace and joy in the Holy Spirit."

At first glance legalism seems hard, but actually freedom in Christ is the harder way. It is relatively easy not to murder, hard to reach out in love; easy to avoid a neighbor's bed, hard to keep a marriage alive; easy to pay taxes, hard to serve the poor. When living in freedom, I must remain open to the Spirit for guidance. I am more aware of what I have neglected than what I have achieved. I cannot hide behind a mask of behavior, like the hypocrites, nor can I hide behind facile comparisons with other Christians.

The Reformed theologian J. Gresham Machen wrote, "A low view of law leads to legalism in religion; a high view makes one a seeker after grace." The ultimate effect of legalism is to lower one's view of God. We tend to think of the stricter denominations and Christian institutions as more "spiritual." In truth, the differences between Bob Jones University and Wheaton College, or between Mennonites and Southern Baptists, are minuscule when compared to a holy God.

I once read that proportionally the surface of the earth is smoother than a billiard ball. The heights of Mount Everest and the troughs of the Pacific Ocean are very impressive to those of us who live on this planet. But from the view of Andromeda, or even Mars, those differences matter not at all. That is how I now see the petty behavioral differences between one Christian group and another. Compared to a holy and perfect God, the loftiest Everest of rules amounts to a molehill. You cannot earn God's acceptance by climbing; you must receive it as a gift.

What's So Amazing About Grace? (209 – 10)

◆

Jolly Beggars

As a child, I put on my best behavior on Sunday mornings, dressing up for God and for the Christians around me. It never occurred to me that church was a place to be honest. Now, though, as I seek to look at the world through the lens of grace, I realize that imperfection is the prerequisite for grace. Light only gets in through the cracks.

My pride still tempts me to put on the best front, to clean up appearances. "It is easy to acknowledge," said C. S. Lewis, "but almost impossible to realise for long, that we are mirrors whose brightness, if we are bright, is wholly derived from the sun that shines upon us. Surely we must have a little—however little— native luminosity? Surely we can't be *quite* creatures." He goes on, "Grace substitutes a full, childlike and delighted acceptance of our Need, a joy in total dependence. We become 'jolly beggars.'"

We creatures, we jolly beggars, give glory to God by our dependence. Our wounds and defects are the very fissures through which grace might pass. It is our human destiny on earth to be imperfect, incomplete, weak, and mortal, and only by accepting that destiny can we escape the force of gravity and receive grace. Only then can we grow close to God.

Strangely, God is closer to sinners than to "saints." (By saints I mean those people renowned for their piety—true saints never lose sight of their sinfulness.) As one lecturer in spirituality explains it, "God in heaven holds each person by a string. When you sin, you cut the string. Then God ties it up again, making a knot—and thereby bringing you a little closer to him. Again and again your sins cut the string—and with each further knot God keeps drawing you closer and closer."

Once my view of myself changed, I began to see the church in a different light too: as a community of people thirsty for grace. Like alcoholics on the path to recovery, we share a mutually acknowledged weakness.

What's So Amazing About Grace? (273)

◆

Declaration of Dependence

Norwegian theologian Ole Hallesby settled on the single word *helplessness* as the best summary of the heart attitude that God accepts as prayer. "Whether it takes the form of words or not, does not mean anything to God, only to ourselves," he adds. "Only he who is helpless can truly pray."

What a stumbling block! Almost from birth we aspire to self-reliance. Adults celebrate when children learn to do something on their own: go to the bathroom, get dressed, brush teeth, tie shoelaces, ride a bike, walk to school.

As adults we like to pay our own way, live in our own houses, make our own decisions, rely on no outside help. We look down upon those who live off welfare or charity. Faced with an unexpected challenge, we seek out "self-help" books. All the while we are systematically sealing off the heart attitude most desirable to God and most descriptive of our true state in the universe. "Apart from me you can do nothing," Jesus told his disciples, a plain fact that we conspire to deny.

The truth, of course, is that I am not self-reliant. As a child I may never have learned to read books, much less write them if a teacher had not stood over me to correct my miscues. As an adult I rely on public utilities to bring me electricity and fuel, vehicle manufacturers to provide me transportation, ranchers and farmers to feed me, pastors and mentors to nourish me spiritually. I live in a web of dependence, at the center of which is God in whom all things hold together.

Prayer forces me to catch sight of this my true state. In Henri Nouwen's words, "To pray is to walk in the full light of God, and to say simply, without holding back, 'I am human and you are God.'"

Most parents feel a pang when the child outgrows dependence, even while knowing the growth to be healthy and normal. With God, the rules change. I never outgrow dependence, and to the extent I think I do, I delude myself. Asking for help lies at the root of prayer: the Lord's Prayer itself consists of a string of such requests. Prayer is a declaration of dependence upon God.

Prayer: Does It Make Any Difference? (33 – 35)

◇

Contract Faith

I have observed that people involved in ministry, perhaps more so than most people, live with an unstated "contract faith." After all, they're giving time and energy to work for God; don't they deserve special treatment in return?

My wife would get irritated when she got a parking ticket while stopping to pick up meat for a soup kitchen or while visiting a shut-in at the hospital. The meter expired for the very reason that she had sensed a need to devote more time to doing God's work. Her reward: a fine and a half-day trip to the city courthouse!

Bud, one of the true "saints" in urban ministry in Chicago, nearly cut off his hand on a power saw while demonstrating to volunteers how to build houses for the homeless. My friend Douglas has lived a Job-like existence in many ways, experiencing the failure of a ministry, his wife's death from cancer, and his own and a child's injuries by a drunk driver. Yet Douglas advises, "Don't confuse God with life."

When doubts arise, I often turn to that great chapter by Paul, Romans 8. "Who shall separate us from the love of Christ?" asks Paul. "Shall trouble or hardship or persecution or famine or nakedness or danger or sword?" In that one sentence, the apostle Paul summarizes his ministry autobiography. He endured all those trials for the sake of the gospel, and yet somehow he had the faith to believe that these "things"—surely not good in themselves—could nevertheless be used by God to accomplish good.

The apostle Paul had learned to see past the hardships of life to a loving God who will one day prevail. "For I am convinced that neither death nor life, neither angels nor demons, neither the present nor the future, nor any powers, neither height nor depth, nor anything else in all creation, will be able to separate us from the love of God that is in Christ Jesus our Lord," the chapter concludes triumphantly. Confidence like that can go a long way towards solving discouragement over a ministry that never quite works out the way we wish.

Church: Why Bother? (92 – 94)

Spur to Action

Prayer may seem at first like disengagement, a reflective time to consider God's point of view. But that vantage presses us back to accomplish God's will, the work of the kingdom. We are God's fellow workers, and as such we turn to prayer to equip us for the partnership. Karl Barth, living in the crisis days of Nazi rule, declared prayer to be "the true and proper work of the Christian," and observed that "the most active workers and thinkers and fighters in the divine service in this world have at the same time, and manifestly, been the most active in prayer."

In modern-day Los Angeles, at the Catholic Worker soup kitchen, the day's work begins with this prayer: "Make us worthy, Lord, to serve our brothers and sisters who live and die in poverty and hunger. Give to them through our hands this day their daily bread and, by our understanding love, give peace and joy."

One volunteer reports that often this initial prayer does not suffice:

> As a result, sometimes I get all caught up in the heavy responsibility of our task, and I have to take a step back to repeat the words of the prayer again. And then I remember, "Oh yes, I'm not in charge. God is. Somehow, there will be enough food; somehow, there will be enough time to prepare it; and somehow, there will be enough volunteers to serve it. Somehow, we will get through this day."

During the food preparation, one person volunteers to go off and pray for an hour. The crew insists on this practice even though the extra pair of hands could be chopping vegetables or making coffee. They want it to be God's work, not theirs. And by eliminating the time for prayer they would be yielding to the workaholism of our culture. In addition, one morning a week the entire community gathers for a half hour of meditative prayer. For activists on the front lines, prayer serves as part oasis and part emergency room.

Prayer: Does It Make Any Difference? (128)

◇

Going Solo

In a tendency that occurs in every religion, the thirst for solitude seems to awaken when society is in a state of collapse. Jewish Essenes retreated into caves in Jesus' day; the Buddha withdrew in order to purge himself of social illusions; the Hindu Gandhi observed a regimen of strict silence on Mondays, a practice he would not interrupt even for meetings with the king of England.

Solitude rips off all masks and disguises, and breaks needless dependence on material goods. Henry David Thoreau insisted, "I never found the companion that was so companionable as solitude."

Thomas Merton was the best apologist for the life of solitude in our century. Merton longed to join those "men on this miserable, noisy, cruel earth who tasted the marvelous joy of silence and solitude, who dwelt in forgotten mountain cells, in secluded monasteries, where the news and desires and appetites and conflicts of the world no longer reached them." Nevertheless, he insisted that "the only justification for a life of deliberate solitude is the conviction that it will help you to love not only God but also other men."

Merton proved that a life of solitude need not lead to isolation or irrelevance. Has our century known a more acute observer of politics, culture, and religion than this monk who rarely spoke and rarely left the grounds of his monastery?

It surprises me that in such a time of moral crisis the church has not responded again with a movement toward solitude. Elijah, Moses, and Jacob met God alone. The apostle Paul, John the Baptist, and Jesus himself escaped to the wilderness for spiritual nourishment.

What if every Christian took a two-hour nature walk each weekend, without speaking? Or if, like Gandhi, we observed a day of silence? He chose Monday; what if we agreed to maintain silence after church on Sunday? More radical still, what if we silenced all Sunday sporting events on television and radio?

I had best stop. As the hermits remind us, these spiritual disciplines can get out of control.

"Back Page" column, *Christianity Today,*
April 6, 1998 (80)

Cosmic Matters

Job presents the astounding truth that our choices of faith matter not just to us and our own destiny but, amazingly, to God himself. Eliphaz taunted Job, "Can a man be of benefit to God?... What would he gain if your ways were blameless?" (22:1–3). At the end, Eliphaz may have chewed on those words as he offered sacrifices through Job and asked forgiveness. Job's faith gained for God a great victory over Satan, who had questioned the entire human experiment.

A piece of the history of the universe was at stake in Job and is still at stake in our own responses. The Bible gives hints, only hints, into the mystery behind that truth:

- A statement by Jesus in Luke 10 that while his followers were out announcing the kingdom of God, "I saw Satan fall like lightning from heaven."
- An intriguing whisper in Romans 8 that we on earth will be agents for redeeming nature. "The creation waits in eager expectation for the sons of God to be revealed" (8:19). Or as Clarence Jordan's *Cotton Patch Version of Paul's Epistles* translates it, "In fact, the fondest dream of the universe is to catch a glimpse of real live sons and daughters of God."
- This phrase from Ephesians: "His intent was that now, through the church, the manifold wisdom of God should be made known to the rulers and authorities in the heavenly realms" (3:10).
- A sweeping assertion from the apostle Peter that "even angels long to look into these things" (1 Peter 1:12).

Such veiled hints reiterate the central message of Job: how we respond *matters*. By hanging onto the thinnest thread of faith, Job won a crucial victory in God's grand plan to redeem the earth. God has given ordinary men and women the dignity of participating in the redemption of the cosmos. God is allowing us, through our obedience, to help reverse the pain and unfairness of this world that Job described so eloquently. We might even say that God agrees with Job's complaints against the fallen world; God's plan to reverse the fall depends on the faith of those who follow God.

The Bible Jesus Read (66–67)

◆

Soul Therapy

The psalms give me a model of spiritual therapy. I once wrote a book titled *Disappointment with God*, and my publishers initially worried over the title, proposing instead *Overcoming Disappointment with God*. It seemed faintly heretical to introduce a book with a negative title into Christian bookstores filled with books on the marvelous Christian life. I found, however, that the Bible includes detailed accounts of people sorely disappointed with God—to put it mildly.

Not only Job and Moses have it out with God; so do Habakkuk, Jeremiah, and many of the unnamed psalmists. Some psalms merit titles like "Furious with God," "Betrayed by God," "Abandoned by God," "In Despair about God." Consider a few lines from Psalm 89:

> How long, O LORD? Will you hide yourself forever?
> How long will your wrath burn like fire? . . .
> For what futility you have created all men!

Or these sentiments from Psalm 88:

> Why, O LORD, do you reject me
> and hide your face from me? . . .
> the darkness is my closest friend.

It may seem strange for sacred writings to include such scenes of spiritual failure, but actually their inclusion reflects an important principle of therapy. A marriage therapist will often warn new clients, "Your relationship may get worse before it gets better." Resentments that have been buried for years may resurface. Misunderstandings must be nakedly exposed before true understanding can begin to flourish. Indeed, the psalms, like psychoanalysis, may help uncover neurotic elements in us.

The odd mixture of psalms of cursing, psalms of praise, and psalms of confession no longer jars me as it once did. Instead, I am continually amazed by the spiritual wholeness of the Hebrew poets, who sought to include God in every area of life by bringing to God every emotion experienced in daily activity. One need not "dress up" or "put on a face" to meet God. There are no walled-off areas; God can be trusted with reality.

For the Hebrew poets, God represented a reality more solid than their own whipsaw emotions or the checkered history of their people. They wrestled with God over every facet of their lives, and in the end it was the very act of wrestling that proved their faith.

The Bible Jesus Read (120–23)

◆

Center Stage

We all experience both an inner life and an outer life simultaneously. If I attend the same event as you (say, a party), I will take home similar "outer" facts about what happened and who was there but a wholly different "inner" point of view. My memory will dwell on what impression I made. Was I witty or charming? Did I offend someone or embarrass myself? Did I look good to others? Most likely, you will ask the same questions, but about yourself.

David seemed to view life differently. His exploits — killing wild animals bare-handed, felling Goliath, surviving Saul's onslaughts, routing the Philistines — surely earned him a starring role. Nonetheless, as he reflected on those events and wrote poems about them, he found a way to make Jehovah, God of Israel, the one on center stage. Whatever the phrase "practicing the presence of God" means, David experienced it. Whether he expressed that presence in lofty poems of praise or in an earthy harangue, in either case he intentionally involved God in the details of his life.

David had confidence that he mattered to God. After one narrow escape he wrote, "[God] rescued me because he delighted in me" (Psalm 18:19). When David felt betrayed by God, he let God know: it was he, after all, who first said the words, "My God, my God, why have you forsaken me?" He called God into account, insisting that God keep up the other end of their special relationship.

Throughout his life David believed, truly believed, that the spiritual world, though invisible to him, was every bit as real as the "natural" world of swords and spears and caves and thrones. His psalms form a record of a conscious effort to reorient his own daily life to the reality of that supernatural world beyond him. Now, centuries later, we can use those very same prayers as steps of faith, a path to lead us from an obsession with ourselves to the actual presence of our God.

The Bible Jesus Read (131)

Advanced School

The process of "letting God in" on every detail of life is one I need. In the busy, industrialized modern world, we tend to compartmentalize our lives. We fill our days with activities—getting the car repaired, taking vacations, going to work, mowing the lawn, chauffeuring the kids—and then try to carve out some time for "spiritual" activities such as church, small groups, personal devotions. I see none of that separation in Psalms.

Somehow, David and the other poets managed to make God the gravitational center of their lives so that everything related to God. To them, worship was the central activity in life, not something to get over in order to resume other activity.

I am learning this daily process of reorientation, and Psalms has become for me a step in the process of recognizing God's true place at the gravitational center. I am trying to make the prayers first prayed by the Hebrew poets authentically my prayers. The New Testament writers did this, quoting Psalms more than any other book. The Son of God on earth did likewise, relying on them as the language of relationship between a human being and God.

I am sure that making the psalms my own prayers will require a lifelong commitment. I sense in them an urgency, a desire and hunger for God that makes my own look anemic by contrast. The psalmists panted for God with their tongues hanging out, as an exhausted deer pants for water. They lay awake at night dreaming of "the fair beauty of the Lord." They would rather spend one day in God's presence than a thousand years elsewhere. It was the advanced school of faith these poets were enrolled in, and often I feel more like a kindergartner. In reading the psalms, maybe some of it will rub off.

The Bible Jesus Read (132)

December

Imagine There's No Heaven

Anthropologists report that every human society discovered believed in an afterlife. I started wondering what a society might look like if it *did not* believe in an afterlife. I let my imagination run, and came up with the following conclusions. For the sake of a convenient label (and with apologies to Samuel Butler, author of *Erewhon*), I'll call my mythical society the backward-spelled Acirema.

Aciremans value youth above all else. Since for them nothing exists beyond life on earth, youth represents hope. As a result, anything preserving the illusion of youthfulness flourishes. Sports is a national obsession. Magazine covers present wrinkle-free faces and gorgeous bodies.

Naturally, Aciremans do not value old age, for elderly people offer a distasteful reminder of the end of life. The Acireman health industry thus promotes cures for baldness, skin creams, cosmetic surgery, and other elaborate means to mask the effects of aging, the prelude to death. In especially callous parts of Acirema, citizens even confine the elderly to their own housing, isolated from the general populace.

Acirema emphasizes "image" rather than "substance." Such practices as dieting, exercise, and body-building, for example, have attained the status of pagan worship rites. A well-formed body visibly demonstrates achievement in this world, whereas nebulous inner qualities—compassion, self-sacrifice, humility—merit little praise. As an unfortunate side-effect, a disabled or disfigured person has great difficulty competing in Acirema.

Acireman religion focuses exclusively on how one fares in the here and now, for there is no reward system after death. Those Aciremans who still believe in a deity look for God's approval in terms of good health and prosperity on earth. At one time, Acireman priests pursued what they called "evangelism," but now they devote most of their energy to improving the welfare of fellow citizens.

Aciremans spend billions to maintain elderly bodies on life-support systems, while they permit, even encourage, the abortion of fetuses. This is not as paradoxical as it seems, for Aciremans believe that human life begins at birth and ends at death.

Just thinking about such a society gives me the creeps. I sure am glad I live in the good ol' U.S.A., where, as George Gallup assures us, the vast majority of the population believes in an afterlife.

I Was Just Wondering (215 – 18)

◆

Not So Modern Despair

I first saw the word on the bright red cover of a book my elder brother brought home from college: *Existentialism Today*. Although I had no clue what *existentialism* meant, that book beckoned me into an arcane world of avant-garde philosophy. I had grown up in airtight fundamentalism, protected from exposure to such dangerous pollutants; the culture of Paris's Left Bank was as alien to me as that of Ouagadougou. Nevertheless, when as a teenager in the 1960s I read that red-covered book and went on to sample the novels of Camus and Sartre, something inside me stirred to life.

Flat emotions, a radical indifference to others, the sensation of drifting, numbness to pain, a resigned acceptance of a world gone mad—all these qualities had somehow seeped through the hermetic shield of fundamentalism. *That's me!* I thought as I read each book of existentialism. I was a child of my age after all.

Looking back now, I can see that I mainly identified with the despair. Why am I living? What is this circus all about? Can one person among billions make a difference on this planet? Those questions pounded me like ocean waves as I read the writings of the French novelists, then Hemingway and Turgenev. All the turbulent questions of the sixties washed over me, and existentialism provided an answer of sorts by insisting they have no answer. I found that more current literature—John Updike, Kurt Vonnegut Jr., John Irving, Jerzy Kosinski, Walker Percy—gave off the same scent of futility, a scent stale as old cigar smoke.

Carl Jung reported that a third of his cases suffered from no definable neurosis other than "the senselessness and emptiness of their lives." He went on to name meaninglessness the general neurosis of the modern era, as people torture themselves with questions that neither philosophy nor religion can answer.

A few years after my adolescent brush with existentialism, and after God had begun to heal some of my feelings of futility and despair, I discovered with an eerie shock precisely the same sentiments, of all places, in the center of the Bible. The mysterious, often-ignored book of Ecclesiastes contains every idea and emotion I had encountered in the writers of existential despair.

[Continued on December 3]

The Bible Jesus Read (143–45)

◆

The First Existentialist

[Continued from December 2]

I wonder if the modern existentialists appreciate the delicious irony of Ecclesiastes 1:9 – 10, which declares, "There is nothing new under the sun," nothing "of which one can say, 'Look! This is something new.'" What seemed like brash iconoclasm in the 1960s, I learned, merely fulfilled the weary prophecies of the ancient Teacher who, three thousand years before, anticipated the full range of human experience and, astonishingly, included his findings in a book that became part of the Bible. Truly, Ecclesiastes was a book for the ages, and I began a search to understand this prescient volume.

Once I got over my sheer amazement about the message of Ecclesiastes, certain nagging questions set in. One struck me immediately, as I read the Old Testament straight through. How can Ecclesiastes coexist with its nearest neighbor, the book of Proverbs? Two more unlike books could not be imagined. Read them back to back and you wonder whether Ecclesiastes was written as a kind of mocking rebuttal.

Proverbs has life figured out: learn wisdom, exercise prudence, follow the rules, and you will live a long and prosperous life. In Ecclesiastes the confident, matter-of-fact tone — *I've got life figured out and you need only follow this sage advice* — has vanished, replaced by resignation and cynicism. Thrifty, honorable people suffer and die just like everyone else. Evil people prosper and grow fat, regardless of Proverbs' neat formulas to the contrary.

> There is something else meaningless that occurs on earth: righteous men who get what the wicked deserve, and wicked men who get what the righteous deserve. This too, I say, is meaningless. (8:14)

This kind of disparity between two adjacent Old Testament books used to annoy and frustrate me. Shouldn't the Bible show more consistency? Over time, though, I came to appreciate the variety as one of the Old Testament's main strengths. Like a very long symphony, it ranges through joyful and somber moods, each contributing to the impact of the whole. It reflects what we all experience, sometimes the trials of Job and sometimes the serenity of Psalm 23, while living in a world that sometimes unfolds according to Proverbial principles and sometimes yields the jarring contradictions of Ecclesiastes.

The Bible Jesus Read (146 – 48)

◆

Eternity in the Heart

I once came across a scene of beauty just a few miles outside Anchorage, Alaska, where I noticed a number of cars pulled off the highway. Whales, a pod of silvery white beluga, were feeding no more than fifty feet offshore. I stood with the other onlookers for forty minutes, listening to the rhythmic motion of the sea, following the graceful, ghostly crescents of surfacing whales. The crowd was hushed, even reverent.

The Teacher would doubtless understand the crowd's response to the whales, for he insists that though we are not gods, we are not solely animals either. God "has also set eternity in the hearts of men." Such an elegant phrase applies to much in human experience. Surely it hints at a religious instinct, an instinct that, to the bafflement of anthropologists, finds expression in every human society ever studied. Our hearts perceive eternity in ways other than religious as well. The Teacher is no nihilist; he sees with dazzling clarity the beauty in the created world.

Ecclesiastes endures as a work of great literature and a book of great truth because it presents both sides of life on this planet: the promise of pleasures so alluring that we may devote our lives to their pursuit, and then the haunting realization that these pleasures ultimately do not satisfy. God's tantalizing world is too big for us. Made for another home, made for eternity, we finally realize that nothing this side of timeless paradise will quiet the rumors of discontent.

The Teacher writes: "He has also set eternity in the hearts of men; yet they cannot fathom what God has done from beginning to end." That is the point of Ecclesiastes. The same lesson Job learned in dust and ashes—that we humans cannot figure out life on our own—the Teacher learns in a robe and palace.

Unless we acknowledge our limits and subject ourselves to God's rule, unless we trust the Giver of all good gifts, we will end up in a state of despair. Ecclesiastes calls us to accept our status as creatures under the dominion of the Creator, something few of us do without a struggle.

The Bible Jesus Read (157–60)

Unconventional Warfare

The books of 1 and 2 Kings, Joel, Jonah, Amos, and Hosea chronicle much of the latter history of divided Israel's first two hundred years. The northern kingdom began sliding away from God during the very first days of its birth. But the Bible devotes far more space to the kings and prophets of the southern kingdom. Of the nineteen men and one woman who rule Judah, at least a handful demonstrate a quality of spiritual leadership unmatched in the northern kingdom. Judah proves more faithful in living up to the covenant with God, and chiefly for that reason it outlasts Israel by nearly a century and a half.

Chapter 20 of 2 Chronicles tells of the extraordinary king named Jehoshaphat, one of Judah's early rulers. No ruler of Judah had a wholly peaceful reign, and as a result much of the action in 2 Chronicles takes place, like this story, on a battlefield. Here is the book's philosophy of war in a nutshell: *If you trust in your own military might or that of powerful neighbors, you will lose. Instead, humble yourself and rely totally on God—regardless of the odds against you.*

As the kings of Judah demonstrate with monotonous regularity, it takes uncommon courage to rely on God alone at a moment of great peril. Even the best of them dip into the royal treasury to purchase help from neighboring allies. But King Jehoshaphat provides a textbook example of the proper response. When invading armies threaten, he calls the entire nation together in a giant prayer meeting. On the day of battle, he sends a choir in front of his army to sing praises to God.

Jehoshaphat's tactics may seem more suitable for a church service than a battlefield, but they work. The enemy forces all turn against each other, and Judah's army marches home victorious. This bright moment of national faith shines out from a very mottled historical record. By his public prayer and personal example, King Jehoshaphat shows what can happen when a leader places complete trust in God.

Meet the Bible (289)

◆

Demanding Answers

Everyone has a built-in sense of justice. If a careless driver runs down a small child and nonchalantly drives on, other drivers will follow in hot pursuit. *He can't get away with that!* We may disagree on specific rules of fairness, but we all follow some inner code.

And frankly, much of the time life seems unfair. What child "deserves" to grow up in the slums of Calcutta or Rio de Janeiro or the East Bronx? Why should people like Adolf Hitler, Joseph Stalin, and Saddam Hussein get away with tyrannizing millions of people? Why are some kind, gentle people struck down in the prime of life while other, meaner people live into cantankerous old age?

We all ask different versions of such questions. And the prophet named Habakkuk asked them of God directly—and got a no-holds-barred reply. Habakkuk does not mince words. He demands an explanation for why God isn't responding to the injustice, violence, and evil that the prophet can see around him.

God answers with the same message given other prophets, that soon the Babylonians will punish Judah. But such words hardly reassure Habakkuk, for the Babylonians are ruthless, savage people. Can this be justice—using an even more evil nation to punish Judah?

The book of Habakkuk does not solve the problem of evil. But Habakkuk's conversations with God convince him of one certainty: God has not lost control. A God of justice cannot let evil win. First, God will deal with the Babylonians on their own terms. Then, later, God will intervene with great force, shaking the very foundations of the earth until no sign of injustice remains.

"The earth will be filled with the knowledge of the glory of the LORD, as the waters cover the sea," God promises Habakkuk (2:14). A glimpse of that powerful glory changes the prophet's attitude from outrage to joy. In the course of his "debate" with God, Habakkuk learns new lessons about faith, which are beautifully expressed in the last chapter. God's answers so satisfy Habakkuk that his book, which begins with a complaint, ends with one of the most beautiful songs in the Bible.

Meet the Bible (322)

◇

Now and Later

A most confusing aspect of the prophets is that they do not bother telling us whether the predicted events — invasions, earthquakes, a coming
Leader, a recreated earth — will occur the next day, a thousand years later, or
three thousand years later. In fact, near and distant predictions often appear in
the same paragraph, blurring together. (Probably the prophets did not know a
timetable — after all, Jesus admitted ignorance of God's schedule while he lived
on earth.)

To complicate matters, sometimes the prophets describe an event that apparently has two different fulfillments, one Now and one Later. Isaiah's famous
prophecy "The virgin will be with child and will give birth to a son, and will
call him Immanuel" (7:14) fits this category. The next two verses make clear
that the sign had a fulfillment in Isaiah's own day (many scholars assume the
child to be Isaiah's own), and yet Matthew links the prophecy's final fulfillment
to the Virgin Mary.

Biblical scholars have names for this characteristic of the prophets: double
or triple fulfillment, part-for-the-whole, creative bisociation. Naturally, such
complicated devices raise questions. How are we to know whether a prophet is
describing something in his own day (Now) or something unfulfilled (Later or
Much Later) or both?

I believe this prophetic device, admittedly confusing, offers a glimpse into
how God views history. As "seers," the prophets have insight into God's perspective, and for a God who lives outside the constraints of time, sequence is a
minor issue. The lamb, says the apostle Peter, "was chosen before the creation
of the world, but was revealed in these last times for your sake" (1 Peter 1:20).
Paul added that God also chose his followers "before the creation of the world"
(Ephesians 1:4). Similarly, our hope of eternal life was promised "before the
beginning of time" (Titus 1:2).

Long before Einstein's theory of the relativity of time and space, the New
Testament writers established some truths as, quite literally, timeless.

The Bible Jesus Read (183–84)

◆

The Prophetic Present

Prophecy paradoxically works best in reverse. A New Testament writer could look back and demonstrate how Jesus fulfilled the terms of the Jewish covenant and the predictions of the prophets, even though most people in Jesus' own day failed to make the connection. Jesus' contemporaries were looking for a new King David to rule over Jerusalem; God sent instead a Servant King to rule over the entire universe.

For this same reason we should approach a book like Revelation with cautious humility. John wrote in terms applicable in his day (horsemen, the harlot Babylon, streets of gold) but no one knows for certain how those prophecies will find fulfillment. We can safely assume, though, that God will fulfill them in a way that surpasses the original promise.

My own reading gradually changed as I began to see how the prophets themselves emphasized a flow in the reverse direction, from Later to Now. They defined human longing and portrayed a glorious future in order to affect Now behavior. They offered a vision of the World as God Wants It for people to cling to even in a time of turmoil and despair.

Formerly, I had turned to the prophets for clues into the future, the Later and Much Later. Will the world end in a nuclear holocaust? Does global warming herald the last days? Rather, their message should primarily be affecting my Now. Do I trust in a loving, powerful God even in our chaotic century? Do I cling to God's vision of peace and justice even when the church is often identified with war and oppression? Do I believe that God reigns, though this world shows little evidence of it?

Instinctively, we want to fly to the future. The prophets point us back to the present, yet ask us to live in the light of the future they image up. Can we trust their vision and accept it as the true reality of earth, despite all evidence to the contrary? Can we live Now "as if" God is loving, gracious, merciful, and all-powerful? The prophets remind us that God is indeed and that history itself will one day bear that out. The World as It Is will become the World as God Wants It.

The Bible Jesus Read (186 – 87)

People of the Book

Nehemiah alone is an impressive leader, but when paired with Ezra, he is downright indomitable. The two make a perfect combination. Nehemiah, emboldened by good political connections, inspires others with his hands-on management style and his fearless optimism. Ezra leads more by moral force than by personality. He can trace his priestly lineage all the way back to Moses' brother Aaron, and he seems singularly determined to restore integrity to that office.

On his arrival in Jerusalem some years before, Ezra was shocked by the Jews' spiritual apathy. Tearing his hair and beard, he threw himself on the ground and began a fast of repentance. His remarkable display of contrition so startled the Jewish settlers that they all agreed to repent and change their ways.

The action in Nehemiah 8 takes place after Nehemiah has completed the arduous task of repairing the wall. The Jews, safe at last from their enemies, gather together in hopes of regaining some sense of national identity. As spiritual leader, Ezra addresses the huge crowd. He stands on a newly built platform and begins to read from a document nearly one thousand years old, the scroll that contains the Israelites' original covenant with God.

As Ezra reads, a sound of weeping begins to rise, spreading through the multitude. The Bible does not explain the reason for the tears. Are the people feeling guilt over their long history of breaking that covenant? Or nostalgia over the favored days when Israel had full independence? Whatever the reason, this is no time for tears. Nehemiah and Ezra send out orders to prepare for a huge celebration. God wants joy, not mourning. His chosen people are being rebuilt, just as surely as the stone walls of Jerusalem have been rebuilt.

The central image of this chapter—a lone figure atop a wooden platform reading from a scroll—comes to symbolize the Jewish race. They were becoming "people of the Book." The Jews had not regained the territory and splendor their nation once enjoyed. But they would never forget the lesson of Ezra. He became the prototype for a new leader of the Jews: the scribe, a student of Scripture.

Meet the Bible (361–62)

What Jesus Read

When we read the Old Testament, we read the Bible Jesus read and used. These are the prayers Jesus prayed, the poems he memorized, the songs he sang, the bedtime stories he heard as a child, the prophecies he pondered. He revered every "jot and tittle" of the Hebrew Scriptures. The more we comprehend the Old Testament, the more we comprehend Jesus. Said Martin Luther, "the Old Testament is a testamental letter of Christ, which he caused to be opened after his death and read and proclaimed everywhere through the Gospel."

In a poignant passage from his gospel, Luke tells of Jesus spontaneously appearing by the side of two disciples on the road to Emmaus. Even though rumors of the resurrection were spreading like wildfire, clearly these two did not yet believe, as Jesus could tell by looking into their downcast eyes. In a kind of practical joke, Jesus got them to repeat all that had happened to this man Jesus — they had not yet recognized him — over the past few days. Then he gave them a rebuke:

> "How foolish you are, and how slow of heart to believe all that the prophets have spoken! Did not the Christ have to suffer these things and then enter his glory?" And beginning with Moses and all the Prophets, he explained to them what was said in all the Scriptures concerning himself. (Luke 24:25–27)

Today we need an "Emmaus road" experience in reverse. The disciples knew Moses and the Prophets but could not conceive how they might relate to Jesus the Christ. The modern church knows Jesus the Christ but is fast losing any grasp of Moses and the Prophets.

The Bible Jesus Read (25)

What God Wants

For two weeks one winter I holed up in a mountain cabin in Colorado. I brought along a suitcase full of books and notes, but opened only one of the books: the Bible. I began at Genesis and when I finally made it to Revelation I had to call for a truck to unbury the driveway.

The combination of snow-muffled stillness, isolation from all people, and singular concentration changed forever the way I read the Bible. Above all else, this is what struck me in my daily reading: in theology books you will read of God's omnipotence, omniscience, and impassibility. Those concepts can be found in the Bible, but they are well buried and must be mined. Simply read the Bible and you will encounter not a misty vapor but an actual Person. God feels delight and anger and frustration. Again and again God is shocked by human behavior. Sometimes, after deciding on one response, God "changes his mind."

If you read the Bible straight through, as I did, you cannot help being overwhelmed by the joy and the anguish — in short, the passion — of the Lord of the Universe. True, God "borrows" images from human experience to communicate in a way we can comprehend, but surely those images point to an even stronger reality behind them.

Jeremiah affected me more than any other book. The image of a wounded lover in Jeremiah is an awesome one that I cannot comprehend. Why would the God who created all that exists willingly become subject to such humiliation from creation? I was haunted by the reality of a God who lets our response matter that much.

When we tame God, in words and concepts filed away under alphabetized characteristics, we can easily lose the force of the passionate relationship God seeks above all else. There may be no greater danger to those of us who write, talk, or even think about God. Mere abstractions, to God, may be the cruelest insult of all.

After two weeks of reading the entire Bible, I came away with the strong sense that God doesn't care so much about being analyzed. Mainly — like any parent, like any lover — God wants to be loved.

I Was Just Wondering (153 – 57)

Jilted Lover

Many people carry around the image of God as an impersonal force, something akin to the law of gravity. Hosea portrays almost the opposite: a God of passion and fury and tears and love. A God in mourning over Israel's rejection.

God uses Hosea's unhappy story to illustrate God's own whipsaw emotions. That first blush of love on finding Israel, God says, was like finding grapes in the desert. But as Israel breaks trust again and again, God has to endure the awful shame of a wounded lover. God's words carry a tone surprisingly like self-pity: "I am like a moth to Ephraim, like rot to the people of Judah" (5:12).

The powerful image of a jilted lover explains why, in a chapter like Hosea 11, God's emotions seem to vacillate so. God is preparing to obliterate Israel—wait, now God is weeping, holding out open arms—no, God is sternly pronouncing judgment again. Those shifting moods seem hopelessly irrational, except to anyone who has been jilted by a lover.

Is there a more powerful human feeling than that of betrayal? Ask a high school girl whose boyfriend has just dumped her for a pretty cheerleader. Or tune your radio to a country-western station and listen to the lyrics of infidelity. Or check out the murders reported in the daily newspaper, an amazing number of which trace back to a fight with an estranged lover. Hosea and God demonstrate in living color exactly what it is like to love someone desperately and get nothing in return. Not even God, with all power, can force a human being to love.

Virtually every chapter of Hosea talks about the "prostitution" or "adultery" of God's people. God the lover will not share the beloved bride with anyone else. Yet, amazingly, even when she turns her back, God sticks with her. God is willing to suffer, in hope that someday she will change. Hosea proves that God longs not to punish but to love.

Meet the Bible (282)

◇

Do I Matter?

I stand in the cashier line of the local supermarket and look around me. I see teenagers with shaved heads and nose rings, picking through the snack foods; a yuppie buying one steak, a few twigs of asparagus, and a baked potato; an elderly woman hunched over from osteoporosis, squeezing bruises into the peaches and strawberries. Does God know all these people by name? I ask myself. Do they really matter to him?

Sometimes when I watch the scenes of abortion protests and counterprotests on the evening news, I try to envision the unborn who are prompting such ferocity. I have seen fetuses on display in museum jars to illustrate the progressive stages of human development. Worldwide, about six million of these tiny fetuses are disposed of each year — *murdered*, say the protestors. The image of God rests inside each one, say the theologians. What does God think of six million human beings who die never having seen the outside of a uterus? I wonder. Do they matter?

Novelist Reynolds Price said there is one sentence all humankind craves to hear: "The Maker of all things loves and wants me." That is the sentence Jesus proclaimed, loud as sweet thunder. The Maker of all things is the Maker of all human beings, an odd species that, unfathomably, is deemed worthy of individual attention and love. God demonstrated that love in person, on the gnarly hills of Palestine, and ultimately on a cross.

When Jesus visited earth in the form of a servant, he showed that the hand of God is not too big for the smallest person in the world. It is a hand engraved with our individual names and engraved also with wounds, the cost to God of loving us so much.

Now, when I find myself wallowing in self-pity, overwhelmed by the ache of cosmic loneliness that is articulated so well in books like Job and Ecclesiastes, I turn to the Gospel accounts of Jesus' stories and deeds. If I conclude that my existence "under the sun" makes no difference to God, I contradict one of the main reasons God came to earth. To the question *Do I matter?* Jesus is indeed the answer.

The Bible Jesus Read (201–6)

◆

Does God Care?

Job reluctantly concluded that, no, God could not care about him or about other suffering people. "How faint the whisper we hear of him," sighed Job. The psalmists cried out for some sign that God heard their prayers, some evidence that God had not forsaken them.

I know of only one way to answer the question *Does God care?* and for me it has proved decisive: Jesus is the answer. Jesus never attempted a philosophical answer to the problem of pain, yet he did give an existential answer. Although I cannot learn from him why a particular bad thing occurs, I can learn how God feels about it. Jesus gives God a face, and that face is streaked with tears.

Whenever I read straight through the Bible, a huge difference between the Old and New Testaments comes to light. In the Old Testament I can find many expressions of doubt and disappointment. Whole books—Jeremiah, Habakkuk, Job—center on the theme.

Almost half of the psalms have a dark, brooding tone about them. In striking contrast, the New Testament Epistles contain little of this type of anguish. The problem of pain has surely not gone away: James 1, Romans 5 and 8, the entire book of 1 Peter, and much of Revelation deal with the subject in detail. Nevertheless, nowhere do I find the piercing question *Does God care?* I see nothing resembling the accusation of Psalm 77: "Has God forgotten to be merciful?"

The reason for the change, I believe, is that Jesus answered that question for the witnesses who wrote the Epistles. In Jesus, God presents a face. Anyone who wonders how God feels about the suffering on this groaning planet need only look at that face. James, Peter, and John had followed Jesus long enough for his facial expressions to be permanently etched on their minds. By watching Jesus respond to a hemorrhaging woman, a grieving centurion, a widow's dead son, an epileptic boy, an old blind man, they learned how God felt about suffering.

The Bible Jesus Read (208–9)

Greatly Troubled

Christmas art depicts Jesus' family as icons stamped in gold foil, with a calm Mary receiving the tidings of the annunciation as a kind of benediction. But that is not at all how Luke tells the story. Mary was "greatly troubled" and "afraid" at the angel's appearance, and when the angel pronounced the sublime words about the Son of the Most High whose kingdom will never end, Mary had something far more mundane on her mind: *But I'm a virgin!*

In the modern United States, where each year almost a million teenage girls get pregnant out of wedlock, Mary's predicament has undoubtedly lost some of its force, but in a closely knit Jewish community in the first century the news an angel brought could not have been entirely welcome. The law regarded a betrothed woman who became pregnant as an adulteress, subject to death by stoning.

In a few months, the birth of John the Baptist took place amid great fanfare, complete with midwives, doting relatives, and the traditional village chorus celebrating the birth of a Jewish male. Six months later, Jesus was born far from home, with no midwife, extended family, or village chorus present. A male head of household would have sufficed for the Roman census; did Joseph drag his pregnant wife along to Bethlehem in order to spare her the ignominy of childbirth in her home village?

Today as I read the accounts of Jesus' birth I tremble to think of the fate of the world resting on the responses of two rural teenagers. How many times did Mary review the angel's words as she felt the Son of God kicking against the walls of her uterus? How many times did Joseph second-guess his own encounter with an angel—*just a dream?*—as he endured the hot shame of living among villagers who could plainly see the changing shape of his fiancée?

The Jesus I Never Knew (30 – 32)

Good News

When the Jesuit missionary Matteo Ricci went to China in the sixteenth century, he brought along religious art to illustrate the Christian story. The Chinese readily adopted portraits of the Virgin Mary holding her child. But when he produced paintings of the crucifixion and tried to explain that the God-child had grown up only to be executed, the audience reacted with revulsion and horror. They much preferred the Virgin and insisted on worshiping her rather than the crucified God.

As I thumb through my stack of Christmas cards, I realize that we in Christian countries do much the same thing. We observe a mellow, domesticated holiday purged of any hint of scandal. Above all, we purge from it any reminder of how the story that began at Bethlehem turned out at Calvary.

In the birth stories of Luke and Matthew, only one person seems to grasp the mysterious nature of what God has set in motion: the old man Simeon, who recognized the baby as the Messiah, instinctively understood that conflict would surely follow. "This child is destined to cause the falling and rising of many in Israel, and to be a sign that will be spoken against," he said, and then made the prediction that a sword would pierce Mary's own soul. Somehow Simeon sensed that though on the surface little had changed, underneath, everything had changed. A new force had arrived to undermine the world's powers.

At first, Jesus hardly seemed a threat to those powers. He was born under Caesar Augustus, at a time when hope wafted through the Roman empire. It was Augustus who first borrowed the Greek word for "gospel" or "good news" and applied it as a label for the new world order represented by his reign. His enlightened and stable regime, many believed, would last forever, a final solution to the problem of government.

Meanwhile, in an obscure corner of Augustus's empire the birth of a baby named Jesus was barely noticed by the chroniclers of the day. Jesus' biographers would also borrow the word "gospel," proclaiming a different kind of new world order altogether. They would mention Augustus only once, a passing reference to set the date of a census that ensured Jesus would be born in Bethlehem.

The Jesus I Never Knew (33 – 34)

◇

How Silently

I remember sitting one Christmas season in a beautiful auditorium in London listening to Handel's *Messiah*, with a full chorus singing about the day when "the glory of the Lord shall be revealed." I had spent the morning in museums viewing remnants of England's glory—the crown jewels, a solid gold ruler's mace, the Lord Mayor's gilded carriage—and it occurred to me that just such images of wealth and power must have filled the minds of Isaiah's contemporaries who first heard that promise. When the Jews read Isaiah's words, no doubt they thought back with sharp nostalgia to the glory days of Solomon, when "the king made silver as common in Jerusalem as stones."

The Messiah who showed up, however, wore a different kind of glory, the glory of humility. "'God is great,' the cry of the Moslems, is a truth which needed no supernatural being to teach men," writes Father Neville Figgis. "That *God is little*, that is the truth which Jesus taught man." The God who roared, who could order armies and empires about like pawns on a chessboard, this God emerged in Palestine as a baby who could not speak or eat solid food or control his bladder, who depended on a teenage couple for shelter, food, and love.

In London, I caught glimpses of the more typical way rulers stride through the world: with bodyguards, and a trumpet fanfare, and a flourish of bright clothes and flashing jewelry. Queen Elizabeth II had recently visited the United States, and reporters delighted in spelling out the logistics involved: her four thousand pounds of luggage included two outfits for every occasion, a mourning outfit in case someone died, forty pints of plasma, and white kid leather toilet seat covers. She brought along her own hairdresser, two valets, and a host of other attendants.

In contrast, God's visit to Earth took place humbly, in an animal shelter with no attendants present and nowhere to lay the newborn King but a feed trough. A mule could have stepped on him. "How silently, how silently, the wondrous gift is given."

The Jesus I Never Knew (36 – 37)

A New Approach

Those of us raised in a tradition of informal or private prayer may not appreciate the change Jesus wrought in how human beings approach deity. In most religious traditions, *fear* is the primary emotion when one approaches God.

Certainly the Jews associated fear with worship. A person "blessed" with a direct encounter with God expected to come away scorched or glowing or maybe half-crippled like Jacob. Among people who walled off a separate sanctum for God in the temple and shrank from pronouncing or spelling out the Name, God made a surprise appearance as a baby in a manger. In Jesus, God found a way of relating to human beings that did not involve fear.

In truth, fear had never worked very well. The Old Testament includes far more low points than high ones. A new approach was needed, a new covenant, to use the words of the Bible, one that would not emphasize the vast gulf between God and humanity but instead would span it.

I learned about incarnation when I kept a saltwater aquarium. It was no easy task. You would think, in view of all the energy expended on their behalf, that my fish would at least be grateful. Not so. Every time my shadow loomed above the tank they dove for cover into the nearest shell.

To my fish I was deity. I was too large for them, my actions too incomprehensible. My acts of mercy they saw as cruelty; my attempts at healing they viewed as destruction. To change their perceptions, I began to see, would require a form of incarnation. I would have to become a fish and "speak" to them in a language they could understand.

A human being becoming a fish is nothing compared to God becoming a baby. And yet according to the Gospels that is what happened at Bethlehem. The God who created matter took shape within it, as an artist might become a spot on a painting or a playwright a character within his own play. God wrote a story, only using real characters, on the pages of real history. The Word became flesh.

The Jesus I Never Knew (37 – 39)

◇

The Underdog

I wince even as I write the word, especially in connection with Jesus. It's a crude word, probably derived from dogfighting and applied over time to predictable losers and victims of injustice. Yet as I read the birth stories about Jesus I cannot help but conclude that though the world may be tilted toward the rich and powerful, God is tilted toward the underdog. "He has brought down rulers from their thrones but has lifted up the humble. He has filled the hungry with good things but has sent the rich away empty," said Mary in her Magnificat hymn.

Laszlo Tokes, the Romanian pastor whose mistreatment outraged the country and prompted rebellion against the Communist ruler Ceausescu, tells of trying to prepare a Christmas sermon for the tiny mountain church to which he had been exiled. The state police were rounding up dissidents, and violence was breaking out across the country. Afraid for his life, Tokes bolted his doors, sat down, and read again the stories in Luke and Matthew. Unlike most pastors who would preach that Christmas, he chose as his text the verses describing Herod's massacre of the innocents. It was the single passage that spoke most directly to his parishioners. Oppression, fear, and violence, the daily plight of the underdog, they well understood.

The next day, Christmas, news broke that Ceausescu had been arrested. Church bells rang, and joy broke out all over Romania. Another King Herod had fallen. Tokes recalls, "All the events of the Christmas story now had a new, brilliant dimension for us, a dimension of history rooted in the reality of our lives. . . . For those of us who lived through them, the days of Christmas 1989 represented a rich, resonant embroidery of the Christmas story, a time when the providence of God and the foolishness of human wickedness seemed as easy to comprehend as the sun and the moon over the timeless Transylvanian hills." For the first time in four decades, Romania celebrated Christmas as a public holiday.

The Jesus I Never Knew (39 – 40)

◇

No Fear

Nearly every time an angel appears in the Bible, the first words he says are "Don't be afraid!" Little wonder. When the supernatural makes contact with planet Earth, it usually leaves the human observers flat on their faces, in catatonic fear. But Luke tells of God making an appearance on earth in a form that does not frighten. In Jesus, born in a barn and laid in a feeding trough, God finds at last a mode of approach that we need not fear. What could be less scary than a newborn baby?

Imagine becoming a baby again: giving up language and muscle coordination and the ability to eat solid food and control your bladder. That gives just a hint of the "emptying" that God goes through.

According to the Bible, on earth Jesus is both God and man. As God, he can work miracles, forgive sins, conquer death, and predict the future. Jesus does all that, provoking awe in the people around him. But for Jews accustomed to images of God as a bright cloud or pillar of fire, Jesus also causes much confusion. How could a baby in Bethlehem, a carpenter's son, a man from Nazareth, be the Messiah from God? Jesus' skin gets in the way.

Puzzled skeptics will stalk Jesus throughout his ministry. But Luke 2 shows that God confirms Jesus' identity from his earliest days. A group of shepherds in a field have no doubt—they hear the message of good news straight from a choir of angels. And an old prophet and prophetess recognize him also. Even the skeptical teachers in the temple are amazed.

Why does God self-empty and take on human form? The Bible gives many reasons, some densely theological and some quite practical. The scene of Jesus as an adolescent lecturing rabbis in the temple gives one clue. For the first time, ordinary people can hold a conversation, a debate, with God in visible form. Jesus can talk to anyone—his parents, a rabbi, a poor widow—without first having to announce, "Don't be afraid!" In Jesus, God comes close.

Meet the Bible (405)

◆

Cosmic Christmas

In Revelation 12 John uses bizarre cosmic symbols: a pregnant woman clothed with the sun; a seven-headed red dragon so enormous that its tail sweeps a third of the stars from the sky; a flight into the desert; a war in heaven. Almost all agree that this chapter has something to do with Jesus' birth and its effect on the universe. When a baby was born, the universe shuddered.

In a sense, Revelation 12 presents Christmas from a cosmic perspective, adding a new set of images to the familiar scenes of manger and shepherds and the slaughter of the innocents. What was visible on earth represented ripples on the surface; underneath, massive disruptions were shaking the foundations of the universe. Even as King Herod was trying to kill all male babies in Palestine, cosmic forces were at war behind the scenes. From God's viewpoint—and Satan's—Christmas was far more than the birth of a baby; it was an invasion, the decisive advance in the great struggle for the cosmos. Revelation depicts this struggle in terms of a murderous dragon opposing the forces of good.

Which is the "true" picture of Christmas? They are the same picture, told from two different points of view. This view of Christ's birth in Revelation 12 typifies the pattern of the entire book, in which John fuses things seen with things normally not seen. In daily life, two parallel histories occur at the same time: one on earth and one in heaven. Revelation, by parting the curtain, allows us to view them together. It leaves the unmistakable impression that as we make everyday choices between good and evil, those choices are having an impact on the supernatural universe we cannot see.

Revelation portrays history through sharply contrasting images: good vs. evil, the Lamb vs. the Dragon, Jerusalem vs. Babylon, the bride vs. the prostitute. But it also insists that, no matter how it appears from our limited perspective, God maintains firm control over all history. Ultimately, even the despots will end up fulfilling the plan mapped out for them by God. Pontius Pilate and his Roman soldiers demonstrated that truth. They thought they were getting rid of Jesus by crucifying him. Instead, they made possible the salvation of the world.

Meet the Bible (682–83)

◆

Parallel Universes

Doubt, for me, tends to come in an overwhelming package, all at once. I don't worry much about nuances of particular doctrines, but every so often I catch myself wondering about the whole grand scheme of faith.

I stand in the futuristic airport in Denver, for example, watching important-looking people in business suits, briefcases clutched to their sides like weapons, pause at an espresso bar before scurrying off to another concourse. *Do any of them ever think about God?* I wonder.

Christians share an odd belief in parallel universes. One universe consists of glass and steel and wool clothes and leather briefcases and the smell of freshly ground coffee. The other consists of angels and sinister spiritual forces and somewhere out there places called Heaven and Hell. We palpably inhabit the material world; it takes faith to consider oneself a citizen of the other, invisible world.

Occasionally the two worlds merge for me, and these rare moments are anchors for my faith. The time I snorkeled on a coral reef and suddenly the flashes of color and abstract design flitting around me became a window to a Creator who exults in life and beauty. The time my wife forgave me for something that did not merit forgiveness — that too became a window, allowing a startling glimpse of divine grace.

I have these moments, but soon toxic fumes from the material world seep in. Sex appeal! Power! Money! Military might! These are what matter most in life, I'm told, not the simpering platitudes of Jesus' teachings in the Sermon on the Mount. For me, living in a fallen world, doubt seems more like *forgetfulness* than disbelief.

I, a citizen of the visible world, know well the struggle involved in clinging to belief in another, invisible world. Christmas turns the tables and hints at the struggle involved when the Lord of both worlds descends to live by the rules of the one. In Bethlehem, the two worlds came together, realigned; what Jesus went on to accomplish on planet Earth made it possible for God someday to resolve all disharmonies in both worlds. No wonder a choir of angels broke out in spontaneous song, disturbing not only a few shepherds but the entire universe.

Finding God in Unexpected Places (34 – 35)

◆

Splitting History

Unlike most people, I do not feel much Dickensian nostalgia at Christmastime. The holiday fell just a few days after my father died early in my childhood, and all my memories of the season are darkened by the shadow of that sadness. For this reason, perhaps, I am rarely stirred by the sight of manger scenes and tinseled trees. Yet, more and more, Christmas has enlarged in meaning for me, primarily as an answer to my doubts, an antidote to my forgetfulness.

In Christmas, the worlds of secular and spiritual come together. If you read the Bible alongside a Civilization 101 textbook, you will see how seldom that happens. The textbook dwells on the glories of ancient Egypt and the pyramids; the book of Exodus mentions the names of two Hebrew midwives but neglects to identify the pharaoh. The textbook honors the contributions from Greece and Rome; the Bible contains a few scant references, mostly negative, and treats great civilizations as mere background static for God's work among the Jews.

Yet on Jesus the two books agree. I switched on my computer this morning and Microsoft Windows flashed the date, implicitly acknowledging what the Gospels and the history book both affirm: whatever you may believe about it, the birth of Jesus was so important that it split history into two parts. Everything that has ever happened on this planet falls into a category of before Christ or after Christ.

In the cold, in the dark, among the wrinkled hills of Bethlehem, God who knows no before or after entered time and space. One who knows no boundaries at all took them on: the shocking confines of a baby's skin, the ominous restraints of mortality. "He is the image of the invisible God, the firstborn over all creation," an apostle would later say; "he is before all things, and in him all things hold together." But the few eyewitnesses on Christmas night saw none of that. They saw an infant struggling to work never-before-used lungs.

Finding God in Unexpected Places (35 – 36)

◆

The Descent

What could be less scary than a newborn baby with jerky limbs and eyes that do not quite focus? The King had cast off his robes.

Think of the condescension involved: the incarnation, which sliced history into two parts had more animal than human witnesses. Think, too, of the risk. In the incarnation, God spanned the vast chasm of fear that had distanced him from his human creation. But removing that barrier made Jesus vulnerable, terribly vulnerable.

> For those who believe in God, it means, this birth, that God himself is never safe from us, and maybe that is the dark side of Christmas, the terror of the silence. He comes in such a way that we can always turn him down, as we could crack the baby's skull like an eggshell or nail him up when he gets too big for that. (Frederick Buechner, *The Hungering Dark*)

How did Christmas day feel to God? Imagine for a moment becoming a baby again. God as a fetus! Or imagine yourself becoming a sea slug—that analogy is probably closer. On that day in Bethlehem, the Maker of All That Is took form as a helpless, dependent newborn.

Kenosis is the technical word theologians use to describe Christ emptying himself of the advantages of deity. Ironically, while the emptying involved much humiliation, it also involved a kind of freedom. I have sometimes pondered the "disadvantages" of infinity. A physical body freed Christ to act on a human scale, without those "disadvantages." He could say what he wanted without his voice blasting the treetops. He could express anger by calling King Herod a fox or by reaching for a bullwhip in the temple, rather than shaking the earth with his stormy presence. And he could talk to anyone—a prostitute, a blind man, a widow, a leper—without first having to announce, "Fear not!"

Disappointment with God (105–6)

The Word Spoke

During the two-week period when I was snowbound in a mountain cabin in Colorado, blizzards closed all roads and I had nothing to do but read the Bible. I went through it slowly, page by page. In the Old Testament I found myself identifying with those who boldly stood up to God: Moses, Job, Jeremiah, Habakkuk, the psalmists. As I read, I felt I was watching a play with human characters who acted out their lives of small triumph and large tragedy onstage, while periodically calling to an unseen Stage Manager, "You don't know what it's like out here!"

Job was most brazen, flinging to God this accusation: "Do you have eyes of flesh? Do you see as a mortal sees?"

Every so often I could hear the echo of a booming voice from far offstage, behind the curtain. "Yeah, and you don't know what it's like back here either!" it said to Moses, to the prophets, most clearly to Job. When I got to the Gospels, however, the accusing voices stilled. God, if I may use such language, "found out" what life is like in the confines of planet Earth. Jesus got acquainted with grief in person, in a brief, troubled life not far from the dusty plains where Job had travailed. Of the many reasons for incarnation, surely one was to answer Job's accusation: *Do you have eyes of flesh?* For a time, God did.

If only I could hear the voice from the whirlwind and, like Job, hold a conversation with God directly! I sometimes think. And perhaps that is why I now choose to write about Jesus. God is not mute: the Word spoke, not out of a whirlwind, but out of the human larynx of a Palestinian Jew. In Jesus, God lay down on the dissection table, as it were, stretched out in cruciform posture for the scrutiny of all skeptics who have ever lived. Including me.

The Jesus I Never Knew (17 – 18)

◆

Jesus on Film

My search for Jesus took off in a new direction when the filmmaker Mel White loaned me a collection of fifteen movies on the life of Jesus. They ranged from *King of Kings*, the 1927 silent classic by Cecil B. De Mille, to musicals such as *Godspell* and *Cotton Patch Gospel*, to the strikingly modern French Canadian treatment *Jesus of Montreal*. I reviewed these films carefully, outlining them scene by scene. Then, for the next two years, I taught a class on the life of Jesus, using the movies as a springboard for our discussion.

The class worked like this. As we came to a major event in Jesus' life, I would scout through the various films and from them select seven or eight treatments that seemed notable. As class began, I would show the two- to four-minute clips from each film, beginning with the comical and stiff renditions and working toward profound or evocative treatments. We found that the process of viewing the same event through the eyes of seven or eight filmmakers helped to strip away the patina of predictability that had built up over years of Sunday school and Bible reading. Obviously, some of the film interpretations had to be wrong — they blatantly contradicted each other — but which ones? What really happened?

Essentially, the films helped restore Jesus' humanity for me. The creeds repeated in churches tell about Christ's eternal preexistence and glorious afterlife, but largely ignore his earthly career. The Gospels themselves were written years after Jesus' death, from the far side of Easter, reporting on events as distant from the authors as the Korean War is from us today. The films helped me get further back, closer to a sense of Jesus' life as seen by his contemporaries. What would it have been like to hang on the edges of the crowd? How would I have responded to this man? Would I have invited him over for dinner, like Zacchaeus? Turned away in sadness, like the rich young ruler? Betrayed him, like Judas and Peter?

The Jesus I Never Knew (21–23)

Who Was This Christ?

In 1971 I first saw the movie *The Gospel According to St. Matthew*, directed by Italian filmmaker Pier Paolo Pasolini. Its release had scandalized not only the religious establishment, who barely recognized the Jesus on-screen, but also the film community, who knew Pasolini as an outspoken homosexual and Marxist.

The impact of Pasolini's film can only be understood by one who passed through adolescence during that tumultuous period. Back then it had the power to hush scoffing crowds at art theaters. Student radicals realized they were not the first to proclaim a message that was jarringly antimaterialistic, antihypocritical, pro-peace, and pro-love.

For me, the film helped to force a disturbing revaluation of my image of Jesus. In physical appearance, Jesus favored those who would have been kicked out of Bible college and rejected by most churches. Among his contemporaries he somehow gained a reputation as "a wine-bibber and a glutton." Those in authority, whether religious or political, regarded him as a troublemaker, a disturber of the peace. He spoke and acted like a revolutionary, scorning fame, family, property, and other traditional measures of success. I could not dodge the fact that the words in Pasolini's film were taken entirely from Matthew's gospel, and their message clearly did not fit my prior concept of Jesus.

About this same time a Young Life worker named Bill Milliken, who had founded a commune in an inner-city neighborhood, wrote *So Long, Sweet Jesus*. The title of that book gave words to the change at work inside me. In those days I was employed as the editor of *Campus Life* magazine, an official publication of Youth For Christ. *Who was this Christ, after all?* I wondered. As I wrote, and edited the writing of others, a tiny dybbuk of doubt hovered just to my side. *Do you really believe that? Or are you merely dispensing the party line, what you're paid to believe? Have you joined the safe, conservative establishment—modern versions of the groups who felt so threatened by Jesus?*

The Jesus I Never Knew (15 – 16)

◆

You Were There

Pulitzer Prize–winning historian Barbara Tuchman insists on one rule in writing history: no "flash-forwards." When she was writing about the Battle of the Bulge in World War II, for example, she resisted the temptation to include "Of course we all know how this turned out" asides. In point of fact, the Allied troops involved in the Battle of the Bulge did *not* know how the battle would turn out. From the look of things, they could well be driven right back to the beaches of Normandy they had come from.

A historian who wants to retain any semblance of tension and drama in events as they unfold dare not flash-forward to another, all-seeing point of view. Do so, and all tension melts away. Rather, a good historian re-creates for the reader the conditions of the history being described, conveying a sense that "you were there."

That, I concluded, is the problem with most of our writing and thinking about Jesus. We read the Gospels through the flash-forward lenses of church councils like Nicea and Chalcedon, through the church's studied attempts to make sense of him. He was a human being, a Jew in Galilee with a name and a family, a person who was in a way just like everyone else. Yet in another way he was something different than anyone who had ever lived on earth before.

It took the church five centuries of active debate to agree on some sort of epistemological balance between "just like everyone else" and "something different." For those of us raised in the church, or even raised in a nominally Christian culture, the balance inevitably tilts toward "something different." As Pascal said, "The Church has had as much difficulty in showing that Jesus Christ was man, against those who denied it, as in showing that he was God; and the probabilities were equally great."

Let me make it clear that I affirm the creeds. But in my writing I hope, as far as is possible, to look at Jesus' life "from below," as a spectator, one of the many who followed him around. I hope, in Luther's words, to "draw Christ as deep as possible into the flesh."

The Jesus I Never Knew (24)

◆

Taming the Lion

Jesus, I found, bore little resemblance to the television Mister Rogers – type fig-ure I had met in Sunday school, and was remarkably unlike the person I had studied in Bible college. For one thing, he was far less tame. In my prior image, I realized, Jesus' personality matched that of a *Star Trek* Vulcan: he remained calm, cool, and collected as he strode like a robot among excitable human be-ings on spaceship earth. That is not what I found portrayed in the Gospels and in the better films. Other people affected Jesus deeply: obstinacy frustrated him, self-righteousness infuriated him, simple faith thrilled him. Indeed, he seemed more emotional and spontaneous than the average person, not less. More pas-sionate, not less.

The more I studied Jesus, the more difficult it became to pigeonhole him. He said little about the Roman occupation, and yet he took up a whip to drive petty profiteers from the temple. He urged obedience to the Jewish law while acquiring the reputation as a law-breaker. He could be stabbed by sympathy for a stranger, yet turn on his best friend with the flinty rebuke, "Get behind me, Satan!" He had uncompromising views on rich men and loose women, yet both types enjoyed his company.

One day miracles seemed to flow out of Jesus; the next day his power was blocked by people's lack of faith. One day he talked in detail of the second coming; another, he knew neither the day nor hour. He fled from arrest at one point and marched inexorably toward it at another. He spoke eloquently about peacemaking, then told his disciples to procure swords. His extravagant claims about himself kept him at the center of controversy, but when he did something truly miraculous he tended to hush it up. As Walter Wink has said, if Jesus had never lived, we would not have been able to invent him.

Two words one could never think of applying to the Jesus of the Gospels: boring and predictable. How is it, then, that the church has tamed such a character — has, in Dorothy Sayers' words, "very efficiently pared the claws of the Lion of Judah, certified Him as a fitting household pet for pale curates and pious old ladies"?

The Jesus I Never Knew (23)

◇

The Main Reason

J esus corrects my fuzzy conceptions of God. Left on my own, I would come up with a very different notion of God. My God would be static, unchanging. Because of Jesus, however, I must adjust those instinctive notions. (Perhaps that lay at the heart of his mission?) Jesus reveals a God who comes in search of us, a God who makes room for our freedom, a God who is vulnerable. Above all, Jesus reveals a God who is love.

Those raised in a Christian tradition may miss the shock of Jesus' message, but in truth love has never been a normal way of describing what happens between human beings and their God. Not once does the Koran apply the word *love* to God. Aristotle stated bluntly, "It would be eccentric for anyone to claim that he loved Zeus" — or that Zeus loved a human being, for that matter. In dazzling contrast the Christian Bible affirms, "God *is* love," and cites love as the main reason Jesus came to earth: "This is how God showed his love among us: He sent his one and only Son into the world that we might live through him."

I remember a long night sitting in O'Hare Airport, waiting impatiently for a flight that was delayed for five hours. A friend, the author Karen Mains, happened to be traveling to the same conference. I was writing the book *Disappointment with God* at the time, and I felt burdened by other people's pains and sorrows, doubts and unanswered prayers.

Karen listened to me in silence for a very long time, and then out of nowhere she asked a question that has always stayed with me. "Philip, do you ever just let God love you?" she said. "It's pretty important, I think."

I realized with a start that she had brought to light a gaping hole in my spiritual life. For all my absorption in the Christian faith, I had missed the most important message of all. The story of Jesus is the story of a celebration, a story of love. It involves pain and disappointment, yes, for God as well as for us. But Jesus embodies the promise of a God who will go to any length to get his family back.

"Unwrapping Jesus," *Christianity Today,*
June 17, 1996 (34)

Ongoing Incarnation

More than two centuries before the Reformation a theological debate broke out that pitted the premier theologian Thomas Aquinas against an upstart from Britain, John Duns Scotus. In essence, the debate circled around the question, "Would Christmas have occurred if humanity had not sinned?"

Whereas Aquinas viewed the incarnation as God's remedy for a fallen planet, his contemporary saw much more at stake. For Duns Scotus, the Word becoming flesh must surely represent the Creator's primary design, not some kind of afterthought or Plan B. Aquinas pointed to passages emphasizing the cross as God's redemptive response to a broken relationship. Duns Scotus cited passages from Ephesians and Colossians on the cosmic Christ in whom all things have their origin, hold together, and move toward consummation.

Ultimately the church decided that both approaches had biblical support and could be accepted as orthodox. Though most theologians tended to follow Aquinas, in recent years prominent Catholics such as Karl Rahner have taken a closer look at Duns Scotus. Perhaps evangelicals should too.

Paul's phrase "in Christ" hints at a reality made vivid in his metaphor of the body of Christ: the church extends the incarnation through time.

In a lovely sermon at Oxford, Austin Farrer asked the question that occurs to anyone who applies Paul's lofty metaphor to the sad actuality of the church: "But what are we to do about the yawning gulf which opens between this Christhood of ours and our actual performance; our laziness, selfishness, uncleanness, triviality and the painful absurdity of our prayers? This gulf which yawns between what Christ has made us and what we make of ourselves."

We do, said Farrer, the very thing Jesus' disciples did: on the first day of the week we gather "and have the resurrection over again." We remind ourselves, to borrow Paul's words, that there is no condemnation for those who are in Christ Jesus, that we are dead to sin but alive to God in Christ Jesus, that if anyone is in Christ, he is a new creation; the old has gone, the new has come! (Romans 8:1, 6:11; 2 Corinthians 5:17). In short, we confront the stunning truth that God gazes on us through the redemptive lens of his Son.

"Back Page" column, *Christianity Today,*
January 2008 (72)

THANKS

Brenda Quinn, who combed through some two million words in various books and articles to make these selections, said to me, "This will be the easiest book you've ever written, Philip." That is true, though only because of a long string of friends, editors, and publishers who have worked with me over three decades. I dare not start naming them individually, for fear of omitting some names, but thank especially the magazine staff at *Campus Life* and *Christianity Today* as well as those who work for the publishers Zondervan, Doubleday, Eerdmans, and Hodder Faith UK. The great majority of selections come from those sources.

Of course, it takes as much effort to edit and publish a compilation book as it does an original book. John Sloan and Bob Hudson and their colleagues at Zondervan found a way to polish words and placement, then convert 366 selections in electronic form into a flat-paper book. Along the way, my assistant Melissa Nicholson cheerfully performed the most tedious and thankless tasks, such as keeping track of all the many excerpts as they migrated to different days and months. And Brenda Quinn stayed involved at every stage, graciously accommodating my arbitrary preferences. To all of you, great thanks.

Philip Yancey

BIBLIOGRAPHY

The Bible Jesus Read (Grand Rapids, Mich.: Zondervan, 1999)

Church: Why Bother? (Grand Rapids, Mich.: Zondervan, 1998)

Disappointment with God (Grand Rapids, Mich.: Zondervan, 1988)

Finding God in Unexpected Places (New York: Doubleday, 2005)

Guidance (Portland, Ore.: Multnomah, 1983)

Helping the Hurting (Portland, Ore.: Multnomah, 1984)

I Was Just Wondering (Grand Rapids, Mich.: Eerdmans, 1989, revised edition 1998)

In the Likeness of God (Grand Rapids, Mich.: Zondervan, 2004)

Indelible Ink: Twenty-Two Prominent Christian Leaders Discuss the Books That Shape Their Faith, Scott Larsen, editor (Foreword by Philip Yancey) (Colorado Springs: Waterbrook, 2003)

The Jesus I Never Knew (Grand Rapids, Mich.: Zondervan, 1995)

John Newton: From Disgrace to Amazing Grace, by Jonathan Aitken (Foreword by Philip Yancey) (Wheaton, Ill.: Crossway, 2007)

Meet the Bible (Grand Rapids, Mich.: Zondervan, 2000)

Money (Portland, Ore.: Multnomah, 1985)

Open Windows (Westchester, Ill.: Crossway, 1982)

Prayer: Does It Make Any Difference? (Grand Rapids, Mich.: Zondervan, 2006)

Praying with the KGB (Portland, Ore.: Multnomah, 1992)

Reaching for the Invisible God (Grand Rapids, Mich.: Zondervan, 2000)

Rumors of Another World (Grand Rapids, Mich.: Zondervan, 2003)

Soul Survivor (New York: Doubleday, 2001)

A Syllable of Water: Twenty Writers of Faith Reflect Upon Their Art, Emilie Griffin, editor (chapter 14 by Philip Yancey) (Orleans, Mass.: Paraclete, 2008)

What's So Amazing About Grace? (Grand Rapids, Mich.: Zondervan, 1997)

Where Is God When It Hurts? (Grand Rapids, Mich.: Zondervan, 1990)

Note: Magazine articles have bibliographical information included at the end of the excerpt.

A DESCRIPTIVE BIBLIOGRAPHY

Books

The Bible Jesus Read (*Zondervan, 1999*)

Like most Christians, I have been baffled and disturbed by parts of the Old Testament. Its books comprise the majority of the Christian Bible, but how should we read them? I select sample books (Deuteronomy, Job, Ecclesiastes, Psalms, Prophets) and describe how I have struggled and then come to terms with each. In the process my own understanding of and appreciation for the Old Testament undergoes a startling change.

Church: Why Bother? (*Zondervan, 1998*)

This short book addresses a question that seems more and more widespread. Churches are morphing into new forms, and surveys show that an increasing number of believers are opting out altogether. I describe my own checkered history with the church, toy with some images of the ideal church, and ponder why the New Testament seems to place so much value on such a motley assembly.

Disappointment with God (*Zondervan, 1988*)

After writing one of my first books, *Where Is God When It Hurts?* I got letters from readers who said something like this: "Thanks for your reflections on physical pain. My situation is different, though. My child has severe disabilities, and I face a constant battle with depression. Prayer doesn't seem to help my emotional pain. When it comes to God, I feel something like betrayal." I settle on three questions, "Is God unfair? Is God silent? Is God hidden?" and scour the Bible methodically, looking for clues. At the time, the publisher questioned the title, so different from the cheery titles that predominate in Christian bookstores. But I wanted to speak to people who were truly disappointed.

Finding God in Unexpected Places (*Moorings/Servant, 1995; Doubleday/ Hodder Faith UK, 2005*)

This book more than any other reflects my career as a roving journalist. (A journalist is a generalist, someone who knows a little about many things but not a lot about any one thing.) I investigate such varied topics as polar bears, sex surveys, Shakespeare, South American prisons, fund-raising appeals, and lousy praise music. The original book went through a major revision in 2005 as I felt the need to add a section on the "clash of civilizations" between Islam and the West.

I Was Just Wondering (*Eerdmans, 1989, 1998*)

The title comes from a "Back Page" column I wrote in *Christianity Today* asking a series of questions, some tongue-in-cheek and some serious, for which I have no real answer. The book gathers together fifty of those columns which cover the emotional spectrum from whimsy to angst.

In the Likeness of God (*Zondervan, 2004*)

Published after Dr. Paul Brand's death in 2003, this volume combines two books that we coauthored: *Fearfully and Wonderfully Made* and *In His Image*. At a time when my own faith was still forming, I was privileged to work for ten years with the brilliant, compassionate surgeon who revolutionized the treatment of leprosy. Our partnership changed forever my thinking about pain. As we worked together and I gave words to his faith, he gave faith to my words. I tell stories from his adventurous life, explore the wonders of the human body, and draw from his rich font of spiritual wisdom.

The Jesus I Never Knew (*Zondervan, 1995*)

I taught a class at my church in Chicago for eight years, the last two of which focused on the life of Jesus. In an attempt to unsettle our preconceptions, we used Hollywood movies based on Jesus as a jumping-off place. My own understanding of Jesus probably went through a more radical change than anyone else's in the class, and this book recounts that change. Jesus changed history more than any other individual and continues to challenge the stereotypes of all who get to know him.

Meet the Bible (*Zondervan, 2000*)

For three years my colleague Tim Stafford and I worked on an edition of the Bible known as *The Student Bible*, which we dubbed "a study Bible for people who would never use a study Bible." Those months of immersion in the Bible nourished the soil for all of my future writing. This book sets out a daily reading program of Bible highlights, drawn from my notes in *The Student Bible* and additional notes written by Brenda Quinn.

Open Windows (*Crossway, 1982; Thomas Nelson, 1985*)

Now out of print, this book brings together essays on a variety of topics: the writing craft, classical music, concentration camps, Francis Schaeffer, televangelism, Somali refugees, and Russian novelists.

Prayer: Does It Make Any Difference? (*Zondervan/Hodder Faith UK, 2006*)

I began with a list of questions: Why pray if God knows everything? Why do so many prayers go unanswered? Does prayer change God? I studied all 650 prayers in the Bible and interviewed scores of people about their own experiences with prayer. The process of writing caused a revolution in my own conception and practice of prayer. I now see it not so much as a way of getting God to do my will as a way of being available to get in the stream of what God wants to accomplish on earth.

Praying with the KGB *(Multnomah, 1992)*

Now out of print, this small book recounts a visit I made to the Soviet Union in the fall of 1991, just as it was collapsing. I went with a group of Christian leaders, invited by then-president Mikhail Gorbachev to help "restore morality to the Soviet Union." I can't report that we accomplished that goal in a week, but we did observe remarkable changes up close during one of the hinge moments of recent history.

Reaching for the Invisible God *(Zondervan, 2000)*

My most personal and introspective book, this one explores times of doubt, silence, and confusion that occur in the Christian life, and gives practical hints on how to cope with the inevitable problems that arise in a relationship with a God who is invisible. It serves as a kind of sequel to *Disappointment with God.*

Rumors of Another World *(Zondervan, 2003)*

I wrote this book for people in the "borderlands" of belief, those who say "I'm spiritual but not religious." I attempt to explain why I continue to believe, in the face of a modern worldview that challenges faith at every turn.

Soul Survivor *(Doubleday/Hodder Faith UK, 2001)*

Sometimes I'm asked, "What is your favorite, of the books you've written?" Each time I point to this one. I felt immensely privileged to draw together profiles of thirteen mentors, some of whom I interviewed (Frederick Buechner, Annie Dillard, Henri Nouwen, and others), some of whom I encountered through their writings (John Donne, G. K. Chesterton, Shusaku Endo, and others). They helped to form my own spiritual autobiography, which the book recounts as well.

What's So Amazing About Grace? *(Zondervan, 1997)*

I had originally conceived a book called *What's So Amazing About Grace and Why Don't Christians Show More of It?* in order to speak to the growing enchantment of American Christians with right-wing politics. Christians were becoming known mainly for what they were *against*: pornography, homosexuality, abortion, and so on. That disturbed me, as I see grace as one of the great, often untapped, powers of the universe that God has asked us to set loose. As I wrote, the book became less about politics and society and more about the wonders of God's grace and how it can transform individuals, families, and even nations.

Where Is God When It Hurts? *(Zondervan, 1977, 1990)*

As I look back on my first real book, I shudder that I had the audacity to tackle one of the most daunting theological questions, the problem of pain, in my late twenties. Yet suffering was one of the impediments to my faith, and it poses questions that confront all of us at some point. This was a book I could not *not* write. Thirteen years after its initial publication, I went back and revised it in view of all I had learned since.

Others

Most of the articles excerpted come from *Christianity Today*, especially a "Back Page" column that I have been writing since 1983. *Grace Notes* also includes excerpted material from several other publications, as noted on the relevant day. The three booklets cited from Multnomah Press (*Guidance, Money,* and *Helping the Hurting*) are now out of print.

SELECTIONS BY SOURCE

What's So Amazing About Grace?
 April 1
 May 19, 20, 21
 June 1, 2, 3
 July 19, 20, 21, 22
 August 7, 8
 September 1, 3, 23, 24, 25
 October 2, 3, 4, 5, 6, 7
 November 3, 4, 5, 6, 20, 21, 22

Where Is God When It Hurts?
 March 22, 23, 25, 26
 May 5, 23, 24
 June 7, 8, 9
 July 12, 13
 August 14
 September 26, 27, 28
 October 15, 16, 17, 18

Selections from Other Books

Indelible Ink (Foreword by Philip Yancey)
 March 6

John Newton (Foreword by Philip Yancey)
 April 7

A Syllable of Water (chapter 14, "The Literature of Fact: On the Writer as Journalist" by Philip Yancey)
 March 7

Articles

Books & Culture: "A Conversation on Books about Islam and the Middle East"
 April 11

Christianity Today articles
 "Angel to the Dying," August 16
 "Bud Ogle, Suburban Transplant," March 31
 "Distress Signals," March 19
 "Do I Matter? Does God Care?" April 13
 "The Penniless Gourmets," January 6
 "A Quirky and Vibrant Mosaic," August 1
 "A State of Ungrace," November 2
 "Unwrapping Jesus," January 14, 15; February 7, 8, 9; March 20; December 30
 "Where Is God When It Hurts," April 16

Christianity Today "Back Page" columns
 January 7, 8, 9
 February 21, 29
 March 1, 8, 13, 30
 April 2, 8, 20
 May 8, 13, 22
 June 30
 July 1, 2, 3, 4, 11, 26, 27, 31
 August 2, 5, 6, 9
 September 10, 17
 October 19
 November 26
 December 31

First Things: "A Goad, A Nail, and Scribbles in the Sand"
 January 12

Miscellaneous

Unpublished Articles and Trip Notes
 February 3, 4
 March 11, 12
 September 29
 October 1

CREDITS

The author would like to thank the following publishers for permission to excerpt passages from their books:

Crossway: *John Newton: From Disgrace to Amazing Grace* (copyright © 2007 by Jonathan Aitken), *Open Windows* (copyright © 1982 by Philip Yancey). Used by permission.

Multnomah: *Guidance* (copyright © 1983 by Philip Yancey), *Helping the Hurting* (copyright © 1984 by Philip Yancey), *Money* (copyright © 1985 by Philip Yancey), *Praying with the KGB* (copyright © 1992 by Philip Yancey). Used by permission.

Paraclete: *A Syllable of Water: Twenty Writers of Faith Reflect Upon Their Art* (copyright © 2008 by The Chrysostom Society). Used by permission.

Random House: *Finding God in Unexpected Places* (copyright © 2005 by SCCT), *Soul Survivor* (copyright © 2001 by SCCT). Used by permission of Ballantine Books and Doubleday, divisions of Random House, Inc.

Waterbrook: *Indelible Ink: Twenty-Two Prominent Christian Leaders Discuss the Books That Shape Their Faith* (copyright © 2003 by Scott Larsen). Used by permission.

Eerdmans: *I Was Just Wondering* (copyright © 1989 by Philip Yancey, rev. 1998). Reprinted by permission of the publisher; all rights reserved.

Zondervan: *The Bible Jesus Read* (copyright © 1999 by Philip Yancey), *Church: Why Bother?* (copyright © 1998 by Philip Yancey), *Disappointment with God* (copyright © 1988 by Philip Yancey), *In the Likeness of God* (copyright © 2004 by Philip Yancey), *The Jesus I Never Knew* (copyright © 1995 by Philip Yancey), *Meet the Bible* (copyright © 2000 by Philip Yancey and Brenda Quinn), *Prayer: Does It Make Any Difference?* (copyright © 2006 by Philip D. Yancey), *Reaching for the Invisible God* (copyright © 2000 by Zondervan), *Rumors of Another World* (2003 by SCCT), *What's So Amazing About Grace?* (copyright © 1997 by Philip Yancey), *Where Is God When It Hurts?* (copyright © 1990 by Philip Yancey). Used by permission.

SUBJECT INDEX